Paul Heger
The Development
of Incense Cult in Israel

Beihefte zur Zeitschrift für die alttestamentliche Wissenschaft

Herausgegeben von
Otto Kaiser

Band 245

Walter de Gruyter · Berlin · New York
1997

Paul Heger

The Development
of Incense Cult in Israel

Walter de Gruyter · Berlin · New York
1997

♾ Printed on acid-free paper which falls within the guidelines of the ANSI
to ensure permanence and durability.

Die Deutsche Bibliothek — Cataloging-in-Publication Data

Heger, Paul:
The development of incense cult in Israel / Paul Heger. — Berlin ;
New York : de Gruyter 1997
  (Beiheft zur Zeitschrift für die alttestamentliche Wissenschaft ;
  Bd. 245)
  Zugl.: Toronto, Univ., Diss., 1996
  ISBN 3-11-015367-X

ISSN 0934-2575

Printed in Germany
Disk conversion: Readymade, Berlin
Printing: Werner Hildebrand, Berlin
Binding: Lüderitz & Bauer-GmbH, Berlin

Acknowledgements

This study was presented as a doctoral dissertation in the Department of Near Eastern Studies at the University of Toronto. I wish to express my gratitude to all the professors of this department who have taught me, granting me of their time and patience and awakening my interest in the classical texts. I wish in particular to thank Professor Harry Fox, my supervisor, who directed my curriculum and advised me from the first day of my arrival at the University of Toronto; his carefully planned range of studies enabled me to write a thesis based on such a wide variety of sources. My deepest appreciation is also due to Professors Tirzah Meacham, John Revell and John W. Wevers of the Department, who read my thesis with great care; their extremely helpful insights and comments have been incorporated into the thesis and so enhanced it. I must also mention the help of Ms. Diane Kriger, who read my thesis and made the appropriate corrections. Last but not least, I wish to thank my spouse for her patience, and to acknowledge with gratitude the concessions which she made during the period of my studies.

Toronto, Ontario, September 10, 1996   Paul Heger

Contents

Introduction

Since the earliest stages of biblical criticism, scholars have debated the assertions in Exodus chapters 30-40. Was an incense ceremony already celebrated twice daily on a specific golden altar in the desert Tabernacle, as these verses suggest? Or was this ceremony introduced into the Israelite cult at a much later time? In the latter case, when was such a ceremony introduced, and what were the historical and social circumstances behind its development?

It has long been proposed that these verses in Exodus which attest to the existence of the golden altar are a retrojection of a much later situation into earlier texts. Wellhausen, for instance, affirmed in his *Prolegomena zur Geschichte Israels*[1] that the institution of the incense ceremony and the construction of the golden altar were post-exilic innovations. He writes (p.65-6): "But the importance which it has attained in the ritual legislation of the Pentateuch is manifest above all from this, that it has led to the invention of a peculiar new and highly sacred piece of furniture, namely the golden altar in the inner tabernacle, which is unknown to history ... the golden altar in the sanctuary is originally simply the golden table." He then proceeds with further doubts concerning the existence of this altar during the Second Temple period, and writes: "It is not to be wondered at if in the post-exilic temple there existed both a golden altar and a golden table (p. 67)." Wellhausen derives his opinion from the mention of the incense altar only in those segments of Scripture attributed to the P editor; as to its absence in the rest of Scripture he comments: "...it could not possibly have been omitted, had it been known (p. 66)." Positing an interchange between the table and the golden altar, he concludes: "Table is the name, altar the function (p. 67)." He corroborates this assertion by noting Ezekiel's synthesis of these two terms in 41: 22: the verse opens with the phrase "the altar of wood," and ends with the phrase "this is the table that is before the Lord."

---

[1] Julius Wellhausen, *Prolegomena zur Geschichte Israels*, Fünfte Ausgabe (Berlin, 1899). The English quotations are from *Prolegomena to the History of Ancient Israel* (New York: The Meridian Library, 1957). Full bibliographic details of these works and all others cited in notes to this essay are listed in the Bibliography at the end of this work.

Since then, scholars have contemplated this issue, expressing different degrees of doubt and agreement with Wellhausen's emphatic pronouncement.[2] Although many scholars[3] still cling, in one way or another, to Wellhausen's postulate, it is not surprising that some scholars, especially in Israel, have attempted to discredit Wellhausen's categorical pronouncement, either on textual grounds or on the basis of archeological findings.[4] Menahem Haran, a well-known scholar in the field of ritual practice in ancient Israel, is typical of such opponents, using both textual and archeological arguments.

The date of the earliest introduction of the incense ceremony into the Israelite cult also remains a contentious issue. There have been two main focal points in this debate: first, the authenticity and the date of certain scriptural verses such as Deut. 33: 10 ישימו קטורה באפך "He offers [the literal translation is "they offer"] incense before you," and I Sam. 2: 28 לעלות על מזבחי להקטיר קטרת "to go up to my altar, to burn incense"; second, the interpretation of archeological finds of small altars, some with burn marks.

It seems to me that the original question posed by Wellhausen (though perhaps not stated with complete clarity and precise demarcation) has been diluted, and the debate among the scholars was expanded to the more general issue of the use of incense in the Israelite cult. I narrowed the scope of the debate, and focused on the following specific areas:

a) The institution of the independent, twice daily, perpetual incense celebration on the particular golden altar, as expressed in the above verses in Exodus.

b) The stages of development of this celebration, from a non-issue in the early scriptural writings, to the great importance it achieved in the late period of the Second Temple. Specifically, I trace the the developmental stages of the incense ceremony in ancient Israel, from the earliest use of fragrant substances as an auxiliary cultic rite, to the enhancement of the incense ceremony to a rite of prime significance in the last part of the Second Temple period. Such development is attested by contemporary his-

---

[2]   See B. Baentsch, *Exodus*, 1903, pp. 259-60; I. Benzinger, *Hebräische Archäologie*, Leipzig, 1927, pp. 365 ff; M. Löhr, *Das Räucheropfer im Alten Testament*, pp.164-165.

[3]   See B. Baentsch, *Exodus, Leviticus, Numeri* (Göttingen, 1902), pp. 259/60; I. Benziger, *Hebräische Archäologie* (Leipzig, 1927), p. 365; M. Löhr, *Das Räucheropfer im Alten Testament*, pp.164-5; Holzinger, *Exodus* (Tübingen, 1900), pp. 144-5; B. D. Eerdmans, *Alttestamentliche Studien*, Vol. IV (1912), pp. 30ff.; M. Noth, *Könige I*, p.122.

[4]   See, for instance, A. Kaufman, כלי המשכן (MA Dissertation, Tel-Aviv University, 1966), pp. 142-167.

torical evidence, and sacred post-biblical writings such as the Apocrypha, the New Testament and rabbinic literature. It may also be deduced from the fact that a single command in the Pentateuch apparently introduced a new institutional practice. Careful analysis of the biblical text of Exod 30: 1-10 reveals that this command is a later interpolation, somewhat carelessly added to the biblical text out of context.

I widened, on the other hand, the "tools" of research, and used in my examination a greater range of textual sources. I also considered the significance and the impact of historical events, and the consequences of relevant practical circumstances, the *Sitz im Leben* of the incense cult. I performed philological studies on various terms relevant to the subject matter, and availed myself of the various classical translations, such as the Aramaic Targumim and the Septuagint. The relevant scriptural pericopes have been critically examined, word for word, to unravel signs of probable changes, substitutions and accretions to the original text, effected with the intention of harmonizing the late interpolation into the text of the pericope (Exod. 30: 1-10) containing the command to construct a specific altar for the daily burning of incense. In addition to the customary methods of biblical criticism, I quoted and examined a number of the most important traditional commentators. In many instances, I derived support from these sources for my deliberations, based on the presence in these sources of ideas and speculations similar to my own; in many cases the questions and perplexities which I raised concerning particular texts had been duly recognized and examined by the Sages and later rabbinic commentators. However, though this fact confirms the validity of my analysis, it does not prevent me from occasionally offering solutions distinctly different from those of the Sages. Their solutions were based on their own particular doctrinal viewpoints; others may discern similar subjectivity in my own solutions.

The absence of any mention of an independent daily incense celebration in the early biblical writings, and the extraordinary significance of this ritual in the later sources, clearly undermine the notion that this rite had been celebrated continuously since early times. On the basis of textual evidence and historical events, I propose that the following represents the probable sequence of the development.

It may be supposed that at a certain juncture in human culture, there appeared a consciousness of the enjoyment to be derived from the fragrant odours emanating from natural substances. Cravings developed for the aroma of certain foods and herbal condiments with pleasant smells. Increased sophistication in dwelling conditions encouraged the use of available fragrant substances, in various forms and applications, to create a more

pleasant environment, and to dissipate the repellent odours of poorly ven-
tilated lodgings and decaying organic substances. I remind the reader that
in the late Middle Ages and even subsequently, perfumes were still used in
great abundance by aristocratic society to mask the offensive smell of long-
unwashed bodies. It is therefore quite logical that when humans came to
believe that they should offer food to the gods, it was also natural to provide
fragrant spices as condiments for the food, and aromatic odours to create a
pleasant environment for the deity's lodging.[5]

Ancient texts and archeological records offer us clear evidence of this
stage in certain ancient cultures, in particular for those which did not develop further on their own, but were superseded by other cultures. On the
other hand, we find only textual traces of this stage in the Israelite sacred
texts, in a culture which continued to develop on its own basis. Biblical
phrases such as ריח ניחח and לחמי לאשי are evidence of this early stage,
remnants of archaic customs and theologies. The fact that we do not find
in earlier biblical sections any specific expression for the creation of a
pleasant aroma through the burning of incense is a central point of this
study; this lack may well reflect the insignificance, if not outright absence,
of incense burning at this stage. This proposition assumes, of course, that
the order of the scriptural texts does not parallel the real chronological order
of the described events, a theory now well accepted among biblical scholars
and thus not requiring further substantiation.

At this point we may start to trace the philological development of the
specific biblical term for the burning of incense; such development, it may
be argued, is closely intertwined with the actual developmental stages of
incense use, both secular and sacral. The root קטר,[6] the general *terminus
technicus* for the incense ceremony, appears in the earlier sections of the
Bible only in non-cultic use: as the noun קיטר "smoke" (Gen. 19: 28), and
the name קטורה (Gen. 25: 1). In Deuteronomy and the later prophets,[7] the
term קטרת (as well as the name קטורה in Deut. 33: 10) is used, but the root
קטר as a description of a cultic ceremony is reserved mainly, if not exclusively, for alien cults. This expanded use of קטר as a cultic term is coinci-
dent with the extension of Mesopotamian political and military influence
in Israel, first in the Northern Kingdom, and later in the Southern Kingdom of Judah, an influence well substantiated by both textual and archeological evidence. One must also not exclude Egyptian influence, due to the

---

[5]   See in this respect chap. 3 note 101, and chap. 4 notes 31, 32 and 35.

[6]   Concerning the etymology of the term קטר, see Chapter One. Its use as a sacral term
       was probably influenced by Akkadian usage.

presence of Jewish settlements in that country from its earliest historical memories and onward; Jeremiah's censure of the incense worship to foreign gods by these Jewish immigrants may bear witness to such a link with that culture, in which incense had been used since early times.

Gradually, however, the Israelite habit of absorbing foreign customs and creeds and refashioning them as their own led to the incorporation of incense into "legitimate" cultic worship. Incense-burning was introduced as an additional element in the bland grain offering of the מנחה. The use of the root קטר to describe such a "legitimate" cultic act appears first in Jeremiah's period, the time of Babylonia's strongest domination of Judah. Such use continued to expand, so that by the Second Temple period the term קטר had come to be recognized as a legitimate expression for sacrificial celebrations in honour of the God of Israel by the foreign nations. Thus we read in Malachi 1: 11 ובכל מקום מקטר מגש לשמי, "In every place incense[8] and pure offerings will be brought to my name." Perhaps this is yet another step in the legitimation of קטר in the Judean cult, beyond its exclusive use to describe the מנחה with frankincense, as we read in Jer. 33: 18: מעלה עולה ומקטיר מנחה ועשה זבח "To offer burnt offerings, to burn grain offerings and to present sacrifices." Here we must interpret the *Minhah* specifically as a grain offering, distinct from the עולה and the זבח, which is another term for שלמים. The use of frankincense as the remembrance offering of the showbread may also have originated in this period.

The next step in this development is reflected in the unusual use of the term קטר in the P section of the Pentateuch to describe all cultic ceremonies in connection with burning. Such use stands in contrast to the term's original etymology and to its previous restrictive meaning. The term thus developed into a single *terminus technicus* for all forms of sacrifice. The use of this unifying term קטר throughout the sacrificial codex indicates its significance; however, it must also cause us to question why this apparently inappropriate term was used for the burning of solid substances. An answer to this question is suggested through a careful examination of the etymology of the verb קטר, through grammatical and exegetical analysis of the various forms of the verb found in the codex, and by a consideration of the various classical translations.

Yet another philological issue is raised in the use of the term מזבח מקטר קטרת for the golden "incense" altar. The specific character of this altar is

---

[7]   The use of קטר in Kings and certain prophetic writings will be discussed in due course.

[8]   I wish to emphasize again that these sources do not specify the substance which was burnt, and this is still an open issue.

particularly emphasized, in that there is a peculiar prohibition against offer-ing materials other than incense on this altar.[9] Yet the term מזבח, from the root זבח "to slay,"[10] is utterly inappropriate for an apparatus restricted exclusively to incense, and with no association to slaughtered substances. In other ancient Semitic languages there are distinct terms for altars on which offerings are burned or exposed before the deity, and for censers used to burn fragrant woods or incense. In none of these languages is a form similar to מזבח used with reference to an incense altar. In Mesopotamia, the offerer imagined that his offerings fed the gods in their temple habitat; the altar was called *passuru*,[11] "table" (פתורא in Aramaic), a piece of furniture upon which the various foods were exposed. The censer was called *nignakk/qqu*, or *maqtarum*, or *kinunu*.[12] The Arabic name for altar is *madbah*, and for the incense altar *mqtr*.[13] The ancient Greek language, although not entirely relevant to our purpose, also had two different terms: βωμός for the altar, and θυμιατήριον for the censer. The *Index Homericus*, by A. Gehring, reveals that in Homer's writing there is only the term βωμός, since there was no incense in Greece in his period. In Herodotus' writings, we find βωμός for altar, and θυμιατήριον associated with the burning of incense, storax and frankincense. The different terms do not reflect differences in the size of the altar, but in use. For instance, in Book VI: 97 of *The Histories*, Herodotus mentions the burning of enormous quantities of frankincense, λιβανωτοῦ τριηκόσια τάλαντα "three hundred talents of frankincense," but these are not burned on a βωμός, The LXX, on the other hand, indis-criminately used θυσιαστήριον for both the holocaust altar and the incense altar, translating literally the Hebrew term מזבח , used as a sacral term in Scripture for both types of altar. The LXX also uses the term θυμιατήριον for the translation of מקטרת when used for illegitimate incense celebrations (II Chr. 26: 19 and Ezek. 8: 11), demonstrating a theological objective in

---

[9]   See chap. 3, sec. 3.3 and note 40.

[10] In Hebrew and other Semitic languages; see Kohler-Baumgartner, *Veteris Testamenti Libros*, s.v.מזבח; *IDB*, s.v. "Altar"; *Theologisches Wörterbuch zum Alten Testament* (Stutt-gart), s.v. מזבח.

[11] *Theolog. Wörterbuch*, and *Reallexicon der Assyriologie*, Ref. "Altar".

[12] *Theolog. Wörterbuch*, but H. Zimmern, in his *Beiträge zur Kenntnis der Babyl. Religion*, translates *kinunu* as "Kohlenbecken," a plain coal basin, distinct from the *nignakku*, the censer bowl. From the context of the translated tablets, one has the impression that Zimmern's translation is the correct one. We should keep this in mind, with respect to the debate concerning archeological finds of bowls with traces of burning; these might be coal burners for heating dwellings or temples.

[13] K. Wigand, *Thymiateria* (Bonn, 1913), p. 15.

its interpretation. These uses therefore cannot serve as an indication of how the term θυμιατήριον was actually used in colloquial Hellenistic Greek. But Hellenistic writers do make a distinction, using the term βωμός for the outer holocaust altar and θυμιατήριον for the incense altar. For example, Josephus has βωμός for the outer holocaust altar in *Ant.* IV: 57, while the term θυμιατήριον is used indiscriminately for the translation of both the censer, מחתה, mentioned in the Korah narration (*Ant.* IV: 32), and the מזבח הזהב "the golden altar" (*Ant.* VIII: 92). Philo also utilizes these terms in like manner, and we read in Moses II: 94 about the tabernacle's furnishings: κιβωτός, λυχνία, τράπεζα, θυμιατήριον, βωμός, ὁ μὲν οὖν βωμός ἱδρυέτο εν ὑπαίθρῳ "the ark, candlestick, table and altars for incense and burnt offerings. The altar for burnt offerings was placed in the open air"; we read further in 101: μέσον μὲν τὸ θυμιατήριον "The altar of incense he placed in the middle." The author of The Letter of Aristeas makes the same distinction. Thus while the indiscriminate use by the LXX cannot serve as evidence that separate terms were not required in Hebrew for the two types of altars, the distinctive terms used by Josephus and Philo do serve as "objective" evidence that such a distinction was made. There is thus no philological or other rationale for the use of the term מזבח for an incense burner.[14]

The philological incongruity in the use of the term מזבח for an altar dedicated exclusively to the burning of incense must lead us to assume that a later and exclusively Israelite motive triggered the creation of a specific sacral terminology, under which the distinct terms קטר, associated with the burning of incense, and מזבח, associated with the burning of animal sacrifices, drew closer together in meaning. At the same time, the term קטר became a *terminus technicus* for all cultic burning. My study suggests that

---

[14] G. Ryckmans, in his essay "Sud-Arabe *Mdbht* = Hébreu *Mzbh* et termes apparentés," in *Festschrift Werner Caskel* (Leiden, 1968), pp. 253-260, writes (p. 254) "Le term *mdbht* peut toute fois s'appliquer a un autel qui n'est pas affecté aux sacrifices sanglants. Il est en même en Hébreu; qu'il suffise de citer II Chron., 26, 16: להקטיר על מזבח הקטרת, pour ne pas parler ici de 'l'autel d'or', dont il sera question plus loin." Similarly, the *Theolog. Wörterbuch,* states: "Zumal *mizbeah* durch semantische Transformation im Hebr. dann auch Räucheraltäre u.a. bezeichnen kann." Ryckmans does not offer any explanation for the derivation of מזבח from the root *dbh*, as he writes : "On sait que la racine *dbh*, en canaéen *zbh*, en araméen *dbh*, signifie 'immoler, tuer une piece de bétail'"; he merely refers to the "questionable" biblical term to substantiate this proposition. The *Theolog. Wörterbuch*, on the other hand, confirms that it is a result of semantic transformation; it leaves open the rationale behind this transformation. J. T. Milik mentions, in *Biblica* 48, (1967) 577, a Semitic deity madbah, but I do not suppose that this occurrence offers a solution to our inquiry.

such changes paralleled an uncompromising and at times brutal struggle in Israelite society for the exclusive privilege of controlling the incense ceremony.

Further evidence of a process of development is derived from a critical examination of those biblical pericopes describing the incense ceremony. Such an examination reveals that the final editing of these pericopes was of a late date, and consisted of a blending of the archaic custom of placing spices with food before the gods with Second Temple realities. Comparative analysis of Mesopotamian sources describing the use of spices and incense in the cult, and the fact that the appearance in Scripture of similar ceremonies with the use of the term קְטֹר coincides with the period of known Mesopotamian military and political dominance, offer credible evidence of foreign influence on the Israelite cult in both language and practice. It also confirms that the initial form of this celebration involved censers, similar to Mesopotamian custom, and in contrast to the later Israelite form of this celebration, as described in Exod. 30: 1-10. Again, such changes offer additional evidence of the development in the Israelite cult.

In the second part of the thesis, I present an hypothesis concerning the motive, circumstances and means by which this extreme change was created, based on the critical examination of the relevant texts – scriptural, post-biblical and historical. I argue that Josiah's reform triggered an overwhelming upheaval in the Israelite cult; the centralization of the cult in a single *locus* and under the control of a limited group had a dramatic impact on the development of the following:

a) the realization of the economic importance and advantages deriving from exclusive control of the cult, and thus the development of an incentive for such exclusive control;

b) the exclusion of other participants in cultic ceremonies, through the introduction of a new concept of a divinely validated genealogical origin as an absolute "entrance" requirement.

The distinct theological and practical aspects of the incense celebration, particularly the control of its supply, lent themselves to the exploitation of these principles. In my thesis I propose a gradual development of the incense ceremony and its significance, in three stages, which led ultimately to the final form of the incense celebration as described in Exod. chaps. 30: 1-9 and 34-38, and to the exclusive control of the incense supply by a restricted priestly clan. In particular, I attempted to delineate the development of the incense ceremony, on the basis of :

a) textual analysis of ancient sources, supported by the opinions of traditional and modern scholars;

b) comparative examination of cultic performances in the surrounding cultures and their influence on Israel;

c) an examination of the impact of Josiah's reform on the Israelite cult in general, and on the incense ceremony in particular;

d) a consideration of the impact of the arrival and wider distribution[15] of frankincense in Israel, and the resulting increase in sophistication of the incense celebration;

e) logical deductions from political and socio-economic principles relevant to my study, collectively subsumed under the concept *Sitz im Leben*.

Critical analysis of biblical texts, and the search for the "kernel of truth" in the relevant narratives as well as their aetiological purpose, served as the "backbone" of my hypothesis and its logical stages. I then considered further textual evidence from primary and secondary sources, and added logical deductions to this "bare skeleton," in order to present a fully-formed theory, grounded in textual evidence.

Philological and textual analysis led me to assume that the institution of the independent, twice-daily incense ceremony on a special altar was a late innovation in the second half of the Second Temple period. The absence of such a celebration in the Temple Scroll, and the dispute concerning the altar on which the frankincense of the showbread was to be burned, provided me with conjectural models, in addition to the logical conclusions derived from the textual examinations. My assumption that only the "establishment" had the power to introduce and successfully impose innovative cultic systems is supported by the opinion of M. Bar-Ilan,[16] in a study concerning the qualification of particular woods for burning on the altar; it is the *Sitz im Leben* which serves as the ground for his conclusion that only the establishment had the power to create significant changes in the cult. Hence, one has to assume that the Temple Scroll group clung to prior custom, under which frankincense was burned with every animal and vegetal offering on the outer altar, and only the frankincense of the showbread was burned, once weekly, on the inner incense altar.

I shall note here some of the textual difficulties which argue against there having been a specific incense altar from earliest times. We have in the Pentateuch three occurrences of the term מזבח הזהב, with no indication of the use of the altar, in Exod. 39: 38, 40: 26 and Num. 4: 11; one occurrence

---

[15]   See also chap. 6, sec. 6.2.4 on this subject.

[16]   M. Bar-Ilan, "Are the Tractates Tamid and Midoth Polemic Documents"? (Hebrew) *Sidra* (1989), pp. 27- 40.

of מזבח מקטר קטרת in Exod. 30: 1, and four occurrences of מזבח הקטרת without the modifier הזהב, "the golden," in Exod. 30: 27, 31: 8, 35: 15 and 37: 25. Only once, in Exod. 40: 5, do we find the association מזבח הזהב לקטרת and in Lev. 4: 7 we find מזבח קטרת הסמים. I analyzed the context of these occurrences in an attempt to find a reasonable explanation for the use of these different expressions concerning the "golden" altar, or a common denominator underlying each different group with the same wording, but have not succeeded. I also examined the corresponding verses in the LXX; the pericope in MT 39: 33-43 appears in the LXX in 39: 13-23, in a different order, but the golden altar does not appear. In v. 15, we find τὸ θυσιαστήριον καὶ πάντα τὰ σκεύη, which seems to be the bronze altar; the MT מזבח הזהב would be translated by the LXX as τὸ χρυσοῦν. Furthermore, the θυσιαστήριον in the LXX must be understood here as the holocaust altar, because it is the only altar mentioned in these verses. The counterpart of MT 39: 39 , which contains the מזבח הנחשת, is missing in the Greek text, but it must certainly be included among the furnishings enumerated in this pericope. Further, the concluding verses of this pericope ככל אשר צוה ה׳ את משה כן עשו (v. 42 in MT), πᾶσαν τὴν παρασκευήν (v. 22 in LXX), and וירא משה את כל המלאכה והנה עשו (v. 43 in MT), πάντα τὰ ἔργα καὶ ἦσαν πεποιηκότες αὐτά (v. 23) must certainly include the holocaust altar. The fact that the second part of v. 16 in the LXX lists the anointing oil and the incense compound, two substances which in MT 39: 38 follow the golden altar, does not compel us to consider the term θυσιαστήριον as referring to the incense altar; it merely demonstrates a tampering with the text. Finally, the phrase θυσιαστήριον καὶ πάντα τὰ σκεύη must refer to the holocaust altar, which has a number of accessories; the phrase can be considered a collective expression for the detailed phrase in the MT ואת מכבר הנחשת אשר לו את בדיו ואת כל כליו, which follows את מזבח הנחשת. The "golden altar" does appear in the LXX in Exod. 40: 26 and Num. 4: 11, as does θυσιαστήριον τὸ χρυσοῦν εἰς τὸ θυμιᾶν, "the golden altar for incense," in Exod. 40: 5. However, the absence of the golden altar in these concluding verses in chap. 39 of the LXX is one of the significant discrepancies between the MT and the LXX concerning the golden incense altar, and is of cardinal importance to this study. The variation from the MT seems to indicate a process by which a central authority added this item to the tradition, and this addition was then not made uniformly in all texts, causing variations among them.

On the other hand, the term מזבח הקטרת, θυσιαστήριον τοῦ θυσιάματος "incense altar," is found in the LXX only in Exod. 30: 27, within the command to anoint the artifacts of the Tabernacle. As Wevers has noted,[17] this term is missing in LXX Exod. 31: 8, where we again find θυσιαστήρια without any further detail, which is supposed to include both the holocaust and the incense altar. The change from the MT text in this regard is remarkable, since there is no other change from the MT in this chapter; this too suggests the possibility that the MT was subject to the revisions of a later editor. Furthermore, the reference to both altars may have appeared to be an elegant solution to the editor, but does not correspond to the order of the implements which appears in other pericopes. In MT chapter 37, the order is: table, lampstand and *incense* altar, then the holocaust altar. In the corresponding chap. 38 in the LXX, the table precedes the lampstand, but the incense altar is missing. In the MT 39: 33-43, we have the same order: table, lampstand, *golden* altar, and bronze altar. In the LXX in the corresponding vv. 16-18, we have a different order, but again no golden or incense altar. The term θυσιαστήριον καὶ πάντα τὰ σκεύη αὐτοῦ points again to the holocaust altar which has many accessories.[18] In the MT 40: 4- 5 we again have the same order: table, lampstand, *golden altar for incense,* and holocaust altar; the LXX text corresponds exactly to the MT. In the MT 40: 22- 29 we have again the table, the lampstand, the *golden* altar and then the holocaust altar. In the corresponding LXX vv. 20-26 we have the same order: table, lampstand, golden altar and holocaust (καπρωμάτων) altar. Thus the listing of the two altars in the LXX 31: 8 before the table and the lampstand is certainly out of place, and suggests the possibility that the translation of this verse was made to conform with the usual formula in the MT text, including Exod. 31:8-9: that is, table, lampstand, incense altar and holocaust altar.

In Exod. 35: 4-29, Moses' report to the congregation of God's commands, the LXX text corresponds exactly to the MT, with the exception of verse 15 concerning the "incense altar," which is entirely missing. The report of Bezalel's accomplishments in the MT Exod. Chs. 37-38 appears in shortened form in chap. 38 of the LXX. Again, the report of the construction of the "incense altar" in Exod. 37: 25 in the MT is missing in the

---

[17] In "Text History of the Greek Exodus," p. 121, Wevers writes: "Exod. compresses the list by adding καὶ τὰ θυσιαστήρια at the beginning of v. 8 but dropping the later ואת מזבח הקטרת ואת מזבח העלה ואת כל כליו."

[18] The MT text in 31: 8-9 has the term ואת כליו, in the appropriate form, for the table, the lamp and the holocaust altar; there are no "accessories" or "utensils" for the incense altar. We observe the same contrast in the MT 37: 17-28 and 39: 36- 38; the expression in the LXX πάντα τὰ σκεύη must therefore refer to the holocaust altar.

corresponding text in the LXX, after the accounts of the construction of the ark, table and lampstand; following the order in the MT, we would have expected the "incense altar" at the end of this list. In conclusion, we have only one mention of the "incense altar" in the LXX, in comparison to four occurrences in the MT.

The fact that in the MT the "incense altar" is described after the ark, table and lampstand is itself bizarre. We would expect it to appear first, right after the ark; this would be appropriate considering its importance, and the fact that according to Exod. 30:6 its position was close to the ark: "ונתתה אתו לפני הפרכת אשר על ארן העדת לפני הכפרת Put the altar in front of the curtain that is before the ark of the Testimony." The occurrence of the term "incense altar" at the end of the verse in Exod. 30:27 and 31:8 leads us to speculate that it is a later revision, placed at the end of a phrase so as to be easier to insert in such a way as not to disrupt the text. If this is an interpolation, it may also have influenced the ordering in other pericopes, in which the incense altar is always mentioned as the last item.

In summary, my analysis did not detect a pattern out of the many oddities in the MT and in the LXX, other than to perceive certain irregularities which demonstrate an intentional editing to insert clauses. M. Haran,[19] in his essay "מזבחות הקטורת" , reflects on these textual issues, and suggests that the terms מזבח הקטרת and מזבח הזהב are simply abbreviations of the complete term מזבח קטרת הסמים (Lev. 4: 7). Haran suggests that the incense altar in the Tabernacle was a type of generic small altar that might be used, outside the Tabernacle, for purposes other than incense; in the Tabernacle, however, it was used specifically for incense, and was thus called מזבח הקטרת. Similarly, the term מזבח הזהב simply reflects the fact that the altar in the Tabernacle was made of gold. I must express my doubts as to the conjecture that only once in the P section (Exod. 40: 5) is the full and explicit term מזבח הזהב לקטרת mentioned, while there are seven occurrences of an abbreviated and inaccurate term. I suggest that these irregularities are not the result of unconcerned variation in phraseology for stylistic purposes alone, but possibly reflect haphazard textual emendation.

The differences between the MT and the LXX in the last six chapters of Exodus (35 to 40) concerning the building of the Tabernacle are also well known, and several scholars[20] have proposed explanations and motivations

---

[19] *Tarbiz* 61/3 (Hebrew) (1992), p. 332.

[20] Among them is an extensive study by John W. Wevers, "Text History of the Greek Exodus," published in *Mitteilung des Septuaginta Unternehmens XXI* (Göttingen 1992),. pp. 117-146.

for these discrepancies. And there are many other discrepancies in the citation of incense provisions in the LXX. For instance, we read in MT Exod. 25: 6 שמן למאור בשמים לשמן המשחה ולקטרת הסמים "Oil for the light; spices for the anointing oil and for the fragrant incense." The LXX omits this verse. This might be explained by the fact that there are separate commands for these items, in Exod. 27:20 for the oil for the light, and the specific commands in Exod. 30: 23-24 and 34-37 concerning the spices for the anointing oil and the incense. On the other hand, it is possible that this verse was added in a later edition of the MT, after the LXX translation. Further, Exod. 35:8 contains the same text as 25: 6, and this is also omitted in the LXX, as Moses recounts God's orders to the people. Similarly, verse 35: 15 in the MT, ואת מזבח הקטרת ... ואת קטרת הסמים "The altar of incense...and the fragrant incense," is missing in the LXX. The pattern of omissions thus appears significant, and suggests the activity of a later editor revising the MT with respect to incense.

I do not believe that my hypothesis is disproved by the theories of such scholars as Sarna or Haran, or by modern archeological evidence. I do not dispute Sarna's theory,[21] set out in his essay *The Psalm Superscriptions and the Guilds* (p. 292), that fragrant substances may have been used with the offering of sacrifices; this would have been similar to Mesopotamian custom, as I describe further in Chapter Three. Incense, however, is nowhere mentioned in earlier books such as Kings. Even in Ezekiel and Jeremiah, in which the terms "incense" or "frankincense" appear, there is no reference to a special "golden" altar; a censer is used by the elders in Ezek. 8: 11, and "incense and oil that belonged to me" is set on a table (Ezek. 23: 41) as a complement to a meal. The "grain offerings and incense" (לבונה in the MT and λίβανος in the LXX) carried by the men in Jer. 41: 5 demonstrate the combining of these two ingredients as one offering, as is specified in Leviticus chapter 2. The burning of fragrant substances, or frankincense at a later date, was a secondary and ancillary element of the cult, until "upgraded" at a later stage. Sarna himself noted (p.290) "...the contrasts between the primary role of sacrifice and the undoubtedly secondary nature of the liturgical music"; yet he seems also to have assigned to incense a similar role to that of music: "singing, dancing and incense are the food of the God (p.287)." One must assume that incense too was originally of "secondary" importance before its exaltation in the Second Temple period.

---

[21] N. M. Sarna, "The Psalm Superscriptions and the Guilds," in *Studies in Jewish Religious and Intellectual History* (Alabama, 1979), pp. 281-300.

I present in this study an extended critical analysis of Haran's theories, in an attempt to show the tortuous way in which he was constrained to proceed in order to harmonize obviously contradictory biblical texts. I shall illustrate here one such difficulty with his reasoning. In his essay כהונה ("Priesthood") in *Encyclopedia Biblica*,[22] Haran suggests that after Solomon's reign the entire cultic system in the Temple was on the decline. He therefore suggests that the incense altar, the table and the lampstand, previously functional items, remained in the Temple, but were no longer used, and had only a "decorative" purpose. Thus, he assumes that the ancient incense ritual, which had been performed before Solomon's period, was rejected from Solomon's period onwards; it was reinstated only in the Second Temple period together with the other rituals of the First Temple, in order to comply with all the biblical commands. He offers no explanation or logical grounds for such a drastic change in the attitude of the people and priests toward the performance of the ritual celebrations in the Temple. Haran is compelled to put forward such farfetched speculations in order to explain the absence of any mention of the incense ceremony in the monarchic period, after the presumed reference to such a ritual in Deuteronomy and I Samuel. He does not carefully examine these two quotations; nor does he question why the incense celebration does not appear in Ezra and Nehemiah among the list of other rituals, or in the narratives concerning Hezekiah and Josiah, described as kings who demonstrated the greatest reverence for the Temple and scrupulously reinstated all biblical commands regarding its rituals.

Haran asserts that verse 22 in Ezekiel chap. 41, which appears to equate the "table" with the "wooden altar," refers to the incense altar; he suggests that the altar was stripped of its golden "overlay" by Nebuchadnezzar, as might be inferred from II Kings 24: 13: ויקצץ את כל כלי הזהב אשר עשה שלמה "... and took away[23] all the gold articles that Solomon king of Israel had made." I do not think it even necessary to dispute Haran's interpretation of the term קצץ as meaning "to strip" the gold off the wood; any idea that the wooden block which served as the inner structure of the "incense altar" remained intact after Nebuchadnezzar's burning of "the temple of the Lord, the royal palace, and all the houses of Jerusalem (II Kings 25: 9),"

---

[22] Encyclopedia Biblica, Vol. IV (Jerusalem, 1962).

[23] I must assume that the translator interpreted the term קצץ differently from its regular meaning "to cut," which is unquestionably the meaning of other biblical occurrences of this term. The NIV translates the phrase וקצתה את כפה in Deut. 25: 12 as "you shall cut off her hand." In a case most similar to ours, in II Kings 18: 16 קצץ ... את דלתות היכל is translated by "stripped off the gold ...[that] covered the doors."

and was kept until the return of the exiles to serve in the new Temple, does
not seem plausible. Moreover, Haran has overlooked the fact that the meas-
urements of the assumed "wooden block of the incense altar" indicated by
Ezekiel do not correspond to those of the incense altar commanded in Exod.
30: 2: "It is to be square, a cubit long and a cubit wide, and two cubits
high." Ezekiel's "altar – table" was "three cubits high, and two cubits square
(Ezek. 41: 22)." The size of this "altar – table" is also not identical with the
dimensions of the table given in Exod. 25: 23, but it is closer to them than
to the much smaller "incense" altar. One might accept different sizes in the
height of the table between Exodus and Ezekiel, but there is no reason to
suppose that an incense altar needed such an enormous surface: two cubits
square (two cubits in length, and since Ezekiel has no indication of its
width, we may assume that it was square, as was the "incense" altar in Exod.
30: 2).

I used this example from Haran as an illustration of the trap one might
fall into in trying to reconcile, by any possible means, conflicting biblical
quotations. The method of biblical criticism, with its conclusions of different, sometimes conflicting, sources as the basis of the canon, and consequent accretions and alterations, is today a proven path, and I need not
defend it. However, as I used this method extensively throughout my thesis, I felt it necessary to illustrate the weakness of the harmonizing theory
used by Haran, a scholar specialized in this field of ritual history.

Archeological discoveries of items which look like incense burners also
do not oppose the postulate of a later introduction of incense into the
"official"[24] Israelite cult;[25] such items might have been burners for heating,
or for burning fragrant woods and other *aromata* in private homes. Even
Haran, who favours the idea of an early Israelite incense cult, expresses
scepticism about the significance of the archeological findings in this respect. In *Temples and Temple-Service in Ancient Israel*[26] he states: "The
truth of the matter is that archeological evidence will remain somewhat
irrelevant to the question of the place of incense in the Israelite cult (as

---

[24] In the Introduction to *Ancient Israelite Religion*, various terms are used to describe cultic
status: *public* and *popular*, *official* and *unofficial*, *normative* and *aberrant*. J. S. Holladay
Jr. has another classification in his essay "Religion in Israel and Judah under the
Monarchy," ibid.: *established*, and *tolerated nonconformist* worship.

[25] Max Löhr, in *Das Räucheropfer im Alten Testament* (Halle, 1927), p. 174 [20], has
already expressed doubts in this regard. Nelson Glueck, "Incense Altars", *Eretz Israel* 10
(1971), pp. 120-125 (Hebrew) describes such altars from the excavation in Tell-el-
Hulefi, dating them from the 5th century B.C.E.

[26] *Temples and Temple-Service in Ancient Israel* (Oxford, 1978), p. 237.

distinct from its secular use in everyday life) until actual remains of Israelite temples eventually come to light." In his later publication,[27] Haran is more explicit, and writes:

ובכל זאת אין בכל 'מזבחות הקטורת' הללו שום ראיה לשימוש פולחני
בקטורת בישראל בתקופת המקרא וכל כך משום שאין בעיני ספק, שהמזבחות
הללו לא שימשו כלל להקטרת קטרת

> And nevertheless there is no evidence from all these 'incense altars' of a cultic use of incense in Israel, in the biblical period. And that, because there is no doubt in my eyes that these altars were not used at all for burning incense.

Such a firm statement, coming from one who accepts the cultic use of incense in the biblical period, confirms that no clear conclusion may be deduced from the archeological artifacts. Several other scholars also discuss the possible uses of these burners (for instance, Nielsen pp. 38-41, W. Zwickel, *Räucherkult und Räuchergeräte*, Chapter II).

On the extra-scriptural evidence regarding the arrival of frankincense in Israel, J. S. Holladay Jr. posits in his essay *The Use of Pottery and Other Diagnostic Criteria, from the Solomonic Era to the Divided Kingdom* on pp.98-99:

> ... it seems reasonable to further hypothesize that this activity [toll collection] was primarily connected with the establishment, under royal aegis, of South Arabian overland trade in incense and spices, consonant with the heavily embroidered biblical traditions concerning Solomon. While Israel, particularly the temple cultus, undoubtedly consumed a minor portion of the trade, the larger part of the business probably involved, as in later days, revenues derived [from the passage to Tell Qasile].

While it is not to be denied that frankincense might have arrived in this way in Israel, and was used in the cult, and that the appearance of קטר in Kings is a result of this arrival, all the occurrences of קטר in Kings refer to illegitimate worship, not to celebrations in the Temple. There is no evidence that frankincense actually arrived in Israel at that period and was used in the Temple in Jerusalem as an independent ceremonial worship. This is demonstrated by the total absence of such celebrations in Kings, in contrast to the narratives of animal offerings. It is interesting to note that according to

---

[27]   *Tarbiz* 61/3 (1992), p. 324.

Holladay's Table 2, in which the artifacts of the various cult sites are classified, incense altars were not found in Samaria, nor in Jerusalem Cave 1
and in Jerusalem Tumuli, the two central sites of the official worship.

At any rate, control of the trading routes by Israel and Judah was lost to
the Egyptians shortly after Solomon's death, as we read in II Chr. 12: 4 :
"He [Shishak – Sheshonk] captured the fortified cities of Judah and came
as far as Jerusalem." Only Amaziah, and his son Azariah- Uzziah, recon-
quered the south for Judah, "and broke down the walls of Gath, Jabneh and
Ashdod...God helped him [Uzziah] against the Philistines and against the
Arabs ...and his fame spread as far as the border of Egypt.... He also built
towers in the desert (II Chr. 26: 6-10)"; but his grandson Ahaz lost everything. We read in II Kings 16: 6: "Rezin king of Aram recovered Elath for
Aram by driving out the men of Judah. Edomites then moved into Elath
and have lived there to this day." In II Chr. 28: 18, we read "... the Philistines
had raided towns in the foothills and in the Negev of Judah. They captured
and occupied Beth Shemesh, Aijalon and Gederoth, as well as Soco, Timnah
and Gimzo." Thus except for a short period, Judah lost control of the
trading routes, and with it probably all means of obtaining frankincense at
reasonable costs. Further, Judah was a small, unimportant and probably
poor country during that period. This does not preclude, however, the
possibility that frankincense was used in minimal quantities in the unofficial cult.

In his essay *The Kingdom of Israel and Judah: Political and Economic
Centralization in the Iron IIa-b (ca 1000-750 B.C.E.)*, p. 34, Holladay
quotes a recently published text "documenting the seizure of a mid-eighth-
century B.C. South Arabian camel caravan ... in the region of the Middle
Euphrates," but "from the goods the camels were carrying, it is obvious they
were heading south"; we therefore do not know the nature of the goods they
were bringing out of South Arabia. Only from the late Pliny do we have
firm evidence of "frankincense caravans" (p. 38). On the other hand,
Holladay offers us an interesting comparison, which may be useful to corroborate my thesis. He states that "during the Achaemenid Period, the self-
administered annual tribute paid to the Empire by the 'Arabian trade'
amounted to 1,000 talents, or about 30 metric tons of incense." He further
compares this fact to the custom in the Old Assyrian trade, when the tribute
was paid in tin. This change in the commodity used for the payment of
tribute does not preclude the possibility that frankincense was already traded
earlier, but it serves as a fairly good indication of the development in this
trade: that is, the increased importance of frankincense, the great demand
for it and the considerable quantities available in the late Achaemenid pe-

riod. Frankincense came to be so important as to dislocate the previously useful and practical tin as the monetary medium. With this exposition I hope to have bridged "the intellectual gap between 'hard' archeological evidence and 'soft' literary traditions"; this, as Holladay concludes in such elegant style in the Endnote to his essay *Religion in Israel and Judah under the Monarchy* (p.298), is an ideal scholarly aim.

Therefore my proposition is not contradicted by the finding of a very few incense burners at sites associated with a temple cult,[28] and dated not later than the eighth century B.C.E. The small chalkstone altars found at cult shrines might have been used for the burning of animal fat and bread, as Zwickel suggests, substantiating this proposition with exegetical analysis.[29] These might represent an ancillary furnishing of the temple, to spread a fragrant odour in the deity's dwelling, cognate to the custom in private

---

[28] As I have noted above, it is interesting that in Holladay's Table 2, p. 272 of his above cited essay, incense burners were not found in the two central cult sites, in the Jerusalem Cave 1 and Tumuli, and in Samaria.

[29] W. Zwickel, *Räucherkult und Räuchergeräte* (Göttingen, 1990), writes on p. 167: "Unter den Altären mit Brandspuren wurden nur bei denen aus 'Arad chemische Untersuchungen der verbrannten Materie vorgenommen; diese belegen, dass auf diesen Kultgeräten tierische Fette verbrannt wurden." ("Among the altars with burn marks, only those from Arad were chemically analyzed; this confirmed that animal fat was burned in these cult paraphernalia.") He further writes on the same page: "Leider lässt sich momentan noch nicht archäologisch erschliessen, ab wann Weihrauch und andere Aromata das in Palästina praktizierte Verbrennen von fetthaltigen tierischen Opfern ersetzten. Hier wird die Untersuchung der biblischen Texte nähere Aufschlüsse vermitteln können." ("Regretfully, it is yet impossible to establish by archeological means from when frankincense and other fragrant substances replaced the sacrificial practice in Palestine of burning animal fat. The examination of biblical texts will provide us here with detailed elucidations.") We may observe the limitations of drawing conclusions solely on archeological considerations, expressed by Zwickel, and the need to consider textual evidence to reach a balanced assumption. Zwickel proceeds with the interpretation of the various biblical quotations (p. 172 ff), and we read on pp. 184-5 his conclusion: "All dies führt zu dem Schluss, dass das Opfern von Brot im vorexilischen Israel ebenso verbreitet war wie in der gesamten altorientalischen Umwelt." ("All this [his preceeding arguments regarding the prohibition against offering leavened bread and honey, as practised by the Canaanites, the bread carried by the pilgrims in I Sam. 10: 3, and the thanksgiving offering with leavened bread in Lev. 23: 17] leads to the conclusion that the offering of bread was widespread in pre-exilic Israel as in the surrounding ancient Near Eastern milieu.") He concludes on p. 195: "Neben dem Räuchern von Fett ist ab dem 8. Jh. mit Am. 4: 5 (vgl. auch Jes. 6: 6 und vielleicht auch Jes. 1: 13) das Verbrennen von Brot belegt." ("In addition to the 'fumigating' of fat, the burning of bread is [textually] proven since the 8th cent. with Amos 4: 5 (cf. also Isa. 6: 6 and possibly also Isa. 1: 13).") It is no wonder that W. G. Dever approaches this issue with great prudence, and writes in his essay "The Contribution of Archeol-

homes; or they might have been auxiliary items on, or at, the altar, a component of the table-setting at which the food for the deity was displayed. We note such a practice in Mesopotamian ritual, and encounter such a description of a table-setting in Ezek. 23:41: ושלחן ערוך לפניה וקטרתי ושמני שמת עליה "...with a table spread before it on which you had placed the incense and oil." Oil and incense were elements of a lavish table setting. The archeological artifacts can in no way serve as evidence for a daily independent and significant incense celebration in Solomon's Temple, or for the existence of a separate golden altar for this specific purpose, the focal point of my thesis. The weak speculations by some scholars,[30] who as a result of these finds opposed Wellhausen's theory and asserted the existence of such ceremony, can scarcely invalidate the textual evidence presented in this study. I shall therefore not elaborate in detail upon the dispute concerning this archeological "evidence"; at this point I shall merely refer to the extremely detailed study on the archeological aspects of incense burners and the cult by W. Zwickel.[31]

Finally, we may turn to historical evidence concerning the spread of frankincense. Nigel Groom, in *Frankincense and Myrrh*,[32] states (p. 33)

---

ogy," *in Ancient Israelite Religion, Essays in Honour of F. M. Cross* (Philadelphia, 1987), p. 233: "The only innovation in the Iron I remains that cannnot be derived from LB is the small four-cornered or 'horned' altar, which may perhaps be considered as evidence for the introduction of incense offerings by the Israelite cult." John S. Holladay Jr. also displays a great sensitivity regarding strong affirmative declarations concerning deductions based exclusively on archeological artifacts. For instance, in his essay "Religion in Israel and Judah under the Monarchy," in *Ancient Israelite Religion*, he writes on p. 251: "...every Israelite and Judean cult center so far identified (whether correctly or not is another story)...." By the use of quotation marks, he notes that the identification of chalices as "incense burners" is not absolute, and in his essay "The Kingdom of Israel and Judah: Political and Economic Centralization in the Iron IIa-b (ca 1000-750 B.C.)" in *The Archeology of Society in the Holy Land*, ed. Th. E. Levy (London, 1994; reprint), p. 62 he writes: "...similar 'chalices', which probably functioned as censers...."

[30] Despite M. Haran's scepticism, noted above, and his later explicit declaration in *Tarbiz* 61 that one cannot deduce the early existence of an incense cult from the archeological artifacts, I wish to note his change of mind in this respect. In Encyclopedia Mikrait IV (Jerusalem, 1954), p. 778, s.v. מזבח, he contradicts Wellhausen's theory that the cultic use of incense was introduced in Israel only from the 7th century B.C.E., and states: אולם כלל זה, יחד עם ההנחה שנוסדה עליו,נתעררו במקצת ע"י הממצא הארכיאולוני "But this principle, together with the hypothesis based on it, were somewhat undermined by the archeological findings."

[31] W. Zwickel, *Räucherkult und Räuchergeräte*.

[32] Nigel Groom, *Frankincense and Myrrh, A Study of the Arabian Incense Trade* (London, 1981).

that the trade in frankincense from South Arabia could not have com-
menced before the domestication of the camel.[33] He then writes: "In the
thousands of cuneiform texts from Mesopotamia the earliest reference to an
Arabian camel dates to the ninth cent. B.C." In his summary (p. 230) he
states: "It is improbable the camel was brought into significant use to transport incense northwards before the first millenium B.C." And he concludes
(p. 231): "The early Bible references to incense and the incense lands cannot
be held as historical evidence .... None of them [the texts] bring the com-
mencing date for the incense trade to any time earlier than is attested by
other sources." The earliest classical author to provide evidence of the use
of frankincense from Arabia is Herodotus, in the fifth century. Jeremiah
attests to its use in Judah in the seventh century, and we have no reason to
doubt the authenticity of his statement. The archeological findings of incense burners in the south of Palestine confirm these circumstances. W.
Zwickel, in *Räucherkult und Räuchergeräte*, writes (p. 17) that the diffusion
of incense burners progressed from the north of Israel to the south, and we
know from Scripture that Mesopotamian influence started earlier in the
north of Israel, in Samaria. He further states (pp. 86-89) that censers were
almost non-existent in south Judah before the seventh century, but enjoyed
a widespread burst of growth after that time. However, the archeological
artifacts do not serve as incontestable evidence of the use of frankincense,
since other, locally available incense[34] could have been used. The broader
distribution of the censers may demonstrate an increased use of incense in
the cult, which could have been bolstered by the availability of the refined
frankincense, as well as by foreign syncretistic influence. On the other hand,

---

[33]   Prof. R. J. Leprohon objects to this declaration, based on Egyptian paleographic evidence
       of the use of incense in much earlier times. Queen Hatshepsut's expedition to Punt in
       the 15th century B.C. to bring `ntyw and sntr, and the story of the shipwrecked sailor
       who landed in Punt where the prince owned `ntyw, are well known, and demonstrate
       the difficulties in bringing these precious substances into Egypt. The Queen therefore
       attempted to transplant trees from Punt to Egypt; however, there seems to be no
       evidence that the experiment succeeded. K. Nielsen, in *Incense in Ancient Israel*, cites
       the problems concerning the correct identification of these two substances `ntyw and
       sntr and the divergent scholarly opinions in this respect. At any rate, the fact that
       frankincense may have already been available in Egypt in the 15th century B.C.E. does
       not absolutely contradict Groom's declaration that regular trade and importing of this
       commodity into the eastern Mediterranean area was a later development because of
       practical transportation problems.

[34]   The availability of incense in Israel is attested in Gen. 37: 25 and 43: 11. These sources
       suggest that it was exported to Egypt. To venture an opinion as to the dating of these
       texts is unfortunately beyond the scope of this thesis. They are generally considered to
       be of an early date.

the archeological evidence as stated by Zwickel accords perfectly with my assertion that the peak of incense celebration was in Jeremiah's period, as is manifest in his book.

Without restricting myself to exact dates, I would speculate that frank-incense as an additive to the grain offering was not introduced into the Judean cult much before Jeremiah's period, that is, in the 6th century B.C.E., since the term לבונה appears for the first time in his writings, as a supplement to the *Minhah*. We have no indication whether the term קטורת mentioned in Isa. 1: 13 was also לבונה, or any fragrant substance added to the grain offering to give the burning a pleasant odour. In that verse, the קטורת is not linked with the *Minhah* as one offering, as it is in Jeremiah, but in any case both terms appear together. The same must be said regarding the occurrences of קטר in Hosea, Isaiah's contemporary in the 8th century B.C.E; these occurrences may have referred to the burning of bread, or of fragrant woods, a custom brought in from Mesopotamia, as will be demon-strated in the further course of the study. From the statement in Amos 4: 5 וקטר מחמץ תודה, one might assume that the custom of burning bread or cakes, also an alien ritual according to Jeremiah, developed in the Northern Kingdom. Concerning the first possible date for the institution of a *twice daily* incense ceremony on a *specific golden altar* (the emphasis is deliberate), there is still no mention of such a ceremony in Ezra, Nehemiah, Daniel and Ben Sira. On the other hand, we have, in addition to Exod. 30: 1-9, the mention of מזבח הקטרת in I Chr. 6: 34, in connection with the genealogi-cal legitimation of Aaron's descendants, and the phrase ולמזבח הקטרת זהב מזקק in I Chr. 28: 18. It is beyond the scope of this study to comment on the date of the writing and final editing of these books, or even of possible later emendations to them;[35] thus, we have no positive evidence with which

---

[35] It is interesting to note that in I Chr. 28: 14-18, in the report of the precious metals given by David to Solomon for the construction of the temple and its furnishings, the incense altar is mentioned at the end of the list of the golden furnishings; it may be that this was done because it was the only appliance made of "refined" gold. On the other hand, in II Chr. 4: 7-8 in the report of the golden furnishings made by Solomon, only the lampstands and tables appear. It is only in the concluding vv. 19-22, which seem superfluous since the previous list of furnishings is repeated, that the golden altar appears. Moreover, contrary to the unexpected order in the Pentateuch, in which the golden altar appears after the table and the lampstand as the last in the list of the interior furnishings, here the golden altar is the first in the list. In the parallel pericope in I Kings 7: 48-49, the golden altar also precedes the table and the lampstand. These differences may betray textual editing; they must also be considered in the context of other problems with regard to these texts, which are discussed in the continuation of this thesis.

to establish an exact date for the institutionalization of the incense ceremony which appears in Exod. 30. We do have extra-biblical evidence of
such a ceremony from the Hasmonean period, in the Apocrypha and
Pseudepigrapha (The Maccabees, Judith, The Testament of Levi and The
Book of Jubilees) as well as Josephus' narratives about that period. Its appearance as a gloss in the MT and in Samaritan and Qumran texts indicates that it was universally added to these scriptural texts some time before
their fundamental division into two or three text types. In the continuation
of Exod. chaps. 35-40, the Septuagint also displays evidence of discrepancies from the MT concerning the incense altar. These are discussed fully in
the continuation of this thesis, as well as by Wevers[36] in a recent study.

Related Issues

One of the tormenting problems which afflict those engaged in the study
and examination of ancient and fundamental Jewish texts is the complex
interconnection of the various issues, and their entangled ramifications.
One cannot escape becoming involved in other topics. A proper consideration of such topics would require an enormously wide-spread knowledge
(which is, alas, scarcely attainable) of the vast body of post-biblical literature
which has accrued over more than two millennia, and the ensuing modern
scholarly research. In order, therefore, to avoid enlarging the scope of the
main issue, I transferred certain detailed discussions of related topics to
Appendices at the end of the dissertation; this allows the reader to skip over
them without interruption of the general flow of the deliberation, and to
revert to the additional data at will. These Appendices are:

I.   List of the 44 occurrences of the verb קטר in the MT Pentateuch.
II.   Financial interests of priests and relations between king – priest.
III. Theophany as cloud, fire and smoke in biblical verses.
IV.   Genealogical requirements for the priesthood.
V.   A study of the hermeneutics of שבט.

One of the largest issues which is inextricably bound up with my subject
is the question of the distinctions in status between Priests and Levites. I
limited discussion of this issue to that necessary for an examination of the

---

[36] J. W. Wevers,"The Composition of Exodus 35 to 40," in *Text History of the Greek
Exodus, Mitteilung des Septuaginta Unternehmens XXI*, (Göttingen, 1992), pp. 117-
146.

authenticity of I Sam. 2: 28. I also avoided the issue of the precise dating of the relevant verses and pericopes, although I believe that my analysis could in some instances offer tangible clues as to the relative sequence of events, if not a definite date for each episode. An examination which has as its scope the precise dating of verses and pericopes must be coupled with a study of linguistic and other parameters, and would have been far beyond the range of this study.

Sources

Quotations from post-biblical sources have generally been taken from the common printed editions; in certain cases I noted alternate readings based on different manuscript evidence. For the Septuagint quotations, I relied on Wevers' critical edition of the Pentateuch, on Ziegler's edition for the available prophets and Ben Sira, on Hanhart's edition of Judith and on Rahlfs' edition for the remaining scriptural books. For the Greek New Testament, the edition published by the United Bible Societies was used. Quotations from Onkelos were taken from the Yemenite Taj edition; difficult readings were also compared with Sperber's critical edition. Quotations from the Samaritan Targum were based on manuscripts J and A of A. Tal's edition, and for the Peshitta, I used the editions of Koster and Hayman. Translations have been provided for each of the biblical verses cited; these have generally been based on the NIV translation of the Bible, and in some cases complemented with my own interpretation. I hasten to emphasize that such translations were provided as a convenience for the reader, and not as evidence of a particular postulate. I also set out my own translations for the quotations from traditional Hebrew writings, and for citations from contemporary scholarly publications in Hebrew, German, French and Italian, as a convenience to the reader.

1. The Association Between קטר and Incense

In its various verbal forms the root קטר appears 116 times in Scripture: 44 occurrences in the P section of the Pentateuch, 19 occurrences in the later Chronicles, 20 times in Kings, 4 times in Samuel,[1] once in Song of Songs (a total of 88), and twice in II Isaiah, once in Malachi, once in Amos, twice in Hosea, once in Habakkuk, and 21 times in Jeremiah.

The study will examine, in detail and in its progressive stages, the exegetical and other aspects of the occurrences of the verb קטר in the P section of the Pentateuch, in its counterparts in Chronicles, and in the later prophets, since these sections of Scripture are the the primary textual sources for the investigation of the developmental stages of the incense ceremony. Concerning the 20 occurrences of קטר in Kings, I shall simply note here that 6 times (I Kings 3: 3, 22: 44; II Kings 12: 4, 14: 4, 15: 4, 15: 35), it appears in a stereotypical phrase concerning the offering on the במות, an evidently late addition after Josiah's reform; 11 times (I Kings 11: 8, 12: 33, 13: 1, 13: 2; II Kings 16: 4, 17: 11, 18: 4, 22: 17, 23: 5 twice, 23: 8), it refers to idolatrous practice, which demonstrates the association of the incense celebration, and the term קטר in ritual practice, with foreign influence. Similarly, II Kings 18: 4 concerns the removal by Hezekiah of the bronze serpent; although the serpent was made by Moses, the context indicates that the editor intended to imply that the removal was a virtuous deed.

On the other hand I do not include in this list I Kings 9: 25 והקטיר אתו אשר לפני ה׳ "burning incense before the Lord." It is obvious that the NIV has interpreted this phrase according to its particular viewpoint, rather than according to the text itself. Jonathan interprets this as ומקטר עלוהי קטורת בוסמיא די קדם ה׳ "And he burns on it incense, which is before God." The MT has vocalized the word אתו to be understood as "with him" or "with it," which does not make sense; therefore Jonathan interpreted it

---

[1] See the later discussion concerning the authenticity of I Sam. chap. 2 on the appropriate genealogy for the priesthood. Since there is strong skepticism regarding verse 28, the core of the discussion, one must apply the same judgement to the three other appearances of קטר in this chapter. Therefore, in my estimation, one cannot consider the appearance of the term קטר in this chapter as evidence of its use in the early writings.

as עלוהי "on it," but did not solve the textual difficulties by this variation. The phrase remains unclear, and we also have no explanation as to why the opening verb of the verse, והעלה, and the closing verb ושלם are in perfect, whereas והקטיר is in participle form, according to the MT vocalization and the Targum, which translates this as ומקטר. These difficulties compelled the traditional commentators to devise additions and interpretations extraneous to the simple meaning of the text. Rashi says: והקטיר אתו. ואותו מזבח הקטורת אשר לפני ה׳ לקטורת הסמים "And that incense altar which [stood] before God for the incense." In order to harmonize the text with his convictions, acquired from other scriptural sources, Rashi interpreted the word אתו "with it," as אותו "it"; moreover, he found it necessary to cut the verse in two, since the first part unequivocally concerns the holocaust altar. Radak, after quoting Jonathan, proposes a lengthy explanation: the verse first records that Solomon offered holocausts on the altar which he built, the bronze altar, and then adds that he also burnt incense on the other altar which was "with him"; since this altar was not in the same place as the other, the verse specifies "which was before God," namely in the Temple itself, and not in the court like the bronze altar.

These commentators have overlooked the fact that according to their interpretation it was Solomon himself, not the priests, who offered the incense. Ralbag, on the other hand, does not attempt to address the same textual issues; he is disturbed rather by the apparent infringement on the priestly privileges. He explains that Solomon brought the incense which was in his own possession, to be burned (by the priests) on the golden altar. Ralbag is also concerned with another textual difficulty in this verse, namely the closing phrase ושלם את הבית; the NIV has translated this as "and so fulfilled the temple obligations," but it means literally "so he finished the House." The phrase apparently does not fit within the context of the verse, which refers to Solomon's offerings. Ralbag claims that Solomon donated out of his personal resources everything necessary for the daily and festive Temple ritual: the animals, flour, wine, oil and incense. The interpretation would thus be: "He completed all the requirements of the Temple." Such an interpretation is supported by II Chr. 2: 3, part of Solomon's letter to Huram:

הנה אני בונה בית לשם ה׳ אלהי להקדיש לו להקטיר לפניו קטרת סמים
ומערכת תמיד ועלות לבקר ולערב לשבתות ולחדשים ולמועדי ה׳

Now I am about to build a temple for the Name of the Lord my God and to dedicate it to him for burning fragrant incense before him, for setting out the consecrated bread regularly, and for making burnt

> offerings every morning and evening and on Sabbaths and New Moons
> and at the appointed feasts of the Lord our God (v. 4 in NIV).

Ralbag understands this latter verse as Solomon's plan to build the Temple and to provide the construction material as well as all the ritual requirements. Perhaps this assumption was inspired by the narrative in Ezra chap. 6, concerning a similar donation by Darius, and in chap. 7, by Artaxerxes. If so, we might conclude that the last phrase in I Kings 9: 25 is a late, structurally inept interpolation.

Concerning the quotations in Samuel, I wish to emphasize that all four quotations appear in I Sam. chap. 2, a narrative which is associated with the exclusion of the house of Eli from the priestly privileges. This text undoubtedly has an aetiological purpose, reflecting genealogical or similar disputes, and we should therefore exercise great caution with regard to the date of the final editing of this chapter, and the specific terms utilized by the editor. As I suggested in the Introduction, the absence of the verb קטר in all sections of the Pentateuch other than P, and the remarkable abundance of this term in Jeremiah, constitute evidence of the period when this type of sacrifice (fumigation) began to gain a foothold and spread in Judah.

We further noted that the meaning of קטר appears to have changed over time; in Jeremiah's period the term seems to be associated with incense, while in the P section of the Pentateuch, the term קטר is used indiscriminately to describe all types of burning related to sacrifice. This issue becomes even more problematic if we keep in mind the following:

a) The root קטר appears to be etymologically associated with fumes, perfume, steam and similar vapours, but not with the burning of materials (such as fat) which were not intended to produce fumes.[2]

b) The verb קטר is not used in association with sacrifices in any other section of the Pentateuch.

c) In the great majority of occurrences in the P section, the verb is used with a directional sense; this is appropriate, not to acts of burning, but to acts of carrying, moving, bringing up and similar activities designed "to put in motion." (This issue will be discussed more fully below).

d) In most of the non-P sources, the verb עלה is used for the wholeburnt עולה, and the verb זבח is used for שלמים.[3]

---

[2]   See the justification in chap. 1, sec. 1.2.6, as well Kjeld Nielsen's evidence in this respect in *Incense in Ancient Israel*, pp.58/59, where he concludes : "It seems to me that there is reason to believe that קטר originally refers to exhalations, be they smoke or odour."

[3]   An examination of some exceptions will be reviewed later; see chap. 3, sec. 3.3.

e) The verb appears generally in Hiph'il or Hoph'al forms; however, it appears in Pi'el only outside the Pentateuch.

1.1 The Meaning of קטר in the Earlier Sources

This issue of the change in meaning of קטר has been discussed by several authors – in particular, Wellhausen, Nielsen and Haran. Wellhausen, in his *Prolegomena*,[4] attempted to correlate the possible meanings of קטר with the different periods of the writings. He states: "Now of this offering [incense]...the older literature of the Jewish Canon, down to Jeremiah and Zephania, knows absolutely nothing. The verb קטר is there used invariably and exclusively of the burning of fat or meal ...it is never used to denote the offering of incense, and the substantive קטרת as a sacrificial term has the quite general signification of that which is burnt on the altar." He adds (Note 2, p. 64): "This verb is used in Pi'el, by the older writers, in Hiph'il by the Priestly Code (Chronicles), and promiscuously in both forms during the transition period by the author of the books of Kings."

It is evident that Wellhausen arbitrarily concluded that, in what he considered to be the earlier writings, קטר in the Pi'el concerns only fat and meal offerings; he did not consider the possibility, evident both from the context and from the standpoint of literary analysis, that the term also applies to incense. Nor did he suggest any reason for the substitution of Hiph'il for Pi'el, or for the shift in the definition of קטר over time.

Both the Targum and the LXX did understand that the references to קטר in the prophetic books included incense. To render the Hebrew קטר, the Targum uses a combination of the verb סלק, in different grammatical forms, with בוסמין;[5] this is found in Isa. 65: 3, 7;[5] Jer. 1: 16; 7: 9; 11: 12, 13, 17; 18: 15; 19: 4, 13; 32: 29; 44: 3, 5, 8, 15, 17, 18, 19, 21,[6] 23, 25; 48: 35; Hab. 1: 16; Hos. 2: 15 (2: 13 in the NIV), 4: 13, 11: 2.[7] In Jer. 33:

---

4   Julius Wellhausen, *Prolegomena*, pp. 64-65, and note 2 on p. 64.

5   I included this passage, although it is considered to be of a later period, since some scholars have also done so in their deliberations: see Nielsen, *Incense in Ancient Israel*, pp. 56-7, and D. Conrad, *ZAW* 80 (1968), pp.232-234.

6   This passage has a direct object את הקטר, contrary to all the others; I included it here since the material is not precisely defined. By its etymology, we may assume that קטר refers to incense.

7   I have not included Amos 4: 5, since its interpretation is questionable, and neither the Targum nor the LXX refers specifically either to meal or to incense offerings for this passage. I shall refer to the passage in I Samuel 2: 28 at a later stage.

18, it is written ומקטיר מנחה. However, this can be considered an exception, since there is an explicit direct object, which the Targum translates
correctly as ומקריב קורבן.

The LXX[8] in most of the above occurrences uses the verb θυμιάω, "to
fill with sweet smells,"[9] to translate קטר. Exceptions occur in Hos. 2: 15
and 4: 13, in which the term θύω is applied. In Hos. 2:15, however, the
Hebrew form is in Hiph'il, not in Pi'el as in all other occurrences of קטר in
Hosea; this fact may justify the exceptional translation, as I shall explain
below. As we have just seen, the Hiph'il is also used in Jer. 33: 18, ומקטיר
מנחה, contrary to all other occurrences of קטר in Jeremiah; however, the
LXX is missing these verses at the end of Jer. (chap. 33), and we therefore
have no comparison for this specific quotation. Nonetheless, we may also
posit that the LXX uses θύω in the translations in Hosea 2:15 and 4: 13
because the interpreter correctly understood that the prophet intended to
express his criticism concerning the worship of alien gods, and not the
specific method of worship. The interpreter thus used the term θύω, which
has the generic meaning "to offer" (Liddell and Scott); this interpretation is
similar to the use of the term ἐπιτίθημι by the LXX and סלק by Onkelos
to translate the term קטר in Num. 17: 5 , in which they understood that
Scripture intended to express a general prohibition of sacrificial worship by
persons other than Aaron and his descendants. It is also possible that in
Hosea 4:13 in the phrase על ראשי ההרים יזבחו ועל הגבעות יקטרו ἐπὶ τὰς
κορυφὰς τῶν ὀρέων ἐθυσίαζον καὶ ἐπὶ τοὺς βουνοὺς ἔθυον, the translator followed the poetic style of the prophet, and used two different terms for
the same performance. At any rate, we observe that the translator used the
specific term θυσιάζω for the translation of זבח, and the generic term θύω
for the translation of קטר. There is a parallel phrase in Hos. 11: 2: לבעלים
יזבחו ולפסילים יקטרון αὐτοὶ τοῖς Βααλιμ ἔθυον καὶ τοῖς γλυπτοῖς ἐθυμίων;
the LXX has again followed the poetic style of the prophet, and used two
different terms. In this case, since he translated the term זבח with the
generic θυσιάζω, he used the verb θυμιάω for the translation of קטר, a
more appropriate term. It is also possible that the translator considered that
in 4: 13 the two verbs refer to the same type of worship to the Baalim, and

---

[8]   *Ieremias*, ed. J. Ziegler, vol. XV (Göttingen, 1976). *Duodecim Prophetae*, vol. XIII
(Göttingen, 1943). *Isaias*, vol. XIV (Göttingen, 1939). *Ezechiel*, vol. XVI (1977). In all
the above instances the verse numbers in the MT and LXX correspond, except Hosea
2: 15.

[9]   Liddell and Scott, *Greek-English Lexicon*, 9th edition (Oxford, 1940).

therefore he utilized two different translations for the sole purpose of variation. In 11:2, on the other hand, the translator may have considered that different types of celebrations were performed to the Baalim than to the γλυπτοῖς "images." From the Greek translation of these parallel structures, it is evident that the LXX intended to affirm the difference between ἐθυσίαζον for the translation of יזבחו, and the verb θυμιάω for the translation of the verb קטר. Thus Wellhausen's assertion that "the verb קטר is there [in the older literature] used invariably and exclusively of the burning of fat or meal," is contradicted by the tradition reflected in the Targum and LXX.[10]

Kjeld Nielsen also proposes that the verb קטר in Pi'el might include the burning of meal and fat. To determine the precise meaning of the Pi'el, (the burning of meal and fat, or incense, or both), he suggests that one should "concentrate on passages in which קטר in Pi'el occurs with other verbs [denoting acts of worship]."[11] He first considered Hab. 1:16, יזבח לחרמו ויקטר למכמרתו. We observe clearly distinct expressions for two different acts of worship, sacrificing (in this case "to its net") and burning incense ("to its dragnet"). It is arguable, however, that the prophet is using a metaphor here which we can reasonably assume to have been known and obvious to his audience. Nielsen then considers the passage in Isa. 65:3: זבחים בגנות ומקטרים על הלבנים; he concludes through literary analysis that "if [קטר] is not incense offering, what can it be"?

Nielsen then looks for similar parallel structures in Jeremiah, and quotes several in which קטר is contrasted with the offering of libations:19:13: לכל) הבתים אשר קטרו על גגותיהם לכל צבא השמים והסך נסכים לאלהים אחרים) 32:29, 44:17 and 44:19a. To these, one must add Jer. 44:18 and 25, in which the same parallelism appears (לקטר למלכת השמים והסך לה נסכים). One must also add 19:4 : ויקטרו בו לאלהים אחרים, and verse 19:5: ובנו את במות הבעל לשרוף את בניהם באש עלות לבעל. There are two distinct acts of worship here – the burning of incense to other gods and the burning of holocausts to Baal. We may also add 48:35: מעלה במה ומקטיר לאלהיו. The verb עלה, as we have seen, usually refers to the burning of עולות, and we have here the same parallelism of two distinct celebrations.

---

[10] Although the interpretations of the LXX and the Targum are of a later date than the original writings, Wellhausen does not offer any reason to interpret them differently, as outlined above.

[11] *Incense in Ancient Israel*, page 54.

Nielsen quotes two further parallelisms, in Jer. 44: 19: וכי אנחנו מקטרים
למלכת השמים ולהסך לה נסכים המבלעדי אנשינו עשינו לה כונים להעצבה
והנשים לשות בצק לעשות כונים למלכת השמים 7:18: and ,והסך לה נסכים
והסך נסכים לאלהים אחרים Here, however, the contrast is between the
making of cakes (עשינו לה כונים in 44: 19 b, and לעשות כונים in 7: 18),
and the pouring of libations, והסך לה נסכים. Nielsen argues that one would
expect קטר in apposition to libations, as in the previous verses; since the
prophet alludes instead to כונים "cakes," Nielsen suggests that "קטר in Pi'el
can mean 'to offer a meal-offering.'" I see no difficulty in admitting that in
Jeremiah קטר might also have the meaning of an offering of meal together
with frankincense, לבונה, a product which appears for the first time in his
writings;[12] this is an issue upon which I shall elaborate more fully in due
course. However, these two verses would still serve as evidence that the verb
קטר as used by Jeremiah refers to the burning of incense.[13]

In reply to Nielsen, it should be noted that in Jeremiah the parallelisms
consisting of the burning of incense and the pouring of libations are two
distinct cult performances, which might have been two elements of a specific cult practice.[14] This might explain the reason for their joint occurrence
in Jeremiah. In addition, however, one may postulate a third type of cultic
celebration, the baking of special cakes.[15] This specific type of worship was
not connected to burning at all, but merely consisted of the baking of cakes
with the deity's image. In these cases, Jeremiah uses the verb עשה, to distinguish the performance of this type of worship, the cake-baking, from the

---

[12] In 6: 20, 17: 26 and 41: 5, appearing each time with מנחה; this would also explain the
expression ומקטיר מנחה in Jer. 33: 18.

[13] It is possible that then, as in the later period, all the לבונה, frankincense, was burned
at the meal offering (with only a small part of the meal, the קומץ "handful"), and
constituted the significant part of the sacrifice. The use of קטר would therefore be
justified.

[14] Max Löhr, in his *Das Räucheropfer im Alten Testament*, p.156, states under the heading
Zweistromland [Mesopotamia], "Mit der Darbringung von Räucherwerk ist häufig
eine Libation verbunden" ("With the offering of incense, a libation is often joined").

[15] See P.A.H. De Boer, "An Aspect of Sacrifices, Divine Bread," *Studies in the Religion of
Ancient Israel*, VTS, XXIII (1972), p. 35: "Cakes stamped with an image of the deity,
baked for sacrifice, are also mentioned in Jeremiah, VII: 18 and XLIV: 19. The prose
tradition in the Book of Jeremiah makes mention of burning incense, pouring out
libations and baking cakes marked with the image of a female deity." See also
Mandelkern's *Concordance*, which explains the term כוונים as cakes baked in the image
of the goddess Astarte.

others, the burning of incense and pouring of libations. This corroborates the proposition that קטר is distinctly dissociated from both flesh and fat sacrifices.

Two further characteristics of Jeremiah's accounts in connection with activities subsumed under the concept of קטר must also be examined in connection with this issue: the place of the celebration –"on the roofs of private dwellings"[16] – and the gender of the celebrants – "women."[17] In Jeremiah's description of the specific cult activities, women tend to be portrayed as participating in, or possibly performing, private celebrations, with limited public exposure.[18]

This would likely exclude the burning of fat from animal offerings, as such sacrifices were offered prominently in public places.[19] Further, the fact that the specific cult was performed on the roofs probably excludes any possibility that animal substances were burnt on an altar, as such a structure would not be appropriate on the roofs of private dwellings. We could, therefore, conclude that the acts celebrated by the women on the roofs were performed with censers and not on altars. This conclusion would then provide us with a reasonable solution to the question posed at the beginning of this Chapter, namely the rationale for the shift in the use of קטר in Pi'el in the earlier writings to Hiph'il in P: the two forms are describing two

---

[16] Jer. 19: 13 and 32: 29, and many other passages in which the specific location, הבתים אשר קטרו על גגתיהם, is indicated.

[17] In Jer. 44, the chapter with the most instances of קטר, women are mentioned together with men in verses 9 and 20-21. In v. 9, the character of the evil deeds is not specified; the prophet merely says; רעותיכם ואת רעות נשיכם. Only in v. 21 are the mischievous acts specified: את הקטר אשר קטרתם. But the prophet speaks here to all people, addressing men and women together: ויאמר ירמיהו אל כל העם על הגברים ועל הנשים; therefore it is possible that the men are blamed only for knowing and approving of the women's deeds. We read in v.15 ויענו את ירמיהו כל האנשים הידעים כי מקטרות נשיהם לאלהים אחרים; in v. 25 the men again made the vows, but the women performed the celebration: אתם ונשיכם ... נעשה את נדרינו אשר נדרנו לקטר, then in the feminine: הקים תקימנה את נדריכם ועשה תעשינה את נדריכם. It seems, therefore, that women were the celebrants of this cult.

[18] A motive for this shift to private cultic celebrations is discussed in Chapter 6.

[19] P. Bird states in "The Place of Women in the Israelite Cultus," in *Ancient Israelite Religion, Essays in Honour of F. M. Cross*: "Animal slaughter and sacrifice, as an action of the worshiper, was reserved for males – as elsewhere generally." With reference to the heterodox cults criticized by Jeremiah, she writes: "Of possible greater significance for an understanding of women's religious participation and the total religious life of the community is the hidden realm of women's rituals and devotions that take place entirely within the domestic sphere and/or in the company of other women."

distinct forms of burnings. The burning-fumigating of pure incense in censers is expressed in Pi'el, while the burning of grain offerings with incense on an altar is expressed in Hiph'il.

The Hiph'il is a causative grammatical form; קטר in Hiph'il means to "bring up for burning." It is possible that for this reason this grammatical form became a technical term for sacrifices "to be brought up" upon an altar, while Pi'el was used for offerings on a censer, or on bricks, as in ומקטרים על הלבנים καὶ θυμιῶσιν ἐπὶ ταῖς πλίνθοις.[20] The incense burnt in a censer was not "brought up"; it was merely put in the censer. On the other hand, the incense to be burnt on the altar, an elevated structure,[21] was indeed "brought up" to be placed on the structure. This "bringing up" would apply both to the burning of pure incense on the altar, and to the burning of the מנחה, a grain offering with incense. Of the latter offering, as we know, only an insignificant component of the grain was burned, but *all* the incense was burnt, as written in Lev: 2: 2 מלא קמצו מסלתה ומשמנה על כל לבנתה, "a handful of the fine flour and oil together with all the incense." Therefore, Jeremiah uses the verb קטר for the burning of the מנחה, since the incense, the לבונה, was the main component of the offering to be burnt; and he uses the Hiph'il, as in chap. 33:18 ומקטיר מנחה, since this sacrifice was burnt on an altar. (Verse 33: 18 is also the only occurrence in Jeremiah of the verb קטר with a well-defined direct object, מנחה). This use thus stands in contrast to the other occurrences of קטר, which are in the Pi'el to describe the burning of incense in a censer. In fact, the only other Hiph'il occurrence of קטר in Jeremiah confirms this proposition: מעלה במה ומקטיר לאלהיו, in chap. 48: 35, demonstrates that at a celebration on an altar, on a במה, where one sacrifices an עולה, and perhaps a מנחה with incense לבונה, the Hiph'il is the correct form. The use of קטר in Hiph'il

---

[20] The NIV translates this as "and burning incense on altars of brick," but this is an interpretation, and there is no mention whatsoever in either the MT or the LXX of an altar. Both forms of worship censured by the prophet, "sacrifices in gardens and burning incense on bricks," are alien to Israelite worship.

[21] It is beyond the scope of this study to investigate the various forms and nature of the altars. For our purpose, it suffices to conclude that an altar was always an elevated object or structure, onto which something had to be raised in order to be placed on it. Textual evidence from the Bible confirms that the altar was an elevated structure: שלש אמות קמתו "three cubits high (Exod. 27: 1)"; Noah as well as Abraham "built" altars, an act described with the term בנה. The Greek equivalent of the מזבח, βώμος, has the generic meaning "any raised platform" (Liddell and Scott), and the common term "altar" from the Latin *altare* derives from the adjective *altus* "high, elevated." The archeological findings corroborate the fact that altars were elevated structures.

in Hos. 2: 15, אשר תקטיר להם, may thus be assumed to indicate an offering on an altar. However, it must be noted that we do not know the type of offering to which the prophet refers. It is also not completely certain whether the verb in this verse was originally stated in Hiphʻil, as the MT indicates, or in Piʻel; I shall refer to this point again.

M. Haran,[22] in contrast to Nielsen, declares that "the verb קטר is, of course, common in biblical passages which do not bear the stylistic stamp of P, but when used in the Piʻel conjugation it nowhere refers to an offering of incense.... Now the Piʻel of קטר is never used of incense, but only of the grain offering....The reason, evidently, is that the grain offering too was sometimes made in the form of a מנחה powder (this time of flour), and moreover had some spice (frankincense) added to it. Hence it could easily come to be associated with the powder which contained nothing but spices, i.e. the קטרת." This reasoning seems inconsistent. The term קטרת is un-equivocally incense, in Haran's opinion, from the root קטר, yet also denotes a grain offering; the latter's appearance is somehow similar to incense in powder form, and "had some spice added to it," "hence it could easily come to be associated" with the powdered קטרת, and with the term קטר in Piʻel. Yet the same verb in Piʻel, according to Haran, "nowhere refers to an [au-thentic] offering of incense." Moreover, as we have seen in verse 33: 18, the only occurrence in Jeremiah in which קטר has a defined direct object,[23] the object is מנחה , a grain offering with the addition of incense, and for that type of offering the prophet employs Hiphʻil, not Piʻel: מעלה עולה ומקטיר מנחה ועשה זבח.[24]

Haran also states "It is not impossible that at times the priests may have seen to it that some spices were scattered on the altar in order to catch fire and mingle with the smoke of the offerings and thus ameliorate the stench of the burning flesh.[25] This would explain the frequent use of the verb קטר

---

[22] Menahem Haran, *Temples and Temple-Service in Ancient Israel*, pp. 233-234, and תרביץ (תשי"ז), p.117, note 4.

[23] The direct object in Jer. 44: 21 does not specify the substance; the object is הקטר.

[24] The NIV interprets "to offer burnt offerings, to burn grain offerings and to present sacrifices." We can observe three distinct technical terms for three diferent types of offerings: the use of the verb עלה for the whole-burnt offering, the verb קטר for the meal offering with frankincense, and the verb עשה for the שלמים offering.

[25] There is no prevailing agreement that burning flesh generates a stench; it is considered as a pleasant odour, by others. However we interpret the many occurrences in the Bible of the expression אשה ריח ניחוח לה', we must acknowledge that in Gen. 8: 21 the odour of the burning flesh of the sacrifices was pleasant. We read there after the

in the Hiph'il conjugation ... characteristic of P's style."[26] Here he suggests that the term קטר was applied "erroneously" to the burning of flesh, merely because some spices (קטרת) might have been added to the sacrifice; yet, as noted above, he also declares that קטר in Pi'el in non-priestly sources is never used of incense.[27] His proposition, it seems to me, is difficult to support on further grounds. There is no etymological reason for the verb קטר in Hiph'il to describe a flesh sacrifice with an addition of incense. In contrast, though he claims that in Pi'el it "is never used of incense," קטר is etymologically linked to קטרת, which is unequivocally incense, according to his thesis. It is true that the verb קטר is used in Hiph'il in the priestly sources, and in Pi'el in most of the non-priestly sources; however, Haran offers no rationale, either for the shift in the verb stem, or for the differences in meaning of קטר in Pi'el and Hiph'il.

In conclusion, none of the three theories cited above has provided a satisfactory definition of קטר in the earlier biblical texts; contrary to their assertions, the term as used in these texts seems clearly associated with incense, and dissociated from the burning of flesh and grain. This stands in contrast to the apparent use of the term in the P section to describe all types of burning.

1.2   קטר in the P Source

As I noted, the verb קטר appears in the P source in relation to all sacrifices; it is used without distinction, both for the burning of bodily or substantial material, such as flesh, fat and vegetable items, and for the going up in smoke of a less solid substance, such as incense.[28] Furthermore, the verb is

---

description of the sacrifices: וירח ה' את ריח הניחח "The Lord smelled the pleasant aroma." This story may have been adopted from the Mesopotamian flood epic, but we encounter a similar opinion in the ancient Greek culture. We read, for example, in Homer's *Iliad*, Book VIII: "They piled up firewood and carried out full-tally hekatombs to the immortals. Off the plain, the wind bore smoke and savour of roasts into the sky" Transl. R. Fitzgerald (Garden City, N. Y., 1975).

[26] Page 230.

[27] Although two different sources are involved, priestly and non-priestly, etymological analysis would not justify such a deviation from the usual meaning of קטר as "fumigation, vaporization" in the Semitic languages.

[28] For the want of a better English term, I shall use "fumigation" to indicate the burning of incense.

used almost exclusively in the P source in the *binyan* Hiph'il;[29] it includes
a) actions with a directional meaning, with a sense comparable to the use of
the English preposition "to", b) actions with a locative meaning, comparable to the use of a preposition such as "on", and c) actions with no directional or locative sense. Further, the various Targumim each use different
verbs for the translation of the Hebrew קטר; I shall demonstrate that these
differences are not trivial, but the result of a profound understanding and
a careful and precise interpretation of the text.

1.2.1 Classification of קטר in the P Source

As a verb, קטר appears 44 times[30] in the Pentateuch, 43 times in the *binyan*
Hiph'il, and once in Hoph'al. (As noted above, Pi'el forms are found only
in the other biblical writings). I examined the context of the 44 Pentateuchal
verses in which the verb קטר is mentioned, and classified them, according
to syntactical and exegetical criteria, into three groups and various sub-
groups, as follows:

Group 1: the verb is used in association with sacrifices of materials of sub-
stance.
Group 2: the verb is used in association with incense.
Group 3: the verb has a generic meaning "to perform sacrifice."

Group 1
Subgroup 1.1 There are 28 occurrences with a directional meaning, according to the context; all occurrences are in association with nouns using the
old ה of direction, such as המזבחה, "to the altar."[31] The verb קטר, as it is
a transitive verb, always has a direct object in the active voice. In some

---

[29] Only once in *binyan* Hoph'al in Lev. 6: 15.

[30] A complete list of the 44 occurrences and their respective translations by Onkelos, the
Samaritan Targum, the Neophyti and the LXX is given as Appendix I at the end of the
thesis.

[31] The only exception is verse Lev. 6: 8 in which the MT has המזבח with no ה at the end,
but from the context it is obvious that it has the directional meaning. The object in
relation to the verb is מטנו, which relates back to the previous clauses; the מזבח could
certainly not be the object of the verb. Onkelos and the Samaritan MS J have appropriately added a ל to the מדבחה in this verse, and I have therefore included it in the
"directional" category.

instances the object is expressed by a noun or by a pronoun suffixed to the verb or to the object marker; however, in other instances the object has been expressed in previous clauses, but is understood or implied in the clause in which the verb in question stands ("null reference").

Subgroup 1.2 There are 4 occurrences in which no object marker is used (object expressed or implied), and in which the relation between the action and the place of its occurrence (the altar) is expressed by על: Lev. 4: 10; 6: 5; 9: 13, 17.

Subgroup 1.3 There are 6 occurrences in which no direction or place of action is indicated, and in which the verb has an explicit direct object:

a) 3 times with the object marker את in Lev. 2: 16; 8: 20 and Num. 18: 17
b) 3 times without an object marker in Exod. 30: 20; Lev. 2: 11 and 17: 6.

Subgroup 1.4 There is one occurrence in Lev. 6: 15, in which the verb is in the Hoph'al (passive voice), and the material to be affected by the action (what would be the subject of the verb in the active voice) is represented by a pronoun.

Group 2
There are 4 occurrences in which there is a specific association with incense:
a) twice with an explicit direct object without object marker and with the preposition על or עליו, in Exod. 30: 7a and 40: 27
b) twice with an explicit direct object, represented by the pronoun suffixed to the verb, in Exod. 30: 7b and 8.[32]

Group 3
There is one occurrence in Num 17: 5, with nominal object, no את and an adverbial phrase לפני ה'; in its context, the verb has the meaning "to perform sacrifice," although expressed in connection with incense.[33] This pericope stresses the exclusive right of persons of the "seed of Aaron" to

---

[32] Although there is an אתנחתא between the verb and the object, one could maintain that the object is explicit because of the context.

[33] Both Onkelos and the LXX have identified this generic meaning of "to perform sacrifice" in the context. Onkelos has therefore translated this with the usual verb סלק for קטר, and the LXX with ἐπιθεῖναι.

perform all the sacrificial rituals, and the prohibition against others doing so; thus it was understood and interpreted in Onkelos' period.[34]

1.2.2 Translation of קטר in the Targumim

Onkelos translated all occurrences of קטר in the MT with the term סלק, except those of group 2.[35] The verbs of this latter group, which refer specifically and exclusively to incense, he translated with קטר. He rendered the Hiph'il forms of קטר in the MT in the *binyan* 'Aph'el; and the form in verse Lev 6: 15, which is in the passive voice Hoph'al, he rendered accordingly in the passive/reflexive 'Itaph'al. We observe therefore a clear distinction made by Onkelos between situations describing the sacrifice of materials of substance, in which he utilizes the verb סלק, and situations describing the burning of incense, which he translated with the verb קטר .

No such distinction is apparent in either the Samaritan or Neophyti Targumim (see Appendix I). The Samaritan MS[36] uses the verb עדי [37] for both burning and fumigating, while the Neophyti[38] invariably uses the verb סדר for the translation of קטר. The Syriac Peshitta,[39] on the other hand, generally[40] makes the same distinction as Onkelos; that is, we find

---

[34] An explanation as to why this generic prohibition was expressed here in connection with incense will be presented later in this essay.

[35] The Onkelos text cited is the *Torah Hadura* פרשה תאג' (Reprint, Jerusalem, 1971.)

[36] As per התרגום השומרוני לתורה, critical edition by Abraham Tal (Tel Aviv, 1982.)

[37] Michael Sokoloff in his *Dictionary of Jewish Palestinian Aramaic* (Ramat Gan, 1990), translates the verb עדי as: "to pass by, to be pregnant," which has an affinity with the meaning of "to carry," suitable for the directional action implicit in the use of the preposition ל in למדבחה. On the other hand, he does not mention an example from the Samaritan Targum in connection with this verb, which always has a peculiar form with an additional ו, such as יועד. But I could find no other verb in his Dictionary under which he mentions these forms from the Samaritan writings, including יעד and ועד. In any case it suffices for our purpose to show that the same verb is used in the Samaritan Targum without distinction for both burning and fumigating.

[38] *Neophyti, Targum Palestinense MS de la Biblioteca Vaticana*, ed. Alejandro Diez Macho (Madrid, 1971.)

[39] *The Old Testament in Syriac, Peshitta, Exodus*, ed. M. D. Koster (Leiden, 1977), and *The Old Testament in Syriac According to the Peshitta Version. Numbers*,. Part I, 2, ed. A. P. Hayman (Leiden, 1991.)

[40] The are two exceptions: in Exod. 30: 20, the Peshitta translates ולמעטרי קורבנא and in Exod. 40: 27 ואסק עטרא. It is possible that in the first case, concerning the priestly washing before any cult service, the translator wanted to make it clear that this was a

the term סלק as the translation of קטר in most of the verses of groups 1 and 3, and עטר [41] in group 2.[42]

The LXX also makes the same distinction as Onkelos. All the occurrences of קטר connected to the burning of material substances are translated by the verbs ἀναφέρω, ἐπιτίθημι, ἐπιτελέω and προσφέρω ; for the 4 occurrences of the verb relating to incense, the verb θυμιάω is used. The expression להקטיר קטרת in Num. 17: 5 is translated with ἐπιθεῖναι, corresponding to the use of סלק in Onkelos. This demonstrates that the LXX, like Onkelos and the Peshitta, interpreted this passage correctly as a general prohibition against lay people celebrating sacrificial rituals, and not specifically against the burning of incense; such an interpretation is evident from the context.

Are the distinctive translations used by Onkelos, the LXX and the Peshitta coincidental, particularly in light of the fact that the other Targumim make no such distinctions? It will be necessary to examine more closely the nature of Onkelos' translation. In particular, I shall look at the grammatical and semantic aspects of the Aramaic terms used in his translation, in an effort to deduce the reasoning behind his particular choice of words. I shall then offer an explanation of the ritual significnce of the terms קטר and סלק.

1.2.3 Grammatical Forms of סלק

In the 40 occurrences in which Onkelos used the verb סלק to translate the MT verb קטר all his grammatical forms appear without the ל of the root and with a *dageš* in the ס. From its appearance in such instances, one might deduce that the root is נסק, as some grammarians perceive it; however,

---

universal precept for all types of celebrations, both on the holocaust and on the incense altar, and therefore used both terms. In the second occurrence, variation may have been the reason for the mixed use. In Num. 17: 5, the Peshitta corresponds exactly to Onkelos' translation.

[41] See Elisha Qimron, ארמית מקראית (Jerusalem, 1993), who writes on p. 12 that the proto-semitic consonant צ underwent a number of transformations until it fused together with ע; in ancient Aramaic it appears as ק (Qimron discusses this issue in greater length). It is therefore unremarkable that the Hebrew קטר adopted by Onkelos appears as עטר in the Peshitta.

[42] See Note 40 regarding the few exceptions. It is interesting to note that in contrast, in *Veteris Testamenti, Fragmenta apud Syros, servata quinque*, ed Paulus De Lagarde (Göttingen, 1880, reprint 1971), the translation for Exodus 40: 27 reads ואעטר עלוהי, as expected, and as it occurs in Onkelos.

Onkelos uses נסק/סלק to translate the Hebrew verbs קטר, סתר, סור, עתק, עלה and הלך according to the context. In these instances there are a number of grammatical forms with the ל (as, for example, סליק for the translation of the Hebrew perfect עלה in its various forms), and other occurrences without the ל (as in the translation of the imperfect of עלה in its various grammatical forms, such as, איסק, תיסק, יסק, יסק etc.).

In the MT, a form of this verb with the ל appears in Aramaic: in Daniel 2: 29 and in Ezra 4: 12 as סלקו, in Daniel 7: 3 as סלקן, and in 7: 8, 20 as סלקת. Different forms, however, appear both in Hebrew (in Psalms 139: 8 as אסק), and in Aramaic (in Daniel 3: 22 as הסקו, in Daniel 6: 24 as הסק, and in the same verse as להנסקה with a נ).

Are there, therefore, two verbs סלק and נסק, each with a different meaning? If, on the other hand, there is only one verb, what is its actual root? Considering Onkelos' translation of the Hebrew עלה with forms both with and without a ל, and examining the context of Daniel 6: 24,[43] we must conclude that there is no difference in the meaning of the verb, whether it is expressed with or without the ל, or with the נ. It would appear, therefore, that the various forms of the verb סלק are regulated not by different meanings in the original Hebrew verb but by the particular tenses and *binyanim*, in compliance with exact grammatical rules. Regarding the root of the verb, modern scholars such as Segert,[44] Kutscher[45] and others[46] regard the original root as סלק, from which נסק arose as a secondary development.

---

[43] We read there: ולדניאל אמר להנסקה מן גבא והסק דניאל מן גבא, "…and commanded that they take Daniel up out of the den. So Daniel was taken up out of the den (v. 23 in the NIV)."

[44] Stanislav Segert, *Altaramäische Grammatik* (Leipzig, 1975). In his Vocabulary at the end of his book, p. 544, the author specifies the verb סלק as the only root for all forms, with and without the נ. He also asserts that this root is present in Early Aramaic, Official Aramaic and Biblical Aramaic.

[45] E.Y. Kutscher, *Toldoth Haaramith, A History of Aramaic, (Biblical Aramaic excepted)* Part I (Jerusalem, 1973), p. 21.

[46] For instance: Wilhelm Gesenius, *Hebräische Grammatik* (Leipzig, 1909), p. 182, Note 66, who states that אסק in Ps. 139: 8 is not from the root נסק, but stands for אסלק and its root is סלק, "to go up"; Klaus Beyer, *Die Aramäischen Texte vom Toten Meer* (Göttingen, 1984), on p. 91, who quotes Kraeling to the effect that מסלק is the etymological form, whereas מנסק is a historical form, from the root סלק; on p. 646, in his Vocabulary, he quotes all the forms of the verb from the root סלק and does not mention any נסק; Franz Rosenthal, *A Grammar of Biblical Aramaic* (Wiesbaden, 1983); in his Glossary, p. 92, the author takes סלק as the root of the various forms of this verb present in Daniel and Ezra.

1.2.4 Semantic Range of סלק and קטר

The various grammatical works attest to the diversity of semantic associations and exegetical possibilities connected with these words:

Klaus Beyer, in his book *Die Aramäischen Texte vom Toten Meer*,[47] offers a particularly detailed insight into the wide-ranging spectrum of meanings of the generic verb סלק in the Aramaic language. He quotes numerous examples for each distinctive sense from the Aramaic Dead Sea scrolls and from Biblical Aramaic. I shall quote a number of these examples:

A. In פעל Pe'al

1. to go up from Egypt (to Canaan), as in Genesis Apocryphon, 1QGenAp, A 20: 33   וסלקת מן מצרין

2. to go up to a higher place, on a rock, as in Genesis Apocryphon, 1QGenAp, A 21: 10   וסלקת למחרתי כן לרמת חצור

3. to come up from the sea, as in Daniel 7: 3   סלקן מן ימא

4. to grow up in height (a horn), as in Daniel 7: 8   קרן אחרי זעירה סלקת ביניהון

5. to go up, with respect to odour, noise, prayer. Odour, as in the Testament of Levi, 1Q21,4Q213,214+CTLevi, 35: 15   סליק די ריח תננהון
Noise, as in Enoch (1Q19),4Q291-207,4QEnastr. 8: 4   וקלא סלק קדם תרעי שמיא
Prayer, as in Enoch 22: 5   עד שמיא סלק ומזעק וקבל

6. to lead up (a spiral staircase), as in Heavenly Jerusalem, 1Q32,2Q24, 4Q, 5Q15,11Q, 3: 3,   בית דרג סחר וסלק

7. to come up (in thought), as in Daniel 2: 29   רעיונך על משכבך סליקו.

B. In אפעל 'Aph'el

1. to bring up something or somebody, as in Daniel 6: 24   להנסקה מן גובא

2. to bring up sacrifices, as in Genesis Apocryphon A 21: 20   ובנית תמן מדבח ואסקת עלוהי עלא ומנחה לאל עליון.

In the Testament of Levi, there are further illuminating examples. In 35: 6-7 we read וכדי תהוי נסב להקרבה כל די חזה להנסקה למדבחה. We can observe here the distinction between the bringing of an offering, which is expressed by נסב להקרבה, and the bringing up of something onto the altar, expressed by להנסקה.

---

[47] Klaus Beyer, *Die Aramäischen Texte vom Toten Meer*, p.683.

In the Testament of Levi 35: 3-5 we read שרי להנסקה אבריה מליחי
ראשה הוי מהנסק לקדמין ועלוהי חפי תרבא. We see here a distinction between the bringing up onto the altar, and the act of covering, חפי, with the
fat. In the same Scroll at 36: 20 we read אעין חזין להקרבה לכל די סליק
למדרבחה. Here, too, there is a distinction, between the verb used for the
bringing up of the wood itself, להקרבה, and that describing everything to
be brought up as a sacrifice to the altar, די סליק.

Beyer translates the noun form of קטר as "knot," as in קשר, and, by
abstract association and extension, as "a difficult problem," similar to the
Gordian knot; in the latter meaning he cites Daniel 5: 12 ומשרא קטרין. The
verb קטר in פעל he also translates as "to bind", and quotes an example from
the Targum of Job, 4Q157,11QtgJob, 39: 10 התקטר [ראם ב]נייריה, for
the Hebrew התקשר ראם בתלם. On the other hand, he translates the אפעל
as "to let it go off in smoke," quoting from Genesis Apocryphon A 10: 15
על מדבחה אקטרת. But the most interesting citation is from the Testament
of Levi 36: 14. We have seen the verb סלק employed in 35: 3-5 for the
bringing of animal parts up to the altar, and later employed in 36: 20 for
the bringing of wood to the altar; we then find in 36: 14 והקטיר עליהן
לבונה. We have here exactly the same distinction as in Onkelos: סלק for
bringing materials of substance, such as meat and cakes, and קטר for
sending frankincense up in smoke.

A. Even-Shoshan, in his *Hamilon Hechadash*,[48] translates the Hebrew
and Aramaic סלק and נסק as "to go up, to climb up," and in הפעיל or
אפעל as "to set alight."

S. Segert[49] in his Glossary translates the Aramaic noun קטר as "knot,"
and the verb סלק in אפעל as "to bring up." He stresses that this latter
meaning occurs in Early Aramaic, in Official Aramaic and in Biblical Aramaic.

F. Rosenthal, in the Glossary of his *An Aramaic Handbook*,[50] translates
the Aramaic סלק in פעל Pe'al as "to go up," in פעל Pi'el as "to remove," and
in אפעל as "to bring up, to lift, to bring." The verb קטר he translates as "to
tie, to harness."

Karl Elliger translates all occurrences of the Hebrew קטר in his book
Leviticus[51] as "in Rauch aufgehen lassen," "to let go off in smoke."

---

[48] Abraham Even-Shoshan, המילון החדש, (Jerusalem, 1974).

[49] Stanislav Segert, *Altaramäische Grammatik*.

[50] F. Rosenthal, *An Aramaic Handbook*.

[51] Karl Elliger, *Leviticus* (Tübingen, 1966).

1.2.5 The Method of Onkelos

I demonstrated that the Pentateuchal קטר covers three distinct situations, which are precisely translated by Onkelos. We have also seen that, like Onkelos, the Aramaic scroll of Levi's Testament, the Peshitta and the LXX have made the same distinction between the burning of materials of substance and fumigation (i.e. the burning of incense), using סלק for the first action, and קטר for the second.

Other scholars have interpreted this type of diversity in language differently. In a study which parallels mine, Bernard Grossfeld[52] examines the issue of the different verbs used by Onkelos in the translation of the Hebrew ברח, and explains the inconsistency by the presence of distinct "strata" and different renderings by various interpreter-translators in the synagogues. Following Churgin he writes, "If, therefore, a word is rendered in one place one way and differently elsewhere, we are certain to have two different Targum recensions." If, however, an alternative explanation can be provided – such as the one suggested above – Grossfeld's "certainty" is clearly not justified. I challenge this pronouncement, declared so forcefully, from both an historical and exegetical aspect; it is, in my opinion, not warranted by the evidence, and certainly contradicts the precision of definition I demonstrated for קטר.

In his Conclusions, Grossfeld writes that the religious authorities of the various synagogues were not concerned with "a consistent and uniform rendering" of the Targum, and therefore "it is difficult to explain why a certain word is in a certain place in the Targum translated by one Aramaic word and by another word somewhere else." Historically, I think we must take seriously the talmudic prohibition against translating the Bible with one's own ideas, as well as the dictum of R. Yehuda, an early *Tanna*, in B.T. Kiddushin 49a, who declared that only "our Targum" (Onkelos) is the correct Targum. Thus, the accurate transmission of the Targum of Onkelos was regarded as reverently by the community as the transmission of the text of the Bible.

We must also take seriously the capabilities of the translators. It is not the issue of this paper to critically analyze Grossfeld's work, but for the sake of contradicting its conclusions, I shall quote one example from Grossfeld's work and propose a different solution. The verb אזל is used by Onkelos to translate the Hebrew ברח לך in Num. 24: 11; this is to be

---

[52]   B Grossfeld, "ערק – אזל," *ZAW* 91 (1979), pp. 107-123.

contrasted with Onkelos' translation of ויברח משה in Exod. 2: 15, where he uses וערק. The context demonstrates, in my opinion, the great difference between these two actions. One cannot translate the exact nuances from one language to another, but one observes in Num. 24: 11 that Balaam was not in danger, he did not need to escape, he was just told, in plain English, "to get lost." He continued to utter prophecies after that, and the chapter ends: ויקם בלעם וילך "And Balaam rose up and went and returned to his place." In Onkelos this phrase is translated וקם בלעם ואזל; there was no running away and no escape. Thus Onkelos similarly translates the ברח in Num. 24: 11 as אזל. On the other hand, in Exod. 2: 15, Moses' flight, ויברח משה , rendered in Onkelos as וערק משה, is anticipated by : "When Pharoah heard of this, he tried to kill Moses." In this case, Moses was in great danger, he had to escape, and the verb ערק is the appropriate translation to describe this flight.

As a further demonstration of the way in which Onkelos extracted precise nuances from the same Hebrew word, we may return to the verb סלק. Most of the occurrences of the Hebrew עלה are translated by Onkelos with the verb סלק, which corresponds to "to go up" in Pa'el and "to be brought up" in 'Aph'el. But in those verses in which עלה means to kindle a light, Onkelos uses the verb דלק: Exod. 25: 37, 27: 20, 30: 8, 40: 4, 25, and Num. 8: 2. Further, for עלתה נצה, "it blossomed" in Gen. 40: 10, Onkelos correctly translates this with נפק, a more appropriate expression. Similarly, I demonstrated in another unpublished study that Onkelos utilized 13 verbs in his Targum to translate the different subtleties of the generic Hebrew verb לקח. Each verb correctly captures the precise intent of the "Author," and harmonizes appropriately with the context. These verbs are: להב, ברי, פלג, סלק, קנה, פרק, שבי,קרב, קבל, דבר, נסב, בזז, פרש. Thus the choice of different Aramaic roots to provide appropriate translations for a single Hebrew root in different contexts is characteristic of the work of Onkelos.

Such subtlety in the use of language should not surprise us; every language has distinct ways to express subtle differences. Certain languages and certain writers have richer and more differentiated ways to describe similar, but not identical, actions, feelings and situations. This is a well-documented reality; one need only refer, for instance, to a lexicon of classical Greek, such as Liddell and Scott, to observe the different nuances attributed to the same word, according to the context. Onkelos, a highly esteemed intellectual, mastered the "finesse" and richness of the Aramaic language, and wrote his Targum accordingly. One might say the question should be reversed: why is the verb ברח , for instance, so indiscriminately used in the MT, both for going away and escaping? Obviously, there are many answers, which are not within the scope of this paper.

Thus we may argue that Onkelos understood the term קטר to include the burning of both solid substances and incense, and translated the term in each verse distinctively according to its context. It is certainly not necessary to attribute such a careful selection of words and expressions to different "strata," or to assume an indifferent attitude toward a correct transmission of the targumic text; rather, we may assume that Onkelos was a translator with a noteworthy literary skill, an impressive mastery of the Aramaic language, and a refined understanding of and sensitivity to the slightest nuances in the text. It was only the Targum of Onkelos, as we have seen in the Talmud, which was revered and meticulously transmitted by the Jewish communities from the date of its composition; this continues to be the case to this very day. The Targum became an entrenched element of the traditionally printed Bibles, its weekly recital in the prayer service a religious duty.

We observe similar subtle distinctions in the Septuagint translation of the Pentateuch. I shall quote one example. In Gen. 16: 4, in the phrase ותהר ותרא כי הרתה, the Hebrew uses the verb הרה for both the first situation, conception, and the second, being pregnant. The LXX recognized the subtle exegetical distinction and translated the first situation with the verb συλλαμβάνω, and the second with ἔχω ἐν γαστρί. This differential translation is not done to enhance variation, but to more precisely emphasize the difference between conception and pregnancy. One can observe the same distinction in other verses. In Gen. 38: 3, for ותהר ותלד בן, "she became pregnant and gave birth to a son," the LXX translates καὶ συλλαβοῦσα; but in 38: 25 לאיש אשר אלה לו אנכי הרה "I am pregnant," the LXX translates ἐγὼ ἐν γαστρὶ ἔχω.

As I already noted, the other Targumim have not used differentiated terms in their translations of קטר; the Neophyti uses the generic term סדר, and the Samaritan Targum the verb עדי. I think we may explain this lack of differentiation by asserting that these Targumim were simply not written in such well-chosen language and refined literary style as that of Onkelos. This said, I would like to avoid the impression that the other translators were careless and provided a crude and unpolished opus. Far from it! They merely had other intellectual associations in the creative process of defining new terms and concepts. The Samaritan translators, for example, while using the term עדי for all ritual bringing or carrying to the altar, use סלק for the Hebrew עלה, "to go up" (for example, Gen. 19: 28, 49: 9, Exod. 32: 30, Deut. 32: 49). Onkelos does not distinguish in these cases between the ritual bringing up of the sacrifices and the generic idea of "going up," and uses the same verb סלק. The verb עדי , on the other hand, is utilized by Onkelos both for the Hebrew סור (Lev. 1: 16; 3: 4, 9, 10 and 15, Deut. 21: 13 and many others), and for הרה (Gen. 4: 1, 17; 16: 4; 21: 2; 25: 21 and many others).[53] The Samaritan Targum uses the verb סטי for the Hebrew סור, whereas the Neophyti uses עבר for the Hebrew סור in connection with sacrifices. On the other hand, the Neophyti uses סדר for the bringing up or lifting of sacrifices and incense, and סלק for the translation of the generic עלה. A particular meaning of עלה, as in Gen. 49: 9, מטרף בני עלית, is translated as הווית משיזב by the Neophyti, but with סלק by Onkelos.

One could enumerate many similar examples, but this is not the purpose of this discussion. Herein I hoped only to demonstrate that every translator, or every territorial segment of the Jewish Aramaic-speaking society, had created by associative imagination different words and expressions for specific concepts. How such processes developed and the reasons for this diversity are problems for linguistic studies; but we can establish the reality of this diversity by numerous examples from everyday language, and by the study of the ramifications of words and concepts from related ancient roots. I shall quote a familiar example, from *Roots, Family Histories of Familiar Words*:[54] from the Indo-European *sal* derive Salt, Saline, Salary, Salami, Salad and Sauce, all by association. This creative process is, in my opinion, the explanation for the distinctive translations of Hebrew words in the MT by the various Aramaic translators, and the reason for the diversity shown by each of them in their choice of specific, dissimilar terms for the same Hebrew word. It is not a matter of inconsistency in form on their part; it is, on the contrary, the result of an intellectual effort to create a faithful interpretation of the Bible,[55] according to their understanding, their literary skill, and their mastery of the Aramaic language.

1.2.6 קטר and סלק as Ritual Terms

Having demonstrated something of the targumic method of distinction in the translation of קטר, I would now like to propose an etymological expla-

---

[53] Onkelos utilizes the verb עדי for the translation of other Hebrew words, but I have quoted only two examples to demonstrate the different associative meanings.

[54] Peter Davies, *Roots, Family Histories of Familiar Words* (New York, 1981), p. 153.

[55] I limited this study to certain translations of the Pentateuch, with particular emphasis on Onkelos. A quest for uniformity among different authors seems to me incompatible with my thesis.

nation for the use of the different Aramaic technical terms סלק and קטר in reference to the ritual celebration. In particular, I shall attempt to explain the association between the idea of "going or bringing up" and Onkelos' term סלק (an association also evident in the verbs ἀναφέρω and ἐπιτίθημι, "to carry" or to "place upon," used by the LXX to translate קטר with reference to sacrifices of materials of substance).

The altar of the עולה , the burnt offering, had a perpetual fire, as it is written in Lev. 6: 6: אש תמיד תוקד על המזבח לא תכבה, "The fire on the altar must be kept burning; it must not go out (6: 12 in the NIV)." This fire was fed with either wood or other materials of substance such as meat or cakes. The flame resulting from the burning of such substances goes straight up. This is probably the reason, or at least one among others, that the whole-burnt offering is named עולה, from the root עלה, which means "to go up." It might also be associated with a belief that the flame, going straight up to the sky, brings the sacrificer in communion with God in heaven. A similar perception is encountered in the Hindu Scriptures, the Rig Veda. The flame of the sacrifices, going straight up, made a connection between the ritual sacrificer and the gods in heaven through the mediation of Agni, the Vedic god of fire.[56]

Therefore the term סלק corresponds with the "going up" of the flame on the altar, when used jointly with מדרבחה, the place from which the fire goes straight up. The 'Aph'el of סלק, the causative mood, means "to bring something up," and when it is expressed in conjunction with the altar, from which the fire goes up, it is understood that something is brought up to be burnt on the altar. In modern English the term altar, whose original context was sacrificial, is now obsolete and is used, for example, in the expression "going to the altar"; similarly, the term מזבח had a precise connotation in the period of our study. It is this connection which may explain the creation of the technical term אסקה למדרבחה, to be brought to the altar for a ceremonial burning. In the book of Genesis and in the first part of Exodus, which refer to an era before the regulation of the institutional cult of sacrifices, neither the verb קטר nor any mention of fire is used with reference to sacrifices. The compound expression composed of לעולה and a form of the verb עלה, commonly used in these chapters, is all that is required to imply that something is to be brought up on the altar for a total burning by a fire. In the same way, the association between אסקה and מדרבחה added to the usual meaning of אסקה, "to bring something up," the idea that the item was also to be burnt up.

---

[56] Nicol MacNicol, "To Agni," *Hindu Scriptures* (London 1938), pp.1, 6, 36-37.

On the other hand, the smoke of incense does not create a straight, upward flame, but a fume which spirals upwards.[57] The term קטר, "to bind around," is thus the appropriate association with fumes which go up in a twisting circular fashion. Therefore Onkelos uses this verb for the ritual of fumigating with incense. Similarly, in Akkadian the verb[58] *qataru* includes the meanings "to rise," "to billow" and "to roll in smoke," and *qutturu* (in the D-stem) includes the meanings "to cause smoke or fog to rise, and incense to billow."

It is probable that the Hebrew verb עטר and the noun עטרה, which appear in the Prophets and Hagiographa but not in the Pentateuch, originate from the same root and etymological association. We have seen that the Syriac Peshitta uses עטר instead of the Hebrew קטר. This verb עטר appears for the first time in I Samuel 23: 26 – ושאול ואנשיו עטרים אל דוד ואל אנשיו לתפשם – and has the meaning "to surround"; the NIV translates this: "As Saul and his forces were closing in on David and his men to capture them," which intrinsically suggests the same meaning as "to surround," that is, "to close them in by surrounding them." In Psalms 8: 6, תעטרהו is translated as "and crowned him (8: 5 in NIV)." We note the connection between a crown, which is around the head, and the lighting of incense whose fumes ascend in spirals.

Finally, as noted above, the term קטר does not appear in Genesis and in the first part of Exodus in any descriptions of sacrifices. This is likely due to the fact that incense was brought from the south of the Arabian Peninsula at a much later date than the ancient cult of sacrifices. This paper does not discuss the issue of the dating of the various segments of the Pentateuch, but the absence of the term קטר and the exclusive use of להעלות עולה in that part of the Bible might contribute some thoughts in this direction.

---

[57] We read in the *Iliad* Book I: 316-17 κνίση δ' οὐρανὸν ἷκεν ἑλισσομένη περὶ καπνῷ "and the steam thereof went up to Heaven, eddying amid the smoke" (transl. J. Thackeray, Loeb Classical Library). Although this passage refers to the smoke of sacrifices, it demonstrates that smoke was considered to go up in spirals. It is possible that in the biblical period and culture, the main symbolic significance of burning sacrifices was given to the smoke and not to the flame, as in other cultures (I shall revert later in the study to the symbolic significance of the smoke of the incense). Therefore, we have the term עולה associated with "going up," while in the Greek world, the comparable sacrifice term is ὁλοκαύτωμα, "burned entirely."

[58] *Chicago Assyrian Dictionary* (Chicago, 1982), vol. 13, s.v. "qataru".

2. Biblical Incense Rituals (Part I): Haran's Classification

My examination of the term קְטֹר has demonstrated that the term under-went a development over the course of time, and we may assume that this also reflects an underlying change in the incense celebrations. We must now examine the disparate quotations in Scripture describing incense celebra-tions, and the various expressions used for such celebrations; here too, many questions, doubts and disputes have been raised.

Haran has attempted to resolve these discrepancies by proposing three kinds of incense used in the cult of Israel:

1) the addition of frankincense to the grain offering, as decreed in P, and probably as an unprescribed complement to all other sacrifices of animal and grain substances;

2) censer incense, as a separate incense offering, a custom which goes back, in his opinion, to an Egyptian custom performed at special occasions; when it was absorbed into the Israelite cult, it became a priestly prerogative, confined mainly to the outer Temple precincts;

3) altar incense, of a special kind and composition, and celebrated exclu-sively by Aaron, the High Priest (not by just any Aaronite priest), in the interior of the Temple, on the special golden altar.

I shall deal with each of these propositions in detail.

2.1 Incense Use as Incidental to Other Sacrifices

Haran 's argument in this case is centred on the phrase ריח ניחוח,[1] "which in biblical descriptions accompanies the burning of sacrifices, and which

---

[1]   It is interesting to note that the expression ריח ניחוח occurs 43 times in Scripture, with all occurrences except Gen. 8: 21 in the P sections (Lev. and Num.) and Ezekiel. All these occurrences are in connection with sacrifices; in most this connection is expressed explicitly, though two cases are derived implicitly from the context. The quotation in Ezekiel 16: 19 apparently deviates from consistent practice, and I will refer to it below. The only Pentateuchal quotation of ריח ניחוח in a non-P section, in Gen. 8: 21 at Noah's sacrifice, can be explained by an exact parallel in the Gilgamesh Epic, Tablet XI, lines 155 ff. See A. Heidel, *The Gilgamesh Epic and Old Testament Parallels* (Chicago 1946), in particular pp. 255ff.

God is accustomed to savour"; he explains this phrase by suggesting that some amount of spices was added to all sacrifices. He proceeds to say that the addition of incense at a sacrifice would explain the association of this expression with the burning of flesh, with grain offerings with frankincense, and even with the burning of those grain offerings to which the addition of frankincense is explicitly prohibited.[2] This addition of incense would also explain why קמר, a term linked specifically with incense, is used in Hiph'il in the P section of the Bible to describe the burning of other types of substances.

I beg to challenge this assumption[3] both from a socio-linguistic and a literary point of view. It seems to me unreasonable that an insignificant and non-commanded addition of spices would have justified a change from the usual term להעלות עולה, used almost exclusively in the non-priestly sections to describe the act of sacrificial offerings, to the term קמר. One might envisage such a change ensuing from an historical event, such as, for example, the availability of a new type of incense, or as the result of some powerful motivation on the part of a personality or a group with some tangible interest and the appropriate position and competence to accomplish such a change. But Haran does not consider any historical or other developments in this respect, and asserts, contrary to Wellhausen[4] and others, that incense was used in the cult of Ancient Israel from early times.

However, the term ריח ניחוח still remains to be explained. The provision of a pleasant odour, the ריח ניחוח, is an important feature of the sacrificial cult, and is mentioned 38 times in the Priestly Code throughout Exodus, Leviticus and Numbers. If incense was to be regularly added to provide such pleasant odour, it would seem strange that there is no reference to any ordinance or custom in this regard, either in the P section, or in the other sections of Scripture, where the notion of smell in connection with sacrifices does not appear.[5] This situation stands in contrast to the addition of salt to every offering; this requirement is not only decreed explicitly in Lev. 2: 13, but is also detailed for each kind of offering, to avoid any misunderstanding: וכל קרבן מנחתך במלח תמלח ... על כל קרבנך

---

[2]   Grain offering as a substitute for sin offering, (Lev. 5: 11) and מנחת קנאות, offered by an unfaithful wife (Num. 5: 15).

[3]   Haran himself discloses in his note 3, p. 231 that "some scholars were baffled by this use of the verb קמר in connection with sacrificial portions of animal offerings."

[4]   *Prolegomena*, pp. 64 ff.

[5]   See note 1 for the only exception.

תקריב מלח. This requirement is also attested in Ezek. 43: 24: והשליכו
הכהנים עליהם מלח והעלו אותם עלה לה'. It is also interesting to observe
that in Gen. 8: 20b- 21a, the only mention of ריח ניחוח in the earlier, non-
priestly section of the Pentateuch, the term קטר is not used; there is merely
the recurrent term עלה, as in the other occurrences of sacrifices in Genesis
and Deuteronomy.[6] In Gen. 8: 20b-21a, it is written: ויעל עלות במזבח
וירח ה' את ריח הניחוח "he [Noah] sacrificed burnt offerings on it [the
altar]. And the Lord smelled the pleasant aroma." Further, Ezekiel, who
knows and uses the term קטר, links the expression ריח ניחוח to sacrifices on
altars, but does not apply the word קטר in this connection. In chap. 6: 13,
it is written: מקום אשר נתנו שם ריח ניחוח לכל, and then: סביבות מזבחותיהם
גילוליהם "around their altars... places where they offered fragrant incense to
all their idols."[7] Thus we see no suggestion of a connection between קטר
and ריח ניחוח.

Another hypothesis is therefore required to offer a tenable solution to
the following questions: a) the use of the inappropriate term קטר for the
burning of sacrifices consisting of grain and flesh, and b) the use of the
expression ריח ניחוח in connection with the burning of such substances.
We must also consider that in the few verses of the Priestly Code which
command the preparation and the use of incense, there is no mention of
ריח ניחוח לה', "an aroma pleasing to the Lord," though, as we have seen,
this phrase is applied 38 times in the Priestly Code to sacrifices other than
incense. For the convenience of the reader, I shall set out the pericopes
relevant to incense preparation, both in the MT version and the NIV translation:

In the opening part of Exodus 30, we read the following verses concerning the incense celebration:

ועשית מזבח מקטר קטרת עצי שטים תעשה אתו :30:1

Make an altar of acacia wood for burning incense.

ונתתה אתו לפני הפרכת אשר על ארן העדת לפני הכפרת אשר על 30: 6
העדת אשר אועד לך שמה

Put the altar in front of the curtain that is before the ark of the Testimony – before the atonement cover that is over the Testimony –
where I will meet with you.

---

6   Gen. 22: 2, 13; Deut. 12: 13, 14; 27: 6.
7   Here again, the NIV interpreted the verse to refer to incense, but the MT does not
    indicate the origin of the pleasant odour; the LXX translates ἔδωκαν ἐκεῖ ὀσμὴν εὐωδίας,
    the usual translation of ריח ניחוח for the burnt sacrifices, without mentioning any
    specific source.

והקטיר עליו אהרן קטרת סמים בבקר בבקר בהיטיבו את הנרת :7 :30
יקטירנה

Aaron must burn fragrant incense on the altar every morning when he
tends the lamps.

ובהעלת אהרן את הנרת בין הערבים יקטירנה קטרת תמיד לפני ה' :8 :30
לדרתיכם

He must burn incense again when he lights the lamps at twilight so
incense will burn regularly before the Lord for the generations to
come.

לא תעלו עליו קטרת זרה ועלה ומנחה ונסך לא תסכו עליו :9 :30

Do not offer on this altar any other incense or any burnt offering or
grain offering, and do not pour a drink offering upon it.

In verses 34-38 of the same chapter we read the following pericope, a
section likely assumed by the editor, and explicitly affirmed by the traditional interpreters and commentators, to constitute a complement to the
above-cited verses:

ויאמר ה' אל משה קח לך סמים נטף ושחלת וחלבנה סמים ולבנה זכה בד
בבד יהיה.
ועשית אתה קטרת רקח מעשה רוקח ממלח טהור קדש.
ושחקת ממנה הדק ונתתה ממנה לפני העדת באהל מועד אשר אועד לך שמה
קדש קדשים תהיה לכם.
והקטרת אשר תעשה במתכנתה לא תעשו לכם קדש תהיה לך לה'.
איש אשר יעשה כמוה להריח בה ונכרת מעמיו.

Then the Lord said to Moses, "Take fragrant spices: – gum resin,
onycha and galbanum – and pure frankincense, all in equal amounts,
and make a fragrant blend of incense, the work of a perfumer. It is to
be salted and pure and sacred. Grind some of it to powder and place
it in front of the Testimony in the Tent of Meeting, where I will meet
with you. It shall be most holy to you. Do not make any incense with
this formula for yourselves; consider it holy to the Lord. Whoever
makes any like it to enjoy its fragrance must be cut off from his people.

These verses together constitute the single command to celebrate a perpetual, twice-daily incense offering, to be burned on the golden altar, which
was dedicated exclusively to this ceremony. This single command stands in
striking contrast to the daily perpetual holocaust offering with its ancillary
Minhah and libation, the command for which appears twice, in two independent pericopes (Exod. 29: 38-42 and Num. 28: 2-8); there is also an
explicit requirement in Numbers chapters 28-29 that it be offered together
with every specific, recurring holiday offering.

The location of our Exodus pericope in chapter 30 is also unusual, six chapters after the commands for the construction of the table and lampstand, the other two furnishings which were placed in the Holy Place.[8] This is particularly so when we consider the following verses and pericopes, in which the table, lampstand and incense altar always appear together in the same verse or in a sequence of verses: Exod. 31: 8; 35: 13-15; 37: 10-29; 39: 36-38; 40: 4-5 and 22-27; Num. 4: 7-12. I have not encountered any scholarly reference to this oddity.

If the purpose of the incense was to provide "an aroma pleasing to the Lord," ריח ניחוח לה' , one would certainly expect to find such a phrase in Exod. 30: 7-10, which commands the burning of incense on the incense altar, or in verses 34-38 of the same chapter, which detail the preparation of the incense. It is equally perplexing to observe that at the dramatic incense celebration in the Holy of Holies on the Day of Atonement, the highest event of the priestly cult, the expression ריח ניחוח, or any similar allusion to odour, is absent. The only reference to the smelling of the odour of incense concerns a human, not the deity; in Exod. 30: 38, it is said: איש אשר יעשה כמוה להריח בה, "Whoever makes any like it to enjoy its fragrance." Again, this absence is all the more astonishing, given the fact that the expression ריח ניחוח in connection with sacrifices other than incense appears 38 times in the Priestly Code. A solution to this dilemma might serve to enlighten us concerning two further issues: the scholarly contro-

---

8   Some traditional commentators also wondered about this "oddity" and attempted to offer solutions. Ramban writes in his Commentary to Exod. 30: 1: "The incense altar should have been mentioned together with the other implements of the "inner" temple, such as the table and lampstand, and indeed it is cited together in Exod. 27: 25-28, right after the table and lampstand." This, he explains, is "because after the commands for the other furnishings in Exod. 29: 45-46 God said that He would dwell among the Israelites, and the incense celebration would be for the glory of God, and it served as a hint to Moses that the incense would stop the plague. It is written about the incense ישימו קטורה באפך 'They offer incense before you', but literally 'in your nose', and the nose is connected with anger: ויחר אף ה' מאוד 'The Lord became exceedingly angry', literally 'His nose burned with anger.' The odour of the incense will appease God's wrath." Seforno has a similar solution, and adds that "the glory of the Lord appeared to all the people" by the "fire...[which] consumed the burnt offering... on the altar (Lev. 9: 23-24)" – that is, on the holocaust altar, not on the incense altar; this corresponds to the phrase in the concluding verses of Exod. 29: 45-46 that God will "dwell among the Israelites," amid the sacred items previously described. Midrash Tanhuma seems also to have addressed this oddity, though implicitly: the incense celebration and the construction of the specific altar were necessary to appease God's wrath because of the sin of the "golden calf", and the incense ceremony serves for forgiveness of sins.

versy regarding the period of the introduction of the incense celebration on the golden altar, and consequently the date of the relevant passages in Exod. 30 decreeing the creation of this specific altar and the composition of a special incense mixture.

2.2 Censer Incense

Haran deduces the existence of a separate censer incense ceremony from certain biblical passages, including three events recounted in the **P** section of the Pentateuch: the death of Nadab and Abihu in Lev. 10: 1-2, the story of the death of Korah's group in Num. 16, and the apotropaic effect of Aaron's use of censer incense regarding the plague in Num. 17: 11-12.[9] I shall excerpt passages from the relevant verses in the MT version and NIV translation; these will be discussed in detail further below:

Lev. 10: 1- 2:   ויקחו בני אהרן נדב ואביהוא איש מחתתו ויתנו בהן אש
וישימו עליה קטרת ויקריבו לפני ה' אש זרה אשר לא צוה
אתם ותצא אש מלפני ה' ותאכל אותם וימתו לפני ה'.

Aaron's sons Nadab and Abihu took their censers, put fire in them and added incense; and they offered unauthorized fire before the Lord, contrary to his command. So fire came out from the presence of the Lord and consumed them, and they died before the Lord.

Num. 16:5- 10(selections):   וידבר אל קרח ואל כל עדתו לאמר בקר
וידע ה' את אשר לו ואת הקדוש והקריב אליו ואת אשר יבחר בו יקריב
אליו. זאת עשו קחו לכם מחתות קרח וכל עדתו. ותנו בהן אש ושימו עליו
קטרת לפני ה' מחר והיה האיש אשר יבחר ה' הוא הקדוש רב לכם בני
לוי. ויאמר משה אל קרח שמעו נא בני לוי. המעט מכם כי הבדיל אלהי
ישראל אתכם מעדת ישראל להקריב אתכם אליו לעבד את עבדת משכן
ה' ולעמד לפני העדה לשרתם. ויקרב אתך ואת כל אחיך בני לוי אתך
ובקשתם גם כהנה.

Then he said to Korah and all his followers: 'In the morning the Lord will show who belongs to him and who is holy, and he will have that person come near him. The man he chooses he will cause to come near him. You, Korah, and all your followers are to do this: Take censers and tomorrow put fire and incense in them before the Lord. The man the Lord chooses will be the one who is holy. You Levites have gone

---

9   Haran quotes these occurrences, it seems, only to demonstrate that there was an incense offering in censers in Israel, without consideration of any common motif underlying the two deaths.

too far!' Moses also said to Korah, 'Now listen you Levites! Isn't it
enough for you that the God of Israel has separated you from the rest
of the Israelite community and brought you near himself to do the
work at the Lord's tabernacle and to stand before the community and
minister to them? He has brought you and all your fellow Levites near
himself, but now you are trying to get the priesthood too.'

Num. 16: 35; 17: 1-5: ואש יצאה מאת ה׳ ותאכל את החמישים ומאתים
איש מקריבי הקטרת. וידבר ה׳ אל משה לאמר. אמר אל אלעזר בן אהרן
הכהן וירם את המחתת מבין השרפה ואת האש זרה הלאה כי קדשו. את
מחתות החטאים האלה בנפשתם ועשו אתם רקעי פחים צפוי למזבח כי
הקריבם לפני ה׳ ויקדשו ויהיו לאות לבני ישראל. ויקח אלעזר הכהן את
מחתות הנחשת אשר הקריבו השרפים וירקעום צפוי למזבח. זכרון לפני
ישראל למען אשר לא יקרב איש זר אשר לא מזרע אהרן הוא להקטיר
קטרת לפני ה׳ ולא יהיה כקרח וכעדתו כאשר דבר ה׳ ביד משה לו.

And fire came out from the Lord and consumed the two hundred and
fifty men who were offering the incense. The Lord said to Moses, 'Tell
Eleazar son of Aaron, the priest, to take the censers out of the
smoldering remains and scatter the coals some distance away, for the
censers are holy – the censers of the men who sinned at the cost of
their lives. Hammer the censers into sheets to overlay the altar, for
they were presented before the Lord and have become holy. Let them
be a sign to the Israelites'. So Eleazar the priest collected the bronze
censers brought by those who had been burned up, and he had them
hammered out to overlay the altar, as the Lord directed him through
Moses. This was to remind the Israelites that no one except a descendant of Aaron should come to burn incense before the Lord, or he
would become like Korah and his followers.

As a general comment, we may note first that Haran does not offer any
historical or other rationale for the development of this specific celebration,
a fact which he himself acknowledges. He merely states: "This manner of
worship would seem to have spread from Egypt to Canaan well before the
Israelites arrived there."[10] He states further: "In the Old Testament, however, such an act [censer incense offering] is clearly depicted as suggesting
an apotropaic meaning...[when it] had been absorbed into the Israelite cult,
it became a priestly prerogative and was confined to the Temple precincts,
though on infrequent occasions the priests would certainly have performed

---

[10]   p. 240.

the rite outside those precincts."[11] Haran also does not suggest a reason for the use of the censer at the incense celebration on the Day of Atonement. He merely states that while the censer incense was of no particular prescribed composition, the altar incense, called סמים, was the exclusive incense to be burnt on the altar; once a year, however, this specific סמים incense was to be used on a censer. In his opinion, the סמים incense was for use in the Temple interior, whereas the other unidentified incense was for use "in the court."

I do not intend to argue at this stage about the logic of this opinion, but contend that it is inadequate to solve the many problems raised by the various verses describing the incense celebrations. For instance, Haran states:[12] "Especially in P and in the Book of Ezekiel, that is, in the writings of the representatives of the priestly school... the existence of a separate spice offering is clearly recognized." But he also states, as noted above, that once "absorbed into the Israelite cult, it [the censer incense offering] became a priestly prerogative and was confined to the Temple precinct."[13] If this were so, one must ask why the P section, which includes so many painstaking instructions about sacrifices, contains no command for such a censer incense celebration, nor any detail about its composition, or its place or manner of celebration. And if, as Haran suggests, the censer incense celebration became a priestly prerogative, one must assume that this group considered it an important element of the cult, and likely struggled against an existing custom, in order to extend their monopoly over this type of worship as well.

Haran sees further evidence that a censer incense ritual was practised in Israel and considered legitimate, in Ezek. 8: 10-11:

ואבוא ואראה והנה כל תבנית רמש ובהמה שקץ וכל גלולי בית ישראל מחקה על הקיר סביב סביב. ושבעים איש מזקני בית ישראל ויאזניהו בן שפן עמד בתוכם עמדים לפניהם ואיש מקטרתו בידו ועתר ענן הקטרת עלה.

So I went in and looked, and I saw portrayed all over the walls all kinds of crawling things and detestable animals and all the idols of the house of Israel. In front of them stood seventy elders of the house of Israel, and Jaazaniah son of Shaphan was standing among them. Each had a censer in his hand, and a fragrant cloud of incense was rising.

A straightforward reading of these verses indicates that it was not the act of offering incense which was criticized, but the idolatrous worship. However,

---

[11] p. 241.

[12] p. 231.

[13] p. 241.

Haran does not discuss whether such a celebration could rightfully be performed, at that time, by lay people, or only by the priesthood. One may
only deduce, following Haran's reasoning, that censer incense was not yet
a priestly prerogative, since Ezekiel condemns only the idolatrous act, and
not the fact that seventy elders of Israel, rather than priests, performed the
incense celebration. Haran does not cite Jeremiah's numerous condemna-
tions of cult performances "on the roofs," described by the term קטר, as we
have seen; he considers them to be grain offerings with incense, and not
strictly incense celebrations.[14] However, I would like to emphasize at this
point, continuing with the same logic, that Jeremiah also does not de-
nounce the cult celebrations by lay people, in whatever form – incense or
grain – they may have taken; he denounces the idolatrous intent: למלכת
השמים, לכל צבא השמים, לאלהים אחרים.

  We may conclude from the above that in the era of Ezekiel and Jeremiah, incense offerings and grain offerings with incense in their own right
were not yet an exclusive priestly prerogative. Consequently, it is likely that
the priesthood would have had to struggle to attain exclusivity in this specific celebration of censer incense, to use the term coined by Haran. Again,
it is astonishing to note, as I stressed above, that there is no hint in all the
P section of any precept decreeing such a celebration, nor any description
of the method and place of its performance. Nor, most importantly, is there
any decree of a priestly prerogative, such as so frequently appears in the
priestly section concerning the other cult celebrations in the אהל מועד or in
the Temple; this is particularly astonishing if one accepts Haran's view that
the censer incense celebration was performed in the Temple precinct. This
absence is even more perplexing, if we consider Haran's opinion that the
incense "...burnt in censers is an 'independent' offering in the full sense of
the word. It is entirely self-contained and involves no other ritual act either
before or after it....In contrast, the סמים or תמיד incense is ...no more than
an inseparable part of a whole complex of acts: it is inextricably bound up
with all the other inner rites of תמיד."[15] According to this statement, Haran
considers the censer incense to be more meaningful, and certainly more
momentous, than the daily תמיד incense offering, especially considering
the dramatic consequences connected with this incense offering in the three
episodes reported in the priestly section: two accounts of death, and, in
contrast, one apotropaic, life-saving outcome. And yet, there is no biblical
command for this independent and consequential offering!

---

[14] p. 234.
[15] pp. 244-45.

Let us now examine in detail the biblical narrations of these three events cited in the priestly sections: the Nadab and Abihu deaths, the Korah insurgence, and the apotropaic effect against the plague. (As noted, Haran does not consider the censer incense celebration of the Day of Atonement to be within the censer incense category, but within the סמים class). It is possible that the motive common to these three strange stories might be the danger connected with the incense celebration, and Aaron's exclusive monopoly over it; it is Aaron alone who turns the danger into salvation.[16] Haran, however, considers the bringing of "strange fire" as the only cause for the capital punishment of Nadab and Abihu and as a secondary cause for the demise of the Korah group.

2.2.1 The Deaths of Nadab and Abihu

Haran's assertion immediately suggests two questions, which he himself attempts to answer: a) What type of transgression is the offering of "strange fire," אש זרה, as it is termed in Lev. 10: 1-3? b) Is there a specific prohibition against such "strange fire"? His answer is taken from Num. 17: 11, in which Moses said to Aaron: קח את המחתה ותן עליה אש מעל המזבח "Take your censer, and put incense in it, along with fire from the altar (16: 46 in NIV)." But it seems inconceivable that an action which carries with it an immediate death penalty is not explicitly prohibited; nor is a command to take fire only from the altar expressly decreed. In Lev. 10: 1, it is written: ויקריבו לפני ה׳ אש זרה אשר לא צוה אותם, "and they offered unauthorized

---

[16] It is more than remarkable that the traditional talmudic midrashim, and not the contemporary scholar Haran, offer a *modern* interpretation of the common ground of these three events, namely the danger associated with unqualified persons performing the incense cult. We read in Exodus Rabba *Parshah* 51: קרח שהיה לוי ובקש ליטול כהונה גדולה "Korah, who was a Levite, wanted to seize the High Priesthood." And we find in Numbers Rabba *Parshah* 4:20: שלא יאמר אדם קשה היא הקטרת,על ידו מתו נדב ואביהוא ועל ידו נשרפו עדת קרח ועל ידו נצטרע עוזיהו "That one should not say incense is troublesome, Nadab and Abihu died on account of it, Korah's company were burnt on account of it, and because of it Uzziah became a leper." The danger associated with incense is even more greatly emphasized in Numbers Rabba *Parshah* 18:8: קחו לכם מחתות קרח וכל עדתו וכל הרי לכם תשמיש החביב מן הכל הוא הקטרת חביב מן כל הקרבנות וסם המות נתון לתוכו שבו נשרפו נדב ואביהוא לפיכך התרה בהם "'Take your censers Korah and all his company': Here you have a function preferred most of all, the incense; [it is] preferred out of all offerings, and the 'spice' of death exists in it, on account [of which] Nadab and Abihu were burnt; therefore, he admonished them." I shall discuss these midrashim further below.

fire before the Lord, contrary to his command." Based on syntactical and exegetical analysis, the latter clause means: "which He did not command them [to offer]"[17] – that is, there was no affirmative command to offer (ויקריבו); but this does not indicate a prohibition.[18] The verb צוה occurs frequently in the P section, and always implies a command to do something, not a prohibition; one such example is זה הדבר אשר צוה ה׳ לעשות (Lev. 8: 5) "This is what the Lord has commanded to be done." A transgression is expressed by the term סרו מהר מן הדרך אשר צויתם (Exod. 32: 8), "They have been quick to turn away from what I commanded them," in which the term צוה again has an affirmative connotation. There is only one other expression of the same sort as in Lev. 10: 1; אשר לא ... וילך ויעבד צויתי isfound in Deut. 17: 3, and occurs often in Jeremiah (7: 31; 14: 14; 19: 5; 23: 32; 29: 23; 32: 35). In Lev. 10: 1, we would thus be going against the plain sense of the text to interpret אשר לא צוה as a prohibition, "which He has prohibited." Further, there is no record of an affirmative command to use the fire from the altar, following the structure of other occurrences of צוה; we find, for example in Lev. 8: 36 ויעש אהרן ובניו את כל הדברים אשר צוה ה׳ את משה, "So Aaron and his sons did everything the Lord had commanded through Moses," which is based on the commands narrated in the preceding pericopes. Nor do we find a prohibition against using "strange fire."[19]

---

17   The NIV translation is an interpretation, which tries to solve the syntactical difficulty of the text. The KJV seems to have translated the phrase literally as "which he commanded them not."

18   Some midrashim are aware of this issue and attempt to find an explanation. We read in Pesiqta deRav Kahana *Ahare Mot* 97: על ההקרבה שהקריבו קרבן מה שלא נצטוו "'...for their offering', because they offered an offering which they were not commanded." This midrash ignores, on the one hand, the simple reading of the cause, the "strange fire" of the text; it seems this remained a puzzle. The midrash did attempt to correctly interpret the expression אשר לא צוה אתם: they brought an offering which they were not commanded to bring. This does not mean that they did what they were prohibited to do, as Haran suggests. Targum Neophyti adds: קרבן יתיר דלא בזמנה "A supplementary offering, not at its time," an attempt to rationalize both the exegetical and syntactical difficulties. This issue will be discussed further.

19   The Sages went so far as to declare that there is an affirmative command to bring profane fire onto the altar. We read in B. T. Yoma 21b and 53a the following *Beraita*: ר"א אומר לא מתו בני אהרן אלא על שהורו הלכה בפני משה רבן מאי דרוש ונתנו בני אהרן הכהן אש על המזבח אע"פ שהאש יורדת מן השמים מצוה להביא מן ההדיוט R. Eliezer says: Aaron's sons died merely because they proclaimed a Halakha in the presence of Moses, their teacher [not because they brought 'strange fire']. How did he deduce it from Scripture ? [Because it is written in Lev. 1: 7] 'And the sons of Aaron the priest shall put fire upon the altar' [hence there is a command to put fire on the altar and,

Further, if there were a specific prohibition against using "strange fire," some warning should have been given to the sons of Aaron, since without it the concept of theodicy, God's righteousness, is violated. The Talmud was aware of this general problem, and we find the following citation,[20] in B.T. Yoma 53a, and in Sifra *Ahare Mot Parshah* 1:13:

ר' אלעזר אומר ולא ימות עונש כי בענן אראה אזהרה יכול יהיה שניהם אמורין קודם מיתת בני אהרן, ת"ל אחרי מות שני בני אהרן. יכול יהיו שניהם אמורים אחר מיתת שני בני אהרן, ת"ל כי בענן אראה על הכפרת. הא כיצד? אזהרה קודם מיתה ועונש אחר מיתה

Rabbi Elazar says: 'Or else he will die' (Lev. 16: 2) is the punishment, 'for I will appear in the cloud upon the atonement cover' is the warning. Is it possible that both [the punishment and the warning] were said before the death of Aaron's sons? [No! because] it says 'after the death of Aaron's two sons.' Is it possible that both [the warning and the punishment] were said after the death of Aaron's two sons? [No! since] it says 'for I will appear [in future] in the cloud upon the atonement cover.' So, how is that possible? [It must be that] the warning [was said] before the[ir] death, and the punishment after the[ir] death.[21]

Thus the nature of the awful sin for which Aaron's sons deserved the death penalty is obscure and mysterious. Many scholars have asked whether there is a kernel of historical truth hidden in that story, and what, if any, is its intended message. The Sages too, it seems, had many questions on this issue, and came up with a great number of arguments concerning the nature of the transgression and the justification for the severe punishment. One trend of argument accepts the literal "strange fire" as the basis of the sin; the remaining arguments do not accept the apparent meaning of the text, and offer a great variety of explanations.[22]

---

therefore, they could not have been punished for performing God's command]. [The answer is] that although the fire came down from heaven, there is a precept to bring profane fire. [Their sin was, therefore, that they declared this ruling in Moses' presence, a transgression punishable by death]."

[20] Note that this midrash considers the sin of Nadab and Abihu to have been the entering of the Holy of Holies, not the bringing of "strange fire". This issue will be discussed below.

[21] In Y. T. Yoma, chap. 1, hal. 5, 7a, we find a complementary dictum: אמר רב זעירא כי בענן נראתי אין כתיב כאן אלא אראה מכאן שאין הקב"ה עונש אא"כ הזהיר "Said Rav Zeira: It is not written here [in Lev. 16: 2] 'for I appeared [in past form]', but 'I will appear [in future]'; from this we learn that God does not punish without having warned."

[22] See "The Sins of Nadab and Abihu in the Sages' Midrashim," (Hebrew), *Tarbiz* 3/4 (1979), pp.201-214. I will later quote some of these "sins."

I shall quote a few of the scholarly deliberations, to demonstrate the complexity of the issue, and the widely-held opinion that a literal interpretation of this narrative, contrary to Haran's opinion, does not offer a satisfying solution. Alfred Bertholet[23] considered the question, as did G. von Rad, who wrote:[24] "And what stands behind the dim narrative of Nadab and Abihu, who brought 'strange fire' and perished therefore"? Bertholet considered the possibility that the story reflects power struggles within the priesthood. Roland Gradwohl speculated[25] that it might reflect the death of Jeroboam's sons Nadab and Abihu, who died young – Abihu by illness (I Kings 14: 1-12), and Nadab killed by Basha after a two-year kingship (I Kings 15: 25-28). Martin Noth[26] also considered the issue and wrote: "Possibly – we might at any rate so construe the story – the lawfulness of 'censing' in the Israelite cult was from time to time contested and stigmatized by the opponents of its use as presumptuous offering of 'strange fire.'" Elliger [27] assumed that the essence of the story was not a literary invention of the author, but was generated by a tradition. But, he asks, what tradition? Had the original story the same scope and motivation as appear in Scripture? Was it originally, he ponders, a tradition which vindicated the exclusion of certain families from the priesthood? Elliger reminds us that in Exod. 24: 1, Nadab and Abihu appear without any mention of their brothers; nor does it state there that they were Aaron's sons. The orthodox scholar Hoffmann[28] quotes the various midrashim and does not take a decisive viewpoint. But he too appears to tend to the interpretation that אש זרה means a non-commanded fire offering. In his opinion, the concept אש זרה is explained by the addition אשר לא צוה אתם in Lev. 10: 1. Hoffmann translates this (as I proposed previously) "which they were not commanded," giving an affirmative meaning to צוה; that is, it was not a regular offering, and was not commanded to be offered on that extraordinary holy day. He then cites the controversy between Rabbi Ishmael and Rabbi Akiva in Sifra Shemini Parshetah 1:32 concerning whether the Scriptural phrase means literally "strange fire," or whether the term is merely symbolic. Rabbi Akiva

---

[23]   A. Bertholet, *Leviticus, Kurzer Hand-Commentar zum Alten Testament*, ed. K. Marti (Tübingen/Leipzig, 1901), p. 291.

[24]   G. von Rad, *Theologie des Alten Testaments* (München, 1962), vol. 1, p. 303.

[25]   R. Gradwohl, "Das Fremde Feuer," *ZAW* 75 (1963), pp. 289-296.

[26]   Martin Noth, *Leviticus* (London, 1965), p.85.

[27]   Karl Elliger, *Leviticus*, p.133.

[28]   D. Hoffmann, *Leviticus*, p. 292-3.

contends that it actually means a "strange fire" brought from a hearth,[29] but according to Rabbi Ishmael "strange" implies that the ceremony was done without consent, or not in its regular time. Hoffmann agrees with Rabbi Ishmael's conception, since, in his opinion, the term אש זרה means: "not commanded by God." We see that even Hoffmann, the traditional scholar, does not hesitate to interpret the term אש זרה in a figurative, non-literal sense. Only John C. Laughlin [30] seems to take the term "strange fire" literally, because of his adherence to a simple interpretation, but he recognizes that, on the other hand, the clause "which they were not commanded" offers some difficulties to a straightforward interpretation.[31] I do not intend to elaborate further on this or other speculations, except by way of footnotes; my intention was only to demonstrate that the issue of the "strange fire" is obscure, and that the term is not taken literally either by the majority of modern scholars (contrary to Haran's proposition), or by the traditional sources.

Before proceeding further, I would only add that the flow of the biblical text itself puts a great strain on our ability to interpret the term אש זרה in Lev. 10: 1 literally. The preceding chapters, 8 and 9, describe the offerings performed by Moses and Aaron, and there we read that they burnt their offerings. In both chap. 8, in which the narration concerns Moses' celebration, and chap. 9, in which Aaron's performances are recorded, the term קטר occurs five times. The question therefore arises: from where did Moses and Aaron take their fire? Further, if they were allowed to bring their own fire, why were Nadab and Abihu punished for the same action?[32]

Other biblical quotations also lead us away from a literal interpretation of the text, and suggest other means of deciphering the nature of the offence

---

[29] It is interesting to note that in Numbers Rabba *Parshah* 2:23, Rabbi Akiva is cited as saying that they were punished for the offering of a non-commanded incense offering, according to a commentator (מהרז"ו).

[30] J. C. Laughlin, "The 'Strange Fire' of Nadab and Abihu," *JBL* 95/4 (1976), pp. 559-65 .

[31] A thorough discussion of Laughlin's propositions would be beyond the scope of this study.

[32] See Noth's statement, p. 83, that the end of chap. 9 and the beginning of chap. 10 are later additions. The biblical editor should have been aware of this obvious contradiction in terms. It may be that this is one of the reasons that the Sages and the traditional Jewish commentators were so keen to search for other than a literal interpretation of the concept "strange fire." As a mattter of fact, the Rashbam, in his commentary to Lev. 9: 17, was probably aware of this inconsistency, and on the expression ויקטר על המזבח, states: שם אותם על המזבח ובבא אש מעלה נקטר "He put them [the *Minhah* offerings] on the altar and when the fire comes from above [heaven], it is burnt."

of Nadab and Abihu, and the motive behind the story. The story of Nadab and Abihu appears four times in the Pentateuch and once in I Chr. 24: 2. In Lev. 10: 1, in Num. 3: 4 and in Num. 26: 61 the "sin" of the "strange fire" is mentioned.[33] In Lev. 16: 1, and in the later I Chr. 24: 2, the "sin" of the "strange fire" is not mentioned. It is interesting that the LXX translation of Lev. 16: 1 adds, probably as an explanation,[34] ἐν τῷ προσάγειν αὐτοὺς πῦρ ἀλλότριον . Similar additions are found in Onkelos and Jonathan. Onkelos states: בקרוביהון אישתא נוכריתא,[35] and Jonathan writes:[36] בזמן קרוביהון אישא בדיא. On the other hand, we read in Targum Neophyti: בקרבותהון קרבן יתיר דלא בזמנה "at their offering a superfluous offering, not at its time." This interpreter certainly added this phrase as an explanation, since it does not correspond to any original biblical text. It does, however, coincide with a midrash found in Sifra *Shemini Parsheta* 1:32:

---

33   Elliger, p. 133 has already observed that the editor of this pericope is lax in the arrangement of the text.

34   It is not likely that they had another original text, since we read in Sifra *Ahare Mot Parshah* 1:2: בקרבתם לפני ה' וימותו ר' יוסי הגלילי אומר על הקריבה מתו ולא מתו על ההקרבה. "...Rabbi Yossi Haglili says: They died [on account] of their approach and they did not die [on account] of their offering." It seems, therefore, that the Sages had a text without any indication of "strange fire" in this verse, and this must have been the text in the possession of Onkelos and Jonathan. We may also assume that the LXX translator added the "strange fire" as an explanation, and not because he had another text. The MT text in the three occurrences has the verb קרב in הפעיל, a causative form, meaning "they brought something [the fire]," whereas in Lev. 16: 1, the verb is in the infinitive קל form, with the meaning "in their approach." The LXX uses, in the three occurrences containing "strange fire," the verb προσφέρω, and in Lev. 16: 1 the verb προσάγω; this might serve as an additional indication that the translator was aware of the difference in the original text, but supplemented his translation with an explanation, as did Onkelos. However, it must be noted that these two verbs are interchangeable, as Prof. J. Wevers enlightened me. It is interesting to note that the Samaritan Bible does not show this addition, and is identical to the MT text.

35   Onkelos does not use the אפעל form in any of his translations of the verb קרב, regardless of the MT form (I have elaborated upon this problem extensively in an unpublished essay). We can therefore deduce nothing, since he uses the same grammatical form in Lev. 16: 1 as he does in the other occurrences.

36   The printed editions read בדיא, which means "invented" and by association also "wrong," according to M. Jastrow, *A Dictionary of the Targumim, the Talmud Babli and Yerushalmi, and the Midrashic Literature* (Philadelphia, 1903), s.v. בדא, בדי, בדה, and the dictionary of M. Sokoloff, s.v. בדי. But in Lev. 10: 1, the Neophyti Targum uses אישא בריה with ר, which means "foreign, strange." There is no contextual or hermeneutic difference between the two readings, and I merely wanted to draw attention to these two readings.

ר' ישמעאל אומר יכול אש זרה ממש ת"ל אשר לא צוה אתם הכניסוה בלא עתה³⁷

"Rabbi Ishmael says: Is it possible that it was actually a strange fire? [No!] since it is written 'which they were not commanded' [which means] they brought [offered] it not in its [right] time." Each offering had its appropriate time. Targum Neophyti has assumed that since the offering was not performed at its appropriate time, as the midrash suggests, the offering must have been superfluous.

There is another interesting supplement to Lev. 16: 1 by both Targum Neophyti and Jonathan. Neophyti adds after "the sons of Aaron" כהנא רבה, "the High Priest," while Jonathan adds כהניא רברביא, "the High Priests," in the plural. The Neophyti addition is a modifier for Aaron, the High Priest, while the addition in Jonathan refers to the sons as the High Priests. These additions are certainly not based on an original text, but serve as an explanatory comment. It may be argued that these interpreters perceived the story of Nadab and Abihu as reflecting an issue of struggle for the High Priesthood. Perhaps such an interpretation was based on their own consideration of the text, or perhaps it followed the various talmudic midrashim, which also point in this direction.

The biblical text in Num. 3: 3- 4 unquestionably refers to the issue of priestly legitimacy. We read there:

אלה שמות בני אהרן הכהנים המשוחים אשר מלא ידם לכהן. וימת נדב
ואביהוא לפני ה' בהקרבם אש זרה לפני ה' במדבר סיני ובנים לא היו
להם ויכהן אלעזר ואיתמר על פני אהרן אביהם.

Those were the names of Aaron's sons, the anointed priests, who were ordained to serve as priests. Nadab and Abihu, however, fell dead before the Lord when they made an offering with unauthorized fire before him in the Desert of Sinai. They had no sons; so only Eleazar and Ithamar served as priests during the lifetime of their father Aaron.

It is obvious from the text that the purpose is to justify the giving of priesthood privileges to Eleazar and Ithamar, notwithstanding that Nadab was Aaron's first-born son, as it is written in v. 2. Therefore the first phrase

---

37 The printed edition has בלא עצה "without counsel," which corresponds to another midrash, but in MS Rome, we read: בלא עתה, "not in its time," "superfluous," which better fits the context. The Ra'avad's commentary on the Sifra in the same printed edition also states הכניסוה בלא עתה: פירוש על האש ועל הקטרת נאמר "they offered it not in its time; this relates to the fire and the incense." The Midrash Hagadol on Lev. 10: 1 also states בלא עתה quoting Rabbi Ishmael.

in this pericope confirms that all four sons were consecrated for the priesthood, but that the first two died without descendants, and therefore the remaining two ministered. Leviticus Rabba 20:11 analyzes the purpose of each phrase in this verse. We read:

ובנים לא היו להם רבי יעקב בר אבין בשם ר' אבין בשם ר' אחא אמר
אילו היו להם בנים היו קודמין לאלעזר ולאיתמר דתנינן תמן כל הקודם
לנחלה קודם לכבוד.[38]

'And they had no children': Rabbi Jacob bar Abin in the name of R. Abin in the name of R. Aha said: If they had children, they [the children of Nadab and Abihu] would come [to be High Priests] before Eleazar and Ithamar, because we learned there ' the one who is first to inherit, is first to honour.'

It is evident that to the midrashic commentator the point of this pericope was the issue of the priestly rights of Eleazar and Ithamar and their descendants.

There are further peculiarities in this pericope which point to underlying issues of legitimacy. At the end of verse 3: 4, we find an unusual expansion: ויכהן אלעזר ואיתמר על פני אהרן אביהם, "so only Eleazar and Ithamar served as priests during the lifetime of their father Aaron." The use of the singular form of the verb כהן with reference to the two sons, the two subjects of the verb, is intriguing.[39] Perhaps there was an influence[40] here from Deut. 10: 6: שם מת אהרן ויקבר שם ויכהן אלעזר בנו תחתיו "there Aaron died and was buried, and Eleazar his son succeeded him as priest." There is the same inconsistency, as we shall observe later, in I Chr. However, there is also a discrepancy between these two pericopes in Numbers and Deuteronomy. In Deut. 10: 6, we read that Eleazar ministered in his [Aaron's]

---

[38] In Sifra *Shemini Pereq* 1:2 a similar homily is brought by Rabbi Shimon ben Gamaliel in the name of Rabbi Eliezer ben Azariah.

[39] Onkelos, Jonathan and the LXX translate this verb in singular form, following the MT text.

[40] It is not within the scope of this study to critically examine and take a position regarding the redaction dates of the different biblical books and their reciprocal influences; I merely wish to draw attention to the fact that the pericope in Deut. 10: 6 might have induced the editor to use the singular form in Num. 3: 4. However, there might also have been two original texts. We read in Deut. 10: 6 that Aaron died in מוסרה, but in Num 33: 38-39, it is said that Aaron died in הר ההר. The Sages noted this as well; we find their questions and answers in Y.T. Yoma, chap. 1, hal. 1, 38b; Y.T. Sotah, chap.1, hal. 10, 7a; in Mechilta dR. Shimon bar Yochai, 15: 22, and in other midrashim.

stead, which is reasonable; after the father's death, his son became priest. But in Num. 3: 4 we read that Eleazar and Ithamar ministered in the sight of Aaron their father, which is illogical: why would the sons minister during the life of their father after the death of their elder brothers?[41] Thus we again observe a hint as to some problem of pretension and counterclaim to priestly titles.

This assumption might shed some light on the addition of the phrase כהניא רברביא by Jonathan, and of the phrase כהנא רבה by Neophyti. Each might have speculated that the story hints at a struggle concerning the duties to be performed by the High Priest. This assumption is more than evident in the flow of the biblical narrative which culminates in the death of Nadab and Abihu in Lev. chap. 10. Exod. 40: 17-33 narrates the setting up and the consecration of the Tabernacle and its equipment, followed by Moses' performance of the sacrificial cult, the offering of the whole burnt sacrifice, the meal (*Minhah*) offering (v.29) and the incense offering (v. 27). The narrative is then interrupted by other issues, in Lev. chap. 1- 7, then resumes in Lev. chap. 8 with God's command for the consecration of Aaron and his sons, and the performance of this command. Chap. 9 follows with Aaron's first performance of the cult, the offering of the various sacrifices; however, there is no mention here of the incense celebration,[42] which we do find at Moses' consecration of the Tabernacle and its equipment, in Exod. 40: 27. We would then expect the incense celebration at the end of chap.

---

[41] In this case too, the Sages were aware of the problematic text, and we find in Numbers Rabba *Parshah* 2:26: "רבי יצחק אמר בחייו ר' חייא בר אבא אמר במותו" "R. Isaac said: 'In his [Aaron's] lifetime'; R. Hija bar Aba said: [they served] after his death." The midrash explains how it would be possible for a son to serve as High Priest during his father's lifetime – that is, when the father was impure.

[42] Actually, we do not find, either in chap. 8 or in chap. 9, a command for the incense celebration, which is in itself strange. This fact might lead us to interesting conclusions regarding the initiatory period of the daily incense celebration, since we may assume that the editor of these chapters would have known the contents of Exod. 30: 7-8 and 40: 27, but nevertheless does not mention them. It seems that the Sages were aware of this oddity concerning the daily perpetual sacrifice, the קרבן תמיד, and we find an interesting midrash in Numbers Rabba *Parshah* 12:15: ר' חנינא הגדול אומר שלשה פעמים בכל יום שנאמר הוקם ויקם להקים אחת לתמיד של שחר ואחת למלואים ואחת לתמיד של ערב "R. Hanina the Great says:Three times [did Moses erect and dismantle the Tabernacle] every day, since the verb to erect [in various grammatical forms] is written three times [in the narration of the erection of the Tabernacle], one for the morning perpetual [offering], one for the consecration [offering] and one for the evening perpetual [offering]."

9, or at the beginning of chap. 10,[43] and we find in 10: 1 that it was performed by Nadab and Abihu; thus it was performed in its right time and sequence, but seemingly not by the right persons.[44] According to the talmudic sources, from which both Jonathan and Neophyti seem to have derived most of their interpretations, there were priestly functions to be performed in the eight days of the consecration of the Tabernacle (seven by Moses, and the eighth by Aaron), and these were the exclusive prerogative of the High Priest.[45] This may explain why the Neophyti described Aaron as "High Priest," while Jonathan did the same for Aaron's sons. These

---

[43] The Sages were apparently also aware of this problem, and we read in Sifra *Shemini Parsheta* 1:30: ויבא משה ואהרן אל אהל מועד. למה נכנס משה ואהרן ביחד ללמד אהרן על מעשה הקטורת "[It is written] 'And Moses and Aaron went into the tabernacle (Lev. 9: 23).' Why did both enter together [since they were already outside the tabernacle, as is clear from the previous verses]? To teach Aaron the incense celebration."

[44] Abarbanel, in his commentary on Lev. 10: 1, has an interesting alternative. He states that Nadab and Abihu each offered incense on two separate censers, that is, two offerings, whereas only one offering was commanded. Actually, the MT text is inconsistent; we read אש ויקחו בני אהרן איש מחחתו ויתנו בהן אש "Aaron's sons Nadab and Abihu took their censers, put fire in them," which clearly means in two censers. The MT text proceeds וישימו עליה קטרת "and added incense" (the NIV avoids the difficulty by omitting the translation of עליה), but here the MT text is in singular, that is, on one censer. Thus we have two censers on which fire was placed, and only one censer on which incense was placed. Onkelos and Jonathan have followed the MT, using first plural and then singular. The LXX is consistent: ἕκαστος τὸ πυρεῖον αὐτοῦ ἐπέθηκαν ἐπ' αὐτὸ πῦρ καὶ ἐπέβαλον ἐπ' αὐτὸ θυμίαμα "Each one [took] his censer [and] put [plural] in it fire and threw [plural] on it incense"; all verbs are in plural, implying each used his own censer. In the Samaritan Bible, we find וישימו עליהן "and they put on them," clearly in plural, implying two censers, just as in Abarbanel's proposition. Prof. J. W. Wevers suggested the possibility that the MT editors had before them two versions, one in plural and one in singular; both would have the same meaning, implying two censers, each to his own censer. The editor tried to maintain both versions, and wrote one part in plural, בהן and one part in singular עליה.

[45] In B.T. Yoma 3b, and in Y.T.chap.1, hal. 1, 38b, the Talmud equates the priestly duties of the Day of Atonement to those of the consecration days. Rashi, in his commentary to the B. T., explains clearly: דנין יום הכיפורים שהיא עבודה ראשונה שהוטלה בכהן גדול בקרבנות ציבור ביום הכיפורים הראשון מעבודת שמיני למלואים שהיא עבודה ראשונה שנעשית ע"י כהן גדול מעולם. "We compare the Day of Atonement, the first performance imposed on the High Priest with respect to the communal sacrifices on the first Day of Atonement, with the duty of the eighth day of the consecration, which is the first celebration ever performed by the High Priest." Moses, who performed the sacrificial cult on the first seven days, is also considered a High Priest for the consecration days celebration, which had to be performed by a High Priest. B.T. Zebachim 101b states: אמר רב משה רבנו כהן גדול "Rav said: Moses, our teacher, [was] a High

Targumim may have deduced from the various midrashim that Nadab and Abihu, by offering the incense, either contested the exclusive prerogative of the High Priest, or considered themselves to be High Priests, with the right to perform the incense celebration. The phrase אשר לא צוה אתם might have the stress on אתם "them"; that is, "they", Nadab and Abihu, were not commanded to perform the incense celebration. It was only Aaron, the High Priest, who was ordered to perform this rite.

This is confirmed by the simple reading of the text in Exod. 30: 7, where it is explicitly written: והקטיר עליו אהרן קטרת סמים בבקר בבקר [46] "Aaron must burn fragrant incense on the altar every morning." Aaron is also mentioned in the pericopes in Lev. 9 and 16 concerning the ministry on the eighth consecration day and on the Day of Atonement. We would therefore expect that all three celebrations – the daily incense, the service on the Day of Atonement and the service on the eight consecration days – should be the exclusive privilege of the High Priest. But in fact we know [47] that while the

---

Priest." We read in Midrash Tanhuma *Parshat Noah* 20: משה התחיל בכהונה ובדוכן "וקרבנות ובתורה, בכהונה גדולה בשבעת ימי המלואים Moses initiated the priesthood, the podium [hierarchy], the sacrifices, the Torah, the priesthood; he served in the High Priesthood on the seven consecration days." And in Exodus Rabba 37:1, we read: רבנן אמרו כל מ' שנה שהיו ישראל במדבר שמש משה בכהונה גדולה וי"א שלא שמש אלא שבעת ימי המלואים "The Rabbis said that all the forty years that [the children of] Israel were in the desert, Moses ministered as a High Priest, and some say that he ministered [as a High Priest] only on the seven consecration days."

[46] The Sages similarly deduced from the phrase ויקרב אהרן אל המזבח in Lev. 9: 8 that the consecration offerings had to be celebrated exclusively by Aaron, the High Priest. Rashi compares the cult service on the Day of Atonement and the consecration days, in B.T. Yoma 3b, and writes: עבודה בכהן גדול ביום הכיפורים מעבודה בכהן גדול במלואים דכתיב ויקרב אהרן אל המזבח "[We deduce] the service by the High Priest on the Day of Atonement from the service by the High Priest on the consecration [days], since it is written 'Aaron therefore went to the altar'."

[47] B. T. Yoma 7a and Horaioth 12b list the differences between the High Priest and the simple priests, and we read there: וכל עבודת יום הכיפורים אינה כשרה אלא בו "And all the service of the Day of Atonement is appropriate [to be celebrated] only by him [the High Priest]." The daily incense celebration does not appear in that list, and we read in Mishnah Tamid, 5:2: אמר להם חדשים לקטרת בואו והפיסו זכה מי שזכה "[The supervisor] said to them: 'New ones [priests who had never before performed the incense celebration] come and cast the lot!' He who won, [served]." We also have corroborating evidence in this respect from Luke 1: 9 :"According to the custom of the priest's office his lot was to burn incense when he went into the temple of the Lord." On the other hand, though we have evidence that a lot was cast for this specific incense celebration, I did not find evidence from other than talmudic sources that a lot was also cast for the other daily cult celebrations, such as the *Tamid* sacrifice and the lighting of the lampstand. From the narration of the priestly operations in *The Letter of Aristeas*, 92-

ministry on the Day of Atonement remained the prerogative of the High
Priest, the daily incense celebration was performed by simple priests. We
can thus verify an inconsistency in the custom, and in the interpretation of
the scriptural commands, and this allows us to speculate that there was a
struggle within the priestly class concerning the privileges of the daily incense celebration. We may assume that such a dramatic change might have
been carried out only after a bitter struggle among the interested groups.
The story of the death of Nadab and Abihu at the incense celebration might
contain an implicit reference to this struggle. Some of the midrashim, as we
have noted, hint at such a "power" struggle; I shall return to the midrashim,
in due course.

Another peculiarity concerning Nadab and Abihu is the text of the later
I Chr. in chapters 5 and 24. In the aetiological chapter 5: 28-30[48] (chap. 6:
3-4 in NIV), we read:

ובני עמרם אהרן ומשה ומרים ובני אהרן נדב ואביהוא אלעזר ואיתמר.
אלעזר הוליד את פינחס פינחס הוליד את אבישוע

The children of Amram: Aaron, Moses and Miriam. The sons of Aaron: Nadab, Abihu, Eleazar and Ithamar. Eleazar was the father of
Phinehas, Phinehas the father of Abishua.

There is no mention of the "sin" of Nadab and Abihu, nor of their death;
both are ignored, as is Ithamar,[49] and only Phinehas,[50] Eleazar's sole de-

---

95, one might even deduce the opposite. Hence, we perceive even in this late period the
rivalry connected with the incense celebration, possibly a remnant of prior struggles, or
due to ongoing issues, as I shall elaborate upon later in this study.

[48] We read in this chapter, in vv. 1-2, the justification for Reuben's loss of firstborn rights,
and the enhanced privileges of Judah and Joseph. We thus have an explanation for the
settlement of the tribes of Reuben, Gad and part of Manasseh on the east side of the
Jordan, and consequent defeat by the Assyrians and forced migration.

[49] Radak, in his commentary to Chr., seems to be aware of this oddity concerning the
disappearance of Ithamar and tries to justify it, stating that Scripture intended here to
illustrate the genealogy of the High Priests. This seems weak, since we also have reference to Miriam in this pericope, who certainly had no connection to the High Priesthood. Moreover, we read in I Chr. 6: 34 that Aaron and his sons exercised the duties
of the priesthood, not of the High Priesthood, and in v. 35 (50 in NIV), Scripture
names the sons mentioned in v. 34 (49 in NIV): ואלה בני אהרן אלעזר בנו פינחס בנו
"And these are the sons of Aaron, Eleazar his son, Phinehas his son." However, it is
clear that Radak too considered this pericope as a justification for the exclusive claim of
Eleazar's descendants to the priesthood.

[50] It is possible that this peculiar type of genealogical record, mentioning only one son and

scendant, is mentioned, in order to confirm Eleazar's descendants as the legitimate High Priests in the Temple. The line is continued through the post-exilic period; we read in v. 36 (6: 10 in NIV): ויוחנן הוליד את עזריה הוא אשר כהן בבית אשר בנה שלמה בירושלים "Johanan the father of Azariah (it was he who served as priest in the temple Solomon built in Jerusalem)." And, after further genealogical records, we read in v. 41 (6: 15 in NIV): ויהוצדק הלך בהגלות ה' את יהודה וירושלם ביד נבכדנצר "Jehozadak was deported when the Lord sent Judah and Jerusalem into exile by the hand of Nebuchadnezzar." Thus the text attests to the legitimacy of the line of priests descended from Eleazar, through Azariah and Jehozadak, and the latter's son Jeshua, who came back to Jerusalem from the exile, as we read in Ezra 3: 2:

ויקם ישוע בן יוצדק ואחיו הכהנים וזרובבל בן שאלתיאל ואחיו ויבנו את מזבח אלהי ישראל להעלות עליו עלות ככתוב בתורת משה איש האלהים

Then Jeshua son of Jozadak and his fellow priests and Zerubbabel son of Shealtiel and his associates began to build the altar of the God of Israel to sacrifice burnt offerings on it, in accordance with what is written in the law of Moses the man of God.

Here then is clear documentation of the post-exilic priestly lineage, tracing itself from Eleazar.

Corroboration of this evidence, and justification for the proposition that the other sons of Aaron, or those who were alleged to be his sons, did not have the priestly privileges, is found in I Chr. 24: 1-2:

ולבני אהרן מחלקותם בני אהרן נדב ואביהוא אלעזר ואיתמר. וימת נדב ואביהוא לפני אביהם ובנים לא היו להם ויכהנו אלעזר ואיתמר

These were the divisions of the sons of Aaron: The sons of Aaron were Nadab, Abihu, Eleazar and Ithamar. But Nadab and Abihu died before their father did, and they had no sons; so Eleazar and Ithamar served as the priests.[51]

---

ignoring all other children, and without further information as to first-born status, was at the root of the Sages' midrash justifying Phinehas as High Priest. B.T. Zebachim 101b states: דאמר רבי אלעזר אמר רבי חנינא לא נתכהן פנחס עד שהרגו לזמרי "Said R. Elazar in the name of R. Hanina: Phinehas was not made a Priest until he killed Zimri."

[51] We observe here a certain inconsistency between the narration in I Chr. 5: 29 and 6: 36, where Ithamar is not mentioned, and I Chr. 24: 2 where Ithamar is mentioned as ministering in a priestly function together with Eleazar. It is possible to reconcile the two verses according to Radak's explanation, as quoted above; but it is also possible that we witness in I Chr. 5: 29 a later development, already hinted at in the verses in I chap.

It is interesting to note that the NIV has added the word "But" at the beginning of verse 2, and the explanatory "so"; the verse is made to imply that only the descendants of Eleazar and Ithamar would be rightful priests, since the others had died without children. Even without these additional words, however, the purpose of this pericope is clear from the text, and is corroborated by the similar quotation in Num. 3: 4:

אלה שמות בני אהרן הכהנים המשחים אשר מלא ידם לכהן וימת נדב
ואביהוא לפני ה' בהקריבם אש זרה לפני ה' במדבר סיני ובנים לא היו להם
ויכהן אלעזר ואיתמר על פני אהרן אביהם.

Those were the names of Aaron's sons, the anointed priests, who were ordained to serve as priests. Nadab and Abihu, however, fell dead before the Lord when they made an offering with unauthorized fire before him in the Desert of Sinai. They had no sons; so only Eleazar and Ithamar served as priests during the lifetime of their father Aaron.

It is only in these parallel verses, Num. 3: 4 and I Chr. 24: 2, that we find mention of the fact that Nadab and Abihu died without children, and thus the justification for the exclusive claim of the descendants of Eleazar and Ithamar to the priesthood. In all other discussions of Nadab and Abihu, there is neither mention of the issue of priestly privilege nor mention of their childless death; thus the deliberate connection of these two topics is evident and serves an aetiological purpose. The main objective of the two chapters, Num. 3 and I Chr. 24, is the legitimation of the priestly geneal-ogy; the continuation of the narrative in I Chr. 6: 34-35 (49-50 in NIV) confirms the exclusive prerogative of Eleazar's descendants to the priestly duties. We read in the latter pericope:

ואהרן ובניו מקטירים על מזבח העולה ועל מזבח הקטרת לכל מלאכת קדש
הקדשים ולכפר על ישראל ככל אשר צוה משה עבד אלהים. ואלה בני
אהרן אלעזר בנו פינחס בנו אבישוע בנו.

24: 3-5. There we read that there were more chief men found of the sons of Eleazar than of the sons of Ithamar; among the former were sixteen chief men and more privileges, whereas Ithamar's descendants had only eight chief men. Thus a hint of the disadvantaged position of Ithamar's successors is already discernible. On the other hand, it is possible that when Solomon demoted Abiathar from his priestly privileges (I Kings 2: 26), the entire clan of Ithamar's descendants, or most of it, was also disquali-fied from the priestly service. Abiathar was a descendant of Ithamar, according to scholarly reference based on a number of citations which relate Abiathar to Ahimelech of the sons of Ithamar (I Kings 24: 3). Thus the absence of Ithamar in the list of Aaron's sons in I Chr. 6: 35 reflects the situation in I Kings 2: 26.

But Aaron and his descendants were the ones who presented offerings on the altar of burnt offering and on the altar of incense in connection with all that was done in the Most Holy Place, making atonement for Israel, in accordance with all that Moses the servant of God had commanded. These were the descendants of Aaron: Eleazar his son, Phinehas his son, Abishua his son.

In these verses, we have definite evidence that only Eleazar's descendants were authorized to perform the priestly duties of offerings on the altar, based exclusively on genealogy. Aaron's other sons are ignored; there is no story of any sin of a "strange fire," or of the early childless death of Nadab and Abihu.

From this detailed scrutiny of the story of Nadab and Abihu, I attempted to construct, from within the available sources, a realistic explanation of this enigmatic biblical narration. We might postulate that some prehistoric disastrous fire was at some point in time linked to the story of Nadab and Abihu, and that this in turn created an aetiology which served to justify the exclusive privileges of the priesthood in general, or the privileges of the specific incense cult, being retained by a group claiming to be Eleazar's descendants. In any event, we may assume from the above analysis that in all probability the story of Nadab and Abihu denotes a struggle for the priesthood offices and their particular privileges.

Before closing this topic, I would like to add the interpretations which Josephus and Philo gave to this narrative. Josephus states in *Ant.* III 209 that the sin consisted in offering incense of a composition other than the one prescribed. Although Josephus does follow the biblical text quite closely in the narration of the cult performances on the Tabernacle consecration days, he has no difficulty in interpreting the biblical "strange fire" as "strange incense."[52] Philo follows his own system of allegorical interpretation and "...interprets the narrative of Nadab and Abihu as a divine exaltation by fire...the fire of Lev. 10: 2 was a sign of divine favour ...alien to creation, but akin to God."[53]

---

[52] Some scholars proposed to interpret the biblical narrative similarly, and were not dissuaded by the textual difficulty, likely because of the more critical questions inherent in the literal interpretation of "strange fire." See John C.H. Laughlin, "The Strange Fire of Nadab and Abihu," *JBL* 95/4 (1976), pp.595-65; the proposition of "strange incense" is discussed and rejected by Laughlin, who supports a literal interpretation. It is not within the scope of this study to debate Laughlin's theory.

[53] The quotations are from an article by Robert Kirschner in *JQR* LXXIII, No. 4 (April 1983), 373-93.

2.2.2 The Korah Insurrection

The second question which Haran poses concerns the reason for the absence of the "strange fire" infraction in the Korah story. His answer is that "... the sin of Korah and his followers in using this fire was overshadowed by their more heinous sin of attempting to usurp the priestly function."[54] Yet such a grave transgression as the use of "strange fire," which carries with it the death penalty, must have been known to the biblical editor, since he placed the story of Korah after the death of Nadab and Abihu. His awareness of this fact is also reflected in Num. 17: 2; the command to Eleazar demonstrates that the latter, not Nadab the first-born, was Aaron's lieutenant, implying that Nadab was already dead at the time of Korah's rebellion. It is not likely that the sin of "strange fire" would have been considered "overshadowed" by this editor, undeserving of even the slightest mention. Nor is it likely that Moses would have ordered the group to commit such an horrendous crime. In Num. 16: 6-7, we note Moses' command: זאת עשו קחו לכם מחתות קרח וכל עדתו ותנו בהן אש ושימו עליהן קטרת "You Korah, and all your followers are to do this: Take censers and tomorrow put fire and incense in them." There is no hint here that Moses is suggesting they take fire from the altar; he is merely commanding them to take their own censers, and place in them their own fire and incense. Moreover, since the death of Nadab and Abihu and the reasons for their punishment were already known at the time of Korah's rebellion, according to the editor's order of events, we must ask whether it is likely that Korah's group would have undertaken this "experiment" with its consequence of certain death. It may have been that they did not know what to expect if their claim to priestly duties was unsuccessful, and therefore they agreed to take the risk; yet they should have known the punishment for bringing "strange fire." It is therefore inconceivable that they would nevertheless have agreed to the trial. These and other questions thus challenge Haran's assertion concerning the absence of the "strange fire" transgression at the Korah group's insurrection.

In disputing Haran's theory concerning the "sin" of the "strange fire" at the death of Nadab and Abihu, I provided a greater amount of textual support; in that case, the "sin" is expressly disclosed in the narration, and the text invites substantial exploration to reveal the real basis of the event, and the purpose of the narrative. Concerning the Korah story, the situation

---

[54] p. 233.

is entirely opposite. Scripture does not mention any transgression of "strange fire"; the only cited wrongdoing is the group's rebellion.[55] Haran finds an affinity between the "sin" of Nadab and Abihu and the "sin" of Korah in their common punishment of death by fire,[56] a fire which came מלפני ה' "from the presence of the Lord (NIV)", or literally "from before the Lord" in the case of Aaron's sons, and מאת ה' "from the Lord (NIV)" in the case of Korah's group; in fact, there is no distinction between these phrases.[57] However, theophany through fire,[58] and death or destruction for sins through God's fire,[59] are common images in Scripture. Thus the fact that different persons may have incurred the same death penalty through fire does not necessarily imply that their sins were the same. I shall therefore attempt to detect any shared aim between the two stories through a literary and critical analysis of the two pericopes, as well as by analogy with certain talmudic midrashim.

Both narratives share the same literary structure: the sin or transgression, the punishment, the moral, and the consequent divine commandments:

---

[55] I have already demonstrated that a) there is no trace of a prohibition against using other fire, b) Moses commanded them to put fire on the censers (v. 7), and c) Aaron and Moses performed the same act. This follows from a close reading of vv. 17 and 18. In both verses, we have two distinct groups who perform in the same way. In v. 17 we read the command: איש מחתתו חמישים ומאתים מחתת ואתה ואהרן איש מחתתו "every man his censer, two hundred and fifty censers; you also and Aaron each of you his censer." And in the following verse 18, we read the deed: ויקחו איש מחתתו ויתנו עליהם אש וישימו עליה קטרת ויעמדו פתח אהל מועד ומשה ואהרן "And they took every man his censer and put fire in them and laid incense thereon and stood in the door of the tabernacle of the congregation with Moses and Aaron." It is evident that Aaron was commanded in v. 17 to take his censer and put incense on it, and did so. Ibn Ezra, in his commentary to Num., supplements the abrupt end of v. 18, ומשה ואהרן, with the explanation עמהם "with Moses and Aaron," as the NIV has correctly translated.

[56] John C. H. Laughlin makes the same comparison in his article, p. 561.

[57] The LXX has in both verses the same preposition παρά; similarly Onkelos uses מן קדם.

[58] I shall quote only a few occurrences: Gen. 15: 17 והנה תנור עשן ולפיד אש אשר עבר בין הגזרים האלה "a smoking firepot with a blazing torch appeared and passed between the pieces"; Exod. 19: 18: והר סיני עשן כלו מפני אשר ירד עליו ה' באש "Mount Sinai was covered with smoke, because the Lord descended on it in fire."

[59] We read in Num. 11: 1: ויחר אפו ותבער בם אש ה' "...his anger was aroused. Then fire from the Lord burned among them," and in Deut. 4: 24: כי ה' אלהיך אש אכלה היא "For the Lord your God is a consuming fire."

Nadab and Abihu	*Korah*
ויקריבו לפני ה׳ אש זרה (Lev. 10: 1)	ומדוע תתנשאו על קהל ה׳ (Num. 16: 3)
And they offered unauthorized fire before the Lord	Why then do you set yourselves above the Lord's assembly
ותצא אש ... וימותו לפני ה׳ (Lev. 10: 2)	ואש יצאה מאת ה׳ ותאכל ... מקריבי הקטרת (Num. 16: 35)
So fire came out ...and they died before the Lord	And fire came out from the Lord and consumed ...[those] who were offering incense
בקרובי אקדש (Lev. 10: 3)	ויהיו לאות לבני ישראל (Num. 17: 3)
Among those who approach me I will be holy	Let them be a sign to the Israelites
יין ושכר אל תשת (Lev. 10:9)	למען אשר לא יקרב איש זר ... להקטיר קטרת (Num. 17: 5)
You and your sons are not to drink wine or other fermented drink	That no one except a descendant of Aaron should come ... to burn incense
ואל יבא בכל עת (Lev. 16: 2)	ושמרתם את משמרת הקדש (Num. 18: 5)
Not to come whenever he chooses	You are to be responsible for the care of the sanctuary
בזאת יבא אהרן (Lev. 16: 3)	ולא יהיה עוד קצף (Num. 18: 5)
This is how Aaron is to enter	So that wrath will not fall

Both narratives have the same motive: to validate God's commands and ensure their fulfillment, through the vivid portrayal of an event demonstrating the punishment of transgressors.[60] It is the particular nature of the

---

[60] We find an interesting midrash in Yalqut Shimoni, Lev. 16: רבי אלעזר בן עזריה אומר משל למה הדבר דומה לרופא שנכנס אצל החולה אמר ליה אל תשת צונן ואל תשכב בטחב. בא אחר ואמר ליה אל תשת צונן ואל תשכב בטחב שמא תמות כדרך שמת פלוני זה זרזו יותר מהראשון "R. Elazar ben Azariah says: To what is it similar? To a doctor who visited an ill person and said to him 'Do not drink cold and do not sojourn in dampness.' [Then] another came and said to him: 'Do not drink cold and do not sojourn in

ensuing commands which outlines for us the nature of the transgression.[61] After the death of Nadab and Abihu, we find a decree restricting to Aaron alone any access into the Holy of Holies to offer incense; a similar command against a stranger offering incense is found after Korah's rebellion.

The threat of the death penalty is also a feature common to both narratives. In Lev. 16, we have a short recapitulation of the death of Aaron's sons, here due to some unspecified transgression (a point to which I shall revert), which continues the chronicle interrupted in chap. 10. This is followed by precise rules detailing the way in which Aaron should approach the Deity with incense, without incurring his sons' fate; ולא ימות "or else he will die," as they did, בקרבתם לפני ה' וימותו "who died when they approached the Lord." The warning ולא ימות is repeated and emphasized at the incense celebration in v. 13: וכסה ענן הקטרת את הכפרת אשר על העדות ולא ימות. It is then followed in chap. 17: 5 by the mention of another exclusive priestly prerogative, the celebration of all animal sacrifices: והביאם לה' אל פתח אהל מועד אל הכהן "They must bring them to the priest, that is, to the Lord, at the entrance to the Tent of Meeting." This command is preceded by the warning in v. 4, to the one who does not obey this command: דם יחשב לאיש ההוא "That man shall be considered guilty of bloodshed." We find the same death penalty prescribed in the Korah narrative for the unauthorized person performing the incense celebration: למען אשר לא יקרב איש זר אשר לא מזרע אהרן הוא להקטיר קטרת לפני ה' ולא יהיה כקרח וכעדתו "That no one except a descendant of Aaron should come to burn incense before the Lord; or he would become like Korah and as his followers [i.e., subject to death] (Num. 17: 5 in MT, and 16: 40 in NIV)." On the death penalty we find similarly in 17: 25 (17: 10 in NIV) ותכל תלונתם מעלי ולא ימותו "This will put an end to their grumbling against me, so that they will not die," and in Num. 18: 7b והזר הקרב יומת "Anyone else who comes near [the sanctuary] must be put to death."

---

dampness, lest you die as X died.' This one warned him more forcefully than the first." The commentators are questioning why the event of Aaron's sons' death was reported again in this chapter, after the apparent end of the narration in chap. 10, and the continuation with other issues.

[61] Based on the command יין ושכר אל תשת "You and your sons are not to drink wine or other fermented drink," which appears shortly after the death of Nadab and Abihu in Lev. 10: 9, certain sages deduced that they had entered the Tabernacle in a state of intoxication. We read in Pesiqta deRav Kahana *Pisqa* 26:9: על שנכנסו שתויי יין במקדש וכתיב יין ושכר אל תשת וגו' ולא תמותו "[Aaron's sons died] because they entered the Temple drunk, and it is written [in Lev. 10: 9]: 'You and your sons are not to drink wine or other fermented drink, or you will die.'"

The Korah narration has no hint of any transgression in worship, as one would expect if the issue were the bringing of "strange fire"; the whole story centres around the issue of whom God has chosen to serve Him exclusively through the incense celebration. Moses' answer and defense is: וידע ה' את האיש אשר לו "the Lord will show who belongs to him (Num. 16: 5)," והיה האיש אשר יבחר ה' הוא הקדוש "The man the Lord chooses will be the one who is holy." God is thus called upon to be the arbiter in the dispute, as is even more apparent from Moses' closing argument in verse 28, before the trial: בזאת תדעון כי ה' שלחני "This is how you will know that the Lord has sent me."[62] This is the core of the conflict – whom God has chosen – and not some flaw in the celebration.

Scripture does not distinguish between Aaron and Korah's group, as I demonstrated, regarding the use of incense censers; they are described in the same way in Num. 16: 17 and 18: ויקחו איש מחתתו ויתנו עליהם אש וישימו עליהם קטרת "So each man [all participants in the trial] took his censer, put fire and incense in it." We thus see that there was nothing wrong in the performance itself; therefore, the censers used were hallowed, because legitimate worship had been performed, though by unauthorized persons. If the fire were a "strange" disqualified one, the censers would not have become hallowed, they would have been blemished; yet Scripture says: כי הקריבום לפני ה' ויקדשו "for they were presented before the Lord and have become holy (Num. 17: 3 in MT, 16: 38 in NIV)." Haran is inclined to interpret the phrase ואת האש זרה הלאה כי קדשו "and scatter the coals some distance away, for the censers are holy (Num. 17: 2 in MT, 16: 37 in NIV)" as referring to "the fire taken from outside the altar area and ... therefore, unfit to continue in ritual use."[63] However, in addition to the contrary arguments mentioned above, this interpretation would conflict with the fact that the censers in which that "blemished" fire was used became hallowed.[64] Thus the death of Nadab and Abihu and the Korah episode have in common the issue of Aaron's exclusive prerogative to approach the Deity with

---

[62] The text contains a further reference to Aaron's privilege, in the story of the blossoming of Aaron's rod; the exclusive choice of Aaron for the incense cult is confirmed by yet another miracle.

[63] p. 232ff.

[64] We find an interesting quotation in B. T. Menahoth 99a: ומנלן דמעלין אמר רב אחא בר יעקב דאמר קרא את מחתות החטאים האלה בנפשתם ועשו אותם רקעי פחים צפוי למזבח כי הקריבם לפני ה' ויקדשו ... בתחילה תשמישי מזבח ועכשיו גופו של מזבח "How do we know that one may enhance [the hallowedness of an object] ? Said Rav Aha bar Yakov: [We know it] because Scripture said: 'The censers of these sinners against their own souls, let them make them broad plates for a covering of the altar; for they offered

or through the performance of the incense celebration, but not the issue of the "strange fire," as Haran suggests. In fact, it seems to me that none of the various scholarly propositions, some of which I quoted, has an impeccable interpretation for this enigmatic term "strange fire"; all have flaws, either textual or logical.

As we have observed, even the traditional interpreters, the midrashim, had problems understanding the exact nature of the violation of Nadab and Abihu, and we find a great number of wrongdoings listed, some of them of a purely moral nature, entirely unrelated to ritual matters.[65] In the various midrashim concerning the common nature of the offense in the Nadab – Abihu and Korah stories, it seems to me that the Sages have expressed a "modern" approach, if we may use this term. There are a number of midrashim which expand upon the particular infringements committed by Nadab and Abihu; most emphasize their rebellious attitude against authority, and their aspiring to seize the power linked to the cult leadership, through their independent offering of incense, an act which was Aaron's

---

them before the Lord, therefore they are hallowed [Num. 17: 3 MT, 16: 38, NIV]'; before [they were covers] they [the censers] were auxiliaries to the altar, now [they are] the core of the altar." We observe that the Sages also interpreted this verse as indicating that the censers were hallowed.

[65] Sifra *Shemini Parshetah* 1, for example, accuses them of arrogance, or even of rebellion, in that they anticipated the moment that they would take over the leadership from Moses and Aaron. Similar reasons relate to their repudiation of Moses' authority, bordering on sedition: they did not take advice from Moses, but acted on their own, or they taught and proclaimed a הלכה, a ruling, before Moses their teacher, a sin punishable by death. Other motives, also unrelated to ritual subjects, are proffered, such as a lack of belief: they did not trust that God would send the fire to burn the sacrifices on the altar, as it is written in Lev. 10: 2 ותצא אש מלפני ה', "And there came a fire out from before the Lord." Other midrashim, for example Leviticus Rabba *Parshah* 20:8, declare that Aaron's sons died for four reasons. The midrash does not use the term חטאים, "sins," but דברים "matters," and enumerates them: their entry into the Holy of Holies, offering an offering [incense] which they were not ordered to perform, bringing in fire from a hearth, and not taking counsel one from the other. Another midrash, Pesiqta deRav Kahana *Pisqa* 26:9, quotes an additional four reasons: they were drunk, they did not wash their hands and feet before the service, they did not wear the prescribed priestly garment, and they did not have sons (or, alternatively, they did not marry). This list has no mention of "strange fire" at all. The common characteristic of all the midrashim is the search for logical reasons to substitute in some way for the vague "strange fire" rationale, and the lack of any prohibition or warning against the use of such fire. There is only one opinion with a literal interpretation; most of the discourses perceive a certain rebellious attitude in their behaviour, which is taken as the root of their sin and punishment.

exclusive privilege. A great number of midrashim also reveal the Sages'
conceptions concerning Korah's rebellion, and I shall quote a few. The
Sages equated Korah's rebellion with the ones who grumbled ("murmured"
in RSV) at the report of the spies sent to search the land of Canaan (Num.
chaps. 13-14). We read in B.T. Baba Batra 118b: מתלוננים ועדת קרח לא
היה להם חלק בארץ "The grumblers and Korah's group had no allotment
in the land." In B.T. Sanhedrin 109b, we read: אין להם חלק לעולם הבא
"They [the grumblers and Korah's group] have no share in the world to
come." In Numbers Rabba *Parshah* 18:1 we read: קרח שחלק כנגד משה
ומרד "Korah who contradicted Moses and rebelled." There is no mention
of any contested issue; the rebellion itself is Korah's crime. We read in
Midrash Tanhuma (Buber) *Parshat Pequdei* 1 : ד"ה אלה פקודי ; קרח שהיה
לוי ובקש עוד ליטול כהונה גדולה "Korah, who was a Levite, aspired to seize
the High Priesthood." It is remarkable that the midrash alludes to Korah's
craving for the High Priesthood, a notion absent in Scripture; this accords
with his desire to perform the incense celebration, the exclusive prerogative
of the High Priest.

There is another common pattern in these two narratives: the exaltation
of Aaron's status, and his relationship with the Deity. Throughout the
Bible we find that God speaks to Moses and commands him to transmit His
decrees to Aaron and his sons: צו את אהרן ואת, or דבר אל אהרן ואל בניו,
בניו; and in some instances God speaks to both Moses and Aaron וידבר ה'
אל משה ואל אהרן. It is only in the case of the two rebellions, of Nadab and
Abihu and of Korah, and the consequent divine commands, that the Deity
speaks directly to Aaron alone. In Lev. 10: 9 and in Num. 18: 8, we read:
וידבר ה' אל אהרן "Then the Lord said to Aaron," and in Num. 18: 1 and
20, we read: ויאמר ה' אל אהרן "The Lord said to Aaron."[66] It is obvious
that the narrator or the editor of these pericopes had as a particular motive

---

[66] It is interesting to note that the Sages perceived this remarkable nonconformity with
the usual formula, and attempted (without much success) to find an explanation or
reconciliation. We read in Sifrei on Num. *Pisqa* 117 on Num. 18: 1: רבי ישמעאל
אומר למי שהדבר מסור, אותו הזהיר "Said Rabbi Ishmael: [God] said [it] to the one to
whom the issue is aimed," that is, to Aaron, who was appointed "to bear the iniquity
of the sanctuary." We read also: וידבר ה' אל אהרן. שומע אני שהיה הדיבור לאהרן, ת"ל
זכרון לבני ישראל, הא למדנו שהדבור למשה שיאמר לאהרן "'Then the Lord said to
Aaron.' I might understand that God spoke to Aaron, but we learn [from the previous
verse on the same subject 17: 5, 16:40 in NIV] זכרון לבני ישראל 'This was to remind
the Israelites,' that God spoke to Moses so that he would speak to Aaron." The
assumption that there was a difference in the character of the commands does not seem
an adequate answer to the question. All commands regarding the performance of the
sacrificial celebrations are certainly directed to Aaron, but were communicated to Moses.

the elevation of Aaron's rank and the demonstration of his superior status versus that of his opponents, a fact which demonstrates the common nature of of the conflict in both episodes.

2.2.3 Hazards of Incense Performance by the Unfit – זר

The death of Aaron's sons and the Korah insurrection share a common pattern with another record in a later biblical book, II Chronicles chap. 26:16-21. This is the story of King Uzziah, who attempted to offer incense, the priestly prerogative, and was immediately punished by leprosy. Various midrashim also connect Korah and Aaron's sons as well as King Uzziah with the unauthorized incense celebration; they grasped the fact that the decisive common characteristic was a confrontation concerning this specific rite. We read in Numbers Rabba *Parshah* 18: 8: קחו לכם מחתות קרח וכל עדתו הרי לכם תשמיש החביב מן הכל הוא הקטרת חביבה מן כל הקרבנות וסם המות נתון לתוכו שבו נשרפו נדב ואביהוא "'You Korah and all your followers are to do this: Take censers....[Num. 16: 6]' Here you have the most desired [cult] service, namely the incense, the most preferred of all offerings, and deadly 'spice' is embodied in it, for which Nadab and Abihu were burned." Another midrash in Numbers Rabba *Parshah* 4:20 has a similar motif, but adds Uzziah's story: שלא יאמר אדם קשה היא הקטרת על ידו מתו נדב ואביהוא ועל ידו נשרפו עדת קרח ועל ידו נצטרע עוזיהו "That one should not say incense is dangerous, on account of it Nadab and Abihu died, on account of it Korah's group were incinerated, on account of it Uzziah became a leper." The common feature of all three is not a "strange fire," but the mere

---

The Malbim, in his commentary to Sifrei on Num. 18: 1, tries to distinguish between occurrences of the verb דבר, which imply exclusive communication to Moses, and the verb אמר, used when God speaks to Aaron. But this attempt does not offer any logical explanation as to why some rules were communicated directly to Aaron, and is in conflict with Rabbi Ishmael's clarification. Moreover, a midrash in Sifra on Lev. 1: 1 asserts that even when it is written that God spoke אל משה ואל אהרן, it really means that God spoke to Moses, who was to repeat it to Aaron. We read in *Vayiqrah Pereq* 2:1: אמר רבי יהודה בן בתירה י"ג דברות נאמרו בתורה למשה ולאהרן וכנגדן י"ג מעוטים ללמדך שלא לאהרן נאמר אלא למשה שיאמר לאהרן "Said Rabbi Jehuda ben Beteira: Thirteen times it appears in the Bible that God spoke to Moses and Aaron, and thirteen times [to Moses alone]. That is to teach us that [even in those occurrences in which both Moses and Aaron are mentioned] God spoke to Moses so that he should speak to Aaron." In light of this midrash, the fact that in the above-mentioned four verses concerning the rebellions of Nadab and Abihu and Korah God spoke directly to Aaron is made to seem even more extraordinary.

fact of the incense celebration. In Midrash Tehilim *Mizmor* 118, there is a further comparison between Korah and Uzziah, their common crime being their rivalry with the Aaronites. We read there: מה עשיתי להם לכל מי שעמד כנגדן קרח עמד וסיעתו בלעה אותם הארץ. עמד עוזיהו ובקש להקטיר את הקטרת וזרחה הצרעת במצחו "What have I done to those who opposed them [Aaron's children]? Korah and his group confronted [them, or him], the earth swallowed them. Uzziah stood and wished to offer incense, and the 'leprosy broke out on his forehead' [II Chr. 26: 19]." I would also emphasize that when the story of King Uzziah's leprosy is recounted in the earlier writing of II Kings chap. 15: 5, the punishment is obviously understood, as are all occurrences in the lives of peoples and kings, as a Godly act: וינגע ה' "The Lord afflicted the king." However, in this earlier citation, there is no reason given for this act, nor does there appear to be any hint of an incense offering or the existence of an incense altar.[67] Thus the sin and punishment in each of these cases is not related to a flawed celebration, but solely to rivalry with the Aaronites, and the attempt to seize their cultic privileges.

2.2.4 אש זרה 'Strange Fire'

As illustrated, there is no convincing and incontestable explanation for the term אש זרה , "strange fire," in Lev. 10: 1. I also call attention to the numerous stylistic difficulties in that verse, as well as in the pericope concerning the fire and censers in Num. chap. 17: 2-3, quoted above. In Lev. 10: 1 it is written: ויתנו בהן אש וישימו עליה קטרת ויקריבו לפני ה' אש זרה אשר לא צוה אתם. "[they] put fire in them, and added incense; and they offered unauthorized fire before the Lord, contrary to his command." I have already discussed the difficulty concerning the word צוה. There are further perplexities. The verse implies that first fire, then incense, were placed in the censers, and only then was "strange fire" offered. If the "strange fire" is the first fire which they put in the censers, then the verse should have opened with ויתנו בהם אש זרה "and [they] put 'strange fire' in them." If, on

---

[67] In Leviticus Rabba *Parshah* 17:3, ten wrongdoings are enumerated for which the punishment is leprosy, and we find there: הגוזל שאינו שלו, מעוזיהו דכתיב ויהי המלך מצורע עד יום מותו "...the one who robs what is not his, [we learn it] from Uzziah, as it is written [in II Chr. 26: 21]:' King Uzziah had leprosy until the day he died.'" This king has different names in the MT, in Kings and in Chr. In II Kings chap. 15, his name is עזריה, transliterated in the NIV as Azariah; in II Chr. chap. 26, his name is עזיהו, transliterated in the NIV as Uzziah.

the other hand, there is a second action, performed after the placing of incense on the fire, what is this second fire?

I therefore suggest another explanation for the term אש זרה, which follows upon our understanding of the sin of Aaron's sons: the term implies an infringement of cultic law and regulation. The incense celebration, as outlined in P, was the exclusive prerogative of Aaron, not of his sons; they were considered זרים, outsiders, with respect to this extremely important performance, despite their exalted status. So too were the Korah Levites, who committed the same crime. The term זר in the Pentateuch is a cultic *terminus technicus*; it appears 15 times in the P section of the Pentateuch, in singular form (זרה, זר, וזר, והזר), each time in reference to something being extraneous to the sanctioned sacrificial cult. That is, the term is used in describing the various prohibitions against lay people enjoying the priestly cultic advantages, and using the things reserved for their exclusive gratification. The following examples illustrate this use: the interdiction against anointing a stranger with holy oil, ואשר יתן ממנו על זר (Exod. 30: 33); the prohibition against eating the holy foods reserved for the priests, וכל זר לא יאכל קדש (Lev. 22: 10); the ban against approaching holy cultic sites, והזר הקרב יומת (Num. 1: 51 and 3: 10); the priest's daughter who married outside her caste,[68] ובת כהן כי תהיה לאיש זר (Lev. 22: 12); and similar sanctions.[69] Thus the term זר has solely a cultic implication in P, though it has broader connotations in other biblical books. In contrast, the idea of other gods is expressed by the term אלהים אחרים, not זרים.

---

[68] The term זר must be seen as a generic expression for anyone not authorized for a specific cult performance, or any other privilege. In some cases, it includes everybody except the Aaronites, as with the anointing oil; in other cases it includes only the Israelites, but not the Levites; and in yet other cases it includes both the Levites and Israelites. In Num 1: 51 והזר הקרב יומת "Anyone else who goes near it shall be put to death," the term זר "stranger" refers only to Israelites; Levites are not included in this death penalty. On the other hand, the same word in Num. 3: 10 also includes the Levites. So I understand this verse. Ibn Ezra, in his commentary to this verse, writes לכהן להיות עם כהונתם ישראלי או לוי יומת "[...with respect to one who approaches] to minister, an Israelite or a Levite should be put to death." Onkelos and Jonathan translate all these occurrences as חילוני, an "outsider" (Jastrow), and LXX translates ἀλλογενής, a "stranger from another race" (Liddell and Scott).

[69] There are two slightly different expressions in Deut., which do not contradict the assumption that the P section understood the term זר exclusively in reference to cultic matters; even these two quotations may be reconciled with the P definition of זר. In Deut. 25: 5, לא תהיה ... החוצה לאיש זר refers to someone who does not deserve an inheritance and is not entitled to it by birthright, similar to the layperson who does not

We may, therefore, suggest that in the three occurrences in which אש
זרה appears with reference to the fire brought by Aaron's sons, as well as in
the phrase קטרת זרה "strange incense," in Exod. 30: 9, the term זר has a
similar meaning: the substance being offered is not of the right type and
provenance,[70] or is offered by one not of the right lineage, as the זר in Num.
17: 5 אשר לא יקרב איש זר, "that no one except a descendant of Aaron
should come to burn incense before the Lord." The placing of incense on
the fire was the essence of this type of worship, to which Aaron alone had
the prerogative; all others, including Aaron's sons, were זרים, outsiders,
with respect to this worship. Therefore, the fire put on the censer by such
a זר becomes itself זרה – alien. In the phrase אשר לא צוה אתם in Lev. 10:
1, which I discussed above, the term צוה would imply, as is usually the case,
a positive command, and the stress would be on the designation אתם ; the
interpretation is: "[an act] which **they** were not commanded to perform,"
but which only Aaron, the High Priest, was. The term זרה, in other words,
may have become entwined with the stories of rebellion against Aaron's
exclusive privilege to perform the incense celebration. As I noted, several
midrashic interpretations impute such rebellious behaviour to Aaron's sons,
including arrogance and failure to take advice from Moses.

Further support for the proposition that "strange fire" was not the primary issue is found in Lev. 16: 1, also in P, which recapitulates the death
of Nadab and Abihu. In this case, the justification for their death is expressed as בקרבתם לפני ה׳ וימתו, "who died when they approached the
Lord (NIV)"; there is no mention here of "strange fire." Although the term

---

have the privilege of the priestly birthright. The phrase in Deut. 32: 16, קנאהו בזרים
בתועבת יכעיסהו , is translated by the NIV: "They made Him jealous with their foreign
gods"; this implies that they provoked Him with cultic transgressions, with sacrifices,
as is elucidated in the next verse, 17: "They sacrificed to demons." Onkelos also emphasizes this in his translation of verse 16: אקניאו קדמוהי בפולחן טעוון,"they provoked
Him by the worship to idols." Usually, the concept of other gods is expressed in Deut.,
in a great number of occurrences, with the term אלהים אחרים, not זרים. Hence, here
too the term זר has a cultic character and implication. There may also be a poetic factor
in this particular verse. I am indebted for this last elucidation to Prof. H. Fox.

[70] B. Levine, in *Leviticus, The JPS Torah Commentary*, considers that the term אש זרה,
"alien fire," refers to the incense itself, and could be translated as "an alien [incense
offering by] fire." He then writes at the end of this issue: "A possible key to the precise
nature of the offense lies in the equivalence of two descriptive terms: אש זרה in our text
and קטרת זרה, 'an alien incense offering', in Exodus 30: 9. If אש זרה is equivalent to
קטרת זרה we may learn from Exodus 30: 9 that it was forbidden to offer on the golden
incense altar anything other than the daily incense offering. Aaron's two sons, then,
violated the law of Exodus 30: 9: Entering the tent for an improper purpose, they met
with death." I have interpreted these texts differently; see sec. 2.2.1.

קרב is also used to express "to bring an offering", as for example in Lev. 1: 2 אדם כי יקריב מכם קרבן "When any of you brings an offering," in this case at least[71] the verb קרב should be translated as "approach." The succeeding pericope after this short introduction decrees precisely the method of approaching the Deity: ואל יבא בכל עת אל הקדש ... בזאת יבא אהרן אל הקדש, "not to come whenever he chooses into the Most Holy Place ...this is how Aaron has to enter the sanctuary area (v. 2)."[72] The traditional commentators took many approaches to this verse. As an example, I shall quote Ibn Ezra, a commentator and grammarian of the Spanish school with a straightforward and literal approach. He states that the term בקרבתם means that Aaron's sons brought the incense within the veil of the Holy of Holies: וזאת הפרשה לאות כי בני אהרן הכניסו הקטרת לפנים מהפרכת.[73] This gives a different perspective on the wrongdoing of Nadab and Abihu; but again, it was the violation of Aaron's exclusive prerogative,[74] in this case to offer incense within the curtain, for which they were punished by a godly fire, just as Korah's group were punished for violating Aaron's exclusive right to offer incense.

---

[71] I do not want at this stage to discuss the meaning of the verb קרב and all its ramifications in the sacral terminology, but the original meaning "to approach" is certainly valid in some verbal forms. The RSV translates here "drew near," similar to the NIV and to Ibn Ezra and other midrashic interpretations (see Note 128). I am indebted to Prof. Revell for drawing my attention to this translation.

[72] The rules on entry into the holy place behind the veil, Aaron's exclusive prerogative to enter this place, and the correct incense celebration are all at the core of this pericope. The core is not the Day of Atonement addendum; the latter is of a later date, according to most scholarly opinion.

[73] Ibn Ezra likely also relies on Rabbi Yossi Haglili's dictum in Sifra *Ahare Mot Parshah* 1:2 that they died because they entered the Holy of Holies.

[74] Haran (p. 244) as well as other scholars consider that the incense offering on the golden altar is the exclusive prerogative of Aaron, and not of his sons, since in Exod. 30: 7-8, the source for the altar incense, Aaron is the only one mentioned; for other priestly duties אהרן ובניו, Aaron and his sons, are indicated. As noted below (Note 47), this is in contrast to rabbinic opinion, expressed in Mishnah Tamid, 5:2: אמר להם חדשים לקטרת בואו והפיסו "[The supervisor] said to them :'New ones [priests who had never before performed the incense celebration] come and cast the lot!'" – that is, every priest had the right to perform the incense celebration once in his lifetime. The High Priest's distinction at the daily incense offering was merely his prerogative to perform it whenever he desired, without any lot-casting. It seems that the Sages were correct, at least insofar as the later period of the Second Temple is concerned. This is corroborated by Luke I: 8-9, where we are told that Zechariah, who was not a High Priest, executed the burning of incense in the Temple interior, on the incense altar, according to his lot. We definitely observe a development in this important ritual, a situation to which I shall refer in due course.

Several midrashim[75] also assert that Aaron's sons entered the Holy of
Holies and that this was the sin for which they were punished. We can in
fact deduce from textual analysis that they entered the Tabernacle, contrary
to Haran's allegation that one offered censer incense in the court, not in the
Temple itself. The expression לפני ה', which appears in all four citations of
the Nadab and Abihu infraction (Lev. 10: 1, 16: 1; Num. 3: 3, 26: 61), is
used typically to indicate the inside of the Temple, or even the inside of the
Holy of Holies, but certainly not the court. As already mentioned, the rules
which are decreed after the sin, in both the Nadab and Abihu story and the
Korah insurrection, are an integral part of the narration, and are meant to
be taken as consequences of the event described in the preceding verses. In
the first pericope in Lev. chap. 10, v. 9 refers to the prohibition against
entering the Temple after having drunk; this rule is stated to apply to both
Aaron and his sons: יין ושכר אל תשת אתה ובניך, "You and your sons are not
to drink wine or other fermented drink whenever you go into the Tent of
Meeting." In chap. 16, as a consequence of the intrusion by Aaron's sons
into the Holy of Holies (following both the talmudic and midrashic interpretations), the text decrees the precise rules regarding access to the holy
place behind the curtain. Such approach to God's presence is limited to
Aaron alone, and that only once a year.[76] The assumption that Nadab and
Abihu offered incense inside the Temple would invalidate Haran's theory
that the crime of Aaron's sons consisted of the use of "strange fire" in
censers, a celebration performed exclusively outside the Temple (according
to his view). Thus it is the violation of specific priestly prerogatives which
is the transgression common to both Aaron's sons and the Korah group.

Haran imputes the crime of "strange fire" to Korah's group from the
expression in Num. 17: 2 ואת האש זרה הלאה כי קדשו, "and scatter the coals

---

[75] Sifrei on Num. *Pisqa* 44, ד"ה ויהי remarks that angels pulled out the corpses of Nadab
and Abihu from the Holy of Holies into the Tabernacle, so that Mishael and Elzafan,
of priestly lineage, could then carry them away. They too were allowed to go into the
Temple to pull them out: שאו את אחיכם מאת פני הקדש (v. 4), but Nadab and Abihu
died in the Holy of Holies: וימתו לפני ה' "and they died before the Lord (v. 2)."
Leviticus Rabba *Parshah* 20:10 has another theory, that they savoured the sight of the
Deity, זנו עיניהם מן השכינה. Here, too, it is assumed that they had entered the Holy
of Holies.

[76] According to scholarly opinions, the limitation to once a year, and the fixing of the
date, are a later addition. (See M. Noth *Leviticus*, p. 126, and Karl Elliger, *Leviticus*, p.
207). Thus the consequential regulations concerning the entrance into the Holy of
Holies are even more firmly connected to the preceding narration of Aaron's sons'
death.

some distance away, for the censers are holy." Here again, it is not clear from the text why the fire should be scattered. The reason indicated does not accord grammatically with the subject to which it apparently refers: האש , "the fire,"[77] is in singular, while כי קדשו, "for the censers are holy," is in plural. The LXX follows the MT and translates it as ἡγίασαν, while Onkelos and Targum Jonathan correct the text and use אתקדשא in singular. The latter interpretation implies that the fire brought by Korah's group was hallowed because incense to God was offered with it; hence it was a legitimate act of worship, since otherwise it would not have been hallowed.[78] Rashi too is aware of the problem in his interpretation: "to scatter away the fire onto the ground [from the censers, since the censers] became hallowed." Other traditional commentators propose different solutions to this passage.[79]

However, the verses following 17: 2 also have literary and grammatical problems. The first phrase of verse 3, את מחתות, "the censers," is out of place stylistically. Then there is the command ועשו אתם "let them make them,"[80] in plural, a mandate initially directed at Eleazar and expressed in singular וירם את המחתות "that he take up the censers." At the fulfillment of the command, we again find the singular form ויקח אלעזר הכהן "so Eleazar the priest collected," but once more the actual work is expressed in plural, וירקעום.[81] Thus we can observe a lack of consistency and unity in this

---

[77] The NIV therefore interprets the phrase as "the coals," in plural, while the "censers" are the subject of the second part of the phrase "for they are holy."

[78] We obtain the same result if we interpret the "censers" as the subject of the phrase כי קדשו, as the NIV has done. Although many translators have interpreted the "censers" as the subject, an approach which is appropriate within the context of the narrative, there remains the stylistic problem; usually the conjunction כי provides the reason for what was said before, and in this case the hallowing of the censers does not explain the reason for the scattering of the fire.

[79] Ramban too relates the causal phrase "because they were hallowed" כי קדשו to the next sentence, which starts את מחתות החטאים האלה "The censers of these sinners." Seforno, on the other hand, relates the phrase to the fire, suggesting that the fire was not to be put where the ashes were disposed outside the camp, because "they" were hallowed (Seforno does not indicate if "they" refers to the fire or the ashes, but since he uses the plural, similar to Scripture, I would suggest that he refers to the ashes).

[80] The NIV has changed the text, translating "Hammer the censers," referring to Eleazar and assuming it is an imperative. The literal translation is "let them make them."

[81] Here again the NIV attempted an elegant solution, and translated "he had them hammered out." Both Onkelos and Targum Jonathan follow exactly the grammatical forms of the MT, in singular and plural, without worrying about the contextual inconsistencies. On the other hand, it seems that the LXX translators had a different text before

pericope,[82] as in the whole Korah narration, which has been discussed and debated at length by many scholars. To deduce from this text that Korah used "strange fire" and that therefore the fire had to be scattered, as Haran proposes, seems unfounded from the standpoint of literary analysis, as well as contradictory to logic, as I argued above.[83]

I also bring further evidence to challenge Haran's assertion that it was the bringing of "strange fire" (i.e., a fire brought from outside and not taken from the altar), for which Nadab and Abihu as well as Korah's group were punished (although in the latter case the "sin" is not explicitly recorded). As we have seen, Haran deduces from Ezekiel 8: 9-12 that incense celebrations were legitimate in Israel, and the prophet's criticism is due only to the idolatrous worship performed by the seventy elders. Now, this type of censer worship was performed outside the Temple;[84] it thus belongs to

---

them, and translated this verse accordingly.There are also inconsistencies in the LXX: ויֵרָם which is in singular is expressed as ἀνέλεσθε in plural, וְעשׂוּ in plural is expressed as ἔλαβεν in singular, and וירקעום is in plural both in the MT and in the LXX, as προσέθηκαν.

[82]   Professor Revell commented that such variation in number, with the singular indicating the individual responsible, and the plural indicating others who did the work, is not at all uncommon in biblical narrative. I accept his comment, but wish to remark that a part of the work done, "and Eleazar the priest took," is also expressed in singular. On the other hand, this may be due to a parallelism in style and reference; God's command וירם in singular corresponds to ויקח, and the mandate ועשׂו אתם in plural corresponds to וירקעום. We also observe that the LXX had a problem with these verses. In any event, my comment on this discrepancy constitutes only one of many points in my opposition to Haran's theory.

[83]   It is interesting to note that the Malbim on Num 17: 2 interprets this command: "Remove the coals – that is what is meant by האשׁ, 'the fire', in the text – from the censers in order to extinguish them"! The Malbim explains that the coals were certainly taken from the altar, as prescribed – that is, both Aaron and Korah's group took the fire from the altar; and since it is forbidden to extinguish the fire from the holocaust altar, the source of the coals taken for the censers, God's explicit command was necessary to instruct Eleazar to nevertheless extinguish these specific coals. According to this interpretation, the Korah group did not commit any transgression of using "strange fire." The Malbim probably reaches this opinion from the text, which links together all the participants in that action: ויקחו אישׁ מחתתו.

[84]   Haran states that this took place "in the temple," possibly in order to avoid this question. I think that the story takes place not in the Temple itself, but in one of the rooms in the Temple precinct, hence in the Temple court. Haran distinguishes this area from the Temple itself, in his three incense celebration categories. Rashi, in his explanation to this pericope, asserts that Ezekiel saw the door of a לשׁכה, an outbuilding in the Temple court, through a hole in the wall. It is also clear from the context that the elders

the second category within Haran's system and hence should have been condemned as the use of "strange fire"! The same consideration should also apply to Jeremiah's numerous reproaches concerning worship.[85] Neither Ezekiel's seventy elders, nor Jeremiah's "women on the roofs," brought legitimate fire from the altar, yet neither group was reproached for this as using "strange fire". It might be argued, following Haran's argument with respect to the Korah insurrection, that because of the more heinous crime, the sin of the "strange fire" was "overshadowed." In that case, one would also expect the prophets to refer to the issue of the priestly prerogative to offer incense, for it would seem that the elders of Israel, the זקני בית ישראל mentioned by Ezekiel, were lay people, not of priestly lineage. Yet they were not accused of the "more heinous sin of attempting to usurp the priestly function," as Haran states (p. 233) with reference to the Korah group.

As I argued above, we might deduce from this passage that incense worship in censers was, in Ezekiel's period, not yet a priestly prerogative, but a legitimate spontaneous custom performed by the people on various occasions, similar to the celebration of animal sacrifices before Josiah's reform; and, obviously they all did not, and could not, for practical reasons, use fire from the altar. That is the simple reason why they were not criticized by Ezekiel for using strange fire, or for usurping the priestly prerogatives. Similarly, Jeremiah reproached only the idolatrous practice, and not the locus of the incense worship, because the prerogative of incense celebration by the priesthood, and its exclusive location in the Temple, were not yet ordained, or firmly established.

---

did not stand in the Temple itself, since we read in continuation: "...the elders of the house of Israel are doing in the darkness, each at the shrine of his own idol." W. Zimmerli states in his *Biblischer Kommentar zum Ezekiel*, p. 216: "Das in [Ezekiel 8] 10-12 geschilderte Geschehen ereignet sich danach ursprünglich im Vorhof, d.h. dem Nordteil des alten Palasthofes...Es ist kaum zufällig, dass in diesem Aussenbereich die Laienvertretung des Volkes zu finden ist." ("The event narrated in Ezek. 8: 10-12 took place accordingly in the outer court, namely the north part of the ancient palace courtyard... It is not by chance that we encounter the lay representatives of the people in that outer precinct.") Zimmerli too asserts that the story took place in the court, not in the Temple, and substantiates his interpretation by his understanding that the seventy lay elders would not have entered the Temple itself, following an established taboo.

[85] Regarding the use of "strange fire" (not from the altar) for sacrificial worship, it would make no difference whether Jeremiah's criticism referred to pure incense, or to grain offerings with the addition of incense.

2.2.5 Summary

While I accept Haran's proposal of a separate censer incense ceremony, I believe I have succeeded in refuting his assertion that it was from the beginning a priestly prerogative. I also suggested that the essence of the Nadab and Abihu and Korah narrations was an issue of legitimacy and not of "strange fire." This suggestion is based on the internal contradictions within the narrations, and based also on the fact that in the numerous biblical references to incense worship, there is no mention whatsoever of the issue of "strange fire," with the exception of the Nadab and Abihu story. I shall further elaborate on this pericope at a later stage, at the examination of the golden incense altar.

2.3 Altar Incense

Haran's third category is the altar incense. I first wish to debate his assertion that the term סמים added to the term קטרת (in those passages concerning the incense to be burnt in the Temple interior, either on the incense altar or in a censer in the Holy of Holies), demonstrates the special character of this incense, and distinguishes it from the "outer" incense, suitable for censer offering. There is apparently a contradiction between this statement and Haran's affirmation that the לבונה, the frankincense ordered to be put on the showbread (Lev. 24: 7), is an integral part of the "inner" incense,[86] like the קטרת סמים, and both are distinct from the censer incense for the "outer" court celebrations. He asserts, just as the Talmud does, that only the frankincense is burned, not the bread, but does not discuss the issue of the appropriate altar on which the offering is made: the inner מזבח הקטרת, the incense altar, or the outer מזבח העולה. B.T. Zebahim 58 a/b declares that the frankincense of the showbread is burned on the outer altar, on the coals of this altar. It states: כל הניטל בפנים לינתן בחוץ שני בזיכי לבונה של לחם הפנים "[What is meant by the phrase] 'what is being taken from inside [the Temple] to be placed outside' ? The two ladles of frankincense of the showbread." Josephus confirms the Talmud's assertion in *Ant.* III, 10: 7.[87]

---

[86] *Temples and Temple Service in Ancient Israel*, p. 210.

[87] "While the incense is burnt on the same holy fire whereon they consume all the burnt offerings." *Antiquities*, transl. H. St. J. Thackeray, R. Marcus et alii (The Loeb Classical Library,1926-1965).

According to Haran this frankincense, since it is located on the showbread, in the inner Temple, should be burned on the inner altar, yet the Talmud and Josephus both state that it was burnt on the outer holocaust altar.

In addition, it seems to me tenuous reasoning to deduce from the presence of the term סמים in some verses that the term applies specifically to "inner" incense, in contrast to an "outer" incense for which we have no formula. First, as there is no command for such an "outer" incense, we could not expect such a formula. Further, it is possible that the formula quoted in Exod. 30: 34 is valid for every type of incense. The mere absence of the term סמים at some occurrences of the term קטרת, in which the latter apparently refers to an incense celebration in the outer court and not in the Tabernacle, does not warrant such a deduction. Finally, in several instances in which one would expect to find a term denoting a distinctive type of incense for an exclusive "inner" use, the term סמים is absent.

For example, if we accept Haran's contention that סמים represents a distinct type of incense, then we would expect to find the term in the introductory verse of the command to construct the specific incense altar. Scripture says: ועשית מזבח מקטר קטרת, "Make an altar of acacia wood for burning incense (Exod. 30: 1)." This is a decree to create an altar exclusively for the burning of סמים, according to Haran, but such a specific use is not mentioned! We see only the term קטרת. Verses 35 and 37 of the same chapter raise similar questions. In v. 34, the word סמים seems to be merely an ingredient, and in v. 35 , where one would expect סמים as the end product of the various elements listed after ועשית אתה קטרת, "and make a fragrant blend of incense," the term סמים is missing. This absence is also noticeable in the prohibition of verse 37; one would certainly expect to see the prohibited type of incense identified specifically, yet we read only: והקטרת אשר תעשה במתכנתה לא תעשו לכם, "Do not make any incense with this formula for yourselves."

Thus if סמים is a technical term identifying a specific type of incense, distinctive in its use and in its place of burning, we would expect to see it at every occasion in which the incense, or the specially designated altar, is mentioned; yet we observe many instances in which it is missing, in addition to those quoted above. Several further examples may be quoted from Exodus. Thus we find in 30: 8 קטרת תמיד, 30: 9 קטרת זרה, 30: 27 ואת, מזבח 30: 35 קטרת רקח, 31: 8; 35: 15, 37: 25 ואת מזבח הקטרת[88]

---

[88] I do not intend, at this stage, to speculate on whether the words ואת מזבח הקטרת at the end of the verses are a late addition.

and in 40: 5 את מזבח הזהב לקטרת. The quotation אשר זר איש יקרב לא אשר
לא מזרע אהרן הוא להקטיר קטרת לפני ה׳ "That no one except a descendant
of Aaron should come to burn incense before the Lord" in Num. 17: 5 (16:
40 in NIV), would imply, if we follow Haran's theory, that the prohibition
against non- Aaronites offering incense refers only to censer incense, and
not to altar incense; this ensues from the fact that the term סמים does not
appear in the narration of the Korah insurrection, nor in the subsequent list
of prohibitions, and the fact that the essence of the rebellion concerned the
prerogative of offering censer incense. If we continue this line of thought,
we must come to the conclusion that the altar incense celebration was not
the contested issue, and was therefore not included in the prohibition against
non- Aaronites, a patently unacceptable deduction; or, we might conclude
that at the period of the redaction of the Korah pericope, the incense altar
was not yet in operation, a possibility I shall explore later. At any rate, we
must recognize that the absence or addition of the term סמים, in itself, does
not enlighten us about the type of incense denoted in the various verses;
other facts and ancillary texts might proffer more helpful clues.

Let us consider the unusual repetition of the term סמים in Exod. 30: 34:
סמים נטף ושחלת וחלבנה סמים ולבנה זכה "fragrant spices – gum resin,
onycha and galbanum; and pure frankincense." The NIV omits the translation of the second סמים of the verse, but the RSV translates this literally
as "sweet spices, stactate, and onycha, and galbanum, sweet spices with pure
frankincense," and I shall therefore use this version, which is more faithful
to the MT. I am not commenting at this stage on the translation of the
three specific spices, but on the fact that both the NIV and the RSV consider the word סמים a generic term for "fragrant spices" or "sweet spices";
the JPS has added the word *these* to the second phrase ("these herbs together
with pure frankincense") in order to make the text understandable, but even
without such an addition, one has to understand the RSV text in the same
manner. Onkelos translates סמים in each case as בוסמין without any change
from the original text. Jonathan, on the other hand, translates this verse
entirely differently, demonstrating an altered interpretation. בוסמי נטף is
used for the first סמים in the construct state; the second phrase is translated
בוסמין בחירין דכייתא מתקל במתקל. The translation would then be: "spices
of [to use the RSV terms] stactate, onycha and galbanum [this follows the
Hebrew order, though a freer translation would be 'stactate, onycha and
galbanum spices'], selected spices, pure, of like weight, should it be." Here
too, the term סמים is understood to be the generic name for incense. To this
term there have then been added the particular kinds of spices, נטף ושחלת
וחלבנה, as well as their required quality – בחירין, "selected."

We observe other problems in the translation of this strange text. The Samaritan Pentateuch has וחלבניה סמים, with a יו"ד. We do not know if this merely indicates a different orthography, or if it is actually a grammatical form with a different meaning, similar to the LXX translation, discussed below. MS J of the Samaritan Targum has וחלבניה סמים, following the Samaritan Hebrew text, but MS A has ולבנתה סמים, which appears to be a qualitative predicate.[89] In Targum Neophyti we read: ראשי קטרן בסמנין טבין קטף שבלה מרייא וחלבנה ולבונה ברירא. The first סמים is translated (in a free translation) as a generic term: "primary types of incense of best quality"; the second סמים is entirely ignored. The LXX translates the first סמים with ἡδύσματα, "flavour, seasoning," in the accusative, followed by the three ingredients, which implies that it is understood as a generic term; the second סמים, however, is a genitive of specification, χαλβάνην ἡδυσμοῦ, explicative of the preceding noun, indicating the quality of the galbanum. It is interesting to observe, in addition to the textual dilemma with which the translators struggled, the fact that the LXX translates סמים with ἡδυσμός, "that which gives a relish," or "flavour, seasoning, sauce";[90] that is, a substance used with food. I shall revert to this question later on. I also draw attention to the text in Exod. 35: 28, where we read: ואת הבשם ואת השמן למאור ולשמן המשחה ולקטרת הסמים "Spices and olive oil for the light and for the anointing oil and for the fragrant incense." We observe that the term בשם, which is used in the composition of the anointing oil (as in Exod. 30: 23 קח לך בשמים "Take the following fine spices"), is also used as a generic word for "spices" (which are listed specifically at the end of verse 30: 23), much as the term סמים is used in Exod. 30: 34-37, the pericope under discussion.[91]

Another point may be raised. If indeed there were different types of incense in the Temple, as Haran suggests, we would expect hints of this in the early translators (LXX and Onkelos), in the writings of Josephus and Philo, and in the Mishnah. No such hint is found in these significant sources. Onkelos and Jonathan translate every occurrence of קטרת with קטרת בוסמין, or בוסמיא, whether or not the Hebrew term occurs with

[89] In addition to the difficult syntax of this text, which many have tried to correct in one way or another, it appears that both the Samaritan Bible (or at least MS A of the Targum) and the LXX also intended to address the issue of the identification of חלבנה, a matter I shall discuss later.

[90] Liddell and Scott, *Greek-English Lexicon*.

[91] The LXX translates both סמים in Exod. 30: 7 and בשמים in 30: 23 (the generic material in the anointing oil) with ἡδυσμα.

סמים. The LXX, on the other hand, translates קטרת alone with θυμίαμα, and קטרת סמים with θυμίαμα τῆς συνθέσεως. In addition to the use of σύνθεσις, which means a "composition," or "compound," we can establish conclusively that the LXX translators understood the addendum סמים as simply a term implying a compound of spices. In Exod. 30: 37, the LXX translates והקטרת אשר תעשה במתכנתה לא תעשו לכם "Do not make any incense with this formula," as θυμίαμα κατὰ τὴν σύνθεσιν ταύτην, Yet more convincing evidence is found in the LXX translation and interpretation of ואת הבשם ואת השמן למאור ולשמן המשחה ולקטרת הסמים in Exod. 35: 28: "Spices and olive oil for the light and for the anointing oil and for the fragrant incense." Although the original text mentions only הבשם, "spices," the translator knows that the spices for the anointing oil are mixed in a compound, as written in Exod. 30: 23-24, and therefore adds the term σύνθεσις, as a clarification. Thus we read: καὶ τὰς συνθέσεις καὶ τὸ ἔλαιον τῆς χρίσεως καὶ τὴν σύνθεσιν τοῦ θυμιάματος. It is evident that the terms בשם and סמים were both considered by the LXX editor as generic terms for a compound of spices, either for oil and condiments, or for incense. It seems that when these terms are unmodified, namely without the notion that they refer to compounds, both בשמים and סמים are translated with the expression ἥδυσμα. We observe this in Exod. 30: 23 ואתה קח לך בשמים ראש, καὶ σὺ λαβὲ ἡδύσματα, and in Exod. 30: 34, where קח לך סמים is translated similarly as λαβὲ σεαυτῷ ἡδύσματα. It is tempting to conclude that the term בשם is used for a compound of spices for oil and condiments, and סמים for the utilization in incense.

Josephus, who lived at the time of the Second Temple, was himself a priest, and boasted of having such a degree of knowledge that the High Priests came to ask him questions about the law.[92] It is likely, then, that he would have known of such distinct types of incense and, through appropriate translations, distinguished among the various classifications. Josephus, however, has one term, θυμίαμα, which he uses indiscriminately: to describe, for instance, the thirteen spices of the incense used in the Temple, in *The Jewish War* 5: 218; for the incense burned in Rome in honour of the Emperor, in *The Jewish War* 7: 71; in the list of spices brought by the people in the desert to build the Tabernacle, in *Ant.* III: 103; and in the list

---

[92] We read in *Life of Josephus*, IX συνιόντων ἀεὶ τῶν ἀρχιερέων καὶ τῶν τῆς πόλεως πρώτων ὑπὲρ τοῦ παρ' ἐμοῦ περὶ τῶν νομίμων ἀκριβέστερόν τι γνῶναι "...insomuch that the chief priests and the leading men of the city used constantly to come to me for precise information on some particular in our ordinances" *Antiquities*, transl. H. St. J. Thackeray, R. Marcus et alii (The Loeb Classical Library).

for the anointing oil, in *Ant.* III: 197. We find the same expression in the Nadab and Abihu narration, in *Ant.* III: 209; in the report of the princes' gifts, in *Ant.* III: 220; and in the Korah story, in *Ant.* IV: 32. In his description of the construction and consecration of Solomon's Temple, we read the same expression in the description of the receptacles in which the incense was brought to the Temple, εἰς τὸν ναὸν (hence implying that the incense was to be burned in the Temple). I used a greater number of quotations from Josephus, because of his undoubted credibility with respect to cult questions, than from Philo, who might be considered less well acquainted with cultic matters, and more interested in the allegorical interpretation of the different cult celebrations. I shall, therefore, merely state that Philo also uses the one term θυμίαμα. The incense altar, for instance, he calls ὁ τῶν θυμιαμάτων βωμός. Finally, we may note that the Talmud also had difficulty interpreting Exod. 30: 34, and deduced from the double citation of the word סמים that the incense was prepared of eleven ingredients.[93] Further in the discussion, use is made of the hermeneutic principle כלל ופרט וכלל, under which the word סמים would be the generic term for incense, and not a specific type of Temple incense, as proposed by Haran. All such instances serve to reinforce my objection to Haran's theory, that one may deduce from the word סמים the existence of a command to prepare a special incense type exclusively for Temple use.

Nielsen [94] was of the opinion that "סמים occurs only in plural and never designates a specific substance." Nielsen notes that Cassuto proposed to interpret בשמים as "fragrant spices" and סמים as merely "spices." It is probable that Cassuto was influenced by the talmudic dictum that one of the ingredients of the incense, חלבנה, has a bad odour,[95] but nevertheless is included in the generic term סמים . On the other hand, the biblical pericope concludes with a prohibition against preparing the described mixture, using

---

93 In B.T. Keritoth 6b, we read: א"ר יוחנן י"א סממנין נאמרו לו למשה בסיני אמר רב הונא מאי קראה קח לך סמים תרי נטף ושחלת וחלבנה הא חמשה וסמים אחריני חמשה הא עשרה ולבונה זכה חד הא חד סרי "R. Yohanan said: eleven spices were told to Moses at Sinai [to use in the incense formula]. Said Rav Huna: From which verse [do we know it]? [From the verse in Exod. 30: 34] 'Take to you sweet spices' [in plural], hence two, 'stactate and onycha and galbanum', we have five, and other spices [of the same number] we have ten, 'and pure frankincense', we have eleven." I have used the literal translation here as being more faithful to the MT and thus rendering the talmudic dictum understandable.

94 p.67.

95 B.T. Keritoth 6b: וחלבנה ... מפני שריחה רע "And galbanum... because of its bad odour."

the words איש אשר יעשה כמוה להריח (Exod. 30: 38) "Whoever makes any like it to enjoy its fragrance"; hence the composition סמים does concern a fragrant matter. Cassuto proposed that the term סמים was repeated to "show that the compound incense consists of two main ingredients: on the one hand, the three spices mentioned between the words סמים, and on the other hand, frankincense." This may be so,[96] but I cannot escape the feeling that the words ולבונה זכה are a later addition to the original text, and, therefore, the second סמים was also inserted later. At any rate, we may conclude that the above scholars do not consider the term סמים a *terminus technicus* to designate a specific Temple incense distinct from other "outer" incense.

It is interesting to note here that Josephus[97] considered the incense to consist of thirteen ingredients, but did not specify them, as the Talmud does. It is possible to reconcile the discrepancy between Josephus and the Talmud by positing that Josephus counted among the ingredients the liquids בורית כרשינא and יין קפריסין, or the salt and the מעלה עשן, the smoke-producing herbs, whereas the Talmud counted only the spices proper among the eleven elements. Hence it is likely that the composition which was narrated in the Talmud was based, in this case, not on a speculative tradition, but on the actual practice during the last part of the Second Temple period. The talmudic sages attempted to find support from Scripture for the actual custom. One can only wonder why Scripture did not enumerate the ingredients in the command in Exod. 30 verse 34,[98] especially if both parts of the verse date from the same period; we may note particularly that at least some of the ingredients cited in the Talmud, such as מר and קנמן, are mentioned in verse 23 of Exod. 30, in the composition of the anointing oil. The expression מר דרור in v. 23 seems to be the same as מור in the Talmud,[99] but in liquid form, necessary for the oil, whereas the quotation in

---

[96] This would imply that the incense was composed of only four elements, which would contradict the talmudic record that the incense had eleven ingredients, as well as Josephus' account of thirteen ingredients.

[97] *The Jewish War* V: 218, τρισκαίδεκα θυμιαμάτων.

[98] The Ramban, in his interpretation of this verse, offers an interesting speculation: it may be that according to God's command only the four enumerated ingredients were absolutely essential to the incense compound. Other unspecified, fragrant spices may and should be added, and that is the purpose of the second סמים. The text, in a free translation, would mean: "Take spices, stactate and onycha and galbanum and other spices and frankincense."

[99] Nielsen, in *Incense in Ancient Israel*, p. 61, quotes A. Dillmann, *Die Bücher Exodus and Leviticus*, (Leipzig, 1897) with regard to this point.

B.T. Keritoth 6a refers to the same spice in powder form, appropriate for the incense. It also seems that מר and לבנה were used together for fumigating, as appears in Cant. 3: 6: מקטרת מר ולבונה כתימרות עשן, "like a column of smoke, perfumed with myrrh and incense." It remains, therefore, enigmatic as to why לבנה appears without מר in Exod. 30: 34. I speculate that this might be explained by assuming, as proposed earlier, that ולבנה זכה was a later addition; the addition of two ingredients, ומר ולבונה זכה, after the concluding generic term סמים, might have seemed even more dissonant than the current wording.

On the other hand, it is possible that the exact composition of the incense was generally unknown[100] and intentionally kept secret by the priestly caste, to reinforce their grip on the Temple worship and their monopoly on the cult. Thus the following story in Mishnah Yoma 3: 11, B.T. Yoma 38a, may contain a kernel of truth: ואלו לגנאי של בית גרמו לא רצו ללמד על מעשה לחם הפנים, של בית אבטינס לא רצו ללמד על מעשה הקטורת "And those [to be remembered] for infamy: the house of Garmu [who] did not consent to teach [others] concerning the preparation of the showbread, the house of Abtinas [who] did not consent to teach [others] concerning the preparation of the incense."[101] This possibility should be considered in our speculation concerning the status of incense worship and its implications regarding the pre-eminent status of the priestly class, during the period of the Second Temple.

---

[100] If Ramban's postulate, described in Note 98, was close to reality, not only was the method of preparation kept secret, as the talmudic source suggests, but even the ingredients of the incense compound would have been unknown. Such a situation may be assumed from the fact that there is a difference in the names of two ingredients of the incense compound, in the Bible and the Talmud. We read in Exod. 30: 34: סמים נטף ושחלת וחלבנה, but in the list in the *Beraita* in B.T. Keritoth 6a, we read: ח"ר פטום הקטורת כיצד הצרי והצפורן והחלבנה והלבונה משקל שבעים. Thus the *Beraita* seems to use הצרי והצפורן instead of the biblical נטף ושחלת. Rashi and certain commentators explain that the terms are identical, but there are questions raised by yet other commentators, which I will not discuss here at length. It is in any event strange that the Talmud does not use the original biblical names, a fact which might imply imprecise knowledge of the incense ingredients.

[101] The legend which appears in the Talmud (B.T. Pesachim 119a, B.T. Sanhedrin 110a, Y. T. Sanhedrin chap. 10, hal. 1, 110a) and many midrashim about Korah's great wealth may similarly be connected to his struggle for the incense celebration, the core of the conflict in the biblical narration.

2.4 Conclusion

In light of the above, it seems to me that Haran's attempt to harmonize the various textual difficulties, without acknowledging a theory of development, is doomed to failure and cannot be sustained. Only an explanation based on long term development, in this particular case as in almost all other human thought and action, can provide us with a plausible solution and a reasonable answer for the varied, sometimes contradictory texts; these texts express in words the actual developmental stages in the incense ceremony, and its relative significance at each level. This is the focus of the following investigation.

3. Biblical Incense Rituals (Part II):
Analysis of Biblical Texts

3.1 General

As I noted in the Introduction, there are numerous textual difficulties inherent in the various biblical pericopes discussing incense. Some of these I
commented upon in my analysis of Haran's classification scheme. I shall
now continue with a review of the textual difficulties apparent in these
pericopes, and shall then discuss in word for word detail the two main
sections in the Pentateuch which describe the incense cult: Exod. 30: 1-10,
and Exod. 30: 34-38.

We may first note the apparently illogical placement in the text of the
command to build the incense altar; this appears in the MT in the first part
of Exod. chap. 30, instead of chap. 25, to which in essence it belongs.[1] In
the Samaritan Bible and in the Exodus Scroll from Qumran,[2] this pericope
appears in chap. 26, after v. 35, but this too is not its logical location. In
Exod. 25: 23-30, we find the command to build the table, and following in
vv. 31-40 the command for the making of the lampstand. Chap. 26 continues with the ordinance for the construction of the Tabernacle; verses 31-
35 follow logically with the division between the Tabernacle's two sections,
and the regulation of the placement of each object: the ark in the Holy of
Holies, and the table and the lampstand in the outer part. One would
expect here the instructions for the placement of the incense altar, which
apparently was also to be placed in the outer part; however at this point the
command to build the altar has not yet been promulgated. In the Samaritan
Bible, in which the command to build the incense altar appears at the end
of chap. 26, the instructions concerning its placement follow this pericope.

The differences between the MT and the LXX in the last six chapters of
Exodus (35 to 40) concerning the building of the Tabernacle are well known,

---

[1] This point was noted by Wellhausen in his *Prolegomena*, p. 65.
[2] Judith E. Sanderson, *An Exodus Scroll from Qumran, 4Qpaleo Exod and the Samaritan
Tradition* (Atlanta: Scholars Press, 1986), p.338.

and several scholars[3] have proposed explanations and reasonable motivations for these discrepancies. Wevers has already stressed the fact that in the LXX the record of the actual building of the incense altar, narrated in MT Exod. 37: 25-28, is entirely omitted. He also noted that in chap. 31, in which God specifies the equipment to be made by Bezalel, verse 8 in the LXX is different, and does not specifically mention the incense altar; only altars, in plural, are mentioned there (see also Introduction), without further details, whereas the MT specifies one holocaust altar and one incense altar.

There are further discrepancies in the citation of incense provisions in the LXX. We read in MT Exod. 25: 6 שמן למאור בשמים לשמן המשחה ולקטרת הסמים, "Olive oil [the literal translation is simply "oil"] for the light; spices for the anointing oil and for the fragrant incense." The LXX omits this verse; this can be considered logical, since there are in fact separate commands for these items. As to the oil for the light, we read in Exod. 27: 20: ויקחו אליך שמן זית זך "to bring you clear oil of pressed olives," and concerning the spices for the anointing oil and for incense, we have the specific commands in Exod. 30: 23-24 and 34-37, which will be fully quoted and discussed below. The omission by the LXX of the command in Exod. 25: 6 is therefore understandable; or, perhaps, this verse was added in a later edition of the MT, after the LXX translation and would therefore verify the existence of a different *Vorlage*. Exod. 35: 8 contains the same text as 25: 6, and this is also omitted in the LXX, as Moses recounts God's orders to the people. Similarly, verse 35: 15 in the MT, ואת מזבח הקטרת ... ואת קטרת הסמים ... "The altar of incense...and the fragrant incense," is missing in the LXX. These significant omissions with reference to the incense again suggest[4] the possibility of a *Vorlage* different from the MT on these matters.

A further textual problem occurs in Exod. 40: 17-33, which recounts the assembly of the Tabernacle, the placement of the various pieces of equipment, and the first cult performance; this includes the burning of incense on the golden altar, as is written in Exod. 40: 27: ויקטר עליו קטרת סמים כאשר צוה ה' את משה, "And burned fragrant incense on it, as the Lord commanded him." After the completion of each act by Moses, Scripture adds כאשר צוה ה' את משה, "As the Lord commanded Moses." We find

---

[3]   Among them is an extensive study by John W. Wevers, "The Composition of Exodus 35 to 40," in *Text History of the Greek Exodus. Mitteilung des Septuaginta Unternehmens* XXI (Göttingen, 1992), pp. 117-146.

[4]   Cf. Wevers' discussion in in *Text History of the Greek Exodus*, in which he attempts to explain the differences between the LXX and the MT without reference to a different parent text.

such commands for these acts in vv. 1-15 of the same chapter, and also, concerning offerings on the holocaust altar, in Exod. 29: 38-41; but in neither of these places is there a command for Moses to burn incense on the golden altar. There is only a command for Aaron to burn incense on the golden altar, in Exod. 30: 7-8, והקטיר עליו אהרן קטרת סמים, "Aaron must burn fragrant incense on the altar," and for Moses to put spices before the Ark, in Exod. 30: 36: ונתת ממנה לפני העדות, "and place it in front of the Testimony."

Exod. chap. 30 contains the two main Pentateuchal sections describing the incense altar and its ceremonies. The pericope in verses 34-38 is assumed to be the postscript and complement to the command for the construction of the incense altar in verses 1-9 of that chapter; it outlines the composition of the incense to be burnt on the incense altar. These seem to be two parts of one coordinated command. But we must note that there is already in the description of the altar in v. 1. a statement of its purpose: מקטר קטרת "for burning incense"; and again in v. 7 the activity to be performed upon it is described as: והקטיר עליו "Aaron must burn fragrant incense." Thus in the first 9 verses there are various forms of the verb קטר, including two instances of יקטירנה; yet in verses 34-38 there is no mention whatsoever of any burning of the incense supposedly dedicated and consecrated to this altar. In the second pericope the activity to be performed with these סמים is described in v. 36 with the verb ונתת "and place it"; there is nothing to indicate burning. Furthermore, in v. 7, it is clearly stated that the incense is to be burned on the altar: והקטיר עליו אהרן קטרת סמים "Aaron must burn fragrant incense on the altar." But v. 36 states: ונתת ממנה לפני העדות באהל מועד "and place it in front of the Testimony in the Tent of Meeting"; there is no precise description of the placement of the incense, and the text certainly does not dictate that it be put on the altar. There is no mention at all of an altar in this latter pericope, despite its containing instructions as to the composition of the incense which is presumed to be burnt upon such an altar.[5]

I have already drawn attention to the prohibition in the concluding v. 38 איש אשר יעשה כמוה להריח, "Whoever makes any like it to enjoy its fragrance," which seems to assume a substance that one merely smells. In

---

[5] Martin Noth has already drawn attention to this inconsistency, in his *Exodus, A Commentary*, transl. J. S. Bowden (London, 1962), p.239, but despite his insight he offers no radically different explanation: " We cannot however understand this to mean anything but 'censing'." He offers no explanation for the lack of the terms "altar" and "burning" in this pericope.

verses 1-9, which clearly describe a material to be burnt, there is no issue of odour; and in verses 34-38 there is no mention of burning. One must come to the conclusion that these two pericopes are not an integral part of one command and do not belong to each other, although one has the impression that the editor attempted to make it seem so. They concern two distinct rules of worship, likely from different periods, which have apparently been put together, presumably with some changes and additions to the original texts to render the narrative more readable. I already pointed to the oddity in verse 34, concerning the probable later addition of סמים ולבנה זכה. On the other hand, the pericope concerning the anointing oil in verses 22-33, and the subsequent verses 34-38 concerning the סמים, display a more obvious affinity and seem to have common features. Oil and fragrant substances are often found in parallel and are mentioned together in many occurrences, an issue to which I shall refer again further on.

3.2 Exod. 30: 6

I now wish to examine in detail the provisions of Exod. 30: 6, which purport to give the exact location of the "incense" altar,[6] and to note the issues inherent in this pericope. Exod. 30: 6 states: ונתת אתו לפני הפרכת אשר על ארן העדת לפני הכפרת אשר על העדת אשר אועד לך שמה, "Put the altar in front of the curtain that is before the ark of the Testimony – before the atonement cover that is over the Testimony – where I will meet you."

3.2.1 פרכת

The first issue which arises is whether there was actually a פרכת, "curtain", in the First Temple. If we consider the general assumption in the scholarly world that the description of the Tabernacle in the desert is a reflection of the First Temple, we must then ask where the incense altar would have been placed in the First Temple. In the description of the Temple built by Solomon, we read in I Kings 6: 31: ואת פתח הדביר עשה דלתות עצי שמן "For the

---

6   I will use the term "incense" in my deliberations, although, as may already be apparent from the discussion, I have reasonable doubts as to whether the pericope in Exod. 30: 34-38 originally concerned incense to be burnt, or fragrant spices, to be used without burning.

entrance of the inner sanctuary he made doors of olive wood." From the context it is clear that the דביר is the Holy of Holies, and the Ark of the Covenant was placed there; we read in v. 19: ודביר בתוך הבית מפנימה הכין לתת שם את ארון ברית ה' "He prepared the inner sanctuary within the temple to set the ark of the covenant of the Lord there." There is no mention of any curtain to divide the rest of the Temple from the Holy of Holies, the דביר, translated by the NIV as "the inner sanctuary." There were only wooden doors at the separating wall, the same as the entrance doors to the Temple itself; in v. 33 we read: וכן עשה לפתח ההיכל מזוזות עצי שמן "In the same way he made foursided jambs of olive wood for the entrance to the main hall."

The Talmud, too, is aware that there is no mention of any curtain in Solomon's Temple. B.T. Yoma 52b refers to the Mishnah, which describes the entrance of the High Priest through the curtain into the Holy of Holies on the Day of Atonement, and asks: במאי עסקינן אילימא במקדש ראשון מי הוו פרוכת אלא במקדש שני מי הווה ארון? "With what are we dealing? If [the Mishnah refers] to the First Temple, was there a curtain? But if [the Mishnah refers] to the Second Temple, was there an Ark"? The Talmud concludes: לעולם במקדש שני ומאי הגיע לארון מקום ארון "Truly [the Mishnah refers] to the Second Temple, and what [does it mean when it says in the Mishnah] 'he reached the ark'? [It means] the place of the ark [i.e. where the ark stood in the First Temple]." The Talmud here thus accepts without dispute that there was no curtain in the First Temple.

In B.T. Yoma 54a the question of the curtain in the First Temple comes up again, in the discussion of another Mishnah which mentions the curtain. There רב אחא בר יעקב answers: לעולם במקדש שני, "Truly [the Mishnah refers to] the Second Temple"; that is, there was no curtain in the First Temple. However, another solution is proposed; an anonymous sage says: לעולם במקדש ראשון ומאי פרוכת פרוכת דבבי דאמר רבי זירא אמר רב שלשה עשר פרוכת היו במקדש שבעה כנגד שבעה שערים ... "Truly [the Mishnah refers to] the First Temple, and what [is meant by] the curtain? The curtain of the gates, as R. Zeira in the name of Rav said: 'Thirteen curtains were in the Temple, seven for the seven gates....'" However, there is no consensus in the Talmud about the number of gates in the Temple,[7] and the number "thirteen", used for various Temple artifacts, is a legendary and symbolic number used frequently in midrash, as we may observe from the various mishnayot in Shekalim chap. 6.[8] We may therefore still con-

---

[7] See B.T. Tamid 27a .

[8] We read in Mishnah 6: 1: שלשה עשר שופרות, שלשה עשר שלחנות, שלש עשרה השתחוויות

clude that according to rabbinic interpretation, there was no biblical evidence of curtains in the First Temple. Even R. Zeira, who theorized that there were curtains, assumed that these were placed along the gates only, and did not contest the idea that there were dividing walls between the Temple, היכל, and the Holy of Holies, the דביר; he also did not speculate as to the side of the doors of the particular gates on which the curtains were hung – that is, on the interior facing the ark, or on the exterior side.

Maimonides in Hilkhoth Beith Habehira chap. 4, Hal. 2 states: אבל במקדש ראשון לא היה שם אלא פרוכת אחת בלבד שנאמר והבדילה הפרכת לכם בין הקדש ובין קדש הקדשים "But in the First Temple there was only one curtain, as it is said: 'The curtain will separate the Holy Place from the Most Holy Place [Exod. 26: 33].'" Maimonides, it seems, could not contemplate the absence in the First Temple of an artifact which was in the Tabernacle, and was an important element in the perpetual cult (for example, in the worship on the Day of Atonement, in which the פרוכת is mentioned many times in Lev. chap. 16, or at the special sin sacrifice of the High Priest, in Lev. chap. 4). He therefore assumed that there was one curtain in the First Temple, and two curtains in the Second. However, the משנה תורה commentator כסף משנה, who, in my opinion, correctly interpreted both the narration in I Kings and the dictum in B. T. Yoma 54a, assumed that although Maimonides said במקדש ראשון, "in the First Temple," he really meant the משכן, the Tabernacle, since there was no curtain in the First Temple. This is an obvious attempt to harmonize Maimonides with an explicitly conflicting talmudic statement, just as Maimonides himself retrojects Second Temple realities. [9]

It is interesting to note that the later II Chr. 3: 14 overcomes this issue of the curtain in the First Temple by inserting, in the description of the construction of Solomon's Temple, the following: ויעש את הפרכת תכלת וארגמן וכרמיל ובוץ ויעל עליו כרובים "He made the curtain of blue, purple and crimson yarn and fine linen, with cherubim worked into it." It is clear from the context that this refers to the dividing curtain at the Holy of

---

היו במקדש "Thirteen shofars, thirteen tables, thirteen prostrations were in the Temple." And in Mishnah 6: 4, we read: שלשה עשר שלחנות היו במקדש "Thirteen tables were in the Temple." Prof. H. Fox suggests that the number thirteen represents the twelve tribes, plus one for all of Israel, or for the priests, similar to the thirteen oxen of the sin offering for a transgression committed by all of Israel. Cf. Mishnah Horaioth 1: 5: רבי שמעון אומר י"ג פרים "Rabbi Shimon says: thirteen oxen."

[9]   For this conclusion, I am indebted to Prof. H. Fox.

Holies; this is also clear from the use of the term פרכת, which is distinct from the outer curtain in the Tabernacle called מסך.[10] There is further corroboration in the almost exact counterpart in Exod. 36: 35, where we read: ויעש את הפרכת תכלת וארגמן ותולעת שני ושש משזר מעשה חשב עשה אתה כרבים "They made the curtain of blue, purple and scarlet yarn and finely twisted linen with cherubim worked into it by skilled craftsmen." The writer-editor of II Chr., aware of the curtain in the Second Temple, interpolated an almost literal quote from the text in Exodus to anachronistically allow a First Temple description to be harmonized with the biblical account of the Tabernacle.

The existence of the curtain in the Second Temple, on the other hand, is validated by many non-rabbinic sources, in addition to the talmudic writings cited above. Philo[11] states in *The Special Laws*, I: 231, at the description of the High Priest's worship on the Day of Atonement: ἀδύτοις καταπετάσματος ἐσωτέρω τοῦ προτέρου,[12] "to sprinkle some of the blood with his finger seven times over against the curtain at the inner shrine, beyond the first curtain." Josephus, describing the Second Temple, states: διείργετο δ' ὁμοίως καταπετάσματι πρὸς τὸ ἔξωθεν[13] "...was screened in like manner from the outer portion by a curtain." On the other hand, in *Ant.* VIII: 75[14] he describes Solomon's Temple in a way similar to R. Zeira in B. T. Yoma 54a, cited above. Although the text is not entirely

---

10   The dividing curtain is also called פרכת המסך, "the curtain of the covering," in Exod. 35: 12, 39: 34, 40: 21, and in Num. 4: 5. On the other hand מסך, by itself, is always the outer curtain of the tent or the court: מסך לשער החצר (Exod. 35: 17, 38: 18, 39: 40, and 40: 8 and 33), מסך פתח (Exod. 35: 15), ואת מסך הפתח לפתח המשכן (Exod. 39: 38; Num. 3: 25, 4: 25), מסך הפתח למשכן (Exod. 40: 5, 28), מסך (ה)אהל פתח שער החצר (Exod. 40: 8, 33). In Exod. 26: 37, we have ועשית למסך, but from the context and the previous verse 36, in which it is written ועשית מסך לפתח האהל, it is evident that this concerns the outer curtain. J. W. Wevers, in *Notes on the Greek Text of Exodus*, p. 427, states: "פרכת is specifically the inner curtain whereas מסך is the outer curtain in front of the tabernacle."

11   Some caution is required, however, in the use of Philo for evidence of Second Temple practice, as he may have been influenced by the account in Exodus, rather than by knowledge of actual practice.

12   *The Special Laws*, transl. F.H. Colson (Loeb Classical Library, 1939), p. 235.

13   *The Jewish War*, V: 219, transl. H. St. J.Thackeray (Loeb Classical Library), p. 267.

14   κατεπέτασε δὲ καὶ ταύτας τὰς θύρας ὁμοίως ταῖς ἐνδοτέρω καταπετάσμασιν "These doors he also overhung with curtains in the same way as those within." *Antiquities*, transl. H. St. J. Thackeray (Loeb Classical Library), p. 610.

precise, it might be that Josephus too could not conceive that the First Temple had no curtain, such an important artifact in the Day of Atonement worship; therefore, he followed the correction made in II Chr. 3: 14.

Notwithstanding this ambiguous citation from Josephus, I think we can safely assume that there was no curtain in the First Temple; this is obvious from an unprejudiced reading of the text in I Kings, and corroborated both by the rabbinic sages and by Maimonides, who surely would have had a strong interest in substantiating the existence of a curtain in the First Temple. I would question why the Rabbis avoided citing the verse in II Chr. in their deliberations concerning the existence of the curtain in the First Temple. Further, I question how the absence of a curtain in the First Temple could have been reconciled with the ongoing cult activities, particularly those decreed in Lev. chap. 4,[15] the sin offerings for the Anointed Priest and the congregation, and in Lev. chap. 16,[16] the cult performance on the Day of Atonement in the Holy of Holies, both of which require a curtain for their accurate performance. Therefore, this substantiation of the absence of the curtain in the First Temple, and its presence only in the Second Temple, offers us a better perspective on the period of the final editing of the biblical P section. It presents us with actual evidence, in support of conclusions derived from textual analysis and critique, that the pericopes which include the term פרכת, the "curtain" dividing the Temple from the Holy of Holies,[17] must emanate, at least in part, from the Second Temple period.

3.2.2 'Before' the Curtain

Proceeding with the analysis of verse Exod. 30: 6, we read: לפני הפרכת אשר על ארן העדת. The NIV translates this as "in front of the curtain that is before the ark of the Testimony," while the RSV translates this as "before the veil that is by the ark of the Testimony." However, על usually means "on", and not "before" or "by"; the translator in each case has thus not translated this word literally but interpreted it in conformity with an opin-

---

[15] Verse 6: והזה שבע and v. 17: והזה מן הדם שבע פעמים לפני ה׳ את פני פרכת הקדש פעמים לפני ה׳ את פני הפרכת "...and sprinkle it before the Lord seven times in front of the curtain."

[16] Verse 12: והביא מבית לפרכת "and take them behind the curtain."

[17] Concerning the presence of another type of פרכת, a "cover" as opposed to a curtain, I shall deliberate in due course.

ion acquired from reading other texts. The primary issue, however, is the meaning and correct translation of "in front of" or "before" the curtain. In Exod. 26: 33 it is stated precisely: ונתת את הפרכת תחת הקרסים והבאת שמה מבית לפרכת את ארון העדות והבדילה הפרכת לכם בין הקדש ובין קדש הקדשים "Hang the curtain from the clasps and place the ark of the Testimony behind the curtain. The curtain will separate the Holy Place from the Most Holy Place"; and it is generally assumed that the curtain was hung from the "ceiling", and served as a division between the main "chamber" and the Holy of Holies. Yet a dividing curtain has two sides, one facing the "Holy Place," and the other the "Most Holy Place"; how then is it possible to know from Exod. 30: 6 on which side the altar was placed, when that verse merely states: לפני הפרכת, "in front of the curtain (NIV)" or "before the veil (RSV)"?

In the above-cited Exod. 26: 33, the place to which the Ark of the Testimony was to be brought is explicit and unequivocal: מבית לפרכת, "behind the curtain (NIV)," or "within the veil (RSV)." The locus of the High Priest's celebration in the Holy of Holies is also precisely specified with the same phrase מבית לפרכת , "behind the curtain," in Lev. 16: 2, 12, 15. The location of the table is similarly clear: מחוץ לפרכת,"outside the curtain,"[18] in Exod. 26: 35, and in Exod. 40: 22, ויתן את השלחן באהל מועד על ירך המשכן צפנה מחוץ לפרכת "Moses placed the Table in the Tent of Meeting on the north side of the tabernacle outside the curtain." The same precision is found with the location of the lampstand in Exod. 27: 21, באהל מועד מחוץ לפרכת, "In the Tent of Meeting outside the curtain," and in Lev. 24: 3, מחוץ לפרכת העדת באהל מועד "Outside the curtain of the Testimony in the Tent of Meeting." In all these occurrences we have the use of exact terms: מבית לפרכת "inside the curtain," and מחוץ לפרכת "outside the curtain"; in our verse, however, we have an ambiguous לפני, "before" or "in front." Our perplexity should lead us to look for a totally different interpretation of this verse.

Onkelos and Jonathan do not help us, as each translates literally using the preposition קדם: ותתן יתה קדם פרוכתא in Onkelos, and קדם פרגודא in Jonathan. The LXX uses ἀπέναντι, which also means "before". On the other hand, we read in the Epistle to the Hebrews, chap. 9: 3-4: μετὰ δὲ τὸ δεύτερον καταπέτασμα σκηνὴ ἡ λεγομένη Ἁγία Ἁγίων, χρυσοῦν

---

[18] The meaning is certainly outside the Holy of Holies, that is, in the Holy Place, on the other side of the veil which divided it from the Holy of Holies.

ἔχουσα θυμιατήριον καὶ τὴν κιβωτὸν τῆς διαθήκης περικεκαλυμμένην πάντοθεν χρυσίῳ "Behind the second curtain was a room called the Most Holy Place, which had the golden altar of incense and the gold-covered ark of the covenant." The RSV and the NAS also have "the golden altar of incense." However, the LXX translates the Hebrew מחתה "censer" with πυρεῖον and uses θυσιαστήριον τοῦ θυμιάματος for the "incense altar".[19] The incense altar is called θυμιατήριον by both Philo (*Moses* II: 94) and Josephus (*The Jewish War* V: 216).[20] We must therefore propose that the writer of Hebrews had in mind the golden incense altar, as is also clear from the context. I do not wish to speculate on the date this Epistle was written, a matter which is beyond the scope of this essay; it suffices to demonstrate that the text is ambiguous, and such an interpretation is possible. It would be difficult to assume that the writer of that Epistle described the location of the incense altar from personal knowledge, since we have many contrary testimonies from writers who actually lived at that period, and did testify from personal knowledge; hence it must be assumed that he merely interpreted the ambiguous text in Exodus as he understood it.

The verse proceeds: הפרכת אשר על ארן העדת. As noted above, the NIV translates this phrase "the curtain that is *before* the Ark," and the RSV translates it as "the veil that is *by* the Ark," which are not strictly correct; the translators have thus interpreted על, which means literally "on" or "upon", with a sense of "near, close to." This was done in order to reconcile the verse with the numerous biblical citations, quoted above, which describe the curtain as a divider, "near" the Ark, but not "upon" it. In contrast, certain of the Targumim translate the phrase literally: Onkelos and Jonathan have דעל ארונא, and the Samaritan Targum also has דעל – i.e. "on" the Ark. The LXX also translates ἐπὶ τῆς κιβωτοῦ, "on", with the noun in the genitive. Although the Talmud has not discussed this verse, it has deliberated on the meaning of על concerning a similar problem in Exod. 40: 3 וסכות על הארן את הפרכת "and shield the Ark with the curtain." The Talmud assumes that the root סכך means "to cover," as in סוכות; we have two interesting discussions about this issue. In B.T. Sukkah 7b, we read: מאי טעמא דרבי יאשיה דכתיב וסכות על הארון את הפרכת פרכת מחיצה וקא קרייה רחמנא סככה "What is the reason for R. Iashia ['s statement concern-

---

[19]   See Introduction p.11.
[20]   I cannot quote a reference from the LXX, since the composite term מזבח הקטרת in the Hebrew Bible is translated as θυσιαστήριον τοῦ θυμιάματος.

ing the amount of shade in a Sukkah]? Because it is written [in Exod. 40: 3] 'and shield the Ark with the *Parokhet*. The *Parokhet* is a dividing curtain, and the Torah calls it a 'cover'." But the Rabbis do not agree with his statement and retort: ההוא דניכוף ביה פורתא דמחזי כסכך "This one [the term סכך in Exod. means] that it is bent a bit,[21] so that it looks like a cover." We see that the Rabbis understood that וסכות implies a placing on top of something, and therefore, to solve the ambiguity, they assumed that the curtain was hanging near the ark, but bent over it; they thus interpreted על as "near or alongside," instead of the usual "on, upon."

This interpretation was also applied to the placing of the frankincense on the showbread. We read in B.T. Sotah 37a, and Menahoth 62a and 98a, almost identical citations: ונתת על המערכת לבנה זכה, רבי אומר על בסמוך אתה אומר על בסמוך או אינו אלא על ממש כשהוא אומר וסכות על הארון את הפרכת הוי אומר על בסמוך "'Along each row put some pure incense as a memorial,' Rabbi says *al* [means] 'near'. Q. You say [that] *al* means 'near', perhaps it [is] not so, but *al* really [means] 'on'? A. When it says 'you should cover with the curtain upon the ark' ['and shield the Ark with the curtain' in the NIV], [just as there you must interpret *al* as 'near', and not 'upon'] so too here, *al* means 'near'." The Rabbis were compelled to interpret על as *near*, concerning the curtain, because of the numerous biblical quotations which unmistakably refer to this item as a dividing curtain. Therefore this issue was clear, and they had no need even of discussion. Having accepted this interpretation as axiomatic, they also deduced that the frankincense had to be put near the showbread, and not upon it.

In light of the above it seems strange that Onkelos and Jonathan, who do make occasional changes in order to harmonize their translations with talmudic interpretations, left על in its original meaning. On the other hand, it seems that concerning the curtain the NIV corrected the meaning

---

[21] From the context, we must take the word ניכוף as a Hebrew נפעל participle from the root כפף, meaning to be bent, and referring to the כפרת. But in that case we would expect it to be written without a י"ד, as נכוף. On the other hand, if we consider it as an Aramaic expression, it would be first person plural, and would mean "we shall bend," which does not make sense here. In fact, in the printed edition, where we find ניכוף, we read in Rashi ליכוף, which would make sense as a Hebrew infinitive, meaning Moses was commanded to bend it; but here again we would expect it to be written without the י"ד, as לכוף. Prof. H. Fox suggests that it should be considered Aramaic, as third person imperfect, in which י"ד and מ"ד sometimes interchange. In fact, MS Munich 140 has the version ליכוף and MS JTS 1608 has דליכוף; the latter, at least, appears to be an infinitive.

of על to "along" and the RSV corrected it to "by", to reconcile this verse with the other citations of a dividing curtain, but they kept the meaning "on" with respect to the showbread, since that case does not conflict with any entrenched opinion. Philo and Josephus took the same view concerning the frankincense on the showbread; either they correctly understood the meaning of the Biblical על as "on", or they recorded actual practice in the Temple. Philo states in *The Special Laws*, I, 175: συνεπιτίθεται δὲ τοῖς ἄρτοις λιβανωτός "On the loaves there is placed frankincense."[22] Josephus states in Ant. III: 256: δύο δὲ χρυσέων ὑπερκειμένων πινάκων λιβανωτοῦ "Two golden platters laden with frankincense are placed over them [the loaves]."[23] Just as Philo and Josephus were not constrained by the "orthodox" limitations governing the Rabbis, which required the latter to reconcile verses, so we too must search for a reasonable answer to these apparent contradictions and inconsistencies.

3.2.3 כפרת

The next problem encountered in this verse is the phrase לפני הכפרת אשר על העדת "before the atonement cover that is over the Testimony." It is perplexing why this location is mentioned at all, since we are already given the exact location in the phrase: לפני הפרכת אשר על ארן העדות "in front of the curtain that is 'before' the ark of the Testimony." As we know from other biblical citations, the כפרת, which the LXX has translated as ἱλαστήριον, the NIV has interpreted, based on hermeneutic analysis, as "atonement cover," and the RSV has translated as "mercy seat," was put on top of the ark. We read in Exod. 25: 21: ונתת את הכפרת על הארן מלמעלה "Place the cover on top of the ark." I would propose that the translation of כפרת should be "cover", which is etymologically feasible,[24] and also expresses the most straightforward meaning in the context. Nevertheless, the additional instruction לפני הכפרת אשר על העדת is only confusing; terms

---

[22] *The Special Laws*, p. 199.

[23] *Antiquities*, p.441.

[24] S. Mandelkern, in his *Concordantiae Hebraicae atque Chaldaicae* (Jerusalem, 1971), states that the word כפר in the meaning of a "village" has its root in the idea of a flexible cover used in the villages and tents, as opposed to the rigid roofs in the cities. Cf. Koehler-Baumgartner, *Lexicn in Veteris Testamenti Libros*, which states that in the Old Testament כפר means "to cover," and W. Baumgartner, *Hebräisches und Aramäisches Lexicon zum Alten Testament*, in which meanings of "smear over," "wipe away," and "expiate" are proposed. Joseph A. Fitzmyer, in his essay "The Targum of Leviticus from

such as "in front," or "before the curtain" and "before the cover," do not contribute any precision as to the exact location. It is possible that it was this latter phrase upon which the writer of Hebrews, quoted above, based his opinion, allowing him to conclude that the incense altar stood within the Holy of Holies.

The traditional commentators, such as Rashi, Ibn Ezra and Rashbam, try to reconcile the contradictions between לפני הפרכת and לפני הכפרת. Since in their opinion פרכת is unquestionably the dividing curtain between the Holy Place and the Holy of Holies, they maintain that the altar was placed in the outer vestibule. On the other hand, the clause לפני הכפרת אשר על העדת indicates a location inside the Holy of Holies, in front of the Ark. Rashi explains, therefore, that this additional instruction is necessary to elucidate that the altar should be placed exactly in the center, facing the Ark, and not to the north or south of it. Ibn Ezra and Rashbam each express the same opinion in a slightly different way. Their conception is obviously founded on the many rabbinic statements concerning the Temple interior, and specifically B.T. Yoma 33b.[25]

The Samaritan Bible and the LXX, on the other hand, have omitted this passage. J. W. Wevers states in *Notes on the Greek Text of Exodus*:[26] "The

---

Qumran Cave 4," *Maarav* 1/1 (October, 1978), pp. 5-23, has drawn attention to the Aramaic כסיא, from the root כסי, "hide, cover," used as a translation of the Hebrew כפרת. Fitzmyer did not consider that this translation might be behind the traditional translation of כפרת as "mercy seat," since the term כסא, a seat/ throne, probably has the same root, כסי. The biblical כסא refers primarily to the throne of God, kings and judges. We also have the expression ה׳ צבאות ישב הכרבים "the Lord Almighty, who is enthroned between the cherubim (I Sam 4: 4; II Sam. 6: 2; Ps. 99: 1; II Kings 19: 15; Isa. 37: 16; and I Chr. 13: 6)." A connection between the throne and the כפרת covered by the cherubim is thus established. The JPS translates כפרת as "cover".

[25] A *Beraita* there states: שולחן בצפון משוך מן הכותל שתי אמות ומחצה ומנורה בדרום משוכה מן הכותל שתי אמות ומחצה מזבח ממוצע ועומד באמצע ומשוך כלפי חוץ קימעא "[The] table on the north, pulled away from the wall two and one half cubits, and the lampstand in the south, pulled away from the wall two and one half cubits, and the altar exactly placed stands in the middle and is pulled a little towards the exterior." This statement goes so far as to oppose the simple understanding of the biblical text. From the Bible we must assume that the altar stood close to the ark, even if not inside the veil, since the ark is mentioned with reference to the place of the golden incense altar, in Exod. 30: 6 and 40: 5. Concerning the place of the table and lampstand, the ark is not mentioned at all, and these items are explicitly located outside the veil. But according to the *Beraita*, the altar stood farther away from the ark than the table and lampstand, pulled to the exterior of the vestibule.

[26] p. 491.

parent text of Exod. had omitted the words due to homoiot." This is certainly possible, but I would suggest the possibility that the phrase was omitted as a bona fide emendation, precisely to avoid the contradiction disclosed above. A more speculative possibility is that the phrase was added at some late stage to the MT, to enhance and exalt the incense celebration with the reference to the כפרת; the latter is the Deity's throne and locus of theophany, as we read: כי בענן אראה על הכפרת "because I appear in the cloud over the atonement cover (Lev. 16: 2)" and ודברתי אתך מעל הכפרת מבין שני הכרבים אשר על ארון העדת את כל אשר אצוה אותך "There, above the cover between the two cherubim that are over the ark of the Testimony, I will meet with you and give you all my commands (Exod. 25: 22)."

As with the issue raised concerning the פרכת, the curtain, we note the absence of the כפרת, the cover, in Solomon's First Temple. The term כפרת appears twenty-seven times in the Pentateuch, and only once again in the rest of the Tanach, in I Chr. 28: 11, similar to the pattern observed for the פרכת. In this instance, the Chronicler's attempt at correcting the omission in the record of the First Temple seems to be rather half-hearted. The text does not say specifically that such an article existed, or was made; it says merely that David gave to Solomon, his son, תבנית האולם ואת בתיו וגנזכיו ועליתיו וחדריו הפנימים ובית הכפרת "the plans for the portico of the temple, its buildings, its storerooms, its upper parts, its inner rooms and the place of the atonement (I Chr. 28: 11)." The absence of mention of the כפרת is especially noticeable in I Kings 6: 23-28, in which the production of the כרובים is described, and in I Kings 8: 3-7, in which the installation of the ark is meticulously described.

From the precise and detailed accounts in the biblical record, we may observe further inconsistencies between the narratives in Exodus, I Kings and I Chr. concerning the description of the Ark's cover. In Exod. chap. 40, we note that it is the פרכת, the curtain, which shields the Ark; thus in v. 3 we read: וסכת על הארן את הפרכת "and shield the ark with the curtain," and in v. 21: וישם את הפרכת ויסך על ארן העדת "and [Moses] hung the shielding and shielded the ark of the Testimony." On the other hand, in Exod. 25: 20 and 37: 9 we observe in almost identical passages that the כרובים, cherubim, shield the atonement cover: והיו הכרבים פורשי כנפים למעלה סככים בכנפיהם על הכפרת "The cherubim had their wings spread upward, overshadowing the cover with them." The phrasing is similar, but again conflicts with the narrations in I Kings 8: 7 and I Chr. 28: 18. In Kings, we read: ויסכו הכרבים על הארון ועל בדיו מלמעלה "The cherubim spread their wings over the place of the ark and overshadowed the ark and its carrying poles." In Chr. we read: הכרבים זהב לפרשים וסככים על ארון ברית ה' "the cherubim of gold that spread their wings and shelter the ark of the covenant of the Lord."

In Exod. 40: 3 and 21, it is the פרכת , the curtain, which covers the ark; in Exod. 25: 21 and 37: 6, it is implied that the כפרת, not the curtain, is to cover the ark, following the clear order in Exod. 25: 21: ונתת את הכפרת על הארן "Place the cover on top of the ark." In these two pericopes the cherubim are a part of the כפרת as it is written (Exod. 25: 19): מן הכפרת תעשו את הכרבים על שני קצוותיו "make the cherubim of one piece with the cover, at the two ends." In I Kings 8: 7 and in I Chr. 28: 18, it seems that there was no כפרת , and the cherubim covered the ark. I would emphasize that in each of these six verses, the same action is described, using the same verb, סכך. We may note that Onkelos uses the same verb, טלל, to translate סכך in all its grammatical forms in the four Pentateuchal verses; hence he too considered this to be the same action. The LXX translates the above six occurrences with different verbs: σκιάζω, σκεπάζω, συσκιάζω and περικαλύπτω; however, all share the basic notion of "to cover."

3.2.4 אשר אועד לך שמה

Exod. 30: 6 continues: אשר אועד לך שמה "where I will meet with you." Although the first two instances of אשר in this verse introduce "locative clauses" indicating placement of the altar, it seems to me that this last occurrence should be interpreted rather as introducing a "purpose clause." That is, the entire last clause appears superfluous, given that the first two clauses have already specified the exact location of the altar; it is thus more logical to interpret the last clause as specifying purpose, despite the presence of the locative שמה. The verb in this last phrase is in future tense, אשר אועד; thus it is not continuing the instruction concerning the placement of the altar, but is merely imparting the information that "I will meet you there." One may note that similar clauses specifying a place of meeting are found after other commands. I suggest that if these clauses do not serve as an indication of the locus of the command, since they are all in future tense, they must serve to indicate causation, or purpose.[27]

---

[27] It is interesting to note that both the LXX and the NIV translate each of the instances of אשר differently, hinting at subtle distinctions. The LXX, which translates only two instances of אשר (לפני הכפרת אשר על העדות is missing) has: καὶ θήσεις αὐτὸ ἀπέναντι τοῦ καταπετάσματος τοῦ ὄντος ἐπὶ τῆς κιβωτοῦ τῶν μαρτυρίων ἐν οἶ γνωσθήσομαί σοι ἐκεῖθεν. In the NIV, we read: "Put the altar in front of the curtain that is before the ark of the Testimony – before the atonement cover that is over the Testimony – where I will meet with you."

In our verse Exod. 30: 6 this additional clause illustrates the importance bestowed upon the incense celebration, as it assigns to the incense altar the status of a meeting place with the Deity. Other meeting places associated with the verb יעד appear in the following verses: Exod. 29: 42 פתח אהל מועד לפני ה׳ אשר אועד לכם שמה "...at the entrance to the Tent of Meeting before the Lord. There I will meet you," and Num. 17: 19 (17: 4 in the NIV) והנחתם באהל מועד לפני העדות אשר אועד לכם שמה "Place them in the Tent of Meeting in front of the Testimony, where I meet with you." In these verses, in which the meeting place is in the Tabernacle, and there is no mention of the כפרת, the Deity meets with more than one person: לכם. In our verse Exod. 30: 6, in contrast, there is the "additional" clause לפני הכפרת, followed by אשר אועד לך, in the singular; in other words, the meeting is to occur only with Moses. We may note other occurrences in which the reference to the כפרת is complemented by a particle in the singular, לך – that is, a reference to Moses only. We read in Exod. 25: 21-22: ונתת את הכפרת על הארן מלמעלה ... ונועדתי לך שם "Place the cover on top of the ark....There...I will meet with you." We read also in Num. 7: 89: וישמע את הקול מדבר אליו מעל הכפרת אשר על ארן העדת מבין שני הכרבים "He [Moses] heard the voice speaking to him from between the two cherubim above the atonement cover on the ark of the Testimony." Thus the כפרת is conjoined with Moses' individual meeting with the Deity; it is also conjoined with the incense celebration, as we observe in Exod. 30: 36:[28] ונתת ממנה לפני העדת באהל מועד אשר אועד לך שמה "Place it in front of the Testimony in the Tent of Meeting, where I will meet with you," and in Lev. 16: 13 וכסה ענן הקטרת את הכפרת "and the smoke of the incense will conceal the atonement cover." There appears, then, to be a correlation among these three elements: the כפרת, incense and theophany.[29]

The succeeding verse 7 of our pericope, however, suddenly interjects an inconsistency into this (almost) exclusive bond between Moses, the כפרת and the incense, a bond which we can perceive in the previous verses of this pericope, and in the succeeding verses 34-38, in which the composition of

---

[28] This is one instance in which the כפרת is not mentioned in connection with a theophany before Moses alone. The other element, the incense, is present.

[29] There is an interesting midrash in this respect, which links the incense altar to theophany. We read in *Otzar Hamidrashim* (Eisenstein) p. 298 ד"ה כיון and in Yalqut Shimoni *Siman* 427: מהיכן היתה שכינה מדברת עם משה רבי נתן אומר מעם מזבח הקטרת, שנאמר ונתח אותו לפני הפרכת "From where did the Deity speak with Moses? R. Nathan says: From the incense altar, since it is said [in Exod. 30: 6] 'And put it before the veil.'" This midrash affirms my proposition that one can observe, through literary analysis, an attempt to link the incense celebration to the theophany.

the incense is described. Abruptly, it is announced that Aaron, not Moses, should perform the incense celebration at the place in which the Deity is to appear to Moses. This remarkable about-face appears only in this verse; in Exod. 30: 34-38, the pericope which is assumed to be the complement to verses 1-9, and which describes the preparation of the incense, Aaron is not mentioned at all. There, all stages of the command concerning the preparation and placement of the incense are explicitly directed at Moses. We read: ... ונתח ... ושחקת ממנה ... ועשית אתה ... ויאמר ה' אל משה קח לך סמים "Then the Lord said to Moses, 'Take fragrant spices...and make ... and grind some of it...and place it.'" I have also previously drawn attention to the fact that in this pericope we have no reference to the burning of incense, merely to the *placing* of it.

3.3 Exod. 30: 7-9

Let us now proceed to an examination of the ceremonies to be performed on the incense altar. (I shall not analyze v. 10 of this pericope, since it is generally acknowledged by the academic community to be a later addition, and has no direct implications for our study at this stage).

In v. 7 we read: והקטיר עליו אהרן קטרת סמים "Aaron must burn fragrant incense on the altar." The RSV also uses the term "fragrant", but the KJV uses the term *sweet*, although the LXX does not use the term ἥδυσμα here, as in Exod. 30: 34, a peculiarity I emphasized previously and shall discuss further on. J. W. Wevers has already noted the different translations of the term סמים in the LXX, and the fact that in Exodus B only τῆς συνθέσεως occurs,[30] but he gives no explanation for this. I shall return to this issue further on; at this stage, I shall merely note again that the KJV idea of *sweet* incense, or the "*sweet* savour" used to translate ריח ניחוח, may have been influenced by the LXX use of ἥδυσμα in Exod. 30: 34. As we have seen, סמים is translated elsewhere in the LXX[31] by συνθέσεως, a "compound", and ריח ניחוח by εὐωδίας, which means a "good" smell, not a "sweet" one; from Liddell and Scott we may note that Aristophanes, for instance, specifically uses ὄζει ἡδύ to stress a "sweet" smell. One wonders whether the conjunction of *sweet* with an odour is a universal association, or whether it appears in Western languages as a result of the LXX and its

---

[30] *Notes on the Greek Text of Exodus*, p. 491.
[31] In Exod. 30: 7; Lev. 4: 7, 16: 12; Nu. 4:16; and in all of Exodus B, as Wevers confirmed.

translations, like so many other concepts and expressions in our daily language which trace their origins from Scripture.

Verses 7 and 8 demonstrate further oddities, which have been observed by certain scholars. M. Noth[32] has analyzed the instructions in these verses concerning the timing of the incense celebrations and the requirement (apparently out of place) that the lamps are to be dressed in the morning and lit each evening; he concluded that these regulations go "beyond the framework given in Chs. 25-28...and thus by themselves reveal the passage to be an addition." Noth does not explicitly state that the same supposition would also apply to the remaining verses of that pericope, but I would assume that he would agree to such an assumption. Further, as Wevers notes,[33] the expression לדרתיכם, "your generations," in v. 8 and v. 10 is not appropriate within the context; this substantiates, if only indirectly, Noth's assumption. (The LXX also noted this inconsistency, and used αὐτῶν, "their", instead of "your").

Verse 9 starts with the prohibition לא תעלו עליו קטרת זרה. The NIV has translated this "Do not offer on this altar any other incense," while the RSV has translated the last phrase as "unholy incense." We have no indication as to what is meant by "any other" or "unholy" incense; we do not know what constitutes "legitimate" or "authorized" incense. We might assume that the editor had in mind the correct incense composition as outlined in vv. 34-36,[34] and refers in verse 9 to incense of another composition; but we would then have expected the term מתכנתה, which would be the logical parallel to the prohibition expressed in v. 37. That verse contains the ban against preparing incense for laic use with the same composition as the holy incense, and our verse 9 would then be an interdiction against burning on the altar any incense of a composition different than the decreed one. But the term זרה "strange" is vague, and does not proffer any clue as to its antonym in this context. I wish to refer to my previous supposition concerning the אש זרה and the deaths of Nadab and Abihu, that the term זר concerning the Temple sacrificial cult has a specific purpose in the P section: it refers to anything other than priestly duties and specific prerogatives. Its synonym would be the term "laic", in the case of common priestly functions, or "unauthorized" concerning the High Priest's exclusive tasks.

---

[32] *Exodus*, p. 235.

[33] *Notes on the Greek Text of Exodus*, p. 492

[34] This too would reveal an odd editing of these two pericopes; the prohibition against using other than the prescribed incense would appear before the details of its composition.

In this case its antonym would include anything of priestly origin; thus the implication in verse 9 would be that the legitimate incense to be burned on the incense altar, located before the כפרת, must be of priestly provenance. Therefore I consider that this passage has no correlation with the prohibition expressed in v. 37.

Another oddity is remarkable in this first part of verse 9: the use of the verb עלה in connection with the burning of incense, לא תעלו עליו קטרת זרה. In chapter 1 I have already drawn attention to the fact that the verb עלה is used in Scripture primarily to describe the offering of an עולה, and I attempted to offer an etymological explanation for the use of the root עלה to designate such a whole-burnt sacrifice (in comparison, for example, with the Greek term ὁλοκαύτωμα). The expression להעלות עולה, in many grammatical variations, is widely used in Scripture to describe the offering of a whole-burnt sacrifice.[35] In most cases it is cited in parallel with לזבוח שלמים; such parallels emphasize the distinct terms used for offering the עולה and the שלמים.[36] In a few instances, the introductory verb עלה is applied to both sacrifices; in such instances the שלמים follows the עולה, and the verb can be understood in a general sense.[37] The same pattern occurs, infrequently, with the pair עולה and מנחה.[38] Never, though, is the verb עלה used for the act of offering incense, with the exception of this verse; elsewhere the appropriate verb קטר is applied. In chapter 1 I raised the question as to why this verb קטר is inappropriately applied to the offering of animal and grain (vegetal) sacrifices. Here we have the one occurrence in which the opposite issue is raised: the use of עלה for the offering of incense instead of the appropriate term קטר .

The next issue is found in the second part of v. 9. The prohibition against offering whole-burnt and *Minhah* sacrifices and libations on this incense altar, ועלה ומנחה ונסך לא תסכו עליו, seems inappropriate, to say the least. The pericope starts with a description of the specific purpose of this

---

[35] Such occurrences are extremely numerous, and I will therefore quote several representative examples: והעלהו שם לעלה (Gen. 22: 2); והעלה הכהן את העלה (Lev. 14: 20); אלף עולות יעלה שלמה (I Kings 3: 4).

[36] For instance, העלו עולות ויזבחו זבחים (I Sam. 6: 15); ויעלו עלות ויזבחו ויזבחו זבחים (Exod. 24: 5); and an interesting quotation in I Sam.13: 9 הגישו אליו את העולה והשלמים ויעל העולה, in which we observe עלה reserved specifically for the whole-burnt sacrifice.

[37] For instance, אשר יעלה עלה או זבח (Lev. 17: 8); ויעלו עולות ושלמים לפני ה' (Jud. 20: 26).

[38] להעלות עליו עולה ומנחה (Jer. 14: 21); וכי יעלו עולה ומנחה (Jos. 22: 23).

altar,[39] מזבח מקטר קטרת, "an altar...for burning incense," and it should be evident that other types of celebrations are not to take place upon it. We have no similar admonition concerning the other altar amid its regulations in Exod. 27: 1-8, and no other prohibitions of this kind. The commands concerning all other cultic implements outline their form, size, locus and purpose, but do not contain prohibitions concerning inappropriate uses. We must conclude that this unique interdiction, and the enumeration of the particular cultic activities prohibited upon this altar, must have a special purpose.[40]

3.4 Excursus: The Table and its Accoutrements

I would like at this stage to refer to another unusual command, which affords us some insight into the oddity in our verse. We read in Exod. 25: 29, which commands the construction of the table and its utensils:

ועשית קערתיו וכפתיו וקשותיו ומנקיתיו אשר יסך בהן זהב טהור תעשה אתם.

Cognate verses are Exod. 37: 16:

ויעש את הכלים אשר על השלחן את קערתיו ואת כפתיו

and Num. 4: 7:

ועל שלחן הפנים יפרשו בגד תכלת ונתנו עליו את הקערת ואת הכפת ואת המנקית ואת קשות הנסך ולחם התמיד עליו יהיה

A further description is contained in I Chr. 28: 16-17:

ואת הזהב משקל לשלחנות המערכת לשלחן ושלחן וכסף לשלחנות הכסף והמזלגות והמזרקות והקשות זהב טהור.

---

[39] We find an interesting midrash in Y.T. Hagiga chap. 3, hal. 8, 79d, and in Leviticus Rabba, *Parshah* 7: 5. Since the text is clearer in the latter, I will quote from that source: אמר רשב"ל אף מזבח הקטורת כן שנאמר ועשית מזבח מקטר קטרת ... המזבח היה מקטיר קטרת, "R. Shimon ben Levi said: The incense altar likewise [has various miracles], since it is written [Exod. 30: 1] 'And you shall make an altar to burn incense upon' ... the altar itself burned the incense."

[40] Noth, in *Exodus*, p. 235 has noted this oddity, and states: "It is now impossible to discover why a warning against the misuse of the altar of incense should have seemed necessary."

A plain reading of these texts – especially that in Chronicles – leads us to conclude that they are describing an ordinary table setting; this is the approach taken by the NIV, which has given a translation faithful to the text. However, there has been a tendency among traditional commentators to move away from a simple reading of the biblical text.

The traditional Jewish commentators interpreted the verb יֻסַּךְ as "cover", from the root סכך, and took קְשׂוֹת as "cover", or as an implement which is the subject of אֲשֶׁר יֻסַּךְ בָּהֵן.[41] This is possibly based on the construct form in Num. 4: 7; or, possibly, the word קְשׂוֹת may have been erroneously associated with the word קֶשֶׁת, the half round bow, which covers what is below it.[42] Although grammatically it is conceivable that in Exod. 25: 29 and 37: 16 the word יֻסַּךְ is the הוּפַעַל form of סכך,[43] this root seems inappropriate in the case of Num. 4: 7, in which the corresponding term is הַנֶּסֶךְ; the וּ"ן would have no justification in a word derived from the root סכך. There are additional difficulties in taking the verb in the sense of "cover", to which I shall refer later. In contrast, the earlier translations took the root as נסך, "to pour libations." The LXX translated the term קְשׂוֹתָיו in all three quotations as σπονδεῖα (note that MT Exod. 37: 16 is LXX 38: 12); the verb יֻסַּךְ in Exod. 25 and 38 is translated by σπείσεις from the root σπένδω, clearly "to offer libation." In Num. 4: 7, the LXX adds the phrase ἐν οἷς σπένδει, an expansion not extant in the MT; however, the LXX addition concerns libation, not cover. Wevers[44] translates σπονδεῖα as "jugs, jars." The Vulgate[45] similarly interprets all three verses as referring to

---

41 As one may observe, the order of the utensils is different in Exod. 25: 29 and in Exod. 37: 16. In the first verse, the order is: וְקַשׂוֹתָיו וּמְנַקִּיּוֹתָיו אֲשֶׁר יֻסַּךְ בָּהֵן, and accordingly we would assume that the covering, or libation, is performed by the מְנַקִּיּוֹתָיו, the adjoining noun. On the other hand, in Exod. 37: 16 the order of the utensils is reversed, and we read וְאֵת הַקְּשׂוֹת אֲשֶׁר יֻסַּךְ בָּהֵן; here the קְשׂוֹת are close to the verb, and hence we would assume that they are the subject of the verb. However, in his commentary to Exod. 25: 29, Rashi states that "'to cover by them' refers to קְשׂוֹתָיו."

42 The term קֶשֶׁת, "bow" has a root with שׁ' (shin), and is associated with the meaning of hardness, whereas the term קְשׂוֹת appears in the MT with שׂ' (sin), and has another root and meaning. It is possible that the KJV interpreted the term קְשׂוֹת as "covers" to harmonize with its translation of יֻסַּךְ as "to cover."

43 In his Concordance, Mandelkern cites the two occurrences of יֻסַּךְ in Exod. 25: 29 and 37: 16 under both נסך and סכך. On the other hand, A. Even-Shoshan in his קונקורדנציה חדשה (Jerusalem, 1989) cites both occurrences under the root נסך.

44 Notes on the Greek Text of Exodus, p. 404. Wevers comments that the Byzantine group has added a doublet φιαλας, "bowls, saucers"; for our purpose this has essentially the same meaning: a container of liquids.

45 Biblia Sacra, Iuxta Latinam Vulgatam Versionem, ex interpretazione sancti Hieronymi (Rome, 1929).

containers for libations. We read in Exod. 25: 29 and Ex 37: 16 for יסך
בהן: *in quibus offerenda sunt libamina*, "in which libations are offered." In
Num. 4: 7 the Vulgate does not add the expansion as in the LXX, and
translates קשות הנסך as *crateras ad liba fundenda*, "bowls for pouring libations."

Onkelos, too, interprets all three verses as referring to containers for
pouring libations. In Exod. 25: 29 and 37: 16 he interprets מנקיתיו as
מכילתה, "container". The term קשות he does not translate, and uses[46] קסות;
אשר יסך בהן he translates as דיתנסך בהן. In Num. 4: 7 he translates
קשות הנסך, which is in construct form, as קסות נסוכא. The Samaritan
Targum also derives the term יסך from the root נסך, "to pour libations."
We read in Exod. 25: 29, in MS A: וכסיו דינסך בהון and in MS J: וכסיו
אד ינסך בון; in Exod. 37: 16 in MS A: וית כסיה דינסך בהון, and in MS J:
וית כסי אד ינסך בהון. In Num. 4: 7 we read in MS A: וית כסי נסכה, and
in MS J וית כאסי נסכה. While the terms כסיות, כסיה, כסי, and כאסי are
ambiguous and might also be understood as cups or covers, the terms ינסך
and נסכה refer unmistakably to libations. Targum Neophyti translates the
phrase in Exod. 37: 16 in a neutral way, without taking any position as to
the nature of the implement: וית קשוותא די ישתמש בהון. However, in Num.
4: 7, we read: וית קשוות נסוכה; here, the Targum clearly means a libation
receptacle.

We thus see that the traditional Jewish commentators interpreted these
verses in complete contradiction to the LXX, Onkelos, Samaritan Targum,
the Neophyti, and, I daresay, to the simple forthright reading of the text;
they considered them as relating only to the showbread and its utensils and
covering. In this regard it seems that they were influenced by certain talmudic
dicta. We read in B.T. Menahoth 97a: אמר רב קטינא אמר קרא ועשית
קערתיוכפתיו וקשותיו ומנקיתיו קערתיו אלו דפוסין כפותיו אלו בזיכין קשותיו
אלו סניפין ומנקיותיו אלו קנים אשר יסך בהן שמסככין בהן את הלחם. "Said
Rav Katina: [Exod. 25: 29 of the] Torah says 'And you shall make...:'
קערותיו are the forms [in which the showbread is placed, either after the
baking[47] or during the baking,[48]] the כפותיו are the בזיכין [the Aramaic

---

[46] In Exod. 25: 29 the MT has וקשותיו in the plural, but Onkelos uses וקסותיה in the
singular. On the other hand, in Exod. 37: 16, the MT reads ואת הקשות, in the plural,
and Onkelos uses קסותא, in the plural.

[47] This translation of דפוסים is according to Rashi's interpretation in his commentary on
Exod. 25: 29. Though in this commentary it is not as explicit, in his commentary to
Mishnah Menahoth 11: 1 he says clearly that the showbread was put in the form after
being taken from the oven. This interpretation is based on a statement in the

term used by the Talmud for the receptacles in which the frankincense for the showbread was placed, as well as the incense for the daily incense celebration], the קשותיו are the posts [to support the bread[49]], מנקיותיו are the canes,[50] אשר יסך בהן, with which the breads are shaded."

B.T. Menahoth 97a interprets קערותיו as דפוסין, "forms". This definition is inconsistent, on both etymological and logical grounds. קערה has its root in קער, which is associated, in Arabic and Syriac, with the idea of "to

---

Mishnah: כשהוא רודן נותנן לדפוס כדי שלא יתקלקלו "when he takes them out of the oven, he places them in a form, to avoid their breaking up."

48 Maimonides states in הלכות בית הבחירה פ"ג, הי"ד והדפוסין שעושין בהם לחם הפנים: הם הנקראים קערותיו "And the forms in which one 'makes' the showbread are those called קערותיו." Rashi does not say explicitly whether the showbread remained in these forms during the entire week during which the loaves remained on the table, but from Maimonides' citation, we can assume that the forms were used only at their baking, or for storage before their placement on the table. I would assume that Rashi held the same opinion, for two reasons:

a) the Talmud does not mention any forms when it describes the system of placing the showbread on the table, in Mishnah Menahoth 11: 3, and in B.T. Menahoth 97a;

b) it is reasonable to assume that the showbread, which according to rabbinic opinion had an intricate shape, would have had to be kept in a special form from Friday, when it was baked, until Sabbath, when it was placed upon the table, which had special implements to support it. According to Mishnah Menahoth 11: 2, the baking of the showbread did not suspend the Sabbath laws, and it was baked on Friday.

49 This interpretation is founded upon Maimonides' citation in הל' בית הבחירה, פ"ג, הי"ג: ארבעה סניפין של זהב היו לשלחן מפוצלין בראשיהן שהיו סומכין בהן שתי המערכות "של לחם הפנים שנים מסדר זה ושנים מסדר זה והם הנאמרים בתורה וקשותיו Four golden posts were at the table, split on their top, by which the two rows of the showbread were supported, two on one side and two on the other side, and these are what are called in the Torah וקשותיו." But Rashi, in his commentary to Exod. 25: 29, states that קשותיו are like half hollow canes split in the middle, which are placed three on top of each loaf, separating the loaves so as to encourage ventilation and avoid mould. Since, as we have seen, Num. 4: 7 has the construct form קשות הנסך, Rashi seems constrained to treat קשותיו as attached to a device which keeps the loaves separated one from the other, like a cover, to justify the derivation of אשר יסך בהן from the root סכך, "to shade". But he runs into difficulties, as we shall see later, and is also forced to admit that his interpretation is in conflict with the citation in B.T. Menahoth 97a, where we read: קשותיו אלו סניפין ומנקיותיו אלו קנים. According to Rashi, קשותיו are the קנים canes, and מנקיותיו are something else, as we shall see shortly. Nonetheless, both Rashbam, explicitly, and Ibn Ezra, indirectly, support Rashi's interpretation.

50 This interpretation is, it seems to me, the most appropriate to the text in the Talmud, and is also quoted by Maimonides in הל' בית הבחירה, פ"ג הי"ג: וכ"ח, where he states: "קנים של זהב מהם כל אחד מהם כחצי קנה חלול היו לו ... והם הנקראים מנקיותיו And twenty-eight golden canes, each one of them as a half hollow cane it had... and these are called

be deep."[51] The term קערה appears elsewhere in the Bible only in the list of the Princes' gifts in Num. 7. We read in Num. 7: 84: קערת כסף שתים עשרה "twelve silver plates," and in v. 85: שלשים ומאה הקערה האחת כסף "Each silver plate weighed a hundred and thirty shekels." It is hardly likely that the Princes gave twelve baking forms as gifts. Nor is it reasonable that such "baking" forms would be of silver, or that the "baking" forms enumerated in our verses would be of gold; these metals are inappropriate for baking forms. Moreover, in Num. 4:7 we read instructions as to how the table and its utensils and the showbread were to be packed and carried: ועל שלחן הפנים יפרשו בגד תכלת ונתנו עליו את הקערת ואת הכפת ואת המנקית ואת קשות הנסך ולחם התמיד עליו יהיה "Over the table of the Presence they are to spread a blue cloth and put on it the plates, dishes and

---

מנקיותיו." Rashi, on the other hand, interprets מנקיותיו, both in Exod. 25: 29 and in Menahoth, as אלו הקנים שמנקין אותו שלא יתעפש canes which clean the bread to deter mould. Rashi probably considered נקה the root of מנקיותיו, but I do not see how מנקיותיו has an affinity with קנה; I suspect that it might be an inversion of נקה. As I noted before, Rashi, who relied heavily on Onkelos, has the difficulty of reconciling his interpretation with that of Onkelos, who translated מנקיותיו as מכילתיה. Possibly because מנקיותיו is joined to אשר יסך בהן, or for some other reason, Rashi assumed that Onkelos' מכילתיה meant posts, סניפין, and looked for an etymological justification for calling posts מכילתיה. This theory was disputed by Ramban, who challenged Rashi's interpretation of מכילתיה as supporting posts; he argued that the term usually refers to measures, and quoted many citations affirming this point. On the other hand, Ramban indicated that he did not understand Onkelos' translation, and assumed that Onkelos referred to the forms in which the dough is prepared, which are different from the forms in which the loaves are baked. He relies on the citation in B.T. Menahoth 94a, שלשה דפוסין הם, "there were three forms." Rashi at Exod. 25: 29 notes that in Menahoth 97a some sages declare that קשותיו are the "posts", creating the impression that it is a contentious issue.

Both the Talmud and the traditional commentators create further complexities in their interpretation of the table's utensils, moving further away from a simple reading of the biblical text; however, I do not think that it is necessary, for the purpose of this study, to consider the issue further. I would only add that these commentators also have difficulty reconciling these verses with the citation in I Chr. 28: 16-17: ואת הזהב משקל לשלחנות המערכה לשלחן ושלחן וכסף לשלחנות הכסף. והמזלגות והמזרקות והקשות זהב טהור ולכפורי הזהב במשקל לכפור וכפור "The weight of gold for each table for conse-crated bread; the weight of silver for the silver tables; the weight of pure gold for the forks, sprinkling bowls and pitchers; the weight of gold for each gold dish." Ibn Ezra states that the quotation in Chr. is flawed; Ramban argues that the utensils enumerated in v. 17 refer to the general instruments assigned to the Temple, and not to the specific utensils for the tables, despite the fact that this verse appears to be related to v. 16, which specifically mentions the tables.

[51] See the *Concordance* of Mandelkern, s.v. קערה.

bowls, and the jars for drink offerings; the bread that is continually there is to remain on it." Here again, it would not be fitting that baking forms and implements be placed upon this table.

We read further in B.T. Menahoth 97a: כפתיו אלו בזיכין "the ladles are the *bazichin*"– that is, the ladles in which the frankincense was placed upon the table.[52] If this is correct, then it is puzzling, to say the least, that in the verses under investigation, in which the presumed receptacles of both the frankincense and the showbread are specified, there is no mention whatsoever of frankincense. This absence might be understandable in Exod. 37: 16, which merely lists the various implements. However, at the end of this chapter in v. 29, we have an account of the preparation of the "consumables": ויעש את שמן המשחה קדש ואת קטרת הסמים טהור מעשה רקח, "They also made the sacred anointing oil and the pure, fragrant incense – the work of a perfumer." Here, therefore, we might have expected to find mention of the frankincense. This expectation is yet more acute in Exod. chap. 25. In v. 29, the utensils of the table are listed, including the presumed frankincense receptacles, followed by v. 30: ונתת על השלחן לחם פנים לפני תמיד, "Put the bread of the Presence on this table to be before me at all times." Here, the absence of the frankincense, the most significant item of the showbread cult and the only part consecrated to be burnt as a fire offering to God,[53] is inexplicable.

The absence of the frankincense is again noticeable in Num. 4: 7, cited above, in which the details concerning the packing and carrying of all the utensils and the showbread are precisely specified. Here there is a specific command that even during the transportation of the table all its utensils and the "consumables" (that is, the bread) must remain on the table; again

---

[52] According to Mishnah Menahoth 11: 5, the ladles with the frankincense were placed on the table between the rows of the showbread. We read there: אבא שאול אומר שם היו נותנים שני בזיכי לבונה של לחם הפנים אמרו לו והרי כבר נאמר ונתת על המערכת לבנה זכה אמר להם הרי כבר נאמר ועליו מטה מנשה "Abba Shaul says: There [in the ventilation spaces between the loaves] were placed the two ladles [with] frankincense. They retorted: Is it not said [in Lev. 24:7] 'Along each row put some pure incense' ? [He] replied: However, it was said [in Num. 2: 20] 'the tribe of Manasseh will be next to them' [and we interpret it as next to them, not on them]." According to Josephus, *Ant.* III : 256, "two golden platters laden with frankincense are placed over them [the loaves]" (translation by H. St. J. Thackeray, R. Marcus et alii of the original δύο δὲ χρυσέων ὑπερκειμένων πινάκων λιβανωτοῦ).

[53] We read in Lev. 24: 7: ונתת על המערכת לבנה זכה והיתה ללחם לאזכרה אשה לה'. "Along each row put some pure incense as a memorial portion to represent the bread and to be an offering made to the Lord by fire."

there is no mention of the frankincense. It seems to me, therefore, that the
כפת, the ladles in the three verses under investigation (Exod. 25: 29, 37:
16, and Num. 4: 7), were not connected with the placing of the frankincense on the showbread, but must have been intended for some other purpose.[54]

The sages quoted in the above citation in B. T. Menahoth 97a , which
is directly concerned with the details of the cult, its utensils and its rules,
were aware of the enigma contained in these biblical verses concerning the
table's equipment and its use, as is evident from their deliberations. A
straightforward interpretation of the terms used in our verses for the utensils, and particularly the receptacles for libation, shows that these verses
stand in sharp contrast to other biblical verses which suggest that the table
was reserved exclusively for the showbread;[55] there is certainly no hint
whatsoever in these verses of any libations to be performed on the table, nor
is any use of plates, bowls and cups indicated. The sages went to great
lengths to reconcile this striking discord, and it is possible that they were
also obliged to avoid any accusations of inconsistency or lack of clarity in
the cult doctrine, as understood in their period. They could not easily
imagine that eating utensils were present on the table in either the Tabernacle or the Temple, and instead conjectured that the verses in question
concerned implements for the baking of the showbread and its placement

---

[54]   One should remark the absence of לבונה, frankincense, an important and, as we know,
expensive substance, in the list of the goods enumerated in the Deity's command to
Moses concerning the types of the gifts to be brought (Exod. chaps. 25ff.), Moses'
communication to the people (Exod. chap.35) and in the account of the work (Exod.
chap. 35). The only occurrence of לבונה in Exodus is in Exod. 30: 34, concerning the
preparation of the incense, the subject of our investigation. This may be further evidence
of a later accretion of the term לבנה to a prior verse. Similarly, it does not appear in
most of the verses concerning the placement of the showbread (Exod. 25: 30; 32: 13;
39: 36; 40: 23; and Num. 4: 7), but only in Lev. 24: 7. As we know, the placing of the
showbread was an ancient custom, much earlier than the arrival of frankincense in
Israel.

[55]   The interpretation of Exod. 25: 29 in Menahoth 97a plunges our investigation into
another controversy. According to Mishnah Menahoth 11: 5, the entire surface of the
table was covered with the showbread. This is the opinion of Rabbi Judah. Rabbi Meir,
however, contended that there were two handbreadths of free space between the two
rows of bread, to allow for aeration, or for placement of the frankincense ladles, according to Abba Shaul. Where, one may ask, would there be extra unencumbered space, to
place these additional utensils? The Mishnah seems not to be concerned with this
problem; however, in the ensuing debate in the Talmud, at B. T. Menahoth 97a, there
is an inquiry concerning the height of the six loaves placed one upon the other, and the
question is raised there concerning the additional height due to the קנים and בזיכין.

on the table. The traditional Jewish commentators followed naturally and understandably in their footsteps;[56] we, however, are not so constrained.[57]

On the other hand, we do find other rabbinic citations in which the nature of the utensils was considered during deliberations on other issues, and which interpreted the terms קשות and אשר יסך בהן according to their simple meaning in context. We read in Mishnah Sanhedrin 9: 6: את הגונב הקסוה ... קנאין פוגעין בו "The one who steals the *Kasva*... the zealots strike him." B.T. Sanhedrin 81b asks מאי קסוה "What is *Kasva*"? and answers

---

[56] It is interesting to observe that one of the later traditional commentators, Abarbanel, who in the 16th century had no concern about anthropomorphic issues, compares the Tabernacle to a royal palace, and its furniture and implements to the equipment of a royal residence. In his commentary on Exod. 25: 23, he states: לפי שנעשה המשכן בדמיון מקדש מלך רב ובית מלכות "because the Tabernacle was made in the likeness of a great king's temple and a royal palace." He then proceeds to describe all of the Tabernacle's furnishings, comparing them to the customary accoutrements of a king. He describes among other things: שם שולחן המלך וכסא והמנורה ושם יכנסו משרתיו ועבדיו לעבדו כי היה השולחן כשולחן המלך בעושר ובמעלה רמה והמנורה נגד ומזבח הקטרת היה במקום כסא מלכותו "...there [stood] the king's table and the seat and the lamp, and there his servants and slaves would enter to serve him; since the table was like the table of an illustrious and rich king, [with] the lamp in front of him, and the incense altar was in lieu of his throne." Within such a conception, the presence of eating implements on the table would be completely understandable. It is noteworthy that Abarbanel equates the incense altar to the Deity's throne. Usually the כפרת with the כרבים, the "atonement cover," is considered God's throne: וישמע את הקול מדבר אליו מעל הכפרת אשר על ארן העדת מבין שני הכרבים "he heard the voice speaking to him from between the two cherubim above the atonement cover on the ark of the Testimony (Num. 7: 89)."

[57] J. Milgrom, in his commentary to Num. 4: 7, attempts to harmonize the simple meaning of that verse, which he correctly translates as "bowls, ladles, jars, and libation jugs," with certain other biblical verses; such verses challenge the presence of such implements on the table, and are contrary to his belief that an anthropomorphic cult, the offering of food to the Deity, was present in the Bible. His explanation of the libation jugs is that they were used on the outer altar, although he admits that those jugs were made of bronze, and the verse of our study refers to golden jugs. He then tries to reconcile this inconsistency, using the talmudic statement that in the Second Temple the libation jugs were made of gold. However, even if we were to accept this argument, which still does not explain the reason for the change from bronze to gold, there is no explanation as to why these jugs for use on the outer altar should be placed on the inner table. Moreover, Milgrom does not attempt to offer a solution to the question he himself poses, regarding the other implements, such as the bowls, ladles and jars, which appear in the same verse. It is surprising to note that Milgrom, an academic, does not admit the possibility of various layers in the biblical writings, a theory which would explain the presence of traces of archaic practice, modified by later changes and substitutions; he apparently possesses a harmonistic image of a single immutable Israelite religion.

אמר רבי יהודה כלי שרת וכן הוא אומר ואת קשות הנסך "Said Rabbi Judah: a serving vessel, and so it says [in Num. 4: 7], ואת קשות הנסך, a utensil for libation." B. T. Sanhedrin does not elaborate specifically on the nature of this utensil; we might, for the sake of harmony with B. T. Menahoth 97a, assume that this utensil refers to the canes which support the showbread, though that does not seem reasonable.[58] However, in B.T. Sukkah 48b we read in a *Beraita*: רבי יהודה אומר שני קשוואות היו שם אחד של מים ואחד של יין, של יין פיה רחב של מים פיה קצר כדי שיהיו שניהם כלין בבת אחת "Rabbi Judah says: there were two receptacles [in the Temple], one for water and one for wine; the [one] for wine [had] a wide opening, the [one] for water a short [i.e.narrow] opening, so that both would be emptied at the same time [when poured]." For our objective, it is not necessary to speculate whether these bowls [59] were firmly attached to the altar, or were separate, free-standing bowls prepared for the libation celebration.[60] For our purpose it suffices to note that Rabbi Judah clearly understood that קשוות was an expression for liquid containers, and that such receptacles were in the Temple. To put it more directly, his opinion was that receptacles for liquids in the Temple were called קשוות.

Y. T. Sanhedrin , chap. 9, hal. 7, 35a, in its commentary on Mishnah Sanhedrin 9: 6, is more specific in connecting the mishnaic word *Kasva* to

---

[58] Rashi does not explain the type of implement. He merely writes in his commentary to the Mishnah הקסוה: מפרש בגמרא"The *Kasva*: it is explained in the Talmud." Maimonides solves the issue in an elegant way; he does not use the term *Kasva* in his הל' סנהדרין פי"ח הל' ו',and states simply: הגונב כלי שרת מן המקדש" "He who steals an implement from the Temple," in a generic way, without specifying the exact type of utensil. Such a generalized interpretation, however, seems in opposition to the Mishnah's intent; the mishnaic text specifies the type of implement used, but does not offer any explanation of the peculiar penalty for the theft of this particular object. H. Albeck, in his *Commentary to the Mishnah*, Sanhedrin 9: 6, offered an explanation similar to that of Milgrom, that the Mishnah refers to the two bowls for the libation of wine and water, as described in Mishnah Sukkah 4: 9. Since the Sadducees apparently opposed the water libation at Sukkoth, a Sadducee might steal the water bowl; in that case, the zealots struck him, since he did not deserve the death penalty for such a theft. (I have argued, however, in an essay to be published, that there is no evidence of the Sadducees' opposition to the water libation in talmudic sources, and offered another explanation for the event recounted in Mishnah Sukkah 4: 9.)

[59] In the relevant Mishnah, Sukkah 4: 9, they are called ספלים, as we read there שני ספלים של כסף היו שם רבי יהודה אומר של סיד היו "two silver bowls were there; Rabbi Judah says they were of lime."

[60] Neither this idea nor Albeck's hypothesis (see note 58) affects my speculation that the contentious issue between the Sadducees and Pharisees, narrated in Mishnah Sukkah 4: 9, originally concerned a determination of where the libation was to be poured.

our biblical verse Num. 4: 7. We read there: קסוה קיסטא רב יהודה אמר כלי משל בית המקדש היה כמה דתימר ואת קשות הנסך "*Kasva* [is] *Kista*, [a measure of liquids].[61] Rav Judah said it was a vessel of the Temple, as it is said ואת קשות הנסך." It is obvious that if the Yerushalmi's interpretation is correct, Rav[62] Judah meant a measured receptacle for liquids, since he, or an Amorah of the same name, supported his interpretation through a biblical quotation which refers to libation.[63] Even if we were to understand קיסטא as "chest", rather than "receptacle", this citation contradicts any suggestion that Rav Judah intended the supporting canes of the showbread (similar to the citation in B.T. Menahoth 97a).

We also read in Sifrei Zuta, *Pisqa* 7: וכן הוא אומר קערותיו וכפותיו וקשותיו ומנקיותיו אשר יסך בהן וכי בהן היו מנסכין והלא כבר נאמר ואת קשות הנסך ומה אני מקיים אשר יסך בהן אלא מלמד שהן מקדשין את הנופל לתוכן "And so it says [Exod. 25: 29]...And did they pour the libation with [those vessels]? Was it not already said [in Num. 4: 7] 'the [vessels] of libation'? Then, why was אשר יסך בהן written? To teach that they [the vessels in Exod. 25: 29] hallow whatever falls into them [that is, an item which falls into the receptacle becomes as holy as the receptacle]." It is obvious from this passage, which also appears in Numbers Rabba, *Parshah* 14: 14,[64] that the author understood the term אשר יסך to refer to the pouring of a libation, and not to a cover for the showbread.

My examination of these verses has demonstrated, on the one hand, that they refer, in their simplest interpretation, to regular eating utensils, an interpretation also evident from the quotation in I Chr 28: 17 cited above;

---

[61] Jastrow's dictionary offers two possibilities: a) a corruption of ξέστης, a measure of liquids, as for example in Genesis Rabba 49:4 where it applies to a measure of wine, or b) a chest containing sacred objects.

[62] In the B. T. Sanhedrin 81b he is cited as Rabbi, and in the Y. T. as Rav.

[63] The interpretation "measured receptacle", from the Greek ξέστης, would also coincide with Onkelos, who, as we have seen, translated קשות as מכילתא, which is a measure. Onkelos also translated איפא ואיפא גדולה וקטנה in Deut. 25: 14 as מכילא ומכילא רבתא וזערתא "several measures, a great and a small." We also find in Y.T. Baba Bathra, chap. 5, hal. 5, 15b רב מנייה ריש גלותא אגרונומוס והוה מחי על מכילתא ולא על שיעוריא "Rav Mania, the Head of the Diaspora, an Agoranomos [officer in charge of the measures in the market] protested with respect to inaccurate measures, but not with respect to overpricing."

[64] We read there: וכן הוא אומר (שמות כה') קערותיו וכפותיו וקשותיו ומנקיותיו אשר יוסך בהן בהן היו מנסכים והלא כבר נאמר ואת קשות הנסך ומה אני מקיים אשר יוסך בהן אלא מלמד שהיו מקדשים את הנופל לתוכן

on the other hand, it has shown the extraordinary effort undertaken by some sages to interpret the verses in a manner removed from their context and their straightforward meaning. Nonetheless, it demonstrates the sages' sensitivity to the potential philosophical danger of a "wrong" interpretation, consistent with their belief that all apparent conflicts in the Bible were to be harmonized; they thus created an interpretation which coincided with their understanding of cult practice as handed down by tradition. They were apparently constrained to avoid any interpretation of the Bible which would give a "vulgar" anthropomorphic aspect to the Deity – for instance, as one to whom food had to be provided. As well, they wished to distance the Temple cult as far as possible from any resemblance to pagan custom,[65] in which various food items were placed before the gods on an "altar", a special raised table. As dishes, spoons, bowls, and forks[66] are the typical utensils for food consumption, and the conventional gadgets of a table setting, these had to be eliminated from the sacred table in the Tabernacle by any possible method of interpretation.

We, however, are free from such limitations. In our attempt to find a reasonable explanation for these apparently "esoteric" verses concerning the table utensils, we must examine the possibility that they are related to the "odd" prohibitions in Exod. 30: 9 against offering not only strange incense,

---

[65] W. Burkert states in "Offerings in Perspective," *in Gifts to the Gods, Proceedings of the Upsala Symposium 1985* (Uppsala, 1987), p. 46: "Feeding the gods has become a conspicuous ceremony in the Temples of Mesopotamia and Egypt," and "In Greece too tables are laid out for the gods with offerings that are finally consumed by the priests." In the same volume, G. Englund in "Gifts to the Gods," p. 57, writes about Egyptian temples: "All over the walls we can see the richly furnished offering tables laden with choice meat, fruit, vegetables, etc."

[66] Added in the parallel list in I Chr. 28: 17 is: והמזלגות, and we evidently are to translate them as forks. The LXX translates here κρεαγρῶν "flesh hooks" (Liddell and Scott), while the NIV translates "forks". This identical utensil is found in I Sam. 2: 13: והמזלג שלש השנים בידו "with a three-pronged fork in his hand." As well, the continuation of that verse describes their use; we read in v. 14: כל אשר יעלה המזלג יקח הכהן "The priest would take for himself whatever the fork brought up," and from the context it is clear that it all concerns the flesh of the sacrifices. This term מזלגות appears in four additional places in Scripture: in Exod. 27: 3 and 38: 3, both times with reference to the bronze altar; in II Chr. 4: 16 without any direct reference to equipment; and in Num. 4: 14, with reference to the מזבח, "altar", without further specification; the context, however, seems to refer to the bronze altar. We might understand that forks would be useful on the bronze altar, to move the pieces of flesh. The use of these gadgets on the golden altar, which was supposed to serve only for the burning of incense, invokes another perplexing problem to which I shall refer later.

but also whole-burnt sacrifices, *Minhah*[67] and libation – food offerings – on the incense altar. In other words, it is the relationship between the table objects and the incense altar which we must investigate. We must also examine the probability that both the verses concerning the table utensils and Exod. 30: 9 are from different periods, and demonstrate the development of the sacrificial cult.[68]

3.5 Exod. 30: 34-36

We may now examine the second pericope, dealing with the incense spices,[69] Exod. 30: 34-38:

ויאמר ה' אל משה קח לך סמים נטף ושחלת וחלבנה סמים ולבנה זכה
בד בבד יהיה. ועשית אתה קטרת רקח מעשה רוקח ממלח טהור קדש.
ושחקת ממנה הדק ונתתה ממנה לפני העדת באהל מועד אשר אועד לך
שמה קדש קדשים תהיה לכם. והקטרת אשר תעשה במתכנתה לא תעשו לכם
קדש תהיה לך לה'. איש אשר יעשה כמוה להריח בה ונכרת מעמיו

Then the Lord said to Moses, 'Take fragrant spices: – gum resin, onycha and galbanum – and pure frankincense, all in equal amounts, and make a fragrant blend of incense, the work of a perfumer. It is to be salted and pure and sacred. Grind some of it to powder and place it in front of the Testimony in the Tent of Meeting, where I will meet with you. It shall be most holy to you. Do not make any incense with this formula for yourselves; consider it holy to the Lord. Whoever makes any like it to enjoy its fragrance must be cut off from his people.'

One observes at first glance the affinity of this text to the previous pericope, vv. 23-33, concerning the anointing oil; there is both a similarity in the literary style, and a resemblance in the interdictions, which prohibit the preparation of the anointing oil and the incense for other than cultic purposes. Both pericopes start with the infrequently used expression קח לך;

---

[67] I do not consider it necessary, at least at this stage, to confront the disputed issue of the actual meaning of *Minhah* in this context.

[68] I examined the various verses in Scripture in which there is mention of either an incense altar, מזבח הקטרת, or a golden altar, מזבח הזהב; see Introduction pp.9ff.

[69] I shall use the common term "incense", although I have some question as to the authentic meaning of the Hebrew terms in this pericope, as I will elaborate upon in my examination.

the NIV again omits the לך and translates "Take", but the literal translation is "take for you." Onkelos, Jonathan and Neophyti translate this literally as סב לך; the LXX in v. 23 translates this as σὺ λαβὲ ἡδύσματα, but
in v. 34, we read λαβὲ σεαυτῷ ἡδύσματα.[70] The association of the verb
לקח with the reflexive pronoun לך, in singular and plural, occurs sixteen
times in the Pentateuch. In the other fourteen instances[71] (that is, with the
exception of the two occurrences in our study), the use of the pronoun is
appropriate within the context, and clearly expresses the intention "to take
for, or to yourself"; in the two commands concerning the anointing oil and
the incense, however, such an interpretation is not accurate, since these
substances are not for Moses' personal benefit. The Talmud, discussing
similar instances in which there are apparently superfluous pronouns such
as לך or לכם, is aware that they are unintelligible; it usually finds a practical
purpose for such use, asserting for instance that לך, משלך "[the meaning
of] 'to you' [is] 'from you[r ownership].'" But in the case of Exod. 30: 34,
the Talmud must admit that the pronoun לך has no specific meaning, and
should be classified among other קיחות בדעלמא, or עשיות בדעלמא, "just
taking" or "just making," without any specific meaning for the pronoun.[72]
I have no explanation for these obscure[73] pronouns in our verses; I merely
draw attention to the similarity of the two pericopes in which these strange
expressions occur exclusively. M. Noth declares, for other reasons, that
both pericopes, in their present form, date from the post-exilic period,[74] but
the recipes may have been taken from older usage, or ancient tradition.

---

[70] J. Wevers, in *Notes on the Greek Text of Exodus*, p. 499 has: "σὺ λαβὲ, which thus fails
      to represent לך, a kind of reflexive pronominal element: with respect to yourself; hex
      supplied σεαυτῷ." Wevers brings to our attention the differences between the MT and
      LXX; we still note that the reflexive pronoun is not appropriate in the context.

[71] Gen. 6: 21, 14: 21, 28: 2, 31: 32, 45: 19; Exod. 5: 11, 9: 8, 12: 21, 30: 23, 30: 34;
      Lev. 9: 2, 23: 40; Num. 16: 6, 27: 18; Deut. 7: 25, 21: 11.

[72] B. T. Yoma, 3a- b, in which the phrases עשה לך and קח לך in singular are also discussed
      and assumed to imply משלך, "from your own possession."

[73] We encounter another strange expression in v. 23, concerning the anointing oil: ואתה
      קח לך Abarbanel noted the unusual addition, and proffered a midrashic explanation.
      We find in B. T.Horaioth 11b: וכולו קיים לעתיד לבוא "and the whole of [the anointing
      oil, prepared by Moses] remains in existence for the future [when the Messiah comes,
      and the same oil will be used then]." Abarbanel considered the additional word ואתה
      "and you," to express a limitation: only Moses may prepare the anointing oil, and it will
      last for ever.

[74] In *Exodus, A Commentary*, p. 238, he states: "The recipe given here for anointing oil for
      sacral anointings may rest upon a tradition of undefinable antiquity, but in the present

I already discussed the oddity of the phrase סמים נטף ושחלת וחלבנה
סמים ולבנה זכה, and the various hermeneutical and exegetical means used
by the Talmud and scholars to reconcile this phrase with their prevailing
approaches to Scripture in general and to the incense issue in particular. I
also challenged the supposition that vv. 34-36 were originally related to vv.
1- 10, and represent the recipe for the incense to be burnt on the incense
altar. The final editor of these pericopes certainly attempted to convey this
impression, arranging them in the same chapter; but the absence in vv. 34-
36 of any mention of קטר "burning", or מזבח "altar", and of any reference
to Aaron, three cardinal elements of the command in vv. 1-10, supports
their distinct origin and purpose, as previously postulated. Further to this
assumption, we must identify and classify the enumerated spices, and investigate whether the three primordial spices, נטף שחלת חלבנה (before the
addition of לבנה), had varied uses, such as in perfumes or condiments, or
were intended exclusively for fumigation. There are obvious problems with
the identification of archaic terms; therefore, I shall not attempt a definite
identification of these spices, which would at best be doubtful, but shall
concentrate primarily on their use.

Onkelos translates these spices as: נטופא, וטפרא וחלביניתא. Jonathan
deviates from this, using: קטף בשת חלבניא, and adds, as already mentioned,
בוסמין בחירין. The Samaritan Targum MS J has: (overscription) קטף
ושללי וחלבניה, and MS A has: קטף ושאבה ולבנתה סמים. Targum Neophyti
changes the text with additional terms: ראשי קטרן בסמנין טבין קטף שבלה
מרייא וחלבנה. The NIV translates the biblical phrase as "fragrant spices: —
gum resin, onycha and galbanum," while the RSV has "sweet spices, stacte,
and onycha, and galbanum."

It is the LXX, as we have seen, which introduces the term ἥδυσμα; this
is not the expected word to describe pleasant odour from burning, which
is usually expressed in the LXX by εὐωδία, the term used for the translation of ניחח . Neither in the Hebrew MT nor in the LXX are the terms
ערב "sweet" or ἡδύς associated with fragrance originating from burning
or fumigation. The terms ערב, ἡδύς and ἥδυσμα are associated in the
Hebrew text and in the LXX with fragrant spices for food, with pleasant
attributes of food and wine, and with an abstract concept of enjoyment
from refined conversation, song, sound sleep, and, possibly, favourable

---

form it doubtless corresponds to post-exilic usage." On p. 239, he adds: "The recipe for
making the material for the 'incense' also may be supposed to come from the post-exilic
period, though it may well have been taken over from an older usage."

dreams.[75] Pleasant odour from burning is denominated in the NT by ὀσμή εὐωδία,[76] Philo associates ἡδύς primarily with abstract pleasure, ἥδυσμα with the agreeable taste and smell of food, and εὐωδία with odour emanating from vapours or incense.[77] He follows the LXX precisely in his

---

[75] ἡδύς

In Esther 1: 7, we read: οἶνος πολὺς καὶ ἡδύς.

In Psalms 135: 3, the Hebrew כי נעים is translated in one MS ὅτι καλόν, and in another ὅτι ἡδύ. In Prov. 12: 11, we read ἡδύς ἐν οἴνων. The end of the verse does not exist in the MT.

In Prov. 14: 23, we read ἡδύς καὶ ἀνάλγητος ἐν ἐνδείᾳ. The Hebrew text is changed here.

In Cant. 2: 14, the term "sweet" is associated with "voice", and the Hebrew קולך ערב is translated as φωνή σου ἡδεῖα

ἡδεῖα.

In Isa. 3: 24, the Hebrew בשם is translated as ὀσμῆς ἡδείας.

In Isa. 44: 16, the exclamation האח, as an expression of pleasure after eating the roast, is translated as ἡδύ μοι.

In Jer. 31: 26, the Hebrew שנתי ערבה לי is translated as ὁ ὕπνος μου ἡδύς. The Hebrew ערב "sweet, or agreeable" is associated with food, sleep, pleasant talk – שיחי יערב עליו "May my meditation be pleasing to him," in Ps. 104: 34 – and sacrifices (וזבחיכם לא ערבו לי) "Your sacrifices do not please me," in Jer. 6: 20).

ἥδυσμα

In Exod. 30: 23, for the Hebrew בשמים (לשמן המשחה).

In Exod. 30: 34, the Hebrew סמים is translated as ἡδύσματα and as an adjective ἡδυσμοῦ. The LXX does not distinguish here between the Hebrew בשמים, for the preparation of the anointing oil in v. 23, and the Hebrew סמים utilized in v. 34.

In I Kings 10: 2, 10, the Hebrew בשמים is translated as ἡδύσματα, and I consider it to mean here spices used for food condiments and fragrances, without burning.

In I Kings 10: 25 and II Chr. 9: 24, the MT reads נשק ובשמים, and in both occurrences the LXX translates this στακτὴν καὶ ἡδύσματα. It seems that the translators had another MS, which read נטף, translated elsewhere as στακτή. Here too, it seems to me, the Hebrew בשם refers to spices for food and fragrance.

In Ecc. 10: 1, the Hebrew שמן רוקח is translated as ἐλαίου ἡδύσματος, and in Ezek. 27: 22, בראש כל בשם is translated as πρώτων ἡδυσμάτων.

[76] We read in the Epistle to the Ephesians 5: 2 καὶ θυσίαν τῷ θεῷ εἰς ὀσμὴν εὐωδίας, undoubtedly the translation of the Hebrew ריח ניחוח, as in the LXX.

[77] ἥδυσμα is associated with: παραρτύω "to season, by addition to food" (Liddell and Scott), in II 275, 17, III 283, 28, III 306, 17, V 54, 2 and VI 65, 21; with ὄψα and μελίπηκτα "relish and honey" in V 42, 15; with κνίσσης "steam from roasted meat," in I 55, 14; with ἐδωδή "food," in III 266, 20; and with μάγειρος and σιτοποιός, "butchers and millers – bakers" in VI 9, 16 and VI 60, 1. εὐώδης and εὐωδία are associated with ἀτμός "vapour" and ἀναθυμιάω "to rise in vapour," the correct term for burning incense, θυμίαμα, in I 293, 24, III 271, 5, V 41, 20, IV 34, 7, I 58, 1, I 71, 17, III 243, 6, and I 186, 21; and with χρῖσμα "scented unguent," in IV 234, 9. (Numbering follows the index to *Philonis Alexandrini Opera quae supersunt*, ed. L.Cohn and P. Wendland, Berlin 1896).

nomenclature, which corroborates the assumption that the term ἥδυσμα is not the usual term applied to incense vapours emanating from burning.[78] I did not find any mention of ἡδύσματα in Josephus' writings. The term ἡδύς appears frequently, but is not associated with fumigation odour; it refers primarily to abstract concepts, similar to the other writings we have seen. I shall quote a few such meanings from the many enumerated by Rengstorff in his Concordance to Josephus: pleasant, sweet, delightful, agreeable, welcome, convenient, soothing, refreshing, well pleasing (to a deity), comfort.[79] Further, we find an interesting phenomenon in the Testament of the Patriarchs. [80] In col. c. of the Aramaic MS, the Aramaic text uses the term בשים to describe the odour of burning fragrant wood די ריח תנגדהון בשים סליק, while the Greek text reads: ὁ καπνὸς αὐτῶν ἡδὺς ἀναβαίνων "whose smoke rises up with a pleasant odour." On the other hand, in col. d., referring to the burning of frankincense, the Aramaic text reads והקטיר עליהון לבונה ויהוון ... לריח ניחוח קודם אל עליון, while the Greek text reads: καὶ θυμίασον ἐπάνω λίβανον τοῦ ἔσεσθαι ... ὀσμὴν εὐωδίας ἔναντι κυρίου ὑψίστου "and burn the frankincense over them ... as a pleasing odour before the Most High God." We observe that the Aramaic בשים, perfume from the fragrant wood, is described by the term ἡδύς, whereas the odour of the frankincense is described by the term ὀσμή εὐωδία.[81] The term סמים occurs in Scripture,

---

[78] It is interesting to note Philo's subtle distinction. In *The Special Laws*, I: 171, concerning the daily incense celebration, he writes ἐπιθυμιᾶται τὰ πάντων εὐωδέστατα θυμιαμάτων "the perfume of the most fragrant kinds of incense is given off" and uses the term εὐωδία, whereas in 175, concerning the frankincense placed on the showbread, the term is used as "relish", and we read: συνεπιτίθεται δὲ τοῖς ἄρτοις λιβανωτὸς καὶ ἅλες, ὁ μὲν σύμβολον τοῦ μηδὲν ἥδυσμα εὐωδέστερον ὀλιγοδείας εἶναι "On the loaves there are placed also frankincense and salt, the former as a symbol that in the court of wisdom no relish is judged to be more sweet-savoured than frugality." Here, the frankincense is both used as a relish and fumigated, and therefore Philo uses both terms, ἥδυσμα for the relish and εὐωδία for the fumigation process.

[79] In the writings of Theophrastus, the third century scientist, we also find the term εὐώδος applied to perfumes, in Περὶ Ὀσμῶν Concerning Odours # 25, and the term ἡδυσμός, concerning the garden herb mint, in Περὶ Φυτῶν Ἱστορίας Enquiry into Plants, VII.7.1, trans. A. Hort (Loeb Classical Library, 1961).

[80] R. H. Charles and A. Cowley, "An Early Source of Testaments of Patriarchs," *JQR* 19 (1906), pp. 574 ff., and English translation by H. W. Hollander and M. De Jonge, in *The Testaments of theTwelve Patriarchs, A Commentary* (Leiden, 1985), p. 463ff.

[81] From this text, it seems that this sect or group required frankincense to be burnt with each sacrifice, on the outer altar, contrary to the plain reading of the scriptural text and mishnaic regulations. Num. 15: 1- 16 describes the regulations and the command

exclusively in **P** texts and in Chr., to indicate the cultic incense, as Haran observed; on the other hand, we find the term בשם in the earlier Kings and in many other writings, and in most occurrences it is clearly unconnected with incense or burning.

The scope of this examination has been extended in order to challenge and to weaken the entrenched opinion that the three spices mentioned in Exod. 30: 34, נטף שחלת חלבנה, were originally intended to be burnt on a censer. The precise character of these spices cannot be ascertained, and doubts persist regarding their correct identification, as well as their probable use in the ancient period in which this composition originated. A particular spice might have been used, as already suggested, as a food additive, or to provide a fragrant odour, or for both. Many edible spices emit fragrant smells without burning, and some of those spices can also be burned to generate a pleasant odour. I shall examine the validity of the various identifications of these spices, and the issue of their use, whether in their natural state or burnt.

We have seen different translations in the Aramaic for the two first-named spices, נטף and שחלת, but their identification with currently known spices remains unclear. The LXX translates נטף, which occurs only once in the Bible, as στακτή, but in other instances, in Gen. 37: 25 and 43: 11, it is the Hebrew לוט which is translated as στακτή. Nielsen[82] states: "As explained earlier נטף is to be connected with צרי , which we identified as storax, and not with stacte as LXX has it." (The LXX translates צרי as ῥητίνη in Gen. 37: 25, 43: 11, Jer. 8: 22, 26: 11 (46: 11 in MT), 28: 8 (51: 8 in MT) and Ezek. 8: 22). Nielsen concludes that נטף is to be connected with צרי, and is therefore storax, on the basis of a statement in B. T. Keritoth 6a, which in my opinion he misunderstood. A *Beraita* in this text enumerates the eleven ingredients of the incense, and appears to start with the four listed in Exod. 30: 34, which are all of the same weight: ת"ר פיטום הקטרת הצרי והצפורן והחלבנה והלבנה משקל שבעים שבעים של שבעים מנה "The Rabbis taught: The preparation of the incense [is as follows]: *Sori,*

---

concerning the special *Minhah,* the cereal and drink offering which has to accompany the animal sacrifices עולה and שלמים. But contrary to the separate *Minhah* cereal offerings decreed in Lev. 2, to which frankincense is specifically commanded to be added, there is no mention of frankincense in this pericope. From the odd position of this chapter, and other peculiarities, it seems that it is of a later date than Lev. 2 (see Noth, *Numbers,* Philadelphia, 1968, p. 114). We read in Mishnah Menahoth 5: 3: מנחת נסכין טעונה שמן ואינה טעונה לבונה "The *Minhah* libation [a technical term in the Talmud for the *Minhah* and libation which accompany animal sacrifices] requires [the addition of] oil, and does not require [the addition of] frankincense."

Siporen, Helbenah and *Lebonah* [each] seventy portions." The two last ingredients correspond to the names mentioned in Scripture, but the first two are different. However, they may be assumed to correspond to Exod. 30: 34, since they are the only ones in the *Beraita* which must be of the same quantity. It seems that Rabbi Simon ben Gamaliel[83] attempted to explain this apparent discrepancy, saying: הצרי אינו אלא השרף הנוטף מעצי הקטף "The *Sori* [of the *Beraita*] is merely the resin which drops from the *Katap* trees." In essence, he suggests that the צרי of the *Beraita* is to be identified with the non-specific biblical term נטף and is a resin which drops from the specified *Katap* tree. צרי is the generic term for resin, and is translated in the LXX as ῥητίνη, an unspecified resin, from the root ῥέω.

M. Zohary[84] proposes to identify צרי with "Liquidambar Orientalis," which "has recently been shown to be specifically identical with the Liquidambar styraciflua." Therefore, he opts for the identification of צרי as "storax". He also states: "The present writer accepts the suggestion of Lagarde (1886) that the Greek name storax derives from the Hebrew Sori."

Similarly, the Hebrew לוט, which the LXX translates as στακτή, from the root στάζω "to drop", denoting "oozing out in drops, trickling, dropping" (Liddell and Scott) indicates a generic term for a substance which is oozed or dropped out. Nielsen states:[85] "On philological grounds, it [לוט] has been compared to Syriac 'ladan', Arabic 'ladan'... the resin from the genus Cistus." He then adds: "The identification is questionable." M. Zohary[85a] proposes to identify לוט with "Cistus incanus," and not the myrrh of the KJV and NIV. He adds that myrrh is a tropical shrub which cannot be grown in biblical Gilead, to which the herbs and delicacies listed in Genesis seem to be native. As we have observed the LXX translates both occurrences of לוט with the generic στακτή, and צרי with the generic term ῥητίνη, not "storax". It is possible that at some point in time the term לוט

---

[82] Nielsen, *Incense in Ancient Israel*, p. 65.

[83] This seems to be R. Simon ben Gamaliel the elder, who was still alive at the time of the Second Temple, and we might assume that he had personal know-how of the ingredients of the incense, but not the "know-how" to prepare it, a procedure kept secret by the Abtinas family. Maimonides, in his interpretation of the first Mishnah in Keritoth, declares that the Abtinas family kept secret the identification of the מעלה עשן plant which produced the required smoke effect.

[84] M. Zohary, *Plants of the Bible*, (Cambridge: Cambridge University Press, 1982), p. 192.

[85] p. 64.

[85a] p. 194.

was known as a resin of a specific plant; but it seems that the LXX did not know to which plant it referred, and used the generic στακτή for the translation of both לוט and the non-specific נטף[86]. On the other hand, the LXX correctly understood that צרי is the generic term for resin which drops from a tree, and translated this as ῥητίνη. That rendering is substantiated by Rabbi Simon ben Gamaliel's explanation, which interprets נטף = צרי as the "flow" from the *Katap* tree.[87] Agreeing with Rabbi Simon's identification, Targums Jonathan and Neophyti, which have a great affinity with each other, interpret נטף as קטף. The Samaritan Targum, possibly with the same insight as Rabbi Simon, also translates נטף as קטף, while Onkelos, as usual following the biblical text strictly, persists with the same, non-specific term נטופא, without indicating the name of the tree. We thus see the difficulties encountered in the identification of the incense ingredients. We can only assume from the above quotations and from the philological associations of the verb נטף that the latter refers to a resin; the Talmud identifies the relevant tree as קטף, whose precise identity is unknown.

The second term שחלת, translated by the LXX as ὄνυξ, has a variety of translations in the various Targumim, quoted above. Nielsen[88] concludes his recitation of the many opinions concerning this term: "But the problem is difficult. It is best to leave it open." We may only assume that the Talmud, which appears to use צפורן as the equivalent of the biblical שחלת, was aware of its identity. In the above quote from Keritoth, there is no questioning of, or explanation for, the apparent discrepancy between צפורן and the biblical שחלת, as there was for צרי and נטף. Furthermore, in the ensuing debate in 6b, we read: ואי כתב ושחלת ה"א גידולי קרקע אין, אבל מין אילן לא אימא "And if [only] *Sehelet* were written, we would have said that [Scripture] intended only [spices] grown in the earth, but not [spices] grown on trees"; hence, the Rabbis identified שחלת – צפורן as an earth-growing fragrant plant.[89]

---

[86] In Περὶ Ὀσμῶν, #29, Theophrastus states: στακτὴ γὰρ καλεῖται διὰ τὸ κατὰ μικρὸν στάζειν "it is in fact called stacte because it comes in drops slowly." This phrase parallels Rabbi Simon ben Gamaliel's dictum.

[87] Maimonides also understood Rabbi Simon's dictum in the same way. In Hil. Klei Hamiqdash chap. 2, hal. 4, he writes: נטף האמור בתורה הוא עצי הקטף שיוצא מהן הצרי "[The] *Natap* mentioned in the Torah are the *Katap* trees, from which the *Sori* flows out."

[88] p. 66.

[89] I do not intend with my limited linguistic and botanical knowledge to solve this riddle, which others more knowledgeable than I could not unravel; I merely wish to draw

The identification of the third ingredient חלבנה (NIV galbanum) is even more perplexing. The various Targumim have kept the original term (with minor changes, as cited above), and so has the LXX, which translates the term as χαλβάνη , a Semitic loan word in Greek.[90] But it seems to me that the common identification of the spice as Ferula entails serious difficulties. B. T. Keritoth 6b, in the debate quoted above, declares that חלבנה generates a bad odour. Zohary[91] affirms that "It [Ferula] is actually a fetid gum." It is therefore improbable that such a product would be used in a preparation of fragrant spices. Further, the pericope in Exod. 30: 34-36, the subject of our examination, concludes in v. 38: איש אשר יעשה כמוה להריח "Whoever makes any like it to *enjoy its fragrance* [emphasis added]." Moreover, we read in Ben Sira 24: 15

ὡς κιννάμωμον καὶ ἀσπάλαθος ἀρωμάτων (δέδωκα
ὀσμήν)[92]
καὶ ὡς σμύρνα ἐκλεκτὴ διέδωκα εὐωδίαν,
ὡς χαλβάνη καὶ ὄνυξ καὶ στακτὴ
καὶ ὡς λιβάνου ἀτμὶς ἐν σκηνῇ,

Like cassia and camel's thorn I gave forth the aroma of spices, and like choice myrrh I spread a pleasant odour, like *galbanum*, onycha and stacte, and like the fragrance of frankincense in the Tabernacle.[93]

The author compares ingredients which have the attributes ἀρωμάτων ὀσμήν "aromatic smells" and εὐωδίαν "pleasant odour," and includes galbanum in this list. Zohary thus concludes: "Despite the Greek, Aramaic

---

attention to the fact that in modern Hebrew, the carnation flower is called צפורן, the term also used for clove. The common dictionary defines "clove" as a dried unexpanded flower-bud of the clove tree, used as a spice. This identification would contradict the talmudic idea that the term refers to an earth-growing plant. It is also interesting to observe in Latin the philological affinity between "fingernail" and "anointing", similar to the Hebrew צפורן, the ingredient of spices. The nail is called *unguis*, and *unguentum* is ointment.

[90]   Nielsen, p. 66, who quotes in his notes I. Loew, *Die Flora der Juden* (Wien – Leipzig, 1928), and J. Feliks, עולם הצומח של התנ"ך (Jerusalem, 1968).

[91]   *Plants of the Bible*, p. 201.

[92]   In Ziegler's edition, *Sapientia Iesu Filii Sirach*, Vol. XII (Göttingen, 1965), these two words are missing; in his apparatus, he indicates the manuscripts in which these words do appear. I have quoted the verses and the translation from Zohary, and left these words in the text because they do not affect my thesis.

[93]   Translation from Zohary p. 201.

and Syriac name *halbane*, cognate with the Hebrew *helbenah*, its identification is not yet firmly established." It is possible that because of this assumed disgusting odour of the חלבנה, Targum Jonathan and the closely related Neophyti added בסמין בחירין and בסמנין טבין, respectively; the LXX adjoined the modifier ἡδυσμοῦ, to differentiate this spice from the fetid one of the same name.

From the above, we must regretfully admit that we have no definite identification for the first three spice ingredients quoted in Exod. 30: 34,[94] and therefore we have no idea whether they were used as condiments for food, whether they were used to generate pleasant odours (either by their mere exposure or through burning on coal), or whether they were used in both ways.[95] Further examination of the context surrounding the "incense" regulations may provide us with more helpful indications as to their purpose. Scripture uses the term רקח both in verses 23-33 in connection with the ointment, and in our verse 35, referring to "incense".[96] The preparation of the "incense" is described in v. 35 as the מעשה רוקח, the art of the "perfumer" in the NIV, but we do not know whether this activity related generally to the preparation of powders and ointments, or specifically to incense. The LXX translates this term as μυρεψός, a "perfumer", from the

---

[94] The traditional commentators do not agree among themselves on the identification of the incense ingredients, and do not provide us with better solutions. See Rashi's interpretation to Exod. 30: 34, and Ramban's dispute. Maimonides indicates Arabic names for all the ingredients, and although we would assume that חלבנה would be called galbanum, as in Aramaic and Syriac, he calls it *Miah*. In his interpretation to Mishnah Keritoth 1: 1, he indicates other names, but also states: ופירוש השמות האלו, יש מהם שהוא מפורסם ויש מהם שנחלקו בו וכבר נתבאר בגמרא שהעשב הזה שקרוי מעלה עשן לא היו יודעין אותו אלא בית אבטינס בלבד "And [as to] the translation of the names [of the incense ingredients], there are some known, and others which were disputed; and it was already elucidated in the Talmud that the plant called *Maaleh Ashan* was known only by the Abtinas family." Hence, Maimonides also admits that the identification of all the ingredients is not known.

[95] In Περὶ 'Οσμῶν, #12, Theophrastus states: "In some of these the smell is only perceived when they are eaten, while some need even to be bruised and broken up, and others to be subjected to fire, as myrrh, frankincense and anything that is burnt as incense." But in # 13 he states: "For, if these substances [frankincense and myrrh] are bruised and crushed, they will indeed present an odour, but it will not be so sweet nor so lasting as when they have been subjected to fire." Theophrastus' statements concerning spices and incense are, it seems to me, relevant to the knowledge and practice in Judah, during the period of the Second Temple and Hellenistic influence.

[96] As I have already noted, there is no indication of burning in this pericope, hence the question remains open whether it refers to incense, or to herbs as condiments or as fragrance.

noun τὸ μύρον, "sweet juice extracted from plants, sweet oil, unguent, balsam" (Liddell and Scott). Onkelos translates this as עובד בוסמנו, and Neophyti as עובד בשם, a "spice artisan." Jonathan translates the term in v. 35 as ממזיג, "mixer [of spices]," exactly as in v. 33, concerning the preparation of the ointment. Hence, we have no indication that the term רוקח describes more than a "perfumer," a professional who pulverizes the various ingredients and mixes them into a compound, which may then be used in powder form, dissolved in a liquid such as water or oil, or fumigated. The numerous occurrences of the root רקח in Scripture do not demonstrate any specific connection to the preparation of incense, but some do suggest the preparation of spiced condiments for food.[97]

The Akkadian term for this profession is *muraqqu* for the male and *muraqqitu* for the female; according to E. Ebeling[98] the root verb is *ruqqu*, "zu Parfüm (Wasser oder -Salbe) verarbeiten," to prepare perfumed water and ointment. We find many similar associations between spices and perfuming in Scripture. We read in Prv. 7: 17 נפתי משכבי מר אהלים וקנמון[99] "I have perfumed my bed with myrrh, aloes, and cinnamon." The use of spices in a dry state to generate a pleasant smell is also suggested in

---

[97] In Ezek. 24: 10, we read התם הבשר והרקח המרקחה והעצמות יחרו "cook the meat well, mixing in the spices; and let the bones be charred." In Cant. 8: 2, we read אשקך מיין הרקח "I would give you spiced wine to drink." Eccl. 10: 1 reads: שמן רוקח "perfume", though a more literal translation might be "the oil of the perfumer." Other occurrences, such as I Chr. 9: 29-30, are not as explicit, but give the same impression that רקח refers to the preparation of spices. We read there: ומהם ממנים על הכלים ועל כל כלי הקדש ועל "Others הסלת והיין והשמן והלבונה והבשמים. ומן בני הכהנים רקחי המרקחת לבשמים were assigned to take care of the furnishings and all the other articles of the sanctuary, as well as the flour and wine, and the oil, incense and spices." Unmistakably, the term רקח refers here to ointment, not to incense, since the frankincense is mentioned separately from the בשמים. This also corroborates my suggestion that בשמים was an ancient concept which referred to spices, and סמים was coined as a *terminus technicus* for the cultic incense. Mandelkern suggests in his *Concordance* that the root רקח should be considered as cognate with רקק, רקע. The term רקע suggests "pounding" and "hammering", as in Exod. 39: 3 וירקעו את פחי הזהב "they hammered out thin sheets of gold"; this is also the activity of the perfumer, as noted above.

[98] E. Ebeling, *Parfümrezepte und Kultische Texte aus Assur*, (Roma: Pontificium Institutum Biblicum, 1950), p. 5.

[99] The LXX translates the verb נפה as διέρραγκα from the root διαρραίνω, "sprinkle". Rashi translates this "to wave and to disperse the odour," but other traditional commentators also translate this "to sprinkle," as does Cassuto. In Cant. 4: 16, we read יזלו בשמיו "that its fragrance may spread about," and in 5: 5 וידי נטפו מור "and my hands dripped with myrrh"; in v. 13, we read again מור נטפות "dripping with myrrh." These verses demonstrate the use of spices in liquid form to generate pleasant odour.

Cant. 1: 13 צְרוֹר הַמּוֹר דּוֹדִי לִי בֵּין שָׁדַי יָלִין "My lover is to me a sachet of myrrh resting between my breasts."[100] None of these quotations refers to incense, merely to aromatic liquids or fragrant spices. If we can deduce anything from a comparison with Mesopotamian practice, it is that the perfumer mainly, if not exclusively, prepared the compounded spices, crushed them into powder and dissolved them in oil or water. As such compounds were used for the well-being of people, so they were also dedicated to the well-being of the gods.[101] It seems, however, that initially pleasant odour was generated by the burning of fragrant wood species, and not by spices, which was a later sophistication. We read in the Gilgamesh Epic[102] and in other ancient tablets[103] that fragrant woods, such as juniper, cedar, cypress and reed, were burned in rituals, to generate a pleasant odour for the gods' enjoyment and to invoke their favourable disposition toward the propitiator. Custom in ancient Israel was probably similar, and there are traces of such custom in Scripture and in other early writings. I shall return to the substantiation of this proposition at a later stage.

Returning to our pericope, we note that verse 35 proceeds with an obscure term, מְמֻלָּח, whose interpretation and purpose is widely discussed and disputed by the various translators and commentators. The NIV translates this as "It is to be salted," but the LXX translates it as μεμιγμένον, "mixed, compounded."[104] Onkelos and Jonathan also translate this as

---

[100] The LXX translates ἀπόδεσμος (τῆς στακτῆς) " girdle, bunch" (Liddell and Scott).

[101] E. Ebeling, p. 4, writes: "Aber man kann gewiss sein, dass bei diesem Glauben von den Göttern die eigene menschliche Vorliebe fur das Parfüm entscheidend gewesen ist." ("But one may be sure that in this belief concerning the gods [that they enjoy an extraordinary satisfaction through pleasant odour], human fondness of perfume was a decisive factor.")

[102] James B. Pritchard, ed., "Akkadian Myths and Epics," in *ANET* (Princeton, 1950), p. 95 : "Upon their pot-stands I heaped cane, cedarwood, and myrtle. The gods smelled the savour, the gods smelled the sweet savour." In the Babylonian Gilgamesh Epic (Ebeling, p. 4) we find the same types of fragrant woods, though in a different order: *qanu tabu*, (cane – מֵרְחָק מֵאַרְדָּץ וְקָנֶה הַטּוֹב, Jer. 6: 20) *asu* (myrtle) and *erinu* (cedar).

[103] Nielsen, p. 25, quotes "a passage from the ritual series SURPU preserved on tablets in the library of Ašurbanipal. In tablet IX we read certain invocations of the means of the ritual such as tamarisk, reed, cedar and juniper." Nielsen then quotes from a Sumerian text, to which I will refer later, referring to incense which comes from the mountains, the fragrance of juniper and cedar.

[104] See J. W.Wevers, *Notes on the Greek Text of Exodus*, p. 503: "μεμιγμένον is an old interpretation of מְמֻלָּח 'salted' in MT, for which compare Lev. 2: 13 (where מֶלַח unequivocally means 'salt')." I propose that the interpretation "mixed" is a later idea than the archaic "salted", and I will elaborate upon this below.

"mixed" מערב, as does Neophyti, using the term ממזג. The Samaritan Targum has an entirely different interpretation: מדוכה, either "crushed" with a pestle, from the root דוך, or "purified" from the root דכי. Since the term מלח has the single meaning "salt" in the Pentateuch, Rashi attempts to reconcile the apparent philological difficulty raised by the translation "mixed" (as in Onkelos). Rashi suggests a similarity to the phrases in Jonah 1: 5 וייראו המלחים ויזעקו "All the sailors were afraid and each cried out," and Ezek. 27: 9 כל אניות הים ומלחיהם "all the ships of the sea and their sailors," where מלחים are sailors; he suggests an association between "mixing and moving" and "sailors" by the fact that the sailors beat the water with the oars, similar to the beating of eggs, or any other liquid compound.[105] Rashbam, among many others, agrees with Rashi, but Ramban and Ibn Ezra interpret ממלח as "salted", and defend their opinion based on B. T. Keritoth 6a, in which it is stated that the incense compound included מלח סדומית רבע "salt of Sodom, a quarter."

It is difficult to understand why Onkelos and the traditional commentators[106] avoided the simple translation "salted", since the Talmud, as we have seen, requires salt to be added to the incense.[107] One might accept that the LXX could not envisage salt as part of an incense compound, but not the traditional translators, who followed the talmudic interpretations.[108]

---

[105] I do not intend to establish a theory concerning Greek etymology, but I would like to draw attention to an interesting comparison between Rashi's association of "sailor" with the "motion" of the waves, and the affinity of "sea" θάλασσα – σάλασσα in Doric – with σαλεύω "to oscillate, to roll like a ship on sea," or σάλος, "a moving motion" (Liddell and Scott). The association between "sea" and "salt" is also documented in Greek: ὁ ἅλς "salt" and ἡ ἅλς " sea". Thus, Rashi's association of these concepts no longer looks strange, or "amusing", an epithet bestowed upon Rashi's "etymological speculations" by V. Hurowitz, in his essay "Salted Incense," *Biblica*, 68. 2 (1987), pp. 178-194. Prof. Wevers comments that the etymology of θάλασσα is unknown, and certainly unrelated to σαλεύω.

[106] Hurowitz, ibid., quotes a great number of these commentators, who avoid the interpretation "salted."

[107] It is interesting to note that Theophrastus states in Περὶ Ὀσμῶν # 25 " Into roseperfume moreover is put a quantity of salt." On the other hand, this admixture of salt mentioned by Theophrastus may have applied only to the preparation of rose perfume, but not to incense.

[108] We have seen that according to the Talmud the incense compound had salt as one of the ingredients, included either in the eleven basic components or as an additive, a contentious issue among the commentators. Furthermore, we find a talmudic dictum that the compounded incense had to be salted again before burning on the altar. We read in B. T. Menahoth 21b this *Beraita*: בשלשה מקומות המלח נתונה, בלשכת המלח, ועל גבי הכבש ובראשו של מזבח ... ששם מולחין הקומץ והלבונה והקטורת ומנחת כהנים וכו'

Hurowitz[109] asks this question and grants it great importance; he writes: "The outstanding problem remaining to be solved is how did the word ממלח come to be taken as 'mixed' rather then 'salted'. There is, to my knowledge, no clear solution nor has anyone ever even addressed the question!" As may be seen from my examination of the relevant verses, I am inclined to consider this pericope as originating in part from an ancient text, changed beyond recognition by deletions and additions. Only through a punctilious critical examination might one attempt to distinguish the older from the newer parts.

I wish to offer the hypothesis that this pericope did not relate initially to incense, but solely to spices as food condiments. I already proposed a number of bases for this postulate, and now offer a further elaboration upon it. It is reasonable to expect that salt, a proven preservative substance, as well as a seasoning for normal usage, was exposed on the table for the meal of the gods, together with other spices used for taste and fragrance. We note the importance of salt throughout the Bible, both with respect to its physical properties and as a symbol. Food without salt was considered flavourless, as we read in Job 6: 6 היאכל תפל מבלי מלח "Is tasteless food eaten without salt," and salt can improve spoiled water, as we see in II Kings 2: 21 וישלך שם מלח ... רפאתי למים האלה "and threw the salt into it ... I have healed this water." The phrase in Lev. 2: 13 ולא תשבית מלח ברית אלהיך מעל מנחתך "Do not leave the salt of the covenant of your God out of your grain," has an aetiological purpose, which seems to be a later interpolation to defend an archaic custom.[110] This "salt" covenant is mentioned several times in Scripture: in Lev. concerning the salting of the offerings, in Num. 18: 19 as a covenant to ensure that the priests receive their part of the offerings, and in II Chr. 13: 5 as a covenant with the House of David for perpetual kingship; all three occurrences have an obvious aetiological purpose.[111] In

---

"In three places salt was deposited: in the salt chamber, on the ascent [to the altar] and on the top of the altar... where the handful [of the *Minhah*] and the frankincense, and the incense and the priest's *Minhah* etc. were salted." Maimonides, in his Hil. Issurei Hamizbeah, chap. 5, hal. 13 omits קטורת from the list of offerings which are salted on top of the altar, but I doubt that he had another MS of the Talmud which omitted this term. It seems that the Tosaphists in Menahoth 21b did have קטורת in their MS; the question is posed as to why the קטרת is salted on the top of the outer altar, since incense was burned on the inner golden altar.

[109] p. 193.

[110] Karl Elliger, *Leviticus*, p. 46.

[111] The midrashim also understood the concept of the "salt covenant" as having an aetiological purpose. We read in the Mekhilta of Rabbi Ishmael Tractate *Pisha, Parshah Bo*

our verse, there is no indication of any covenant, and it seems to me that the simple motive of serving salt as a condiment is a reasonable explanation.[112] Similarly, at the offering of the showbread, the LXX has added the word "salt" in its translation. In Lev. 24: 7, we read: ונתת על המערכת לבנה זכה, but the LXX translates: καὶ ἐπιθήσετε ἐπὶ τὸ θέμα λίβανον καθαρὸν καὶ ἅλα. It would be difficult to disregard as irrelevant this data from the LXX, which was created during the Temple period. One might assume that this was the customary procedure, founded on ancient tradition, which was changed at a later date, and the text adjusted accordingly. If such a conjecture is correct, it would further substantiate my hypothesis.

The Talmud too considers salt an indispensable accompaniment to food.[113] This linkage between salt and food did not appeal to the traditional interpreters, because the idea that this pericope might refer to food seasoning, and the consequent anthropomorphic aspect of offering food to the deity, were not in harmony with their opinions. I demonstrated the pains which most of the interpreters took to obliterate any association between the table in the Tabernacle and a display of food and eating utensils; the relevant verses had, as we have seen, undergone heavy-handed interpretation, which has left open many questions. The traditional interpreters were

---

1, ד"ה בארץ מצרים: "Until Aaron was chosen, all of Israel was appropriate for priesthood; after Aaron was chosen, all Israel was excluded, since it says 'it is a covenant of salt for ever before the Lord to you and your descendants.'" Similar midrashim on this verse also appear in Sifre on Num. 118-119, and in Tanhuma *Parshah Bo*. In Midrash Tanhuma *Parshah Lekh Lekha*, we find a midrash which links Aaron's "salt covenant" to David's covenant; as Aaron's covenant for priesthood is perpetual, so is David's kingship. Both possess the "salt covenant."

[112] Hurowitz, who interprets this pericope as referring to incense, postulates that salt was indeed added to incense "to influence the rate of burning or smoking of the incense or fumigant (p.192)." I do not intend to discuss this hypothesis, since my theory evolves from an entirely different starting point; I only wish to mention that in my opinion the evidence he brings from a Mesopotamian tablet, concerning the placing of a lump of salt in a censer, is not conclusive. The tablet in question refers to an incantation to drive out demons, and the lump of salt is described as "created in a pure place"; this demonstrates that it was specifically a lump of salt originating from a mountainous mine which was necessary, not salt to enhance the burning. Pure salt from a mountain, which indicates purity in Mesopotamian ritual texts, had a ceremonial purpose, namely to exorcize demons.

[113] We read at B. T. Berakhoth 5a מלח ממתקת את הבשר "salt sweetens (softens) the meat," and at 40a ואחר כל אכילתך אכל מלח "and after each meal, eat salt"; here salt has an apotropaic effect. In Y. T. Horaioth chap. 3, hal. 5 we read אפשר לעולם לחיות בלי פלפילין, אי אפשר לעולם בלי מלח "the world can exist without pepper but cannot exist without salt."

certainly aware of textual difficulties and inconsistencies, similar to the
questions raised by modern Bible critics; they offered answers and solutions
appropriate to their credos. For instance, Onkelos, the usually straightforward interpreter, changed the simple anthropomorphic phrase ריח ניחח
לה', with reference to the sacrifices, to דמתקבל ברעוא קדם ה' "[a sacri-
fice] which is received with goodwill before the Lord." It is no wonder that
Onkelos, with his great sensitivity in expunging all anthropomorphic associations, especially concerning the sacrificial cult, has interpreted ממלח as
"mixed", instead of "salted", which could be connected to food; most of the
other interpreters followed him. Rashi explicitly refers to Onkelos, in justifying his interpretation as "mixed" instead of the expected "salted".

Proceeding to v. 36, we read ונתתה ממנה לפני העדת באהל מועד אשר
אועד לך שמה "And place it in front of the Testimony in the Tent of
Meeting, where I will meet with you." I already deliberated at length regarding the issue of the location of the incense altar, indicated in v. 30: 6
to be לפני הכפרת אשר על העדת, and its linkage with God's place of meeting
with Moses. Our verse has a great similarity to v. 6, both in style and in the
special emphasis on the meeting place. But again we must come to the
conclusion that the original text intended the "spices" to be placed, literally,
"before" the ark; they could not have been placed on the incense altar, since
this was outside the Holy of Holies. The phrase לפני העדת occurs twice
more in the Pentateuch, and in both these instances, based on the context,
it is associated with the ark; this was also the understanding of the Rabbis.[114] I already demonstrated that it is Moses, not Aaron, to whom verses
1-6 and verses 34-38 in Exod. chap. 30 are addressed. This contrasts with
v. 7 in that chapter, in which it is Aaron who is commanded to burn the

---

[114] We read in Num. 17: 19 (17:4 in NIV), regarding Aaron's rod, והנחתם באהל מועד
לפני העדות אשר אועד לכם שמה "Place them in the Tent of Meeting in front of the
Testimony, where I meet with you." As in our verse, there is the apparently unnecessary
mention of the meeting place; this, I suggest, must be associated with the ancient
tradition of the Tent which served as the place to seek oracles, as described in Exod.
33: 7-11, quite different from the Tabernacle of P (see G. von Rad, *Old Testament
Theology*, New York, 1962, p. 234 ff). In Num. 17: 25 (17:10 in NIV), we read השב
את מטה אהרן לפני העדות "Bring Aaron's rod again before the testimony." A *Beraita*
in B. T. Yoma 52 b and B. T. Keritoth 5b recounts: משנגנז ארון נגנזה עמו צנצנת המן
וצלוחית שמן המשחה ומקלו של אהרן ושקדיה ופרחיה "When the ark was hidden, the
pot of manna, the carafe of the anointing oil and Aaron's rod with its almonds and
blossoms were hidden with it." The Talmud connects the pot of manna and Aaron's
rod, which were placed לפני העדות with the ark. I shall not elaborate in this essay upon
the distinctions between the Tent and the ark, a significant and much debated subject.

incense on the golden altar. I have also drawn attention to the fact that our later pericope uses the words ונתתה ממנה "and place it" – that is, place it before the Testimony, with no reference to burning, or to the golden altar, or to מזבח מקטר קטרת,"the altar to burn incense upon," which one would expect if the spices were to be burnt.

3.6 Exod. 30: 37-38

We come now to the strange and unique prohibition in verses 37-38 against preparing a mixture identical to the "incense" compound , קטרת; this is the same type of interdiction as declared in v. 33 concerning the preparation of the anointing oil. We have observed the overall parallelism of these two pericopes, in their literary, structural and functional aspects and in the exceptional ban against making the relevant items. Both pericopes start with the unusual קח לך; the first pericope ends in v. 33 with איש אשר ירקח כמהו ואשר יתן ממנו על זר ונכרת מעמיו "Whoever makes perfume like it and whoever puts it on anyone other than a priest must be cut off from his people," and in v. 38, we read איש אשר יעשה כמוה להריח בה ונכרת מעמיו "Whoever makes any like it to enjoy its fragrance must be cut off from his people." The similarity of the literary style, the prohibition and the chastisement are striking, as is the association in each of the pericopes between the particular cultic rite and the exclusivity of the priesthood.

Aaron and his descendants are the only family to be anointed with the holy oil,[115] similar to the anointing of the Tabernacle's furnishings, a practice which excluded all others from the sacrificial cult. With this uniqueness is associated – through the analogy suggested by the arrangement of the two pericopes in the same style – the interdiction against preparation of incense, and by implication the control of its supply and celebration. The ban against anointing with the holy oil was not decreed with the aim of forbidding the physical enjoyment of a material prepared for sacral use – a small change in its composition would allow the same enjoyment – but rather to prevent use

---

[115] We observe the different terms applied to the anointing of the priests and the Temple furnishings, and for the spreading of lotion on a layperson. In the first case, in vv. 25-31, we find the verb משח, which is used almost exclusively in Scripture for the consecration of priests and kings, whereas in v. 32, in the phrase על בשר אדם לא ייסך "Do not pour it on men's bodies," we find the verb סוך, a neutral term for a cosmetic smearing of balm.

of the oil to initiate inappropriate persons into the priestly duties and privi-leges.[116] Similarly, the purpose of the prohibition against preparing and smelling the incense odour was not to impede the physical enjoyment of a thing reserved for the Deity.[117] Here too, a small change in its formula could allow this; its motive was to ban any inappropriate person, as far as possible, from connection with the preparation of the anointing oil[118] and the incense procurement and celebration. I do not know of any other such drastic prohibition against preparing a substance which was used in the cult. One might comprehend a simple interdiction against use; but it seems to me that the specific ban against preparation is unique, and demonstrates an extraordinary resolve to maintain and safeguard special "monopolistic" interests. It is not unreasonable to assume that specific events and circum-stances dictated such excessive restrictions on two significant priestly privi-leges: the investiture of a single clan into the perpetual priesthood, and their exclusive control of the highest charismatic positions and most rewarding functions, and specifically the incense celebration. I shall elaborate upon this issue further.

---

[116] We find an interesting *Beraita* in B. T. Keritoth 6b: הסך בשמן המשחה לבהמה וכלים פטור לעובדי כוכבים ולמתים פטור "Whoever anoints an animal and utensils with the anointing oil is not liable [to be cut off from the people]; [whoever anoints] idolaters and corpses is not liable." The Talmud emphasizes that the prohibition is not connected with the enjoyment of a thing reserved for the Deity; it is directed against the anointing of someone not eligible for consecration.

[117] In contrast to the prohibition against eating the fat reserved for the Deity, כל חלב לה׳. ... כל חלב וכל דם לא תאכלו "All the fat is the Lord's....You must not eat any fat or any blood (Lev. 3: 16-17)," there is no suggestion that the odour "belongs" to the Deity; as already emphasized, the common phrase ריח ניחוח לה׳ "an aroma pleasing to the Lord " is missing. The remarkable absence of this phrase in the "incense" ritual, a rite involving a fragrant substance, leads us to assume that the final editing of this pericope was effected at a late date, and any archaic anthropomorphic implication was intentionally omitted. I. Knohl, מקדש הדממה (Jerusalem: Magnes Press, 1992), pp. 162-3 states similarly that the phrase ריח ניחח does not occur with the sin sacrifice so as to eliminate any anthropomorphic suggestion. He has overlooked the sin sacrifice for an individual, in Lev. 4: 31, where we do read: והקטיר הכהן המזבחה לריח ניחח לה׳ וכפר עליו הכהן "...and the priest shall burn it on the altar as an aroma pleasing to the Lord. In this way the priest will make atonement for him."

[118] See note 73, concerning the midrash which states that only Moses prepared the anoint-ing oil, which lasted forever.

4. The Development of the Incense Cult (Part I)

4.1. Fragrant Woods Versus Incense

We may now reconsider the issue of the relationship, in ritual, between the burning of fragrant wood species and the use of spices, both in Israel and in Mesopotamian cultures. We have noted briefly the Gilgamesh Epic, in which we read that the burning of such woods was practised to please the gods, and we find in Scripture and in other ancient Jewish documents a similar importance bestowed on the wood to be burned on the altar. I have discussed this issue elsewhere in connection with B. T. Tamid,[1] and I shall summarize here the critical details of that discussion.

In Gen. 22: 3, part of the mythical narrative of the sacrifice of Isaac by Abraham, we read[2] ויבקע עצי עלה "When he had cut enough wood for the burnt offering."[3] In v. 6, the term עצי העלה is repeated, again in construct

---

[1] We read in Mishnah Tamid 2: 1 כל העצים כשרין למערכה "All [types] of wood are suitable for the order [of the wood on the altar]." It may be that this regulation was a later development, after the introduction of the daily incense celebration, which had diminished the significance of the fragrant woods. I shall elaborate upon this hypothesis in due course.

[2] H. Gunkel in his *Genesis, Handkommentar zum Alten Testament* (Göttingen, 1922), p. 237 quotes Holzinger, who assumed that this phrase was added at the wrong place; it should have been in v. 6, before the phrase "and Abraham took the wood." In any event, one may observe the importance given by the editor to the splitting of the wood.

[3] The translation of the NIV is not exact, since עצי עלה is a construct form; hence the literal meaning is "burnt-offering wood," namely a specific wood suitable for such an offering, and not merely wood for offering. The LXX is not explicit; we read ξύλα εἰς ὁλοκάρπωσιν, and εἰς can also mean "for" a particular end (Liddell and Scott). On the other hand, Prof. Wevers does not consider that the construct (bound) form automatically means that it is an adjectival genitive, and in his opinion the phrase should be interpreted as "wood for the holocaust offering." However, he would not object to interpreting the phrase as implying that there was a special wood used for the holocaust offering, especially as we have evidence for this from other sources. Onkelos, who would not interpret Scripture contrary to the Talmud, translates וצלח אעי לעלתא, and we observe that the interpretation "wood for a burnt offering" is written with a למ"ד, and not in a construct form as in the Hebrew. Jonathan, who often includes the talmudic midrashim and interpretations, has וקטע קיסין דקיתא ותאנתא ודיקלא דחזיין לעלתא "and he split slim splinters of fig and palm [wood], which are appropriate for the burnt offering." Jonathan understood Scripture to be referring to special woods

form. The significance of the wood is evident in the entire pericope; in v. 9, we find again וַיַּעֲרֹךְ אֶת הָעֵצִים "and arranged the wood on it," and וַיָּשֶׂם אֹתוֹ עַל הַמִּזְבֵּחַ מִמַּעַל לָעֵצִים "and laid him on the altar, on top of the wood." Gary Anderson suggests[4] that a mythical text preserves a more archaic meaning in its language, even when the older purpose has already been suppressed. We ought therefore to concede serious significance to these apparently superfluous details.[5] The Rabbis sought meaning and purpose in every apparently unnecessary word in the Bible; so too Gunkel, in his *Introduction to Genesis* (p. XXXIV), states that no biblical stories contain any words or details which are not necessary for the idea or the spirit of the story.

In Leviticus, we also observe the significance assigned to the wood and its arrangement upon the altar. We read in Lev. 1: 7 וְנָתְנוּ בְּנֵי אַהֲרֹן הַכֹּהֵן אֵשׁ עַל הַמִּזְבֵּחַ וְעָרְכוּ עֵצִים עַל הָאֵשׁ "The sons of Aaron the priest are to put fire on the altar, and arrange wood ["arrange" implies an ordering] on the fire." The command to lay the wood, and the additional mandate to lay the wood in order, both seem to be superfluous.[6] For the burning of the *'Ola*

---

required for the offering, and quoted the talmudic regulation. It is beyond the scope of this essay to reconcile this dictum with that in Mishnah *Tamid* which states that all woods are suitable.

[4]   Gary A. Anderson, *Sacrifices and Offerings in Ancient Israel* (Atlanta: Scholars Press, 1987), p. 35.

[5]   Among the main traditional commentators, only Ramban, as far as I am aware, wondered why Abraham hauled wood with him. He suggested that Abraham was not sure whether he would find wood on the mountain, and, eager to fulfil God's command, he ensured a supply of wood; or, since wood with worms would not be suitable for an offering, he made sure to carry appropriate wood. The Torah describes this, to demonstrate Abraham's love for God and his zeal to comply with His command. Abarbanel disputes this assumption, and offers another explanation; it suffices for our purpose to demonstrate that these details about the splitting and carrying of the wood appeared superfluous to these keen commentators.

[6]   The Rabbis in Y. T. Yoma chap. 2, hal. 1, 39c deduce from this phrase מִצְוָה לְהַקְדִּים אֵשׁ לְעֵצִים, שנא' וְעָרְכוּ עֵצִים עַל הָאֵשׁ. קִדֵּם עֵצִים לָאֵשׁ "The command is to have the fire precede the wood, as it is said: 'and arrange wood on the fire'; [in the command] wood precedes the fire." In effect, the fire must be put on first and only then the wood. This order is inflexible, according to the Talmud, and if done the other way round, the arrangement of the wood is to be removed and redone in the right sequence. At any rate, we observe the significance of the wood, an integral element of the sacrificial cult, in the talmudic literature. A further corroboration of the fact that in the opinion of the Rabbis the placing of the wood had a ceremonial importance is found in B. T. Yoma 26b: תַּנְיָא רשב"י אוֹמֵר מִנַּיִן לַתָּמִיד שֶׁל בֵּין הָעַרְבַּיִם שֶׁטָּעוּן שְׁנֵי גִזְרֵי עֵצִים בִּשְׁנֵי כֹהֲנִים שֶׁנֶּאֱמַר וְעָרְכוּ עֵצִים "It is taught in a *Beraita*: Rabbi Simeon bar Johai says: Whence do we know that for the evening *Tamid* [there is an obligation] for two logs of wood [to

a fire is of course necessary, and as suggested in the first part of the verse, the wood is only a means to keep the fire burning. However, the subsequent mandate to arrange the wood evidently demonstrates an additional purpose. In v. 8, the priests are further commanded to arrange the dissected animal parts על העצים אשר על האש "upon the wood that is on the fire,"[7] again a seemingly superfluous rule.[8] During the Second Temple period, it

---

be set] by two priests? Since it is written 'lay the wood in order' [both the verb 'lay' and the object 'wood' are in the plural, therefore two priests and two logs of wood are required according to the text]." We have no concrete evidence that this rule was actually performed in the Temple, but it is possible that this *Tanna*, who lived about 60 years after the destruction of the Temple, might have known the practice there. This would accord with the literary style of his question: "Where is it written in Scripture that we need two logs and two priests, as was the *practice* in the temple [emphasis added]."

[7]   This is the literal translation of the MT, which also corresponds to the RSV and to the LXX ἐπὶ τοῦ πυρός. I do not have any explanation for the NIV translation "on the altar," instead of "on the fire."

[8]   Rendtorff, *Studien zur Geschichte des Opfers im Alten Israel*, p. 106, writes: "Aus diesen Stellen geht hervor, dass das Holz für das Feuer, in dem die 'Ola verbrannt wird, Gegenstand besonderer Beachtung war und dass man dafür u. U. Dinge von besonderer Bedeutung verwendete." (In free translation: "From these citations it follows that the wood on which the 'Ola was burnt was a subject of extraordinary significance, and in some circumstances, one used for it things of particular importance.") Rendtorff quotes additional evidence from Scripture to substantiate his thesis: the *Ashera*, the holy tree which Gideon was commanded to cut down and use for the burning of the sacrifice (Jud. 6: 26), the cart in which the ark was returned by the Philistines, whose split segments were used for the 'Ola (I Sam. 6: 14), the threshing instruments donated by Araunah for the holocaust sacrifice (II Sam. 24: 22), and the wood used by Elijah (I Kings 18). These citations do not contradict my thesis, but also do not confirm it unequivocally, and therefore I did not quote them. The term ערך "to arrange in order" appears only in the citations which I have quoted, whereas in the Elijah story the term שים "to place" is utilized. Rendtorff is aware of this distinction, but does not grant significance to it. The term ערך in the Pentateuch has a limited and well-defined meaning, namely to "arrange in a prescribed manner." It is used once with respect to arranging an army for battle (Gen. 14: 8), and all the remaining occurrences are associated with ritual procedures: the method of kindling the lampstand (Exod. 27: 22, 39: 37; Lev. 24: 3, 4), and the order of placing the showbread (Exod. 40: 4, 23; Lev. 24: 6, 7, 8). Further, the reference to the wood in Elijah's narration has a clear purpose: to demonstrate that everything was burnt by the miraculous flame from heaven. The cutting and burning of the *Ashera*, in Gideon's story, also has a purpose: to demonstrate the ineffectiveness and powerlessness of Baal and his ancillary altar and *Ashera*, which are both destroyed to provide for the worship of the real God. The Philistines' cart could not have been used whole and had to be split; this procedure thus is a natural element of the story. The details of Araunah's donation show that he offered everything necessary for the sacrifice, without asking for remuneration.

seems that the offering of wood was officially "established," as we read in
Nehemiah 10: 35 'והגורלות הפלנו על קרבן העצים ... לבער על מזבח ה "We
... have cast lots ... a contribution of wood to burn on the altar of the Lord
(v. 34 in NIV)"; and in 13: 31, when Nehemiah asks God to remember his
virtuous deeds, he includes the performance of the wood offering בעתים
מזמנות "at designated times."

We also have corroboration of wood's significance in the cult from the
Damascus Scroll. We read there: אל ישלח איש למזבח עולה ומנחה ולבונה
ועץ ביד איש טמא "Let no man send to the altar a burnt-offering or a grain-
offering or frankincense or wood by the hand of any man affected with any
of the types of uncleanliness."[9] It is interesting to note the remarkable and
somewhat suspicious absence of incense in this list; frankincense is mentioned, but not קטורת, the "incense" compound, a cult element of cardinal
importance in the Second Temple period, as is well documented. The absence of incense in the Damascus Scroll may assist us in our speculation as
to whether the absence of the incense celebration in the Temple Scroll is due
simply to missing text, or to the possibility that the sect did not acknowledge this ritual.[10] The importance of the wood offering is even more emphasized in the Temple Scroll, in which we read that special sacrifices had
to be offered on the festival of the Wood Offering, which lasted for six
days.[11] J. Milgrom asserts that the Temple Scroll group attributed the institution of the Wood Offering festival, among others, to the "Sinaitic

---

[9]   Critical text and translation by Ch. Rabin, *Zadokite Documents*, (Oxford, 1954), pp.
      58-59.
[10] Y. Yadin, *The Temple Scroll*, with reconstructed texts, does not mention the daily
      incense celebration. The incense altar is recorded in the scroll: its construction is com-
      manded (page 3), as is the burning of the frankincense of the showbread on the incense
      altar (p. 8). I wish to note here that this decree is contrary to the talmudic ruling that
      the frankincense of the showbread is to be burnt on the holocaust altar, and to Josephus'
      corroborating narrative, as I have shown elsewhere. There is no reference to the in-
      cense, either in the original text, or in the reconstruction of the incense celebration in
      the ritual described for the Day of Atonement (pp. 25-27). There is also no reference
      in connection with the kindling of the lampstand (at the end of p. 9, or at the top of
      p. 10), where one would expect it, analogous to Exod. 30: 8 ובהעלת אהרן את הנרת
      בין הערבים יקטירנה "He must burn incense again when he lights the lamps at twilight."
      I suggest that such absence of details on the incense celebrations, in places where one
      would expect them, cannot be attributed merely to chance. I wonder that Yadin, who
      diligently compared the details of the sacrifices of the Day of Atonement with those in
      Scripture in his מבוא Commentary, pp. 106 ff., did not draw our attention to the
      missing incense celebration.
[11] See Yadin, *The Temple Scroll*, (Hebrew), pp. 34-35 and 74-75.

revelation of God to Moses," that is, they appended "Qumran's Wood Offering festival to Leviticus chap. 23."[12]

We thus see the importance of wood in the sacrificial cult in Israel, and we have questioned the definition of עצי עולה "*Ola*-wood," the specific wood mentioned in Gen 22. An answer to this question may be found in the Apocryphal literature. We read in the Testament of Levi (1Q21, 4Q213,214) 35: 14-21:[13]

ומהקריב אעין מהצלחין ובקר אינון לקודמין מן תולעא ובאדין הסק אינון
ארי כדנה חזיתי לאברהם אבי מיזדהר מן כל תרי עשר מיני אעין אמר לי
די חזין להסקה מנהון למדבחה די ריח תננהון השים סליק ואלין אינון
שמהתהון ארזא ודפרנא ושגדא[14] ואתלא ואשוחה וארנא וברותא ותאנתא
ואע משחא וערא והדסה ואע חנתא אלין אינון די אמר לי די חזין להסקה
מנהון לתחות עלתא על מדבחא

And offer split wood and examine it first for worms and then offer it up, for thus I saw my father Abraham acting with care. Any of all twelve kinds of wood which are fitting he told me to offer up on the altar, whose smoke rises up with pleasant odour. And these are their names – cedar, juniper, almond, fir, pine, ash, cypress, fig, oleaster, laurel, myrtle and asphaltos. These are those that he told me are fitting to offer up beneath the holocaust upon the altar.

Further, the quantity of wood for each sacrifice is also established. This clearly demonstrates the significance of wood in the cult;[15] the high cost of supplying expensive fragrant woods is the likely motive behind defining the minimum required quantity. We read: לתורא רבא ככר אעין <חזה> ליה במתקל ואם תרבא בתחודוהי סליק שיתה מנין ואם פר תורין הוא די סליק [חמשין מנין] "For a large bull: a talent's weight of wood (is fitting) for it;

[12] J. Milgrom, "Qumran's Biblical Hermeneutics: The Case of the Wood Offering," in *Révue de Qumran* 16, (1994), pp. 449-456.

[13] Aramaic text from Klaus Beyer, *Die Aramäischen Texte vom Toten Meer* (Göttingen, 1984), p. 199, and *JQR* 19 (1906-7), pp. 566-583. English translation from *The Testaments of the Twelve Patriarchs*, p. 463.

[14] Beyer has made some emendations to the names of the trees, but Charles and Cowley, the editors of the text in *JQR*, left the text unchanged. Since such differences do not matter to our study, I shall not elaborate further on this issue.

[15] Josephus calls it "the sacred timber"; we read in *The Jewish War* V :36 τὴν ἱερὰν ὕλην εἰς πολεμιστηρίων κατασκευὴν "[John] actually misappropriated the sacred timber for the construction of engines of war."

and if the fat alone is offered up,[16] six minas, and if a bull is offered up [50 minas].[17] A similar list of fragrant woods, with a strong admonition to use them exclusively for their fragrance, is found in the Book of Jubilees, 21: 12- 14.[18]

In this pericope from the Testament of Levi we observe that it is the fragrant odour emitted by the burning of the specific wood species which is of primary importance in their selection for the sacrifices. The burning of the wood provides the ריח ניחוח לה׳, "the sweet savour unto the Lord" required at the sacrifices; and as we have seen, this element is remarkably absent in the "incense" pericopes. We must also take note of the fact that in the Testament of Levi the requirement to offer split wood is independent of the examination for worms; that is, it is a separate requirement. We observe a similar requirement in the Samaritan Targum; the term עצים, wood for the construction of the tabernacle and its various implements, is translated by the common אעי, but the wood for the altar is called קצמי, "chipped" or "cut" wood. Targum Jonathan interprets ויבקע עצי עולה in Gen. 22: 3 as וקטע קיסין דקיתא דתאנתא ודקלא דחזיין לעלתא "and he split thin splinters of fig and palm[19] [wood] which are suitable for the 'Ola." In

---

[16] Until now, we saw a requirement for specific wood types only for the burning of the 'Ola; now, we observe that the same rule also applied to other sacrifices, שלמים or חטאת, where only the fat was burnt.

[17] Beyer reconstructed these two last words. Though the Aramaic text ends there, the Greek text follows, according to Hollander and De Jonge, with "and for the second bull fifty minas, and for its fat alone, five minas. And for a full grown bullock, forty minas," and then proceeds with the exact quantities of wood for the sacrifice of a ram, a he-goat, a lamb, a goat kid, and their fat alone. Thus the wood is an intrinsic element of the sacrifice.

[18] "And as regards the wood of the sacrifices, beware lest you bring [other] wood for the altar in addition to these: cypress, bay, almond, fir, pine, cedar, savin, fig, olive, myrrh, laurel, asphaltus. And of these kinds of wood lay upon the altar under the sacrifice, such as have been tested as to their appearance, and do not lay [thereon] any split or dark wood, [but] hard and clean, without fault, a sound and new growth; and do not lay [thereon] old wood [for its fragrance is gone] for there is no longer fragrance in it as before. Besides these kinds of wood there is none other that thou shalt place [on the altar], for the fragrance is dispersed, and the smell of its fragrance goes not up to heaven." R. H. Charles, ed., The Apocrypha and Pseudepigrapha of the Old Testament, Vol. II (Oxford, 1913), p. 44.

[19] The use of palm tree wood is contrary to the quoted mishnah in Tamid, which does not allow this species of wood for the burning of the 'Ola. At the burning of the Red Heifer, we read in Mishnah Parah 3: 9 a dispute concerning the type of wood with which one must kindle the fire, and Rabbi Akiba declares that branches of palm tree are correct. It is interesting to note that in Mishnah Parah 3: 8 four species of wood are prescribed

certain Mesopotamian myths,[20] we find that fragrant wood was burnt on censers, *niknakku*; from the numerous pictures[21] on seals, we note that these implements were small and could physically contain only small chips of wood. Moreover, the smaller the fragments, the more pronounced the odour, and this might be the reason for the requirement to split the wood. Also of interest is the presence of an equivalent custom in Greek mythology.[22]

It seems to me that the association between sacrifice and the burning of fragrant woods can be unquestionably established in the ceremonies of ancient Israel and the surrounding cultures. This phenomenon would answer the various questions posed above, including the meaning of the term עצי עולה, and the regular mention of ריח ניחוח in connection with the burnt sacrifices. One has the impression that this archaic custom was invalidated by the official priestly establishment, at a certain point in the Second Temple period, and replaced by the daily incense celebration. We have

---

for the burning of the Red Heifer, עצי ארזים וארנים וברושים ועצי תאנה חלקה "cedar, pine, cypress and smooth fig woods"; these four species are included in the types of wood enumerated in the apocryphal writings.

[20] I shall quote only one well-known passage from James B. Pritchard, ed., "Akkadian Myths and Legends," in *ANET* (Princeton, 1950), p. 95, lines 158-161: "Upon their pot stands I heaped cane, cedarwood, and myrtle, The gods smelled the savour, The gods smelled the sweet savour, The gods crowded like flies about the sacrificer." There is no consensus among scholars as to whether the fire to burn the sacrifice was sustained by these fragrant woods, or whether they were burnt on separate censers. I would opt for the second possibility, since we note from other Mesopotamian tablets that the sacrifices were placed on a table – altar, *passuru*, and the fragrant wood was burnt on a separate stand. I quote this procedure from H. Zimmern, *Beiträge zur Kenntnis der Babylonischen Religion* (Leipzig, 1901), a study to which I shall refer again.

[21] See K. Galling, *Der Altar in den Kulturen des Alten Orients* (Berlin, 1925), pp. 32-35 concerning various Babylonian altars, their forms and uses. There is reference to a large altar for the placing of the food before the deity ("Absatzaltar"), on top of which a censer was placed; and square altars, too small for burning food, probably for incense. On p. 37, he states that pleasant odour was created by the burning of fragrant wood kindled by the flame of a torch, and not by incense shed on a coal censer. The description of Assyrian illustrations (p.40) is similar. There is no fire on the table with the food, and only the censers show a flame going up (p. 48); this demonstrates that tiny bits of wood were burnt, not incense powder on coal, which produces only smoke, not a flame.

[22] We read in The *Iliad*, Book I: 462 that the old man burned the sacrifices καῖε δ' ἐπὶ σχίζης ὁ γέρων. σχίζα is "a piece of wood cleft off, a splinter" (Liddell and Scott). F. A. Paley, in his *English Notes to Iliad* (London, 1866), emphasizes that this expression "was also a technical term," and quotes examples.

observed that the writers of the Apocrypha still required the burning of
fragrant wood, and we must assume that they were not creating a new
custom. The odd dialogic style of Mishnah Tamid 2: 3 וכי כל העצים
כשרים למערכה? "Are all types of wood suitable for the ordering of the wood
[on the altar]?" and the answer הין "yes", suggests the existence of a previous
custom, which allowed only specific wood types on the altar.[23] We must ask
why this custom was eliminated, and whether it was partially or totally
replaced by the incense celebration.

Although the Israelite cult developed its particular ritual elements, in
my opinion, in response to the continuous change in its theology, and
probably also to differentiate itself, at a certain stage, from the surrounding
cultures (a recurrent theme in the Bible), most of the basic ceremonies
retained their ancient forms. We know that many old pagan feasts subsist
in the monotheistic religions, retaining their external archetypes, but with
a totally different inner meaning. We observe even today that people without religious creed cling eagerly to many religiously ingrained ceremonies,
and that modern-thinking people, far from superstitious thought, still ad-
here to archaic, superstitious habits. I suggest, therefore, that we may learn
basic principles from a comparison with the customs of neighbouring people.

It seems that the practice of sacrifice was once a universal idea, and we
may assume that Israel was influenced by Mesopotamian habit,[24] particularly with respect to the incense issue, which was introduced into Scripture
at a late stage.[25] As I noted above, there are few occurrences of the term קטר

---

[23] L. Ginzberg, in his conclusive essay "Tamid, the Oldest Treatise of the Mishna,"
Journal of Jewish Lore and Philosophy, I (1919), p. 267, considers this passage a later
gloss. A. Brody, in his *Der Mishna Traktat Tamid* (Uppsala, 1935), p. 113, does not
think that the literary style alone justifies considering it a gloss, but he too notes that
contrasting rules are evident in other writings. The Mishnah forbids merely the use of
olive and vine wood, and the Talmud argues about the motive behind this interdiction.
There is a charming midrash in Leviticus Rabba 7: 1 to the effect that the burning of
these two species is forbidden since they are honoured: their products, oil and wine, are
utilized in offerings to God.

[24] See B.A. Levine and W. Hallo, "Offerings to the Temple Gates at Ur," *HUCA* 38
(1967), pp. 17-58, regarding the comparison between the permanent closing of the
outer, eastern gate in the Jerusalem Temple with the custom at the Ur temple. On the
other hand, it is interesting to note that there is no mention of an incense ceremony
in the early texts examined in that study, dating from the Hammurapi period.

[25] In defence of my hypothesis, I shall refer to the biblical occurrences of the term קטר
which apparently originate from earlier periods.

in writings of the 8th century B.C.E.; use of the term becomes prolific by
the time of Jeremiah, in the 6th century. In that period, as is well known,
Israel and Judah were under the influence of Assyria and Babylonia. We
have concluded, based on scholarly viewpoints and further arguments, that
the prophets did not object to the incense ceremony *per se,* but disapproved
rather of the worship of foreign gods. We find no protest in any of the prior
prophets against such cult practice. We may therefore assume that the
burning of incense was a kind of worship "imported" together with the
deities, in one "parcel"; some people used it in the worship of the God of
Israel, while others also embraced the foreign deities. We have noted above
the worship on roofs, the celebration by women, the baking of cakes; all are
alien to forms of worship in Israel and Judah, as described in earlier writings, or as reprimanded by the earlier prophets.

Much has been debated and written about the origin of sacrifices generally and specifically concerning the Semites. I do not think that we can
exclude from our deliberations the simple motive of feeding the gods as one
of the foundations of early human thought in this regard.[26] Even the theory
proffered by Robertson Smith[27] of sacrifice as a communion, a meal consumed by the group in communion with the deity, has an intrinsic element
of food, consumed together by god and man. Whether the זבח, in which
"god and his worshippers are commensals," or the עולה, "the holocaust,"
was the earliest sacrificial worship in Israel,[28] or whether these forms were

---

[26]   W. W. Hallo writes in his essay "the Origins of the Sacrificial Cult" in *Ancient Israelite
Religion,* ed. P.D. Miller Jr. et alii (Philadelphia,1965): "Indeed, if there is one common
thread running through both Sumerian and Akkadian myths about the relationship
between gods and men, it is that men were created to relieve the gods to provide for
their own food (p.7)." See also "Excursus 65: The Tamid," *The JPS Torah Commentary.
Numbers,* by J. Milgrom: "In its outer form, the Tamid resembles the daily offering of
Israel's neighbours, for whom, at least symbolically, it formed the daily diet of the
gods." The burning of food offered to gods implies a certain sophistication in thinking,
since obviously they did not consume it. It may have started, as certain scholars suggested,
as a sublime idea of some worshipper, who, being far away from the god's temple or
statue which he venerated, was inspired by the flame or smoke which dissolved in the
atmosphere to consider these as a symbolic medium through which his offering reached
the deity.

[27]   See W. Robertson Smith, *The Religion of the Semites* (New York: Schocken Books,
1972), p. 349: "...the flesh is given to the priests because they minister as the representatives of the sinful people... the act of eating it is an essential part of the ceremony,
exactly as in the old ritual of communion."

[28]   We find an interesting debate in B. T. Zebahim 117a: ר"א ורבי יוסי בר חנינא, חד אמר
קרבו שלמים בני נח וחד אמר לא קרבו "Rabbi Elazar and Rabbi Jose bar Hanina disa-

brought in by either of the two founding groups (the southern and the northern or the nomadic and the sedentary), or whether the Israelites absorbed Canaanite custom,[29] need not engage us in this study. Walter Burkert states in his essay *Offerings in Perspective:*[30] "Feeding the gods had become a conspicuous ceremony in the temples of Mesopotamia and Egypt." He then adds: "In Greece too tables are laid out for the gods with offerings that are finally consumed by the priests." F. Thureau-Dangin[31] has translated certain Akkadian tablets in which the particulars of a ritual meal for the gods are described. René Labat describes a similar ritual from a Babylonian creation epic.[32] In this poem translated by Labat we observe two cardinal theological doctrines: a) the concept of "taking care" of the gods implies the offering of food, and b) conditions on earth are a reflection of those in "heaven".[33] This idea is similar to the concept in Greek mythology that gods are similar to men, have the same desires and needs, but on a larger

---

greed; one said that the Noahides offered *Shelamim*, and the other one said they did not." That is, both agree that they offered עולות "whole-burnt sacrifices"; one may consider this passage as a philosophical speculation concerning the primeval idea of sacrifices.

[29]   R. de Vaux, in *Ancient Israel, Its Life and Institutions* (London, 1973), states on p. 441: "The custom of burning either the whole or part of the victim upon an altar obtained in Canaan before the Israelites came to Palestine. On the other hand, there is no certain proof that the Israelites practised the custom when they were semi-nomads, and perhaps the oldest form of sacrifice they practised is the type which survived in the offering of the Paschal lamb."

[30]   "Offerings in Perspective,"in *Gifts to the Gods*, p. 46.

[31]   F. Thureau-Dangin, in *Rituels Accadiens* (Paris, 1921), p. 99, states: "Dans la cour sur des sièges ils assiéront, puis ils attendront Lugal-marda et Nin-sun. Le grand repas du matin à Anu, Antu et à tous les Dieux sera offert." ("They [the gods] will take their places in the courtyard on the seats, and then will await [the arrival] of Lugal-marda and Nin-sun. The great morning meal will be offered to Anu, Antu and to all the gods.")

[32]   René Labat, *Le poème Babylonien de la création* (Paris, 1935), p. 153. We read in Tablet VI: "Qu'il fixe pour ses pères de grandes offrandes rituelles, Qu'on accomplisse leurs rites, qu'on observe leurs fêtes, Qu'il fasse humer l'encens et recevoir leur nourriture, Image sur terre de ce qu'il faut dans les cieux." ("Let him establish great ritual offerings for his fathers, let him perform their rites, let him observe their holidays, let him fumigate the incense and cause them to receive their food, a reflection on earth of what is necessary in heaven.") We read further on p. 155: "Qu'à sa parole ils prennent soin de leur déesse! Que des offrandes soient apportées, pour leur dieux et leurs déesses." (At her command, let them take care of their goddess! Let offerings be brought, for their gods and their goddesses.")

[33]   Compare ויאמר אלהים נעשה אדם בצלמנו כדמותנו "Then God said, 'Let us make man in our image, in our likeness (Gen. 1: 26).'"

scale. Following this principle, the gods need not only a dwelling place,[34] furniture, food and drink, but also a table arrangement with eating utensils, condiments, and foods with a pleasant, fragrant odour. We find such descriptions in Mesopotamian mythology[35] and traces of similar concepts in Scripture,[36] both in the earlier writings[37] and in the P source.[38] Further, the

---

[34] See V. Hurowitz, *I Have Built You an Exalted House* (Sheffield, 1992), p. 126, who states that the pattern of Solomon's Temple is similar to Mesopotamian descriptions of temple buildings; the Tabernacle, on the other hand, a mobile sanctuary, resembles Arab traditions. We observe here the synthesis of the two traditions, the sedentary Mesopotamian, and the nomadic Arabian.

[35] H. Zimmern, *Beiträge zur Kenntnis der Babylonischen Religion*, gives on pp. 94-95 a summary of the usual equipment necessary for a ritual offering in Babylon, which he derived from written descriptions on tablets, and pictures from seals: a table *passuru*, with a bowl; a censer *niknakku*, a narrow high utensil, kindled with a torch *diparu*; a laver *egubbu*. The offerings usually consisted of an arrangement of twelve (or three times twelve) loaves of sweet (unleavened) bread, (לחם הפנים?), wine, sesame wine, intoxicating drink, butter, oil, fine oil (*šamnu tabu*), honey, milk, dates and salt. For fumigating, cypress, cedar and flour were used. For animal offerings, which were not frequent, the right shoulder was placed on the table. One cannot escape comparison with Lev.7: 34 כי את חזה התנופה ואת שוק התרומה לקחתי מאת בני ישראל מזבחי שלמיהם ואתן אתם לאהרן הכהן ולבניו לחק עולם מאת בני ישראל "From the fellowship offerings of the Israelites, I have taken the breast that is waved and the thigh that is presented and have given them to Aaron the priest and his sons as their regular share from the Israelites." We have here a sophisticated expression of the reality that food offered to the Deity is consumed by the priests, God's chosen servants. Similar sublimations abound in the sacrificial cult, and I shall refer to such occurrences in due course. H. Schmökel states in *Ur, Assur und Babylon* (Stuttgart, 1955), p. 39: "Aber die Götter benötigen auch Tisch, Bett, Sessel und Lade." ("But the gods also require table, bed, stool and ark.")

[36] I have already made reference to several such concepts: for example, the table, שלחן (פתורא in Aramaic, similar to the Akkadian *passuru*), and its implements and utensils, which I discussed concerning the actual interpretation of קערתיו ואת כפתיו ואת מנקיתיו ואת הקשות אשר יסך בהן in Exod. 37: 16, Num. 4: 7, and other occurrences.

[37] For instance, the narration of Gideon's offering in Jud. 6: 18-24. At the end of the story, it is God's angel who is the protagonist who receives and burns the meat and the cakes with his touch; however, there is no rigid demarcation in the pericope between the two concepts, מלאך ה' and ה', which are intermingled throughout. We find a similar event in Jud. 13: 15-23 concerning the offering of Manoah and his wife, Samson's parents.

[38] For instance, the expressions: את לחם אלהיך הוא מקריב "because they offer up the food of their God (Lev. 21: 8)"; את קרבני לחמי לאשי "the food for my offerings made by fire (Num. 28: 2)"; and the numerous occurrences of ריח ניחוח לה' "an aroma pleasing to the Lord," or "a sweet savour to the Lord."

admonitions against such ideas by some of the prophets[39] attest to their existence in the people's imagination.

4.1.1 Conclusion

It is therefore conceivable that in ancient Israel the table standing before God was to have all necessary eating utensils, and customary condiments such as oil and spices. A further innovation – as a result of refinement or foreign influence – might have been a fumigating bowl with fragrant wood, on the table, or on a special stand close by. Man's craving for fragrant odour in his dwelling, and specifically at his table to improve the smell of the food, led him to impute to the Deity similar desires, and to arrange His table accordingly. But we must bear in mind, based on the various cited texts and additional texts which I shall discuss shortly, that the arrangement of powdered spices and fragrant wood species was merely an auxiliary practice designed to enhance and perfect the deity's meal, similar to the supply of oil and salt; these substances were not independent offerings in themselves. H. Zimmern[40] offers us a description of a great oracle ritual, transcribed from Babylonian tablets, in which the fragrant wood chips were kindled with the fire of a torch; there is no mention of powdered incense ingredients burned

---

[39]   Isaiah 1: 11 שבעתי עלות אילים וחלב מריאים "I have more than enough [the exact translation of the Hebrew term is "I am satiated"] of burnt offerings, of rams and the fat of fattened animals"; Hosea 6: 6 כי חסד חפצתי ולא זבח ודעת אלהים מעלות "For I desire mercy, not sacrifice; and acknowledgment of God rather than burnt offerings." We read also in Psalms 50:12-14 אם ארעב לא אמר לך כי לי תבל ומלאה. האוכל בשר אבירים ודם עתודים אשתה "If I were hungry, I would not tell you; for the world is mine, and all that is in it. Do I eat the flesh of bulls, or drink the blood of goats"?

[40]   p. 101 (free translation from German): "At the onset, you should arrange the offering outfit, sprinkle holy water, place one fumigating bowl east before Marduk, one fumigating bowl east before the Patron god, one fumigating bowl east before the Patron goddess, place one table behind the fumigating bowl which stands before Marduk, put forth four pitchers of wine, set up three times twelve wheat loaves, spread on a puree of honey and butter, sprinkle salt." The same procedure is repeated for the other gods, and then: "Scatter [with cypress and cedar spices] the fumigating bowl standing before Marduk, grasp the hand of the offerer and speak so: 'Your servant and that one (the offerer) wish to bring you an offering in the morning hour,' raise the cedar rod, step before Shamash; may it be benevolently received by the great deity, in sight of this lamb, which is entirely of unblemished meat, and impeccable form. Then you should bring the offering, he (the offerer) should keep the lamb, you should do the sprinkling, advance one step towards the slaughtered lamb, scatter the fumigating bowl on the rear, which stays before the Patron god [and the other gods]…then wash the right shoulder

on coal, nor of spices as food condiments. Thureau – Dangin[41] offers us a
description of fragrant powder strewn on the meat offering; these spices
were not burned or fumigated, they merely served as food condiments.
Other accounts of ritual celebrations noted by Thureau – Dangin describe
a diffusion of aromas, produced by burning resins which emit vapours.[42]
We may note that in these accounts the offering ("un sacrifice") consisted
of the animal parts, and the diffusion of odours took place at the site of the
offering ("sur le lieu des offrandes") to create a pleasant ambience at the
deities' table. G. Furlani[43] suggests that every religious ceremony, burning
of food, or libation in Assyria and Babylonia had to be accompanied with
incense fumigation; here too it is evident that the burning of incense was
merely an accessory to the offering, and not an independent celebration.
We may therefore presume that at a time when offerings to God were
considered in ancient Israel as food donations, the provision of condiments
and fragrant odours for a pleasant environment would have been common
practice. The various scriptural texts previously cited certainly do not contradict such a postulate; some, on the contrary, support it.

Based on the critical examination of the various texts concluded in the
previous segment of the study, I shall now summarize my hypothesis concerning the development of the incense celebration in Israel. The form of
the two main pericopes of our investigation (Exod. 30: 1-9 and Exod. 30:
34-38) is unquestionably the result of a variety of accretions and eradications
which occurred over an extended period, following developments in meta-
physical thought concerning sacrificial rites, and changes consequent upon

---

in the consecration bowl, scatter salt on it, place it on Marduk's table, set alight the
fumigation bowl [and the same procedure for the other gods]…let the offerer raise his
hand, pray, prostrate himself; [you should] clean up Marduk's table." We observe that
the lamb and the other food substances constitute the actual offering, and the fumigation is auxiliary.

[41] p. 96. We read: "Il renversera sur le coeur une écuelle d'or (pleine) de poudre
(aromatique) *mashatu*. Avec une vase de vin il fera une libation sur la tête du mouton."
("He will empty on the heart a golden bowl with (aromatic) powder *mashatu*. He will
perform a libation with a vase of wine on the sheep's head.")

[42] p. 95. We read: "Sur le lieu des offrandes il fera une effusion (d'aromes), puis un
sacrifice de boeuf et de mouton devant Anu il offrira: le coeur du boeuf et la tête du
mouton il placera devant (Anu)." ("On the site of the offerings he will make a diffusion
(of aromas), then a sacrifice of an ox and a sheep before Anu he will offer: the heart of
the ox and the head of the sheep he will place before (Anu).")

[43] Giuseppe Furlani, *Il Sacrificio nelle Religione dei Semiti di Babylonia e Assiria* (Roma,
1932), Serie VI, Vol. IV, Fascicolo III, p. 353.

such developments and upon influences from surrounding cultures and internal political circumstances. We can identify in these pericopes phrases which can be attributed to early antiquity, such as the tent as the site of the oracle,[44] and the notion of food presented to the Deity.[45] On the other

---

[44] We read in Exod. 33: 7: ומשה יקח את האהל ונטה לו מחוץ למחנה הרחק מן המחנה וקרא לו אהל מועד והיה כל מבקש ה׳ יצא אל אהל מועד אשר מחוץ למחנה "Now Moses used to take a tent and pitch it outside the camp some distance away, calling it the 'tent of meeting'. Anyone inquiring of the Lord would go to the tent of meeting outside the camp." It is obvious that this tent is not identical with the construction of the אהל מועד described in Exod. 40, where the term משכן is sometimes added to אהל מועד. The LXX had difficulties with the correct interpretation of these two terms. In MT Exod. 39: 33, we read: ויביאו את המשכן אל משה את האהל ואת כל כליו "Then they brought the tabernacle to Moses: the tent and all its furnishings"; in the LXX, the corresponding verse is Exod. 39: 14, and we read there καὶ ἤνεγκαν τὰς στολὰς πρὸς Μωυσῆν καὶ τὴν σκηνὴν καὶ τὰ σκεύη αὐτῆς "And they brought the garments to Moses and the tent and its furniture." (See J. W. Wevers, *Notes on the Greek Text of Exodus*, p. 639.) Onkelos translates both משכן and אהל מועד with the term משכנא: ואיתיו ית משכנא למשה ית משכנא.

The traditional commentators were also aware of the odd language in Exod. 39: 33, and in the related narration in I Kings 8: 4, cited below. Rashi quotes a midrash, which appears in Exodus Rabba 52: 4 and Midrash Tanhuma *Pequdei* 11, explaining the strange idea that the Tabernacle was brought to Moses, and the apparent duplication of the terms משכן and אהל, which were considered identical objects. The midrash recounts that Moses was grieved by the fact that he did not take part in the building of the Tabernacle, and therefore God decided to let him raise it up; the builders could not do it, and had to bring the Tabernacle to Moses. Miraculously, Moses single-handedly erected the Tabernacle. Thus, the text is understood as: "They [the builders] brought the elements of the Tabernacle to Moses [and then they are cited]: the tent and all its furnishings, its clasps, frames, crossbars, posts and bases, etc." Ramban, Seforno, and Abarbanel offer another solution. They interpret המשכן as "the curtains of fine twined linen," and the term אהל as "curtains of goats' hair." According to this interpretation the text should be understood as: "They brought the linen curtains and the goats' hair curtains [two distinct objects]." Ramban suggests one read the verse as if there were a conjunctive ו"יו attached to the term אהל. We again observe that the traditional commentators asked the same questions as modern analysts; they merely offered different answers, to reconcile the obscure texts with their fundamental beliefs. These commentators encounter the same dilemma in I Kings 8: 4 ויעלו את ארון ה׳ ואת אהל מועד ואת כל כלי הקדש אשר באהל "And they brought up the ark of the Lord, and the Tent of Meeting and all the sacred furnishings in it." A simple reading of the text would imply that the אהל מועד the Tabernacle, was also placed in Solomon's Temple, an unsustainable position according to the traditional view that the אהל מועד always refers to the constructed Tabernacle. Therefore, Rashi and other commentators explain that the Tabernacle was not brought into the Temple but was hidden; only its vessels were brought in. They refer to Tosefta Sotah 13: 1: משנבנה בית הראשון נגנז אהל מועד קרשיו קרסיו ועמודיו ואדניו, אע"פ כן לא היו משתמשין אלא בשולחן ומנורה שעשה משה

hand, there is reference to a daily, independent incense celebration, a later development, and there is the absence of any anthropomorphic expression such as ריח ניחוח לה׳ "a sweet savour to the Lord"; as noted, such absence

---

"When the First Temple was built, the Tabernacle was hidden – its frames, clasps, posts and bases. Nevertheless they used only the table and the lampstand which Moses made." It seems strange that the incense altar is not mentioned; the ark is specifically cited in the verse, but the incense altar, which may be included in the term "vessels", is not expressly listed together with the lampstand and the table.

The commentators also have difficulties with the אהל מועד in v. 4 since at the beginning of the chapter, in v. 1, the Tabernacle is not mentioned at all; we read there: אז יקהל שלמה את זקני ישראל ... להעלות את ארון ברית ה׳ מעיר דוד היא ציון "Then king Solomon summoned into his presence at Jerusalem the elders of Israel... to bring up the ark of the Lord's covenant from Zion, the city of David." They therefore explain in their comments to v. 4: "They brought the ark from Zion, and the Tabernacle from Gibeon, where it was located." They refer to I Kings 3: 4, where it is said וילך המלך גבענה לזבח שם כי היא הבמה הגדולה "The king went to Gibeon to offer sacrifices, for that was the most important high place." According to their doctrine, they had to disregard the fact that the verse does not state that the Tabernacle was in Gibeon, only the great *Bamah*. They also had to ignore the fact that David placed the ark in a tent which he himself pitched especially for the purpose of housing it, as we read in II Sam. 6: 17: ויבאו את ארון ה׳ ויצגו אתו במקומו בתוך האהל אשר נטה לו דוד "They brought the ark of the Lord and set it in its place inside the tent that David had pitched for it." The expression נטה אהל is always used for the pitching of a tent, and not the construction of a tabernacle. In Gen. 33: 19 we read: אשר נטה שם את אהלו "where he pitched his tent," and in Gen. 26: 25, the phrase ויט שם אהלו "There he pitched his tent." The term נטה is never used in the narration of the Tabernacle's construction.

This issue, with emphasis on the relation between Ark and Tent, has been thoroughly deliberated by a number of scholars. Thomas Stäubli writes about the issue in *Das Image der Nomaden* (Freiburg, 1991), pp. 225 ff; he quotes several biblical verses, but his thesis relies mainly on a comparison with the artifacts of other nomadic tribes. Martin Noth, in *Könige* (Neukirchen, 1968), pp. 176 ff. thoroughly examines the above-quoted verses in I Kings chap. 8, and determines that the first eleven verses are such a fusion of pre- and post- deuteronomic strata that it is impossible to divide them (p. 174). Noth does not argue about the distinction between the Tabernacle and the Tent, but asserts that it is most unlikely that the Tent was brought into Solomon's Temple (p.177). G. von Rad writes in *Old Testament Theology* (New York, 1962), p. 235, concerning the pericope in Exod. 33: 7 –11, about the tent "which Moses pitched outside the camp, and which served as the place to seek oracles from Jahwe and had the name אהל מועד. Although it has the same name, this tent is quite different from the tabernacle of P. Here we are dealing with a much older source." I have attempted to corroborate this postulate by a critical examination of the various cited verses. J. Morgenstern, in his book *The Ark, The Ephod and Tent of Meeting* (Cincinnati, 1945), asserts that משכן is the more recent name of the Tabernacle and אהל מועד is the older name for the Tabernacle in the wilderness; they are not synonymous (p.132). He also declares that Moses was the regular priest of the אהל מועד (p. 142). Morgenstern

is remarkable here, in contrast to the habitual utilization of such a phrase in the P source of Scripture in connection with the burning of sacrifices.

According to this postulate, the difficult questions posed during the examination of these pericopes attain a logical solution. We may now understand the expressions לפני העדת, "*in front of* the Testimony (Exod. 30: 36)" and לפני הפרכת אשר על ארן העדת, "*in front of* the curtain that is **before** the ark (Exod. 30: 6)." The altar and "incense" were ultimately placed in the Temple itself, not near the ark, but on the outer side of the curtain which divided the ark (the Holy of Holies, since there was no ark in the Second Temple) from the main area of the Temple; in the archaic oracle tent, however, there was only the ark, covered by a curtain, which accounts for the statement that the curtain was *on* the ark, not *before* or by the ark, as translations may have it. Moses, the oracle keeper, was ordered to put the spices before the ark, God's throne, together with the food, and therefore nothing is said about burning them. In this tent Moses encountered the Deity, a phenomenon which is emphasized in both pericopes by the apparently redundant phrase אשר אועד לך שמה "where I will meet with you," and extensively described in Exod. 33: 7-11; this explains the total absence of Aaron in the pericope concerning the spices, verses 30: 34-36, and in verses 30: 1-6 referring to the construction of the "censer".[46] Aaron appears only at the end of the first pericope, in the later addendum, together with the more recent ritual of the Day of Atonement.

I did not find textual evidence to ascertain whether use of spices and/or fragrant wood without burning, for food condiments or pleasant scents, was prevalent prior to the practice of burning such substances to create aromatic fumes, or whether all such practices existed simultaneously in ancient Israel. That spices were used is evident from early sections of Scripture; there is mention of them in Gen. 37: 25, 43: 11[47] and in I Kings chap. 10, the story

---

integrates his hypothesis with his theory of a change in the theology of Israel. I propose that we must consider the core part of Exod. 30: 34−36 and possibly some components of the pericope in Exod. 30: 1-6 as originating from the same archaic period as the pericope in Exod. 33: 7-11.

[45] This issue was thoroughly discussed with respect to the types of spices, the absence of any reference to their burning, and the addition of salt.

[46] I assume that these verses were also thoroughly reworked at a later date, when the incense celebration was institutionalized, and the burning apparatus was given the technical term מזבח, an issue to which I will revert.

[47] I wish nevertheless to remark that scholars have divergent opinions concerning the dating of the Joseph story. See Nielsen, note 31, who lists them. There are also problems with the interpretation of the terms in these two verses. We read in Gen. 37: 25

of Solomon and the Queen of Sheba,[48] but we have no hint as to their manner of use. In Exod. 30, we encounter both uses, the burning of incense in vv. 1-6, and their use as fragrant food condiments in vv. 34-36; however, since both sections have been reworked and edited, as is apparent from their common characteristics, it is now impossible to trace their original sequence.

נכאת וצרי ולט "spices, balm and myrrh"; the LXX translates this as θυμιαμάτων καὶ ῥητίνης καὶ στακτῆς. We observe that the LXX translates נכאת as "incense", and לט as στακτή, whereas in Exod. 30: 34 the latter term is used for the Hebrew נטף. We find the same terms in a different order in Gen. 43: 11, and the equivalent Greek terms. Onkelos in both verses translates נכאת as שעף, צרי as קטף, and לט as למוס. Jonathan translates the terms similarly to Onkelos with a slightly different orthography (שעוה instead of שעף, which may be identical; however; Jastrow translates שעף as gum traga-canth and שעוה as wax). There is also an addition to the term צרי; Jonathan does not merely translate this as קטף but adds שרף קטף the resin of the *kataf.* This interpretation corroborates my understanding above of the dictum of Rabbi Simeon ben Gamaliel in Keritoth, that צרי is the generic term for resin. I think that the LXX translated the term נכאת as incense, merely because of its appearance together with other spices which are used both as incense and for perfume and medicinal purposes. The LXX translator of II Kings 20: 13 and Isa. 39: 2 translated בית נכחה as οἶκον τοῦ νεχωθα, which demon-strates that he was unaware of its real meaning. נכאת "tragacanth" is not used as incense, according to M. Zohary in *Plants of the Bible,* p. 195, and H. Gunkel in *Genesis,* p. 408. The latter adds that it was used in Egypt as glue for the preparation of the mummies, an explanation in harmony with the biblical narrative that the Ishmaelite caravan was carrying it to Egypt. Mandelkern, in his *Concordance,* offers a number of explanations for נכאת: an "aromatic powder," etymologically similar to נכה in other Semitic lan-guages, or from the root נכא, meaning "finely crushed", which would here imply a generic term for powdered spices. The term נכאתה in Kings and Isaiah he considers as originating from the root נכה, "treasure house," from Assyrian. Rashi translates נכאת in Gen. 37: 25 as an "accumulation of spices," כל כנוסי בשמים הרבה קרוי נכאת. I suggest interpreting the statement in this way, rather than as a "compound", because in II Kings and in Isaiah Rashi states בית נכחה – בית גנזי בשמיו "storage chamber of spices." Oddly, in Gen. 43: 11, Rashi translates נכאת as שעוה, "gum", similar to Onkelos and Jonathan. The latter probably derived their translation from a midrash in Genesis Rabba 9:11, where Judah bar Rabbi says נכאת – שעוה. Ibn Ezra quotes another inter-pretation in the name of Rabbi Moses the Spaniard: נכאת – דבר נחמד "a decorous thing," referring to בית נכחה in II Kings, which he understands as a facility to house decorous items. It is interesting to note that in modern Hebrew, a museum is also called בית נכאות. In New Zealand, the newly coined Maori term for museum is also a philo-logical expansion of the Maori word for a household box containing precious things.

48 We read in v. 2 : ותבא ירושלמה בחיל כבד מאד גמלים נשאים בשמים וזהב "Arriving at Jerusalem with a very great caravan – with camels carrying spices, large quantities of gold." Although there might be doubts about the dating of this pericope, it refers to an early period. On the other hand, it concerns בשמים "spices", and we have no reason to assume that this was incense.

As we have seen, the term בשם appears in Scripture as a fragrant ointment for cosmetic and healing purposes, and these utilizations are either definitely without burning, or with no indication of their method of use; these citations do not offer us a clear answer to our question.

On the other hand, we do find an association between food and incense in Scripture. In Ezek. 16: 18, we read: ושמני וקטרתי נתתי לפניהם "you offered my oil and incense before them." This verse refers unmistakably to food, as we ascertain from the following v. 19: ולחמי אשר נתתי לך סלת ושמן ודבש האכלתיך ונתתיהו לפניהם לריח ניחח "Also the food I provided for you – the fine flour, olive oil and honey I gave you to eat – you offered as fragrant incense before them." Some traditional translations have interpreted לחמי as "meat" based on hermeneutical principles,[49] since the term לחם is used in Scripture with reference to animal sacrifices, but the simple meaning here is actually "bread", or the generic "food", as is clear from the specified types of food which follow.[50] A more pronounced connection between the arrangement of a table and incense is found in Ezek. 23: 4: ושלחן ערוך לפניה וקטרתי ושמני שמת עליה "with a table spread before it on which you had placed the incense and oil that belonged to me." The oil and the incense were components of the preparation of a table for a meal, to perfect its presentation, as we see also in Prv. 27: 9: שמן וקטרת ישמח לב "Perfume and incense bring joy to the heart (NIV)," or "Oil and perfume[51] rejoice the heart (RSV)."

---

[49] I am indebted to Prof. Revell who informs me that "in King James' time 'meat' was often used where we would use 'food'. Cf. Hamlet's reference to 'funeral bake-meats' and the term 'sweetmeat' in common use, until more recently shortened to 'sweet' (candy or dessert)."

[50] The LXX has translated καὶ τοὺς ἄρτους μου "my bread," and the Targum has וטובי דיהבית ליך "and the good things which I gave you."

[51] The NIV has interpreted שמן as "perfume," while the RSV translated this as "oil", the simple meaning of the word. It is possible that the NIV followed the LXX, which has μύροις καὶ οἴνοις "myrrh and wine," probably on the basis of a different original Hebrew text than the MT, which has no wine in this verse. On the other hand, the association with wine in the LXX should also lead us to consider the oil in Prv. 27: 9 as a food condiment, parallel to wine. Rashi has for Prv. 27: 9 "fragrant balsam oil," without specifying its use, but Ibn Ezra interprets it as שמן למשחה "oil for anointing." Midrash Tanhuma *Tezaveh* 15 associates the pericope in Exod. 30: 1-10 concerning the incense altar with the verse in Prv., and relates it to the High Priest. We read there: כהן גדול וכל ישראל מרתיתים בשעה שכ"ג נכנס לפני ולפנים עד שהיה יוצא משם בשלום. כיון שהיה יוצא היתה שמחה גדולה בישראל שנתקבל ברצון שנאמר שמן וקטרת ישמח לב. שמן זה כ"ג שנמשח בשמן המשחה, וקטרת אלו ישראל "The High Priest and all of Israel were trembling when the High Priest went into the Holy of Holies, until he emerged safely. When he came out, there was a great joy in Israel, [since it was a sign] that he

While we do not have concrete textual or other evidence to ascertain which practice preceded the other (that is, the use of fragrant substances in their natural state, or for burning), it seems to me that we may deduce from Scripture that the burning of spices was a later development. We must assume that the desire for pleasant odour is an ancient human craving, which was satisfied by the use of various plant substances in their natural state. As we have established, we do not encounter the use of the verb קטר associated with burning in the oldest segments of Scripture. The initial, and rare, occurrences of the verb קטר[52] are found in the later prophets Hosea, Amos[53] and Habakkuk, mainly in connection with celebrations to idols. More frequent occurrences are encountered in Jeremiah and in Third Isaiah;[54] this illustrates the broad penetration of this new and alien ritual about two centuries later. Though, as we have determined, the prophets did not consider the act of burning incense, or cakes, as an illegitimate ceremony, these texts demonstrate that the custom reached Israel in the form of a foreign influence; we do not encounter such a celebration in the Israelite cult before the middle of the eighth century, and Mesopotamian dominance in Israel's affairs. We may therefore deduce that the burning of fragrant substances of any kind in ancient Israel was a later fashion. Gradually, aromatic materials came to be utilized in both methods: in their natural state, and for burning.

At a certain stage, as is evident from biblical and various post-biblical texts, incense burning became a legitimate, institutionalized ritual ceremony

---

was well accepted [by God], as it is written 'oil and incense rejoice the heart'; 'oil' is the High Priest, anointed with the anointing oil, and 'incense' is Israel." It is possible that this midrash influenced traditional commentators into interpreting this verse as referring specifically to ointment, rather than to oil as a condiment. In Gen. 49: 20, the Hebrew מאשר שמנה לחמו is interpreted in the LXX as Ἀσηρ πίων αὐτοῦ ὁ ἄρτος "Asher's bread is fat"; we observe the association of oil with food, as improving its taste and delight. The Targum translates משחא ובוסמא "oil and perfume," without any further specification. It is also possible that the parallelism of the pericopes in Exod. chap. 30 concerning the anointing oil and incense, which I have demonstrated above, influenced the commentators into connecting them in this verse as well. They might have overlooked the fact that the "editor" combined the two concepts, and used the verb ישמח, in singular, to indicate that each one was to separately rejoice the heart (Rashi emphasizes this detail in his commentary to Jos. 2: 4). There is no literary exigency to join the two substances.

52 I will revert to the citations in Sam. and Kings.

53 For the quotations of these texts, see chap. 6, sec. 6.1.1.

54 I have quoted at the beginning of the chapter the citations from Jeremiah; the term קטר appears in chap. 65:3-7, both occurrences concerning idol worship.

in Judah. Our objective must now be to explore the various phases of this development in the cult, and attempt to ascertain how an "imported" foreign ritual became the most holy ceremony in the Temple cult, and its most exclusive privilege, so fiercely contested. The next section will attempt to substantiate the following postulates: a) there was no independent incense ceremony and no specific incense altar during the First Temple period; b) at the end of that period, on the other hand, לבונה, frankincense, was used as part of the legitimate Israelite cult as an auxiliary additive to the grain offering. I shall then argue that it was the introduction of this refined incense into the cult which served as the forerunner of the specific and independent incense ceremony.

4.2 Incense Celebrations in the Period Prior to the Second Temple

I do not think it necessary to repeat at length Wellhausen's theory that puts into question the existence of the golden or incense altar even during the Second Temple period,[55] or the opposing theories of various scholars. Haran is typical of such adversaries of Wellhausen; his arguments, set out in his *Temples and Temple – Service in Ancient Israel*, are based on two biblical verses,[56] which in his opinion are to be considered more trustworthy in light of archeological evidence. At this point, however, I simply wish to adduce further evidence in support of the proposition that there was no independent incense celebration prior to the Second Temple period.

In his study, Wellhausen has noted a number of instances in Scripture, other than the **P** source, in which one would expect to find reference to the

---

[55] See relevant quotations from his *Prolegomena* in the Introduction to this study, p. 1.

[56] The two verses are Deut. 33: 10: ישימו קטורה באפך וכליל על מזבחך "He offers incense before you and whole burnt offerings on your altar," and I Sam. 2: 28: ובחר אתו מכל שבטי ישראל לי לכהן לעלות על מזבחי להקטיר קטרת לשאת אפוד לפני "I chose him [your father] out of all the tribes of Israel to be my priest, to go up to my altar, to burn incense, and to wear an ephod in my presence." It is at any rate interesting that Haran does not rely for his thesis on the frequent occurrences of the term קטר in Kings, such as מזבח ומקטיר "he offered sacrifices and burned incense (I Kings 3: 3)," or מזבחים ומקטרים בבמות "The high places... the people continued to offer sacrifices and burn incense there (I Kings 22: 44 in MT and 43 in NIV)," a stereotypical phrase often repeated in Kings; he concludes: "If anyone wishes to prove the antiquity of this use, but does not consider the traditions recorded by **P** as ancient enough for his purpose, he can safely stand on such evidence as Deut. 33: 10; I Sam. 2: 28."

specific incense altar. I already examined some of the textual difficulties and inconsistencies which lead to the same assumption, and I shall reinforce his statement by noting further instances in which the absence of the altar or incense is remarkable.

It is inexplicable that even in Ezra and Nehemiah we encounter no mention of a daily celebration of incense; these books narrate circumstances in the early period of the Second Temple, when incense was already employed in ritual, as we have seen, and לבונה, "frankincense" was available in the Temple chambers (Neh. 13: 5, 9). Nor do we find the terms קטורת or סמים in these books.[57] We read in Ezra 3: 2-6 an exhaustive report concerning the ritual celebrations performed by the returnees:

ויבנו את מזבח אלהי ישראל ... ויעל עליו עלות לה׳ עלות לבקר ולערב
... ועלת יום ביום במספר כמשפט ... ואחרי כן עלת תמיד ולחדשים ולכל
מועדי ה׳ ... מיום אחד לחדש השביעי החלו להעלות עלות לה׳

... [they] began to build the altar of the God of Israel to sacrifice burnt offerings on it ... they built the altar on its foundation and sacrificed burnt offerings on it to the Lord, both the morning and evening sacrifices ... with the required number of burnt offerings prescribed for each day. After that they presented the regular burnt offerings, the New Moon sacrifices and the sacrifices for all the appointed sacred feasts of the Lord ... .On the first day of the seventh month they began to offer burnt offerings to the Lord.

We notice that the sacrificial cult was already in an advanced stage of institutionalization, with precise rules for the daily and festive occasions, but there is no hint of the building of an incense altar, nor of a daily incense celebration. Just as the returnees offered burnt sacrifices on the altar, one would expect them to offer incense on the appropriate altar, if there were already such a daily, specific and independent ritual in effect. In the narration of the Temple dedication, in Ezra 6: 17, we find a precise list of the sacrifices brought on that occasion, and in the following verses a discussion of the Passover celebration; again, there is no mention of an incense celebration. This is analogous to the record in I Kings 8, where we find a list of the numerous sacrifices at the consecration of Solomon's Temple, but no express indication of an incense celebration. The same lack of incense is noticeable in the list of sacrifices enumerated in Ezra 8: 35.

---

[57] Nor do we find these terms in the Apocryphal Ezra.

There are yet further confirmations in Ezra and Nehemiah. We read in Ezra 7: 17 that the Persian king ordered all the necessary funds to be provided for the Temple worship: תקנא בכספא דנה תורין דכרין אמרין ומנחתהון ונסכיהון "With this money be sure to buy bulls, rams and male lambs, together with their grain offerings and drink offerings." Incense is not mentioned! In v. 22, we find a detailed list of goods to be bought: חנטין כורין מאה ועד חמר בתין מאה ועד בתין משח מאה ומלח די לא כתב "a hundred cors of wheat, a hundred baths of wine, a hundred baths of olive oil, and salt without limit." This is a precise list, from the most expensive products to the least expensive salt; but again there is no provision for incense, an expensive material according to all sources, and required for use twice daily, if the rule in Exod. 30: 7-8 were in effect. We read further in Nehemiah 10: 34 the list of the public offerings financed by the third part of a shekel imposed on all the people: ללחם המערכת ומנחת התמיד ולעולת התמיד השבתות החדשים למועדים ולקדשים ולחטאות "For the bread set out on the table; for the regular grain offerings and burnt offerings; for the offerings of the Sabbaths, New Moon festivals and appointed feasts; for the holy offerings; for sin offerings (v. 33 in NIV)." This is an elaborate and sophisticated schedule of the sacrificial cult, corresponding to the detailed program in Num. chaps. 28-29; it deals only with public offerings, not individual donations, and incense is once more entirely absent. According to the explicit rules in Scripture regarding the "official" incense cult, incense is exclusively a public offering; there is no rule for an individual offering of incense.[58] Incense is described as קטרת תמיד "perpetual incense," in Exod. 30: 8, and one would certainly expect to find such a "perpetual" daily

---

[58] On the issue of individual offerings of incense, we find throughout Num. chap. 7 the phrase קטרת מלאה זהב עשרה אחת כף "one gold dish weighing ten shekels, filled with incense," donated by each of the twelve princes. The Talmud has a problem with this incense donated by the princes. We read in a *Beraita* in B.T. Menahoth 50a זהו ת"ר קטרת שעלתה ליחיד על מזבח החיצון הוראת שעה היתה "The incense which was brought up for an individual on the outer altar was a one-time, exceptional rule." Rav Papa comments on 50b לא מיבעיא ציבור על מזבח החיצון דלא אשכחן ולא מיבעיא יחיד על מזבח הפנימי דלא אשכחן אלא אפילו יחיד על מזבח החיצון דאשכחן בנשיאים, הוראת שעה היתה "[The verse from which we learned this prohibition of an individual offering of incense] is not needed concerning a public offering on the outer altar, which we do not find, nor for an individual offering on the inner altar, which we do not find, but for an individual [offering] on the outer altar, which we do find with respect to the princes; that was an extraordinary rule [and is not to be repeated]." We may also observe the special concern of the Talmud to assert that the incense brought by the princes was not burnt on the inner altar, merely on the outer one. The inner altar was reserved exclusively for the public offering of incense. Midrash Tanhuma goes even further, and

celebration together with the other "perpetual" celebrations enumerated in Neh. 10: 34: מנחת התמיד and עולת התמיד. Further, in the succeeding verses of Neh. chap. 10, we do find listed numerous individual offerings: obligatory tithes and donations to the priests and the Temple, such as the wood offering, the first-fruits, the first-born, the first of the dough, wine and oil – but even here there is no incense.[59] This absence suggests that no such incense celebration yet existed.[60]

According to talmudic opinion, there was a rule that incense must continue to be offered on the site of the golden altar, if it had been moved from its place. We read in B.T. Zebahim 59a: מזבח שנעקר מקטירין קטורת במקומו "[If the] altar is shifted, one burns incense on its site." Maimonides repeats this dictum in his הלכות תמידין ומוספין פ"ג ה"ב. We do not have a similar rule for the other altar; hence, if such incense offering had been in effect, one might assume that the returnees from exile should have attributed even more importance to this rule. We need not reject this evidence as deriving *ex silentio*, given the various items of positive confirmation that there was no independent incense offering.

As I shall argue more fully below, the incense celebration had attained profound significance by the end of the Second Temple period. Among other characteristics, it was associated with prayer,[61] and no person was

---

we read in *Parshat Naso* 8: אלו שלשה דברים שעשו הנשיאים שלא כהונן וקבל הקב"ה, "These are the ואלו הן שאין יחיד מתנדב קטרת והביאו כל אחד קטרת ... ד"ה ויהי ביום: three things which the princes did incorrectly, and to which God conceded, that an individual should not offer incense, and each of them brought incense...."

59 Prof. Fox has commented that if incense was a priestly monopoly, then it is obvious that it could not be offered by lay people. This is exactly what I have attempted to show: the fact that it was not included in the list of the tithes and donations demonstrates either that the ceremony was not yet performed, or alternatively, it already had a special status, and incense could not be donated.

60 The absence of incense in the list of the king's donations cannot be interpreted as evidence that there was a prohibition against donating it. The prohibition against donating incense, discussed in the previous note, does not forbid donation of money to acquire the incense to be offered on the altar as a public offering; it prohibits only its offering *in naturalibus* by an individual. The king donated money for the procurement of other animals and substances for the *Tamid*, a public offering, and would have included incense, another public offering, if it were already celebrated. As I have argued, the difference between the עולת תמיד and קטרת תמיד is that an *'Ola* could be offered by an individual, whereas "incense" could never be offered by an individual.

61 See Luke 1: 10: "And when the time for the burning of incense came, all the assembled worshipers were praying outside." We read in Psalms 141: 2 תכון תפלתי קטרת לפניך "May my prayer be set before you like incense," and in Numbers Rabba, *Parshah* 13: 18: תפלה משולה לקטרת "Prayer is comparable to incense."

allowed inside the Temple, or even in the court between the Temple and the outer altar, at the time of the incense celebration.[62] Thus it seems inexplicable that, in contrast to the abundance of texts and minute details which we find in Scripture concerning the various sacrifices, we have only two short, incomplete, and ambiguous pericopes concerning the incense celebration. A comparison of the data concerning the various meal offerings in Lev. chap. 2, or the rules of procedure for the celebration of a whole-burnt sacrifice in Lev. chap. 1 and in other occurrences, with the sparse regulations in our two pericopes, must attract our attention to this astonishing circumstance.

For instance, we find in Mishnah Tamid 3: 1 a list of priestly duties which were awarded by casting lots. Among them, we find מי מדשן מזבח הפנימי "who will remove the ashes of the inner [incense] altar." In Mishnah 1: 4 we learn that there was a permanent place, near the steps of the outer altar, where the ashes of the incense altar were deposited: מקום שנותנים מוראות העוף ודישון מזבח הפנימי ודישון המנורה "the site where the crops of the fowls, the ashes of the inner altar and of the lampstand are disposed." In Lev. 6: 3-6 we do find scriptural evidence of a precise procedure regarding the removal of ashes, the special garments to be worn at that occasion, and the tending of the fire, but only with respect to the holocaust altar; one would have expected to find rules for similar assignments concerning the inner "incense" altar, if there were one. The removal of the ashes from the holocaust altar cannot be considered merely a trivial act of cleaning: the precise rules decreed for its execution attest to its cultic significance. Further, there are also no precise instructions in the Bible regarding the performance of the incense celebration on the altar: did one, for instance, spread the coals on the altar and sprinkle the incense upon them, or keep

---

[62] Although the scriptural prohibition against the presence of human beings in the Tabernacle is associated implicitly with the celebration on the Day of Atonement, the sages ruled that no one, not even a priest, was allowed to remain during the daily incense celebration. We read in Mishnah Tamid 6:1: פרשו העם והקטיר "the people withdrew and he offered the incense." Maimonides explains the Mishnah as saying that all the priests had to leave the court between the Temple and the outer altar, according to the dictum in Mishnah Kelim 1: 9: ופורשין מבין האולם והמזבח בשעת ההקטרה "And one withdraws from between the Temple and the altar at the time of the incense offering." B. T. Yoma 44a explains: בהיכל פורשין בין בשעת הקטרה ובין שלא בשעת הקטרה ומבין האולם והמזבח אין פורשין אלא בשעת הקטרה "In the Temple one withdraws both at the time of the incense celebration and when it is not the time of the celebration; and between the Temple and the altar, one withdraws only at the time of the incense celebration."

the coals on the fire-pan,[63] sprinkle the incense upon them, and place the fire-pan with the incense on the golden altar? Thus the lack of precise instructions for the incense celebration on the altar, and for the cleaning of the incense altar, a most sacred implement, is quite puzzling. Such discrepancies again lead us to a fundamental conclusion concerning the period of introduction of the daily incense celebration in Israel: a late interpolation of the few phrases concerning the incense celebration can account for this and the other discrepancies noted above.

Finally, I already cited in the Introduction some of the differences between the MT and the LXX texts of Exod. chaps. 35-40, and noted that this

---

[63] As a matter of fact there is an apparent disagreement between two rabbinic sources concerning the correct method. We read in Mishnah Tamid 6: 2: מי שזכה במחתה צבר את הגחלים על גבי המזבח ורדדן בשולי המחתה והשתחוה ויצא "The [priest] who obtained [by lot] the right to [bring in] the coal-pan, heaped the coals upon the altar and spread them evenly with the edge of the coal-pan, and he prostrated himself, and left." In Mishnah 3, concerning the actions of the priest who obtained the right to burn the incense, we read התחיל מרדדן ויוצא "he started to spread them [the incense grains] evenly [on the coals upon the altar], and walks out." The Ra'avad explains with respect to Mishnah 2: פירוש צוברן יחד ע"ג המזבח ורדדן בשולי המחתה: כלומר היה משוה אותן ע"ג המזבח בשולי המחתה "...he heaps them [the coals] together upon the altar, and straightens them upon the altar with the edge of the coal-pan," and for Mishnah 3 he reiterates ונותנו על גבי הגחלים שעל המזבח "and he puts [the incense] on the coals upon the altar." It results unequivocally from these mishnaiot that the coals were spread directly upon the altar. We find further substantiation of this method in B. T. Erubin 19a and Hagiga 27a, which quote an utterance of Resh Lakish: מזבח הזהב שאין עליו אלא כעובי דינר זהב כמה שנים אין האש שולטת בו "The golden altar which had only a thin layer of gold [on top of the wood] withstood the fire for many years." On the other hand, we read in Numbers Rabba *Parshah* 4:16: מה היו כליו כף ומחתה כף לקטורת סמים ומחתה להכניס בה שבכף גחלים; היה מניח המחתה של גחלים על גבי המזבח ומערה הקטורת לתוכה על גבי הגחלים "What were its [the golden altar's] implements? a ladle and a coal-pan; the ladle for the incense, and the coal-pan to put coals into it. He [the priest] placed the coal-pan with the coals upon the altar, and emptied the incense of the ladle on it, upon the coals." According to this midrash, the coals were not placed directly upon the altar, and therefore, the midrash, in its extended homily, does not describe any removal of the ashes from the golden altar before it was covered, prior to the moving of the Tabernacle and its furnishings. It is possible that the midrash came to the conclusion that such was the method of burning the incense, since Scripture decrees the removal of the ashes from the holocaust altar in Num. 4: 13: ודשנו את המזבח ופרשו עליו בגד ארגמן "They are to remove the ashes from the bronze altar, and [then] spread a purple cloth over it," whereas concerning the golden altar covering, there is no similar provision, and we read: ועל מזבח הזהב יפרשו בגד תכלת "And upon the golden altar they shall spread a cloth of blue." Thus it was assumed that if there had been ashes on the golden altar, there would have been a command to remove them, as for the holocaust altar.

phenomenon has been amply discussed by many scholars, especially Wevers.[64] I also emphasized that the most striking absences in the LXX are of the phrases concerning the "incense" altar. It seems that these peculiar deficiencies continue in the LXX translation of I Kings 6: 20- 22, in the narration of the building of the golden altar; the LXX text is much shorter and offers a different version of events than the MT. Martin Rehm[65] elaborates upon these verses, and declares that the MT text reveals changes and additions, executed before and after the LXX translation. He suggests that the date indicated at the beginning of the chapter, 480 years after the exodus from Egypt, demonstrates that this phrase belongs to the post-exilic period, and notes that similar views are held by de Vaux, van den Born, Gray, and others (p. 66). Rehm emphasizes that similar late editorial changes in the MT, occurring after the translation of the LXX, also exist with regard to I Kings chap. 8, concerning the transfer of the ark and the other cultic furnishings into the Temple (p. 78 ff). It is beyond question that we observe in the MT a systematic attempt, with varying degrees of skill, to modify texts concerning the golden "incense" altar, in order to reconcile the ancient writings with the later P segments. Therefore, despite numerous opinions to the contrary, discussed in detail in Rehm's study, we are unable to utilize these adjusted texts to serve as evidence regarding the specific issue of the incense altar and celebrations.

Further evidence of the lack of an independent incense offering in the earlier period is derived from the fact that when we do encounter the לבונה, frankincense, a significant and indispensable element of the "incense" in Exod. 30: 34, it is in association with the מנחה, the "meal offering", and not an independent offering. We have seen that לבונה occurs for the first time in Jeremiah, and there it is combined with the מנחה. In 17: 26, we find: "מבאים עלה וזבח ומנחה ולבונה"...bringing burnt offerings and sacrifices, grain offerings,[66] incense," and in 41: 5: ומנחה ולבונה בידם"...bring-

---

[64] J. W. Wevers,"The Composition of Exodus 35 to 40," pp. 117-146; see also Introduction p. 13.

[65] Martin Rehm, *Das Erste Buch der Könige, Ein Kommentar* (Eichstätt, 1979) p. 63ff.

[66] The term מנחה is in this case specifically a grain offering. The "marks" in the MT, עלה וזבח on מרכא טפחא, and ומנחה ולבונה on מנח אתנחתא, demonstrate that the words in each group are paired, though זבח is generally considered as the independent offering שלמים. In Jer. 17: 26, the Targum translates the term as ונכסת קודשין, but the LXX, which probably had another version, translates φέροντες ὁλοκαυτώματα καὶ θυσίαν καὶ θυμιάματα καὶ μαναα καὶ λίβανον. On the other hand, the Targum translates מנחה not by the usual מנחתא but as the neutral קורבנין.

ing grain offerings and incense with them."[67] We read further in Nehemiah 13: 5: ושם היו לפנים נתנים את המנחה הלבונה "to store the grain offerings and incense," and in v. 9: ואשיבה שם כלי בית האלהים את המנחה והלבנה "and then I put back into them the equipment of the house of God, with the grain offerings and the incense."

4.2.1 Conclusion

I suggest that the frankincense which was brought together with both the regular *Minhah* and the ancillary *Minhah* attached to the holocaust or peace offering[68] was burnt on the outer altar, whereas the frankincense of the *Tamid* and of the showbread was burnt, at some period, on the inner golden incense altar. The similarity of the phrase קטרת תמיד "perpetual incense (Exod. 30: 8)" to עלת תמיד "continual burnt offering (Exod. 29: 42)" might have been the factor which suggested that the incense accompanying the daily holocaust should be burnt on the incense altar, similar to the frankincense of the showbread. Further, the pattern of the pericope in Exod. 30: 1-8 regarding the incense, and that of the pericope in Lev. 24: 5-9, dealing with the showbread, are identical. The commands to prepare the altar and the bread are directed at Moses; the act of offering, and the burning of the incense, are meant for Aaron. In Exod. 30: 34-38, concerning the spices, Aaron is not mentioned. The various sects might have observed this peculiarity, and interpreted the incense rules to accommodate it. We, too, might conjecture that the verses addressed to Aaron are a later addition, corresponding to a change in cult practice: the elevation of the daily independent incense celebration to the highest significance, as opposed to its previous auxiliary role, and the consequent priestly exclusivity regarding this now major act of worship.

---

[67] I do not consider it necessary to enter into a discussion of the etymology of מנחה in other than the P source, it is obvious from the context that in the books of Ezra and Nehemiah, מנחה is not associated with the burnt offerings, and this specific meaning is also corroborated by the quotations from Jeremiah. In 17: 26 מנחה must unequivocally be regarded as a "cereal" offering, being separated from the first two animal offerings. Therefore, we must assume that the other mention of לבונה in association with מנחה in Jer. 41: 5 is also a "cereal" offering.

[68] According to the rules of the Temple Scroll, the public sin offerings brought with the *Mussaf* offerings also required an attached *Minhah* and libation. See Yadin, *Temple Scroll*, (Hebrew) p. 18, column 33, p. 56 and the Introduction, p. 114.

5. Significance of the Incense Celebration in the Second Temple Period

We have seen the philological problems and the textual inconsistencies encountered when one attempts to harmonize all the scriptural accounts of the incense celebrations, an approach which assumes the existence of a golden incense altar and a daily perpetual incense celebration in the earliest stages of ancient Israel's cult history. Before presenting my hypothesis concerning the development of this ritual, I would like to juxtapose and compare the absolute lack of reference to such celebrations in the early writings with the monumental significance which the incense ritual attained in the later period of the Second Temple, and its promotion to the foremost rank of priestly duties. I have already drawn attention to the first element of the comparison, and quoted several occurrences regarding the second component; I shall now proceed with additional observations and quotations in this respect.

5.1 The Biblical Text

5.1.1 Interjections

We may first observe certain phrases in Chronicles which are clear interjections. We find in I Chr. 6: 34 a verse introduced among genealogical data: ואהרן ובניו מקטירים על מזבח העולה ועל מזבח הקטרת לכל מלאכת קדש הקדשים "But Aaron and his descendants were the ones who presented offerings on the altar of burnt offering, and on the altar of incense in connection with all that was done in the Most Holy Place (v. 49 in NIV)." This verse does not have a counterpart in the Pentateuch, and its odd position suggests that it is a definite attempt to equate both celebrations. We also observe the use of the term קטר for the burning on the holocaust altar, in contrast to the term להעלות עולה utilized in Scripture, other than in the P segments. In Exod. 24: 5, we still find: עלת ויזבחו זבחים שלמים ויעלו, and the first linkage of the term קטר with עולה is found in Exod. 29: 18, concerning the consecration ceremonies of Aaron and his sons. A similar interjection, without a counterpart in the Pentateuch, is found in the

genealogical record in I Chr. 23: 13: קדש קדשים הוא ובניו עד עולם להקטיר
לפני ה׳ ויבדל אהרן להקדישו" Aaron was set apart, he and his descendants
forever, to consecrate the most holy things, to offer sacrifices – להקטיר –
before the Lord." The ability to perform incense celebration is thus seen as
the primary purpose behind Aaron's distinction.[1]

---

[1]   The NIV interpreted the term קטר here in a generic manner, understanding that
      Scripture tried to emphasize that only Aaron and his descendants were to perform all
      forms of sacrificial worship. Although the substance is not explicitly stated in the MT,
      it seems that the Sages understood that in this verse the term להקטיר refers to the
      incense celebration. We read in Pesiqta Rabbati 14:11 (ed. Ish Shalom, Wien, 1880,
      reprint Jerusalem, n.d.), p. 63b, and in a number of other midrashim כל אותן ארבעים
      שנה שהיו ישראל במדבר לא נמנע משה מלשמש בכהונה גדולה, הה"ד משה ואהרן בכהניו,
      רבי ברכיה בשם רבי סימון שמע לה מן הדא ובני עמרם אהרן ומשה ויבדל אהרן להקדישו
      קדש קדשים "In all those forty years in which Israel was in the desert, Moses served as
      a High Priest, as it is written 'Moses and Aaron were among his priests [Ps. 99: 6].'
      Rabbi Berakhia in the name of Rabbi Simon learned it from [the verse] 'The sons of
      Amram: Aaron and Moses; Aaron was set apart, he and his descendants forever, to
      consecrate the most holy things [I Chr. 23: 13].'" The exclusive incense celebration was
      the privilege of Aaron. Midrash Tanhuma *Parshat Korah* 10 links I Chr. 23: 13 with
      the Korah rebellion, which specifically concerned the incense celebration. We read
      there: ד"א בקר להקדישו וכשם שהבדיל בין האור ובין החושך... כך הבדיל אהרן, שנא׳
      ויבדל אהרן "Another homily: [It is written 'In the morning the Lord] will show who
      belongs to him [Num. 16: 5].' And as [God] has separated between light and
      darkness...so He separated Aaron [from the Levites], as it says 'and Aaron was set
      apart.'" According to this midrash, it is evident that the separation of Aaron in this
      verse concerns the incense ceremony. Moreover, I would consider this interpretation
      the correct one, since in the following verses I Chr. 23: 28-32 the Levites' duties are
      described, and they include all the offerings except the incense celebrations. We read in
      v. 31, with regard to the Levites' functions ולכל העלות עלות לה׳ לשבתות לחדשים
      ולמעדים במספר כמשפט עליהם תמיד לפני ה׳ "And whenever burnt offerings were
      presented to the Lord on Sabbaths, and at New Moon festivals and at appointed feasts.
      They were to serve before the Lord regularly in the proper number and in the way
      prescribed for them." I do not wish to elaborate, at this stage, upon the struggle between
      the Levites and Aaronites, but it is possible that the narrative in this chapter bears
      witness to an intermediate period, during which the Levites still offered sacrifices, and
      only the incense celebration was the exclusive privilege of the Aaronite clan. Some
      traditional commentators were aware, it seems, of the blatant inconsistency between
      this verse and the traditional concept that only the Aaronites offered sacrifices, and
      attempted different interpretations. Rashi interpreted the verse to imply that the Levites,
      who were responsible for the various chambers and storage places, would bring the
      correct number of animals for the prescribed sacrifices on the various days. Radak
      proposed to consider this verse as a continuation of the previous one, which states that
      the Levites had the duty to stand and praise the Lord; his interpretation was that they
      were to praise the Lord at the offering of the sacrifices by the Aaronites. For our
      purposes it suffices to demonstrate that the simple meaning of these verses is not as
      these commentators suggested, but as I have proposed.

There are a number of seemingly parallel pericopes in the books of Chronicles and Kings, in which a distinct pattern is observable. For instance, we have noted Uzziah's punishment by leprosy for usurping the priestly prerogative of the incense celebration, narrated in II Chr. 26: 16-19; the leprosy is also recorded in II Kings 15: 5, but here there is no mention of the grounds for this punishment. In I Chr. 28: 18 the golden vessels made by Solomon are recalled; we read there ולמזבח הקטרת זהב מזקק "And the weight of the refined gold for the altar of incense," but in the parallel verse I Kings 7: 48, we find only the neutral מזבח הזהב "the altar of gold," without any indication of its purpose.[2] In II Chr. 2: 3-5 Solomon writes to Huram and describes the functions of the house he desires to build: בית לשם ה' אלהי... להקטיר לפניו קטרת סמים ומערכת תמיד ועלות לבקר ולערב "a temple for the Name of the Lord ... for burning fragrant incense before him, for setting out the consecrated bread regularly, and for making burnt offerings every morning and evening." This verse offers evidence of a well-established, institutionalized routine in the late period, and the incense celebration is at the top of the list. In the parallel narration in I Kings 5: 19, the same description of the house is used, בית לשם ה' "a temple for the Name of the Lord (NIV 5: 5)," but without any list of the ceremonies to be performed there. In II Chr. chap. 13, a debate between Abijah and Jeroboam is recorded, and in v. 11 Abijah describes the priestly functions in his kingdom in Judah: ומקטרים לה' עלות בבקר בבקר ובערב בערב וקטרת סמים ומערכת לחם על השלחן הטהור ומנורת הזהב ונרתיה "Every morning and evening they present burnt offerings and fragrant incense to the Lord. They set out the bread on the ceremonially clean table and light the lamps on the gold lampstand every evening." The parallel pericope in I Kings 15: 7 recounts the war between Abijah and Jeroboam, but the debate concerning the priestly duties is not mentioned.[3] That the purpose of the narrative in II Chr. is to validate the legitimacy of the Aaronite priesthood, and its exclusive prerogatives, is evident: the incense celebration, and the indiscriminate use of the term קטר for both burnt sacrifices and incense, stand in the forefront of the narration.

---

[2]   Concerning the various terms used for the "golden", "incense" altar, see Introduction pp. 9-12.

[3]   This entire pericope in II Chr. is in total contradiction to the facts narrated in I Kings; there Abijah "committed all the sins his father had done before him," whereas in II Chr. he is represented as the true defender of the genuine priesthood, who prevailed over Israel " because they relied on the Lord, the God of their fathers (II Chr. 13: 18)."

In II Chr. 29, Hezekiah's exhortation to the priests and Levites, we read the following in v. 7: גם סגרו דלתות האולם ויכבו את הנרות וקטרת לא הקטירו ועלה לא העלו בקדש "They also shut the doors of the portico and put out the lamps. They did not burn incense or present any burnt offerings at the sanctuary of the God of Israel." In v. 11, we read: כי בכם בחר ה' לעמד לפניו לשרתו ולהיות לו משרתים ומקטרים "for the Lord has chosen you to stand before him and serve him, to minister before and to burn incense." We observe in the first verse the importance of the incense ceremony, which is listed before the burnt offerings, and in the second verse the significance of the incense celebration is emphasized yet more strongly. It is the function for which the priests were chosen. This entire pericope is missing in the appropriate chapters of II Kings which refer to Hezekiah. The intentional addition of the term קטר in Chronicles to parallel references to the altar in Kings is convincingly evident in a comparison between II Chr. 32: 12, II Kings 18: 22 and Isa. 36: 7, the Rabshakeh's discourse. The verse in II Kings is almost identical with the verse in Isaiah: וכי תאמר[ון] אלי אל ה' אלהינו בטחנו הלוא הוא אשר הסיר חזקיהו את במתיו ואת מזבחתיו ויאמר ליהודה ולירושלים[4] לפני המזבח הזה תשתחוו [בירושלם] "And if you say to me, 'We are depending on the Lord our God' – isn't he the one whose high places and altars Hezekiah removed, saying to Judah and Jerusalem, 'You must worship before this altar [in Jerusalem]?'" In II Chr. 32: 12, which is similar in style and composition, we read: הלא הוא יחזקיהו הסיר את במתיו ואת מזבחתיו ויאמר ליהודה ולירושלם לאמר לפני מזבח אחד תשתחוו ועליו תקטירו "Did not Hezekiah himself remove this god's high places and altars, saying to Judah and Jerusalem, 'You must worship before one altar, and burn sacrifices[5] on it.'" It is evident that all three citations relied on the same common primary source; but the later editor of Chronicles has intentionally added the burning of incense as the principal ritual on the altar in Jerusalem.

In conclusion, we must recognize that this great number of intentional additions to the ancient texts demonstrates a major shift in the Temple cult, specifically concerning the incense celebration, as well as a conspicuous attempt to exalt the incense cult, and justify the transformation. It is interesting to note in this respect that notwithstanding the barely concealed aim

---

[4] The characters in square brackets do not appear in Isa. 36: 7.

[5] The NIV also interprets the term קטר here in a generic manner, as in the P section of the Pentateuch; but the contrast between the uses in the parallel sentences in Kings and Chronicles attests to the intentional use of the specific ritual term קטר in Chr. to enhance its importance in the cult.

of the Chronicles editor to emphasize the permanence and significance of the incense celebration, he has omitted, possibly by oversight, to interject the existence of the incense altar or the ceremony in some instances where one would expect it. For instance, in the continuation of Hezekiah's exhortation in II Chr. 29, we read in v. 18 a report of the priests' and Levites' accomplishments: ויאמרו טהרנו את כל בית ה׳ את מזבח העולה ואת כל כליו ואת שלחן המערכת ואת כל כליו "and [they] reported: 'We have purified the entire temple of the Lord, the altar of burnt offering, with all its utensils, and the table for setting out the consecrated bread, with all its articles.'" The Chronicles editor has neglected to insert the incense altar, which was probably not included in his primary source. Verses 21-36 recount the cult activities performed in the Temple for the consecration ceremonies; though in v. 7 there is a remonstrance against failure to perform the incense ceremony, וקטרת לא הקטירו , we again find no trace of such a celebration in the long and detailed list of the priestly offices. This too was apparently overlooked by the editor. On other occasions, we observe a "sloppy" interpolation, as, for example, in II Chr. 4: 19: ויעש שלמה את כל הכלים אשר בית האלהים ואת מזבח הזהב ואת השלחנות ועליהם לחם הפנים "Solomon also made all the furnishings that were in God's temple: the golden altar; the tables on which was the bread of the Presence."[6] The beginning of the

---

6   An almost identical verse appears in I Kings 7: 48, and there too it seems to be a later interjection. The structure of the chapter, which decribes in great detail the construction of the lower rank bronze furnishings, and then compresses a description of the most hallowed golden items, such as the golden altar, table, and lampstand, into two short, laconic verses, emphasizes the different style of these latter verses. We encounter in I Kings 6: 17-22 the same tampering with the text; the Masoretic text is totally incomprehensible from the aspect of style and syntax. The LXX has changed the text entirely, to make it understandable; both Rehm in *Das Erste Buch der Könige* and Noth in *Könige* have discussed this matter in detail. Noth attempted to find an explanation for the MT irregularities by presuming that the LXX originally had a different text, which was later corrupted through errors in copying. While this is possible, I suggest that the text before the LXX translator had already been corrupted by the deliberate interjection of the golden altar for incense among the Temple's artifacts, instead of a wooden table-altar which stood in front of the ark in the *Dabir*. The LXX attempted to create order out of the confusion by eliminating part of the MT text, thus offering a plain and comprehensible version of these verses. Moreover, we do not find the golden altar and the lampstand in Ezekiel's description of the Temple, which further substantiates the postulate that they were a later addition. M. Rehm, *Das Erste Buch der Könige*, p. 80, writes: "In v. 14 und den vv.48-50a ist der Einfluss der Priesterschrift erkennbar." ("In v. 14 and verses 48-50a the priestly code influence is noticeable.") Another question is raised with reference to the P narration: why did Solomon need to build the golden altar, the table and the lampstand, all pieces of equipment built by

chapter records in great detail the construction of all the other furnishings, as well as their location, but the golden or incense altar is suspiciously absent there; the interjection of the altar[7] into this later verse is obvious, but fails to indicate its size and exact location, as for the other implements.[8]

5.1.2 Absence of the Celebration in Ezekiel

In Ezekiel, the complete absence of any mention of the incense altar or the daily incense celebration in the Temple is even more striking. Ezekiel was himself a priest, and his book contains a fully detailed code for the construction of the Temple, its furnishings, and its rituals, parallel to the Priestly code in the Pentateuch.[9] In chap. 43, the prophet describes in minute detail the consecration rituals for the Temple, which are similar to the Pentateuchal

---

Moses for the Tent of the Congregation; Solomon did not rebuild the ark, which still remained from that period, and one would expect the same for the other furnishings. There might be an explanation for the table and lampstand, since Solomon constructed ten of each, and these could have been in addition to the originals, but such a solution is not appropriate regarding the golden altar, a unique piece of equipment. The Rabbis, it seems, were aware of this issue, and we find in a *Beraita* in B.T. Menahoth 99a, and a similar pericope in Y.T. Sheqalim chap. 6, hal. 3, 24b, an indirect answer concerning the tables and lampstands: ת"ר עשרה שלחנות עשה שלמה ולא היו מסדרין אלא על של משה שנא' ואת השלחן אשר עליו לחם הפנים זהב. עשר מנורות עשה שלמה ולא היו מדלקין אלא בשל משה שנא' מנורת הזהב ונרותיה לבער בערב "The Rabbis taught: Solomon made ten tables, but only on the one [made by] Moses was [the showbread] arranged, as it is said: 'The golden table on which was the bread of the Presence [I Kings 7: 48]'; Solomon made ten candlesticks, but they would kindle only the one [made by] Moses, as it is said 'and light the lamps on the gold lampstand every evening ([II Chr. 13: 11].'" There is a dispute in the Talmud, in B.T. Menahoth and Y.T. Sheqalim; in the B.T. Rabbi Eleazar (in the Y.T. it is Rabbi Jose bei Rabbi Judah) contends that all ten tables and lampstands were used. For our purpose it suffices to demonstrate that the Rabbis believed that the furnishings made by Moses in the desert subsisted and were placed in Solomon's Temple. On the other hand, they did not ask the obvious question: what was the purpose of the second golden altar made by Solomon, in addition to the one made by Moses?

7   Professor Fox commented here that this item is secondary to Chronicles, which has consciously added the incense offering in its reworking of ancient traditions, but added the golden altar only in its own re-editing, making it the latest element in this series of enhancements of the incense offering.

8   For the absence of קטרת in Daniel 9: 27, I have no explanation other than the possibility that the author or editor belonged to a school with a similar conviction as the group who created the Temple Scroll, who apparently did not celebrate the daily incense ceremony.

regulations,[10] but the incense celebration is absent. In chap. 44, we find a description of the functions of the Levites: המה ישחטו את העולה ואת הזבח לעם "they may slaughter the burnt offering and sacrifices for the people (v.11)," and of the priests, Zadok's descendants: המה יקרבו אלי לשרתני ועמדו לפני להקריב לי חלב ודם "[they] are to come near to minister before me, they are to stand before me to offer sacrifices of fat and blood (v. 15)." Further particulars of the sacrifices performed and consumed by the priests appear in v. 27: יקריב חטאתו "he is to offer a sin offering," and in v. 29: המנחה והחטאת והאשם המה יאכלום "They will eat the grain offerings, the sin offerings and the guilt offerings." Again, there is no mention of an incense celebration. Similarly, chap. 46 records the routine ritual for the daily, Sabbath and festival sacrifices, and again there is no indication of an

---

9   The regulations do not correspond exactly to the priestly code, and there is a debate among scholars as to which writing is earlier. See עיונים בספר יחזקאל (Jerusalem, 1982), p. 4 ff. It is interesting to note that M. Haran, who participated in these discussions, emphasizes the fact that there is no mention of the incense altar, or of the lampstand, in Ezekiel (p. 6). As we have seen, in Haran's essay on incense he relies on the phrase in I Sam. 2: 28 to validate the existence of the incense ceremony at the early stage of this book's composition. It seems to me that he overlooked the fact that the phrase in Samuel refers to an incense celebration on an altar, לעלות על מזבחי להקטיר קטרת "to go up to my altar, to burn incense." I shall refer to the quotation in Samuel in defence of my hypothesis. The Rabbis were also aware of the extreme inconsistencies between the Pentateuchal sacrificial rules and Ezekiel's ordinances, and we find interesting dicta in B. T. Menahoth 45a: א"ר יוחנן פרשה זו אליהו עתיד לדורשה "Said Rabbi Johanan: This pericope [Ezek. 45] will be interpreted by Elijah"; אמר רב יהודה אמר רב זכור אותו איש לטוב וחנינה בן חזקיה שמו שאלמלא הוא נגנז ספר יחזקאל שהיו דבריו סותרין דברי תורה "Rav Judah said in the name of Rav: This man by the name of Hanina son of Hezkiah should be remembered well for his accomplishment, since if it were not for him, the book of Ezekiel would have been concealed because it contradicts the teachings of the Torah."

10   In B. T. Menahoth 45a we read: רב אשי אמר מילואים הקריבו בימי עזרא כדרך שהקריבו בימי משה "Rav Ashi said : At the time of Ezra, they offered consecration [offerings] as they offered in Moses' time." Maimonides offers an interesting commentary on and interpretation of the apparent contradiction between the Pentateuch and Ezekiel, in הל' מעשה הקרבנות, פ"ב הי"ד: כל שיעורי הנסכים האמורין בספר יחזקאל ומנין אותן הקרבנות וסדרי העבודה הכתובים שם כולם מלואים הן ואין נוהגין לדורות אלא הנביא צוה ופירש כיצד יהיו מקריבין המלואין עם חנוכת המזבח בימי המלך המשיח כשיבנה בית שלישי "The measures of the libations mentioned in the book of Ezekiel, and the number of the offerings and the order of the rituals written there, are all consecration [rituals] and are not authoritative for all periods; the prophet merely commanded and interpreted the manner in which the consecration [offerings] should be offered at the consecration of the altar at the time of the King Messiah, when the Third Temple will be built."

independent incense celebration in the Temple, by the priests. However, as I discussed above, Ezekiel does record in chap. 8 an incense celebration in censers performed by elders, and employs the term קטרת, strong evidence that the substance was then available in Judah, and familiar in cultic usage.

5.2 Apocryphal and Historical Writings

Inconsistencies in the Temple Scroll and apocryphal writings deepen the perplexities concerning the incense celebration and its introduction and development in ancient Israel. There is first the strange absence of any reference to the daily incense celebration in the Damascus Scroll and in the Temple Scroll; it would be quite implausible that the absence of references where one would expect them has occurred purely by chance. According to the rules of the Temple Scroll[11] the frankincense of the showbread was burnt on the inner incense altar, contrary to the actual procedure in the Temple, where it was burned on the outer altar, as confirmed by Josephus and the Talmud. Is it possible that these sects did not make a distinction between the לבונה "frankincense" and קטרת סמים "incense compound"? Perhaps they considered the verses in Exod. 30: 34-35 as describing not a complex compound of eleven or fourteen spices, but rather a frankincense compound, with or without some minor additions of herbs, to be burnt on the holocaust altar with each מנחה, meal offering, attached to the holocaust offering; we must consider that there is no mention of any altar in that pericope. Or perhaps they had a different text for Exod. 30: 34 than the MT, without the addition of the phrase סמים ולבנה זכה discussed above; this alternative seems more likely. Such a text would give a coherent reading, referring only to spices, and would have some affinity with the LXX term ἥδυσμα "that which gives a relish or flavour." As we have seen, neither the term מזבח הקטרת nor the term קטרת appears in Ezra and Nehemiah, and we encounter there only the term לבנה.[12]

---

[11] Yadin, p. 26, reconstructed: עמוד ח׳ והיתה ה[ל]לבונה הזאות ללחם לאזכרה [אשה לה׳
והקטרתה ביום השבת ביום השבת ע[ל מזבח הקטרת בהסירכ]ה את הלחם "And this frankincense should be a memorial for the bread, an offering made by fire to God, and you should burn it on the Sabbath, on the Sabbath upon the incense altar at the removal of the bread."

[12] It is also possible that they had another version of the pericope Exod. 30: 1-8, and were missing vv. 7 and 8 with the command to burn the daily incense upon the golden altar. In general, the edicts of the Temple Scroll do not flagrantly contradict the biblical texts;

In The Testament of Levi, we find an interesting rule regarding the burning of frankincense. In the Bodleian MS, col. d line 30, following the rules for the placing of the salted meat parts on the altar, we read: ובתר דנה [כל] נישפא בליל במשחא ובתר כולא חמר נסך והקטיר עליהון לבונה ויהוון עובדיך בסריך וכל קרבניך לר[עו]א "After that , fine meal mixed with oil, after that pour out the wine and burn the frankincense over them;[13] and let [all] your actions follow due order and all your sacrifices be [acceptable]." The addition of frankincense to the *Minhah* (מנחת נסכים) which is obligatory with every holocaust and peace offering is not mentioned in the MT text, in Num. 15: 2- 16. It is also in express opposition to the rabbinic dictum in Mishnah Menahoth 5: 3: מנחת נסכין טעונה שמן ואינה טעונה לבונה "The *Minhah* of the libation requires oil and does not require frankincense."

Another intriguing rule regarding this issue is found in the continuation of the above text, which exists only in Greek. I shall therefore cite the English translation:[14] "Six shekels of frankincense for the bull and half of that for the ram and a third of that for the kid. And all the mixed up fine flour, if you offer it up alone and not upon the fat, let two shekels' weight of frankincense be poured out upon it (verse 45)." The editor of this document has established a precise quantity of frankincense for the regular *Minhah* offered without an animal sacrifice – two shekels' weight. Scripture does not define the quantity of the frankincense for the independent *Minhah* offering,[15] saying only ונתן עליה לבנה "and put frankincense thereon (Lev.

---

they merely show another interpretation of the same text (see note 17). It would therefore be extremely unlikely that they would have disregarded the clear command in vv. 7 and 8, if they had had the same text as the MT. Such a possibility would confirm a late accretion of these verses to this pericope.

[13] We find a similar description of the procedure for offering a holocaust together with the *Minhah*, libation and incense, in the story of Noah's sacrifice in the Book of Jubilees, 6: 2-3 (see note 15).

[14] *The Testaments of the Twelve Patriarchs, The Testament of Levi, A Commentary*, Greek MS *e*, vv. 32b-66.

[15] The editor of the Book of Jubilees, it seems, also required incense to be burnt with every sacrifice, together with the flour, oil and wine libation. In chap. 6: 3, we read of Noah's offering after the flood: "And he offered them holocaust on the altar and put on them a *Minhah* mingled with oil, and poured on wine and put incense on it, and brought up a sweet savour, an offering made by fire to God." The author projects his own views about the correct ritual onto Noah's offering, since in the Pentateuchal story there is no indication of these additions to the holocaust. In the Temple Scroll, the addition of incense is not explicitly stated, but the style of the text on Page 34, Plate 49 is very similar, as is the requirement that the various ingredients be put one on top of the

2: 1)." In Mishnah Menahoth 13: 3, we read: המתנדב מנחה יביא עמה קמץ לבונה ושני בזיכין טעונין שני קמצים "If someone pledges to offer a *Minhah*, he should bring with it a handful of frankincense. And the two platters [on the showbread] require two handfuls." The Rabbis established the approximate quantity of frankincense, a "handful," required equally for all *Minhah* offerings which demanded frankincense.[16] The group to which our Testaments editor belonged established different quantities of frankincense for each *Minhah*, when brought as an ancillary to an animal sacrifice, in the same way that Scripture distinguished the quantities of flour, wine and oil for these offerings; according to the Rabbis, there was no frankincense offered with such ancillary *Minhah* offerings, as we noted above.

Josephus' detailed description of these offerings, in *Ant.* III 233-234, does not mention frankincense. He records, exactly as in Leviticus, the required measures of flour, wine and oil, but nothing else. We must assume, therefore, that in his time this was the actual practice in the Temple. On the other hand, there is a strong possibility that certain sects maintained different interpretations of the scriptural texts, as we know them, or had access to other texts, unknown to us. It is unlikely that the rules of the sects were deliberately made contrary to the biblical texts; these groups did not intend to contradict Scripture, but merely interpreted scriptural dicta in a different way than the "establishment".[17] Or, if they had other texts in their possession, they may have objected to the alteration of these texts by official institutions. Accusations of false modifications of Scripture were a common practice, dating from the split with the Samaritans and continuing until the Middle Ages. I do not intend to present an argument as to which party induced the changes, but point out that logically it would most likely be the powerful "establishment" which would initiate modifications of ingrained custom. A small group would not have had the fortitude and audacity to

---

ומקטירים אותמה על האש אשר על המזבח פר פר ונתחיו אצלו ומנחת סולתו עליו ויין :other נסכו אצלו ושמנו עליו והקטירו הכוהנים בני אהרון את הכול על המזבח אשה ריח ניחוח לפני ה' "And one burns them on the fire upon the altar, each bullock and its pieces with it, and its fine flour *Minhah* on it, and its wine libation with it, and its oil upon it, and let the priests, Aaron's sons, burn [fumigate?] everything on the altar, a fire offering, a sweet savour before the Lord."

[16] In Sheqalim 50b, there is a discussion as to whether the handful of the priest or of the offerer is meant; in any case, a handful is not an exact measure.

[17] In Yadin's Commentary to the Temple Scroll, he suggests that it was the editor's different interpretation of the biblical text which led to the group's divergent rules. Yadin is of the opinion that the group followed the biblical text, and did not flagrantly oppose it.

introduce innovations into the official cult, and would be more likely to struggle against them. Such a social theory needs substantiation, which is beyond the parameters of this study.[18] Nonetheless, we observe crucial variations in the incense offerings among the sects, a fact which unequivocally suggests changes in existing practice, and a series of innovations. It is possible that the groups responsible for the apocryphal writings and the Temple Scroll had some common conceptions concerning the incense celebration.

Apocryphal writings also offer us an insight into the significance of the incense ceremonial in their period, by their retrojection of such performances into such narratives as the editors considered appropriate, though the corresponding scriptural narratives record no such performances. Rabbinic midrashim also employ such retrojections to describe the Patriarchs' fulfillment of the Torah's precepts, including the offering of sacrifices;[19] however, the pre-eminence of the incense celebration on these occasions is

---

[18]   I am indebted to Prof. Revell for the following useful elucidation: "There is (perhaps) a parallel in language. Much change is initiated in the cultural centre. When such changed usage has become normative, speakers at the centre assume that those at the periphery are ignorant and uneducated, but the usage at the periphery continues the earlier standard usage." See also my assumption (Introduction p. 9), confirmed by the thesis of Bar-Ilan, that only the "establishment" had the power to introduce and successfully impose innovative cultic systems.

[19]   We read in Genesis Rabba 34:9: ויבן נח מזבח לה׳ ויבן כתיב נתבונן; אמר מפני מה צווני הקב"ה וריבה בטהורים, אלא להקריב מהן קרבן, מיד ויקח מכל הבהמה הטהורה. רבי אליעזר בן יעקב אומר על מזבח הגדול שבירושלים ששם הקריב אדם הראשון "'Then Noah built an altar to the Lord '[Gen. 8: 20]; 'he built' is written [with a similar root to] 'he contemplated'; he said 'Why has God commanded me to increase the number of the clean [animals to be brought into the ark] ? Surely to bring offerings from them.' Immediately, '[he took] some of all the clean animals.' Rabbi Eliezer ben Jacob says [the term 'altar' refers to] the great altar in Jerusalem, where Adam made an offering." In Yalqut Shimoni 101 on Gen. 22:9, we read a further midrash: ויבן שם אברהם את המזבח מזבח אין כתיב כאן אלא את המזבח, המזבח שהקריבו בו קין והבל הוא המזבח שהקריבו בו נח ובניו "'And Abraham built an altar there' [Gen. 22: 9]; it is not written 'an altar', but 'the altar' [with a definite article, in the Hebrew text]; it is the altar upon which Cain and Abel offered, and this is the altar upon which Noah and his sons offered." In B.T. Yoma 28b, we read אמר ... אמר רב קיים אברהם אבינו כל התורה כולה רבא ואיתימא רב אשי קיים אברהם אבינו אפילו עירובי תבשילין שנא' תורותי אחת תורה שבכתב ואחת תורה שבעל פה "Said Rav: Abraham our father performed all [the precepts] of the Torah...Rava, and possibly Rav Ashi, said: Abraham our father performed even the precept of *Eiruvei Tavshilin* [a rabbinic stipulation to allow the preparation of food on a feast day, for the following Sabbath], since it is written '[Abraham obeyed me, and kept my requirements, my commands], my decrees and my laws' [in plural; Gen. 26: 5]: the written Torah and the oral Torah." Midrash Tanhuma offers us, with

most evident in the Apocrypha. In the Book of Jubilees[20] we find a great number of such retrojections. In 3: 27, we read: "And on that day on which Adam went forth from the Garden, he offered as a sweet savour an offering, frankincense, galbanum, and stacte, and spices in the morning with the rising of the sun from the day when he covered his shame." In 4: 25, we read that Enoch offered incense: "And he (Enoch) burned the incense of the sanctuary (even) sweet spices, acceptable before the Lord of the Mount."[21] In 6: 3, we read in the description of Noah's offering: "...and sprinkled wine[22] and strewed frankincense over everything, and caused a goodly savour to arise, acceptable before the Lord." In chap. 7, the sacrifices offered by Noah on the first day of the first month[23] correspond to the scriptural offerings of the first day of the seventh month, and here too we find:"...and he placed incense on the altar and caused a sweet savour to ascend."

In chap. 15, we read the manner in which Abraham celebrated the Feast of Weeks:[24] "...their fruit offerings and their drink offerings he offered upon the altar with frankincense (v. 2)."[25] In chap. 16: 20- 24, we have a

---

another interpretation of the same verse, an insight as to why Abraham was ordered to leave Haran, his homeland: We read in *Parshat Lekh Lekha* 1: ... 'ותורותי', והלא תורה אחת היא אלא שהיה מדקדק אחר כל מצות שבתורה, אמר הקב"ה אתה מדקדק אחר מצותי, ותשב אצל עובדי ע"ז, צא מביניהם "'My statutes [in plural]' – though there is only one statute (Torah), [Abraham] performed punctiliously all the Torah's precepts. Said God: 'You perform my precepts punctiliously, and you will dwell among the idolaters? Depart from among them.'" The Patriarchs kept the Torah, and offered sacrifices, but the midrashim do not add that they offered incense.

20 The English texts are from R. H. Charles, ed., *The Apocrypha and Pseudepigrapha of the Old Testament* (Oxford, 1913).

21 These quotations do not unequivocally point to a daily incense ceremony at that period, but suggest that there was such a celebration on special occasions; this procedure prevailed in an intermediate period, as I shall propose later on.

22 From the style and language of Gen. 9: 20, Scripture seems to imply that Noah was the first to plant grapes for wine, and this was after his sacrifice. We read there: ויחל נח איש האדמה ויטע כרם "Noah, a man of the soil, started and planted a vineyard." Onkelos translates ויחל as שרי, which is to be understood as "he began". Jonathan relates that Noah started to plough the earth and found a vine which the river had carried from the Garden of Eden; thus, this author also understood the verse to imply that there were no vineyards before this time.

23 This divergence corresponds to the dispute as to whether the first month is Nissan or Tishrei.

24 According to the calendars of various sects, this feast is celebrated on the fifteenth day of the third month.

25 We observe that the frankincense was offered together with the sacrifices on the holocaust altar.

description of Abraham's celebration of the Feast of Tabernacles, and, after the specific offerings, we read in v. 24: "And morning and evening he burnt fragrant substances, frankincense and galbanum, and stacte, and nard, and myrrh, and spice, all these seven[26] he offered, crushed, mixed together in equal parts (and) pure."[27] Chap. 32 describes Levi's consecration to the priesthood by his father Jacob, and the offerings celebrated on that occasion. In v. 6, we read: "And when the fire had consumed it, he burnt incense on the fire over it." In chap. 50: 10, concerning the Sabbath, we read: "...and rest thereon from all labour which belongs to the labour of the children of men, save burning frankincense and bringing oblations and sacrifices before the Lord";[28] the burning of frankincense is placed in first position. We may grasp from these retrojections the significance bestowed upon the incense celebrations;[29] in the belief of the editors, these were a

---

[26] Since Scripture is vague concerning the composition of the incense, we encounter varied opinions as to the ingredients, as I have noted above; seven are listed here, eleven are listed by the Rabbis, and fourteen by Josephus. It is interesting to note that Theophrastus remarks in Περὶ Ὀσμῶν, XII: 57: "The more numerous and the more various the perfumes that are mixed, the more distinguished and the more graceful will be the scent." Perhaps the various commentators agreed with this thought, and this might be the reason for the constant increase in the number of the mixed spices.

[27] In the other quotations, it is obvious that the incense is an element of the sacrifice, similar to the libation, and is burned together with the sacrifice on the holocaust altar. It is remarkable that even here, where one has the impression that the editor is describing an independent offering of incense in the morning and evening, parallel to the scriptural command, there is no indication as to where it should be burnt: on a separate incense altar, or on the holocaust altar. In v. 20, we read: "And he built there an altar," and we must suppose that there was only one altar. Such a procedure would correspond to provisions in sectarian writings and regulations that incense should be burned together with the animal sacrifice on the holocaust altar, precisely like the frankincense of the meal offering, as explicitly decreed in Lev. chap. 2.

[28] This dictum seems in disagreement with the citation in the Damascus Scroll, quoted above: "Let no man offer on the altar on the Sabbath except the burnt offering of the Sabbath; for thus it is written: 'apart from your Sabbath-offerings.'" On the other hand, if we assume that the incense was burnt together with the animal offering on the holocaust altar, and was an integral element of the daily perpetual or Sabbath offering, then it could be included, in the view of the author, in the term "Sabbath offering"; the prohibition against offering other sacrifices would not exclude the addition of incense to this offering, in the same way as it would not exclude the ancillary Minhah offering. We have seen that according to sectarian writings, incense is an integral and essential element of the ancillary Minhah.

[29] We encounter a similar aetiological retrojection in the Book of Jubilees 6: 17 concerning the institution of חג השבועות, the Feast of Weeks. Here the feast is said to be a remembrance of the covenant made by the Deity with Noah after the flood, in contrast

necessary part of the various events. We also acquire an awareness of the extent to which references to incense celebrations are lacking in Scripture, other than in the P segments. A remarkable perspective, illustrating the significance ascribed to the incense celebration, is found in the Testament of Levi, chap. 8, at Levi's consecration ceremony. Seven men in white raiment perform the ritual in seven steps, but the climax is the incense performance (v. 10): "The seventh placed on my head a diadem of priesthood, and filled my hands with incense, that I might serve as priest to the Lord God." The incense ritual, in other words, consummates the ordination as a priest.

We also encounter a linkage between the incense celebration and prayer – that is, an assumption that the time of this celebration is a propitious time for prayers to be offered to the Lord. Judith seems to have timed her prayer for the success of her dangerous venture to coincide with the incense celebration. We read in Judith 9: 1: καὶ ἒν ἄρτι προσφερόμενον ἐν Ἱερουσαλὴμ εἰς τὸν οἶκον τοῦ θεοῦ τὸ θυμίαμα τῆς ἑσπέρας ἐκείνης, καὶ ἐβόησεν φωνῇ μεγάλῃ Ἰουδὶθ πρὸς κύριον[30] "And the incense of that evening was

---

to its character as a popular agricultural feast in the Pentateuch. The rabbinical writings also changed the character of this holiday, and proclaimed it as a remembrance of the Sinai event and the conferring of the Torah; see B.T. Shabbath 86b: בששי בחדש ניתנו עשרת הדברות לישראל. רבי יוסי אומר בשבעה בו "On the sixth of the month [Sivan] the ten commandments were given to the Israelites. Rabbi Jose says: On the seventh." In the Mekhilta of Rabbi Ishmael Tractate *Bahodesh* 3 we read: זה, והיו נכונים ליום השלישי, יום ששי, שבו נתנה התורה "'and be ready by the third day [Exod. 19: 11]', this is the sixth day [of the month of Sivan] when the Torah was given." The Book of Jubilees, 34: 12-19 also retrojects the institution of the Day of Atonement, including the self-denial of the people, and the sacrifice of a goat as a remembrance of Jacob's anguish on seeing Joseph's robe dipped in the blood of a goat slaughtered by his brothers. In both cases, the retrojection had a significant aetiological motive. The character of the Feast of Weeks was changed from a popular feast, which has no fixed date in the Pentateuch, no prohibition of work as with other holidays, and no mention in Ezekiel, into a religiously motivated holy day, associated with a covenant with the Deity. The Rabbis too linked the Feast of Weeks with the Sinai event, a milestone in the narrative of the covenant between God and Israel. The association in the Book of Jubilees of the Day of Atonement with the misdeeds of Jacob's sons serves as a justification of the utmost cleansing of sins commanded for that day, and as the foundation for its specific and exceptional cultic celebrations. The Torah offers historical grounds for other holidays, such as Passover and the Feast of Tabernacles, but has none for the Day of Atonement; the Book of Jubilees thus retrojects the institution of this holiday to the Patriarch, in the same manner as the Book of Chronicles retrojects to David many topics regarding the construction of the Temple and the division of labour between the priests and Levites.

[30] Greek text ed. R. Hanhart (Göttingen, 1979).

now being offered at Jerusalem in the house of God, and Judith cried to the Lord with a loud voice."[31]

However, it is also remarkable that in Ecclesiasticus, written by Ben Sira as late as the second century B.C.E., there is no mention of a daily incense celebration at points where one would expect it. In chap. 50: 11-22 the entire course of the High Priest's ritual performance is vividly described with all relevant details, almost precisely as it appears in B.T. Tamid chaps. 6-7; only the incense celebration is missing. Yet in chap. 50: 8 we note that frankincense is explicitly associated with the *Minhah*: וכאש לבונה על המנחה "and as the flame of the frankincense on the *Minhah*."[32] Further, chap. 45

---

[31]   English text from *The Apocrypha and Pseudepigrapha of the Old Testament*, ed. R. H. Charles. It is interesting to note that A. Kahana, הספרים החיצונים (Tel Aviv, 1959), the translator of the Apocrypha into Hebrew, remarks here that although the Greek text reads θυμίαμα, he suspects that the original Hebrew text reads מנחת הערב and that the later translator negligently translated this as if it were קטורת הערב. Kahanah does not elaborate upon the basis of his assumption, but I suspect that he doubted whether during the period of the original author of the story a daily evening incense celebration linked to a propitious time for prayer was already an established custom. Moreover, the narrative of Judith's appeal to God is similar in its nature to Elijah's prayer for a miracle in I Kings 18: 36, where we read ויהי בעלות המנחה. The Greek text uses προσφέρω, a verb usually referring to sacrifices, but not to the burning of incense; for the latter, as we have seen, the term θυμιάω is utilized in the LXX. The NIV has a neutral interpretation, "At the time of sacrifice," but the Hebrew text which was before Judith's translator emphasizes the evening sacrifice. The translator might have changed the text to adapt it to the practice prevailing during his lifetime, when the daily incense ceremony was already a fundamental custom.

[32]   The Greek text in Ziegler's edition, verse 9, reads ὡς πῦρ καὶ λίβανος ἐπὶ πυρείου; however, there is difficulty with this translation, since we have observed that in Jeremiah the לבונה appears joined as a complement to the *Minhah*, the grain offering. The Jerusalem Academy of the Hebrew Language has in fact emended the unreadable text here so that it is the same as Cassuto's text cited above. See *The Historical Dictionary of the Hebrew Language: Ben Sira, The Origin, Concordance and Analysis of the Thesaurus* (Jerusalem, 1973). We encounter the same Hebrew reading in M. Z. Segal, ספר בן סירא השלם (Jerusalem, 1972), in A. Kahana's Hebrew translation of the Apocrypha הספרים החיצוניים, and in the *Anchor Bible, The Wisdom of Ben Sira* (New York, 1987). In the latter we read: "Like the blaze of incense at the sacrifice," and in the relevant Comment, p. 552, the linkage of the incense with the grain offering is emphasized in the following phrase: "Heb. Minha is the cereal offering on which frankincense and oils were placed; part of this combination was then burned on the altar (Lev. 2: 1-2; 6: 7-8) [the verses in which the grain offering is commanded]." Only the *New Oxford Annotated Bible with the Apocrypha* (New York, 1991) follows Ziegler's Greek text, and we read there: "like fire and incense in the censer." I therefore definitely prefer the Hebrew version.

describes the choosing of Aaron for the priesthood, and in v. 14 we read the purpose of his election: ‏להגיש עולה וחלבים ולהקטיר ריח ניחוח ואזכרה‎[33] "to offer holocaust and fat, and to burn sweet savour and remembrance."[34] The term ‏אזכרה‎ appears six times in Scripture. In three occurrences it refers to the handful of flour with frankincense[35] taken from the *Minhah* offering, to be burnt on the altar. In one occurrence frankincense is simply not mentioned,[36] and in two occurrences[37] the omission of frankincense is explicitly indicated. It is obvious that in Ecclesiasticus frankincense and the term ‏קטר‎ are linked, and both refer to the meal offering. The only mention of ‏קטרת‎ ‏סמים‎ in the Hebrew text, and its equivalent σύνθεσιν θυμιάματος in the Greek text, refer to the merit of Josiah: ‏שם יאשיהו כקטרת סמים‎ "Josiah's name is like sweet incense"; and μνημόσυνον Ἰωσίου εἰς σύνθεσιν θυμιάματος "the memorial of Josiah [is] as sweet incense."

Josephus likewise confirms the extreme sanctity of the incense celebration and its veneration; it was the catalyst for divine revelation, the stage of prophecy. We read in *Ant.* XIII 282:

παράδοξον δέ τι περὶ τοῦ ἀρχιερέως ὑρκανοῦ λέγεται τίνα τρόπον αὐτῷ τὸ θεῖον εἰς λόγους ἦλθεν, φασὶ γὰρ, ὅτι κατ' ἐκείνην τὴν

---

[33] Hebrew text edited by A.S. Hartom, following Cassuto (Tel Aviv, 1963), from Hebrew manuscripts, where available. Greek texts from Ziegler's *Septuaginta*.

[34] Here too the Greek text is somewhat different than Cassuto's text; verse 16 reads προσαγαγεῖν κάρπωσιν κυρίῳ θυμίαμα καὶ εὐωδίαν εἰς μνημόσυνον. I prefer the Hebrew version, in which the original was written, and the emendation executed by the Jerusalem Academy of the Hebrew Language, as quoted by Cassuto. We encounter the same Hebrew reading in M. Z. Segal, ‏ספר בן סירא השלם‎ and in A. Kahana's Hebrew translation of the Apocrypha ‏הספרים החיצוניים‎. The *Anchor Bible, The Wisdom of Ben Sira* and *The New Oxford Bible* follow the Greek text instead. In the first we read: "To burn sacrifices of sweet odour for a memorial," and in the latter we read: "Incense and a pleasing odour as a memorial portion." In fact these interpretations do not oppose my proposition that Ben Sira referred to the grain offering in this verse, and the *Anchor Bible* interpreter also declares in his Comment, p. 522: "The wording of 45: 16c comes from Lev. 2: 2,9 [the rules for the grain offering]." One also observes that the Greek translator has changed the flow of the Hebrew text, and has omitted the verb for the "incense" offering, if such occurred in the original text. The verbs ‏נגש‎ and προσάγω, respectively, are not appropriate for the burning of incense. On the other hand, the term ‏קטר‎ is appropriate for the burning of incense, and as we have seen, is used to equate the two parallel but distinct cult activities ‏קטר‎ and ‏זבח‎.

[35] Lev. 2: 2; 2: 16 and 6: 8.

[36] Lev. 2: 9 referring to the baked *Minhah*.

[37] Lev. 5: 12, referring to the sin *Minhah*, and Num. 5: 26, referring to the jealousy *Minhah*.

ἡμέραν καθ ᾽ἣν οἱ παῖδες αὐτοῦ τῷ Κυζικηνῷ συνέβαλον αὐτὸς ἐν
τῷ ναῷ θυμιῶν μόνος ὢν ἀρχιερεὺς ἀκούσειε φωνῆς ὡς οἱ παῖδες
αὐτοῦ νενικήκασιν ἀρτίως τὸν ᾽Αντίοχον,

Now about the high priest Hyrcanus an extraordinary story is told
how the deity communicated with him, for they say that on the very
day on which his sons fought with Cyzicenus, Hyrcanus, who was
alone in the temple, burning incense as high priest, heard a voice
saying that his sons had just defeated Antiochos.

Philo, who interprets all the Pentateuchal laws allegorically, establishes the
incense celebration at a higher echelon than the animal offerings, as it
consumes a "divine" rather than a "human" substance. In *The Special Laws*,
I: 171, we read:

ὡς εἶναι τὰ μὲν ἔναιμα εὐχαριστίαν ὑπὲρ ἡμῶν τῶν ἐναίμων τὰ δὲ
θυμιάματα ὑπὲρ τοῦ ἡγεμονικοῦ τοῦ ἐν ἡμῖν λογικοῦ πνεύματος
ὅπερ ἐμορφώθη πρὸς ἀρχέτυπον ἰδέαν εἰκόνος θείας.

Thus the blood offerings serve as thanksgivings for the blood elements
in ourselves and the incense offerings for our dominant part, the rational spirit-force within us which was shaped according to the archetypal
form of the divine image.[38]

As reflected in the Mishnah, the daily incense celebration on the special
golden altar had become firmly established by the Second Temple period.
We can establish this from citations in tractates Tamid and Yoma, in which
exact rules and practices are described to the smallest, seemingly unimportant details.[39] The only dispute which is reflected between the Pharisees and
Sadducees concerned the archaic incense ceremony on a censer, which in
their period was celebrated once yearly on the Day of Atonement. It is
natural that we would encounter divergent opinions on an obsolete performance celebrated only once yearly, whereas the new daily custom became
familiar and was accepted by all.

---

[38]   Trans. F. H. Colson (London: Loeb Classical Library, 1939).

[39]   For example, we read in Mishnah Tamid 5: 2: אמר להם חדשים לקטורת באו והפיסו
"[The supervisor] said to them: New ones [priests who had never before performed the
incense celebration] come and cast the lot!"; we then read in the following mishnaiot
of the way in which the winner was to proceed, the precise form and size of the incense
spoon, the manner in which the coals were to be taken from the holocaust altar, and so
forth. A specific procedure for the removal of the ashes from the incense altar was
introduced, although Scripture indicates such a procedure only for the holocaust altar.

The utmost significance of the incense celebration in the period of the Second Temple is also confirmed by the New Testament. We read in Luke 1: 9-11:

> κατὰ τὸ ἔθος τῆς ἱερατείας ἔλαχεν τοῦ θυμιᾶσαι εἰσελθὼν εἰς τὸν ναὸν τοῦ κυρίου, καὶ πᾶν τὸ πλῆθος ἦν τοῦ λαοῦ προσευχόμενον ἔξω τῇ ὥρᾳ τοῦ θυμιάματος. ὤφθη δὲ αὐτῷ ἄγγελος κυρίου ἑστὼς ἐκ δεξιῶν τοῦ θυσιαστηρίου τοῦ θυμιάματος.

> He [Zechariah] was chosen by lot, according to the custom of the priesthood, to go into the temple of the Lord and burn incense. And when the time of the burning of incense came, all the assembled worshippers were praying outside. Then an angel of the Lord appeared to him, standing at the right side of the altar of incense.

We observe here details of the same type as in the Mishnah, which attest to the extreme significance of the incense ceremony: the casting of a lot among the priests for the privilege of performing the celebration, and its glorification in the eyes of the people, who gathered for prayer at the same time as the incense celebration, as it was considered the most propitious time for supplication. And, as in Josephus' narration, Zechariah experienced communion with the Deity, receiving His message through an angel, who stood "at the right side of the altar of incense." Theophany is thus linked to the incense ceremony. The danger associated with the incense ceremony is similarly attested in verse 21: καὶ ἦν ὁ λαὸς προσδοκῶν τὸν Ζαχαρίαν καὶ ἐθαύμαζον ἐν τῷ χρονίζειν ἐν τῷ ναῷ αὐτόν, "Meanwhile, the people were waiting for Zechariah and wondering why he stayed so long in the temple"; the people, in other words, were worried[40] that something harmful had occurred to him during his encounter with the Deity

I quoted in this study[41] a passage from the Epistle to the Hebrews which describes the location of the golden altar of incense in the Most Holy Place, thus demonstrating its importance. We read there in 9: 3-4: μετὰ δὲ τὸ δεύτερον καταπέτασμα σκηνὴ ἡ λεγομένη Ἅγια Ἁγίων χρυσοῦν ἔχουσα

---

[40]   The term θαυμάζω can be understood as "to marvel" or "to be astonished," the context determining whether in a good or a bad sense: W. Bauer, *A Greek English Lexicon of the New Testament and Other Early Christian Literature* (first edition of Preuschen's dictionary of 1910 revised by Bauer 1928, reprinted Chicago, 1979). I think that according to the context in this case, one must consider the term as "to be astonished" in a negative sense. Many scriptural and talmudic quotations discussed in this study corroborate such an interpretation.

[41]   Chap. 3, sec. 3.2.2. .

θυμιατήριον καὶ τὴν κιβωτὸν τῆς διαθήκης "Behind the second curtain was a room called the Most Holy Place, which had the golden altar of incense and the gold-covered ark of the covenant." There is no other source which confirms the placement of the incense altar in the Holy of Holies, but the fact that the writer of this Epistle describes it so, as well as his comparison of the annual ceremony of the High Priest with the sacrifice of Jesus, indicate the significance bestowed upon this altar.

We encounter another occurrence attesting to the glorification of the golden altar and the incense ceremony in Revelation chaps. 8-10. There, an angel with a censer stands at the center of the grand, mystical "happening" in heaven. I shall quote only short excerpts from the pericope "The Seventh Seal and the Golden Censer":

> καὶ ἄλλος ἄγγελος ἦλθεν καὶ ἐστάθη ἐπὶ τοῦ θυσιαστηρίου ἔχων λιβανωτὸν χρυσοῦν, καὶ ἐδόθη αὐτῷ θυμιάματα πολλά, ἵνα δώσει ταῖς προσευχαῖς τῶν ἁγίων πάντων ἐπὶ τὸ θυσιαστήριον τὸ χρυσοῦν τὸ ἐνώπιον τοῦ θρόνου, καὶ ἀνέβη ὁ καπνὸς τῶν θυμιαμάτων ταῖς προσευχαῖς τῶν ἁγίων ἐκ χειρὸς τοῦ ἀγγέλου ἐνώπιον τοῦ Θεοῦ,

> Another angel, who had a golden censer, came and stood at the altar. He was given much incense to offer, with the prayer of all the saints, on the golden altar before the throne. The smoke of the incense, together with the prayers of the saints, went up before God from the angel's hand.

Thus we find the same pattern: the linkage of the incense with prayers, the proximity of the golden altar to the throne (as suggested by the above citation from the Epistle to the Hebrews), and the incense as the vehicle which conveys prayer to the Deity.

There is thus solid evidence demonstrating the utmost significance of the incense celebration in the later period of the Second Temple. Further, I postulate that the scriptural references to an "independent" incense celebration on an altar, as described in Exod. 30: 1-6, cannot be extended backwards in time; from the absence of reference to such celebrations in all ancient texts other than the P segments, we must assume that there were no such celebrations before that period. We must therefore speculate on the historical environment which might have provoked such a significant shift in the sacrificial cult; similarly, we may examine if, and to what extent, the change in ritual influenced modifications in other aspects of life in Judah, in that period.

6. The Development of the Incense Cult (Part II)

6.1 The Historical Factors

Throughout our analysis of the existing literary sources, we have seen the difficulties created by the traditional assumption that there was a daily incense celebration dating from the early period of the Tabernacle and continuing through the Second Temple period. I shall now present the opposing assumption. My hypothesis contemplates historical and cultural conditions prevailing in ancient Israel which fostered the introduction of a daily, distinct incense celebration and advanced its development; this led to the establishment of the punctilious ceremonial which attained its cardinal significance in the final period of the Second Temple, as we have seen in later texts. Although we have observed scattered suggestions of incense celebrations before Josiah's reform of the sacrificial ritual, the appearance of these celebrations is absolutely evident after this reform, in the many references in the book of Jeremiah. In addition to Josiah's reform, this period is marked by Mesopotamian influence, military and cultural. Another factor to be considered, specifically with regard to the incense celebration, is the arrival and greater availability of frankincense on the international market, including Judah, in this same period. It is the coincidental occurrence of these three elements which brought about the introduction of the incense ritual in Judah, and I shall now elaborate upon this postulate.

6.1.1 Foreign Influence and the First Occurrences of קטר in the Biblical Text

As verified by the numerous citations, the first use of the term קטר appeared during a period of Assyrian and Babylonian influence, first on the Northern Kingdom and then on the Kingdom of Judah.[1] Military and political dominance can induce cultural changes, and sometimes even a total cultural transformation; this postulate has been well corroborated in scholarly

---

[1] Concerning the various forms and occurrences, see chapter 1, p. 23, and sections 1.2.3, 1.2.4 and 1.2.6.

circles. I wish only to add that Scripture itself is aware of the cultural impact of the surrounding and dominant societies.[2] Reference to the burning of incense as worship to foreign gods appears first in the exhortations of the prophets active in the Northern Kingdom.[3] We read in Hosea 2: 15: את ימי הבעלים אשר תקטיר להם "the days she burned incense[4] to the Baals (2: 13 in NIV)"; in 4: 13: ועל הגבעות יקטרו "and burn offerings on the hills"; and in 11: 2: ולפסילים יקטרון "and they burned incense to images." In Amos 4: 5 we find the obscure phrase וקטר מחמץ תודה "Burn leavened bread as a thank offering." In Habakkuk 1: 16 we find the term קטר specifically connected to an alien cult: יזבח לחרמו ויקטר למכמרתו "therefore he sacrifices to his net, and burns incense to his dragnet". This connection is overwhelmingly prominent in Jeremiah, where the term is explicitly linked to alien gods, and associated with unusual practices, heretofore unknown. We read in 7: 9: וקטר לבעל והלך אחרי אלהים אחרים אשר לא

---

[2] Scriptural quotations are too numerous to cite. I will limit myself to a few representative verses. We read in Exod. 34: 15: פן תכרת ברית ליושב הארץ וזנו אחרי אלהיהם "Be careful not to make a treaty with those who live in the land; for when they prostitute themselves to their gods and sacrifice to them, they will invite you and you will eat their sacrifices"; in Deut. 6: 14: לא תלכון אחרי אלהים אחרים מאלהי העמים אשר סביבותיכם "Do not follow other gods, the gods of the people around you." The command to destroy the seven peoples of the land in Deut. 7: 1-4 has as its motive כי יסיר את בנך מאחרי ועבדו אלהים אחרים "For they will turn your sons away from following me to serve other gods." In Jud. 2: 12, we read: וילכו אחרי אלהים אחרים מאלהי העמים אשר סביבותיהם "they followed and worshiped various gods, of the peoples around them"; in II Kings 17: 15: וילכו אחרי ההבל ויהבלו ואחרי הגוים אשר סביבתם "They followed worthless idols and themselves became worthless. They imitated the nations around them." Recognition of the persuasive influence of a dominant power is encountered in Deut. 28: 64: והפיצך ה' בכל העמים מקצה הארץ ועד קצה הארץ ועבדת שם אלהים אחרים אשר לא ידעת אתה ואבתיך עץ ואבן "Then the Lord will scatter you among all nations, from one end of the earth to the other. There you will worship other gods — gods of wood and stone, which neither you nor your fathers have known."

[3] We have only one mention of קטרת from that period which does not apparently fit in this category, and that is in Isa. 1: 13 קטרת תועבה היא לי "Your incense is detestable to me." But one exception does not invalidate the rule; it is possible that the incense ritual, brought in from other cultures, penetrated slowly from the Northern Kingdom into Judah, and started to be used there in the legitimate worship of the God of Israel; therefore Isaiah included it in his exhortation against all ritual celebrations by unrepenting wrongdoers.

[4] See the next note. It is possible that in Jeremiah the term קטר may also have included the burning of frankincense לבונה, since this item appears for the first time in his writings; in the writings of the earlier prophets, it may well refer to fragrant woods, similar to the custom in Mesopotamia, as previously discussed.

ידעתם "burn incense to Baal, follow other gods you have not known"; in
11: 12: וזעקו אל האלהים אשר הם מקטרים להם והושע לא יושיעו להם "and
cry out to the gods to whom they burn incense; but they will not help
them"; in 18: 15: לשוא יקטרו ויכשלום בדרכיהם שבילי עולם ללכת נתיבות
דרך לא סלולה "they burn incense to worthless idols, which made them
stumble in their ways and in the ancient paths, they made them walk in
bypaths, and on roads not built up"; in 19: 4: ויקטרו בו לאלהים אחרים
ואסיקו ביה) אשר לא ידעום המה ואבותיהם "they have burned sacrifices (ואסיקו ביה
בוסמין in the *Targum,* "burning incense" in the RSV, and ἐθυμίασαν in the
LXX) in it to gods that neither they nor their fathers nor the kings of Judah
ever knew"; in 44: 3: ללכת לקטר לעבד לאלהים אחרים אשר לא ידעום "by
burning incense and by worshiping other gods that [neither you nor your
father] ever knew"; in 44: 8: לקטר לאלהים אחרים בארץ מצרים "burning
incense to other gods in Egypt."

The novel practice of burning incense[5] on the roofs,[6] the participation
of women in these particular rituals,[7] the distinctive nomenclature for the
rituals[8] and for the gods,[9] as well as the linkage of קטר "incense" with נסכים
"libations"[10] in Jeremiah and II Isaiah, all corroborate the postulate that we
have before us a new and recently introduced type of worship, established
in Judah as a result of foreign influence. Out of twenty-one occurrences of
the verb קטר in Jeremiah, twenty refer to idolatrous practices, and are
without a direct object. The only exception is verse 33: 18, which is a
legitimate celebration and has a well-defined direct object: מעלה עולה
ומקטיר מנחה, "to offer burnt offerings, to burn grain offerings." This corresponds to Ecclesiasticus, in which the term קטר refers to the *Minhah.*
One has the impression from the contrasting utilizations of קטר in Jeremiah that the use of incense for the legitimate worship of the God of Israel

---

5   I translate the Hebrew term קטר here as "burning incense," without confirming at this
    point the nature of the burnt or fumigated substance.

6   Jer. 19: 13; 32: 29; Isa. 65: 3.

7   Jer. 44: 15; 44: 25.

8   In Jer. 44: 19, in connection with אנחנו מקטרים, we read: עשינו לה כונים "that we were
    making cakes like her image." The same term כונים "and make cakes," לעשות כונים is found
    in 7: 18, without the term קטר, but associated with libations to "the queen of heaven,"
    as in 44: 19. The worship to this goddess consisted of special cakes which were burnt
    on the roofs, and libations were offered together with them.

9   The name of the goddess, מלכת השמים, appears only in Jeremiah: once in 7: 18, quoted
    above, and 4 times joined to the verb קטר in 44: 17, 18, 19 and 25.

10 In Jer. 19: 13; 32: 29; 44: 17, 18, 19, and 25.

was only at its beginning stages, and the term was applied exclusively to the burning of the bland, odourless grain of the *Minhah* with frankincense. On the other hand, in the later Malachi, we encounter קטר as a celebration to honour Israel's God: ובכל מקום מקטר מגש לשמי ומנחה טהורה "In every place incense and pure offerings will be brought to my name (1: 11)." I emphasize again that these citations do not specify the substance which was burnt, and this is still an open issue. From this textual evidence we may assume, with almost complete certainty, that the introduction of the incense ritual in Judah corresponds to the period of greatest Mesopotamian influence.

6.1.2 The Short-Term Impact of Josiah's Reform

I shall now approach the wider issue of Josiah's radical reform[11] of the cult and its implications for the development of Israel's forms of worship. The motive behind the abolition by Josiah and Hezekiah of all the *Bamoth*, including those dedicated to the legitimate worship of God, has been amply debated and need be of no concern to this study. My focus is on the people's reaction to these extreme measures, which were intended to drastically change the worship patterns of the masses. Moshe Weinfeld[12] has analyzed the kings' motives, and the probable reaction of the people. He writes (in free translation): "... this revolution, if it lacked an important goal – the issue of our research – would cause a rebellion of all the people against the reformer and the royal dynasty itself. In the realm of the people, the reform – without a valid motive – could be understood as a desecration of the holy, and not as a deed agreeable to the Deity. And surely such an attitude is evident from the Rabshakeh's discourse: 'And if you say to me: We are depending on the Lord our God – isn't he the one whose high places and altars Hezekiah removed, saying to Judah and Jerusalem: You must worship before this altar in Jerusalem (II Kings 18: 22).' We must conceive in our imagination the fatal consequences of this reform: a people attached with all its soul and its sacral custom to the local holy sites (the *Bamah* and

---

[11] I do not intend to elaborate on the reform movement which actually started with Hezekiah's actions, described in II Kings 18: 4: "He removed the high places, smashed the sacred stones, and cut down the Ashera poles. He broke into pieces the bronze snake Moses had made"; but the final drastic and brutal measures were taken by Josiah, and, in academic historical jargon, Josiah's "paternity" prevailed.

[12] Moshe Weinfeld, מיהושע עד יאשיהו (Jerusalem, 1992), pp. 156ff.

small temple) is suddenly removed from them by force, and for their replacement is offered another central Temple, to which the pilgrimage from
distant localities is not easy, and, for certain people (old and feeble), impossible. Moreover, a central Temple, with all its rigid established pattern,
removes and forcibly excludes the spontaneous and intimate religious experience to which they were accustomed at the small holy temples scattered all
over the land. The implication of the prohibition against the *Bamoth* at that
period was that the majority of the population was deprived of intimate
religious experience, and a religious vacuum was created among the people." M. Noth[13] has expressed essentially the same opinion.

Weinfeld contemplates the long-range effects of this reform, but I wish
to speculate on its short-term implications. The *Sitz im Leben* in Israel and
the attachment of the people to the local temples and holy places, as so
vividly described by Weinfeld, must lead us to consider the people's immediate reaction to these stern measures. We must assume two significant
factors: a) the likelihood that drastic and forced change generated an equally
strong reaction, and b) the probability that the new regulations were not
completely enforced by the king and his government at that stage of development of the administrative system. Under the most favourable conditions we could expect, as a result of the official prohibition, the disappearance of the *Bamoth* in public places,[14] but the government had no way of
eliminating personal cult celebrations,[15] such as the burning of cakes or

---

[13] M. Noth, *The History of Israel* (London, 1960), pp. 276-7: "The abolition of the local
      sanctuaries was an exceedingly violent infringement of the traditional religious life of
      the people. The limitation of all cultic activity to the one and only holy place in Jeru-
      salem reduced the number of cultic observances to an extraordinary degree and inevitably
      brought about a separation between everyday life and religious activity between which
      there had hitherto been a very close bond."

[14] Weinfeld writes in note 6, p. 157: "We have no evidence that 'Bamoth' were again
      rebuilt after Josiah's death," and quotes in this respect Y. Kaufmann, תולדות האמונה
      הישראלית, Vol. III (Tel Aviv, 1984), pp. 385-6. There is no affirmative evidence, but
      this does not preclude *Bamoth* having been rebuilt in some remote locations.

[15] Seventy years ago an extended debate took place on the origin of Deuteronomy and the
      reform; the main point of contention was whether Josiah's reform was practicable. See
      G. Hölscher, "Komposition und Ursprung des Deuteronomiums," *ZAW* 40 (1922),
      pp.161-255. K. Budde, who argues with Hölscher in his essay "Das Deuteronomium
      und die Reform König Josias," *ZAW* 44 (1926), pp. 177-244, does not deny the
      inherent difficulties and risks in executing the reform; he is merely disputing the
      assessment of Hölscher that the priests would not have tried to carry it out. He
      writes: "...sie gar nicht daran denken konnte, das abzulehnen, sondern, ob leicht oder
      unter Schwierigkeiten, ob mit gutem Gelingen oder mit allen möglichen Beschwerden,
      und die gestellte Aufgabe herantreten musste." ("[The priesthood] could not conceive

incense in private enclosures on roofs and in courtyards.[16] Such practices would be expected, considering the magnitude of the resentment against the abolition of the customary local sanctuaries, and such practices in fact occurred. The numerous reprimands by Jeremiah and the last Isaiah against the burning of cakes or incense[17] by the people, on the roofs[18] and in gardens,[19] serves as compelling evidence of this consequence of the reform. For instance, we read in Jeremiah chap. 7: וקטר לבעל "and burn incense to Baal (v.9)"; "The children gather wood, the fathers light the fire, and the women knead their dough and make cakes of bread for the Queen of Heaven. They pour out drink offerings to other gods (v.18)." It is also noteworthy that Ezekiel describes a "conspiratorial" mood in the narration of an incense celebration to the idols. We read in Ezek. 8: 12: "... have you seen what the elders of the house of Israel are doing in the darkness, each at the shrine of its own idol? They say, the Lord does not see us." Jeremiah also tells us of deeds performed in secret: "Can anyone hide in secret places so that I cannot see him? declares the Lord (Jeremiah 23: 24)." It is possible that this type of ritual started as worship to the God of Israel, as a reaction to the prohibition against the *Bamoth*, and was not opposed by the prophets, as discussed above; but later on, the pursuit of an alien custom degenerated and developed into idolatrous worship. And, as often happens, the trend of alien worship continued and grew in intensity, and possibly culminated in the performance of idolatrous rituals in public.

We read in Jeremiah 11: 13: "...and the altars you have set up to burn incense to that shameful god Baal are as many as the streets of Jerusalem"; and in 19: 5: "They have built the high places of Baal to burn their sons in the fire." These verses are not incontrovertible evidence of a reaction to Josiah's reform, since it is possible that the prophet was addressing events which took place during Manasseh's reign (which are clearly recounted in

---

of declining [the reform]; rather, whether effortlessly or with difficulties, whether with [a chance] of success or with all kinds of adversities, they had to proceed toward the execution of the assigned task.")

[16] Cf. N. M., Sarna, "The Psalm Superscriptions and the Guilds," in *Studies in Jewish Religious and Intellectual History* (Alabama, 1979), p. 281, at p. 292, re "the impact of the reformism of Hezekiah and of Josiah."

[17] As analyzed in the first part of the study, the verb קטר is usually used without a distinct object, and from the text it is not clear to what substance it refers.

[18] "All the houses where they burned incense on the roofs to all the starry hosts (Jer. 19: 13)."

[19] "A people who continually provoke me to my very face, offering sacrifices in gardens and burning incense on altars of brick (Isa. 65: 3)."

II Kings 21: 3-7),[20] and not after Josiah's reform. On the other hand, from a careful reading of Jeremiah's reproaches and chastisements, as well as the censures in II Kings of the last kings of Judah who reigned at that period, we gain a sense that it was not the kings who were the instigators of the idolatrous worship, but rather that it was the people who introduced and practised such rites. We do not know whether the kings could not, or would not, employ all their power to eradicate these cults, and whether that was the motive behind Jeremiah's censure of them. In contrast to Elijah, who confronted Ahab directly about his initiatives in introducing and practising idolatrous worship,[21] or to the prophet who castigated Jeroboam for his illicit sacrificial worship,[22] we do not find a similar approach in Jeremiah's encounters with the kings of his period. An attentive reading of the expressions used by the editor of Kings, in the condemnation of each monarch for his deeds, will also reveal a peculiar pattern with respect to the last kings of Judah. There is a marked difference between the precise reproaches directed at Manasseh and his son Amon, and the indefinite, stereotypical accusations against Jehoahaz[23]and the succeeding kings. The stereotypical nature of this accusation is particularly noticeable in the case of Jehoahaz. According to II Kings 23: 30, Jehoahaz[24] was the son of Josiah, of whom it is said: "Neither before nor after Josiah was there a king like him who turned to the Lord as he did – with all his heart, and with all his soul, and with all his

---

[20] "He also erected altars to Baal (v.3)"; "He sacrificed his own son in the fire (v.6)."

[21] "I have found you, he [Elijah] answered, because you have sold yourself to do evil in the eyes of the Lord (I Kings 21: 20)"; "He behaved in the vilest manner by going after the idols, like the Amorites…when Ahab heard these words (vv.26-27)."

[22] "By the word of the Lord a man of God came from Judah to Bethel, as Jeroboam was standing by the altar (I Kings 13: 1 ff)."

[23] We read in II Kings 21: 2-7: "He [Manasseh] did evil in the eyes of the Lord, following the detestable practices of the nations the Lord had driven out before the Israelites. He rebuilt the high places his father Hezekiah had destroyed; he also erected altars to Baal…he built altars in the temple of the Lord…he sacrificed his own son in the fire…He took the carved Ashera pole he had made and put it in the temple." We further read in II Kings 21: 20-22: "He [Amon] did evil in the eyes of the Lord, as his father Manasseh had done. He walked in all the ways of his father; he worshiped the idols his father had worshiped…He forsook the Lord, the God of his fathers." On the other hand, concerning Jehoahaz, it is written in II Kings 23: 32: "He [Jehoahaz] did evil in the eyes of the Lord, just as his fathers had done," with no specification of the nature of the alleged wrongdoings.

[24] It is interesting to note that in II Chron. 36: 1-4 the story of Jehoahaz is told with the same content as in II Kings, but the sentence "he did evil in the eyes of the Lord" is omitted.

strength (II Kings 23:25)"; however, we then read "He [Jehoahaz] did evil in the eyes of the Lord, just as his fathers had done (v.32)." The father, Josiah, was a most pious man, and yet here his son is accused of doing all the evil of his fathers![25]

The same obscure allegation is raised in II Kings against Jehoiakim, Josiah's next son, again with the phrase "all that his fathers had done,"[26] in plural. In II Chr. 36: 8, the accusations against him are also of an unspecified nature: "The other events of Jehoiakim's reign, the detestable things he did and all that was found against him...." Only in Jer. chap. 22 do we find specific charges against Jehoiakim; these are all of a moral nature,[27] and specified to be the basis of his punishment.[28] Chapter 36, telling of Jehoiakim's cutting of the scroll, also refers to political and moral issues, not to idolatry. Jehoiakim's son Jehoiachin is accused of having acted as badly as his father.[29] When it comes to Zedekiah, who was possibly also a son of Josiah,[30] the editor of II Kings carefully added to the stereotypic sentence that Zedekiah did evil "according to all that Jehoiakim had done" – not that his father had done, or his predecessor, Jehoiachin.

---

[25] One cannot escape the impression that this stereotypical sentence was corrected here to appear in plural, as was also done with respect to Josiah's other son, Jehoiakim, in v. 37. This was probably in order to avoid the "gaffe" which would appear if it were left in singular, as it does in the same phrase regarding Jehoiachin, 24: 9: "just as his father had done."

[26] II Kings 23: 37.

[27] I shall quote a few of the expressions used: "Woe to him who builds his palace by unrighteousness, his upper rooms by injustice (v.13)"; "But your eyes and your heart are set only on dishonest gain, on shedding innocent blood and on oppression and extortion (v.17)."

[28] "Therefore this is what the Lord says about Jehoiakim...they will not mourn for him... he will have the burial of a donkey (vv.18-19)."

[29] In II Kings 24: 9 the stereotypical phrase appears again, ending with "just as his father had done." In II Chr. 36: 9, we read only: "he did evil in the eyes of the Lord," with no mention of his father.

[30] We read in II Kings 24: 17: וימלך מלך בבל את מתניה דדו תחתיו ויסב את שמו צדקיהו "He [the king of Babylon] made Mattaniah, Jehoiachin's uncle, king in his place and changed his name to Zedekiah." Jehoiachin was the son of Jehoiakim, who was the son of Josiah, hence Zedekiah was Josiah's son; therefore, the editor had to change the usual expression "just as his fathers had done," and referred instead to what his brother Jehoiakim had done. The Hebrew text does not state explicitly that Mattaniah was Josiah's son (though the KJV in fact suggests this was the case); it merely states "his [Jehoiachin's] uncle," as the NIV translates it, which could also be Jehoiachin's mother's brother. However, a midrash in Keritoth 5b corroborates that Zedekiah-Mattaniah was Josiah's son. We read there הוא שלום הוא צדקיה ... ומה שמו מתניה "Shalom is the

The Historical Factors 199

It is obvious that these kings were not idolaters, and that their "sin" was their political perspective and their opposition to Jeremiah's policies and admonitions. This fact is clearly stated with respect to Zedekiah in II Chr. 36: 12-13: "He did evil in the eyes of the Lord his God and did not humble himself before Jeremiah the prophet, who spoke the word of the Lord. He also rebelled against King Nebuchadnezzar, who had made him take an oath in God's name." A talmudic midrash also attests to Zedekiah's right-eousness.[31] On the other hand, the subsequent verse II Chr. 36: 14 makes it clear that the people did sin with idolatrous practices: "Furthermore, all the leaders of the priests and the people became more and more unfaithful, following all the detestable practices of the nations and defiling the temple of the Lord, which he had consecrated in Jerusalem." (It is not clear which of the priests sinned: those outlawed by Josiah, which would be under-standable, or others).

Thus textual analysis supports the postulate that the masses did not willingly accept Josiah's reform and did not comply with the royal decree. It is probable that the later kings did not proceed against the transgressors with the same severity as did Josiah,[32] and were censured for this failure; for

---

same as Zedekiah...[in I Chr. 3: 15, we read 'The sons of Josiah: Johanan the first born, Jehoiakim the second son, Zedekiah the third, Shallum the fourth]'...and what was his name? Mattaniah." This would correspond to Jer. 1: 3: "Zedekiah son of Josiah king of Judah." On the other hand, we read in II Chr. 36: 10: "...king Nebuchadnezzar sent for him and brought him [Jehoiachin] to Babylon, together with articles of value from the temple of the Lord, and he made Zedekiah his *brother* king over Judah and Jerusalem." (This is the exact translation of the MT text, which has here אחיו, and so the KJV and the RSV have translated it. The NIV, however, interprets here "and he made Jehoiachin's *uncle*, Zedekiah, king," probably because of the LXX, which reads ἀδελφὸν τοῦ πατρὸς.) Based on this verse as it appears in the MT, Zedekiah was the son of Jehoiakim, not Josiah. It is not the purpose of this study to investigate the king's genealogy; I merely wished to justify the expression "possibly."

31   In the above midrash in Keritoth we read: ת"ר הוא שלום הוא צדקיה ולמה נקרא שמו שלום שהיה שלם (נ"א משולם) במעשיו "The Sages said: Shallum is the same as Zedekiah, and he was called Shallum because he was complete in his deeds." This midrash also appears in B.T. Horaioth 11b, and Rashi explains there: צדיק גמור הוה בעל מעשים טובים "He was a completely righteous person who did good deeds." There appears in Horaioth another inference: איכא דאמרי שלום ששלמה מלכות דוד בימיו "Others said Shallum, because the kingdom of the house of David came to completion [i.e. finished] in his days"; but there is certainly no hint that he was an evil king, even in this second talmudic opinion, notwithstanding the stereotypical sentence in Kings and Chr.

32   We observe pronounced differences in Jeremiah's accusations. With respect to the king's social injustice, Jeremiah denounces him personally, as in Jer. chap. 22, which starts: "This is what the Lord says: Go down to the palace of the king of Judah and proclaim his message there: Hear the word of the Lord, O king of Judah, you who sit

our purpose it suffices to have established indications that the masses replaced the forbidden worship at the local sanctuaries with other cultic ceremonies, and that the burning of cakes or incense in private dwellings became an ideal way to achieve a personal and intimate religious experience. As I argued above, the descriptions of these activities suggest that they were private cultic performances by the people, effected in an almost conspiratorial way; there is no indication of any public or official consent or encouragement. Nor is there any reference to animal sacrifices, which would have exposed the people in public, but only to fumigation of incense and cakes.

6.1.3 The Arrival and Diffusion of Frankincense in Judah

The third element which likely encouraged this specific aspect of the cult was the arrival and diffusion of frankincense in Judah at about this period. The first appearance of לבונה in the biblical books, other than in the P source, occurs in Jeremiah,[33] which demonstrates a certain, if only restricted, availability and use in Judah at that period (the end of the seventh and the first half of the sixth centuries). It is possible that some limited quantities of frankincense reached Judah earlier,[34] in the period of Azariah in the middle of the eighth century B.C.E. This king "was the one who rebuilt Elath and restored it to Judah (II Kings 14: 22)," and consolidated his father's conquest of the south of Judah,[35] defeating the Edomites: "He [Azariah] was the one who defeated ten thousand Edomites in the Valley of Salt and captured Selah in battle (II Kings 14: 7)." Azariah could therefore open the trade routes to Arabia and take control of the caravans bringing frankincense,[36] among other products. It is possible that the reference in II

---

on David's throne." On the other hand, in his chastisement of the people for their social injustice and idolatry, Jeremiah's censure in chap. 7 is directed to the people: "Stand at the gate of the Lord's house and there proclaim this message: Hear the word of the Lord, all you people of Judah who come through these gates to worship the Lord (v.2)." "Will you steal and murder, commit adultery and perjury, burn incense to Baal, and follow other gods you have not known (v.9)."

[33] Other occurrences are in II Isa. 43: 23, 60: 6, and 66: 3. We find a suggestion of greater supplies in Neh. 13: 5 and 9, where frankincense is already stockpiled in the Temple chambers.

[34] See Introduction p. 5.

[35] The report of his great army and conquests is expanded in II Chr. 26: 6-15. One may assume that trade and economic expansion were the motives behind his wars.

[36] למה זה לי לבונה משבא תבוא "What do I care about incense from Sheba (Jer. 6: 20)."

Chr. 26: 16 to his incense-burning ("... and entered the temple of the Lord to burn incense on the altar of incense") is anachronistic, but still has some kernel of truth; that is, frankincense was first introduced to Judah in his reign as a result of his conquest of the Arabian trade routes. However, since Judah lost Elath after a short period, in the reign of Ahaz,[37] it is probable that the availability of frankincense on the market was drastically reduced, or disappeared entirely, to reappear with increased volume and frequency in Jeremiah's period at the end of the seventh century. These suggestions concerning the earliest arrival of frankincense in Judah and its wider distribution in the sixth century are also supported by other scholars.[38] We may, therefore, affirm this state of affairs with respect to the arrival of frankincense in Judah.

6.2 The Centralization of the Cult and its Implications for the Priestly Status

It seems to me that another significant consequence of Josiah's reform of the cult and its centralization has been overlooked: the gradual transition from a sacrificial cult performed mainly by lay people to an exclusively priestly celebration system. The reform therefore had the full assistance of the Jerusalemite priests,[39] who foresaw its great advantages to them. The centralization of the sacrificial cult in one city, Jerusalem, and in one temple, instituted a "division of labour" within the system, which in due course also affected the incense celebration.

---

[37] It is beyond the scope of this study to investigate the bizarre report in II Kings 16: 6, that Rezin king of Syria "recovered Elath for Aram by driving out the men of Judah. Edomites then moved into Elath." See Martin Rehm, *Das Zweite Buch der Könige* (Eichstatt, 1979), p. 160, who discusses this matter and quotes other scholars. It suffices for our purpose to verify that Judah lost the south.

[38] See citations in Introduction p. 19-20.

[39] Adam C. Welch writes in "The Death of Josiah," *ZAW* 43 (1925) p. 259: "Obviously it [Josiah's reform forbidding worship at any centre other than the Temple at Jerusalem] would have the support of all the influential priesthood at the capital." Welch concludes his essay: "Patriotism and religion, as well as the interests of two organised bodies, the court and the priesthood, found it the natural means of effecting their common ends."

6.2.1 The Shift in Functions

The initial impact of Josiah's reform in this respect is a much debated issue,[40] and it is beyond the scope of this essay to investigate this impact on a broad basis. It will suffice to draw attention to the reported dismissal of certain priests, who had until then ministered in the local temples, from various sacrificial duties and privileges. The extent of their exclusion from the priestly functions is not clear from the text in II Kings 23: 9: "Although the priests of the high places did not serve at the altar of the Lord in Jerusalem, they ate unleavened bread with their fellow priests"; such exclusion seems in conflict, as scholars have observed,[41] with the law in Deut. 18: 6-8,[42] the theological basis of Josiah's reform, which grants to the provincial Levites similar rights to minister and partake of tithes. Josiah's reform created a two-tier system of priests, and set boundaries on the various cult performances, but one may assume that this process developed gradually, and probably in opposition to ingrained practice and conventions.[43] We may observe this progression in the contrast between the description of the "second class" priests in II Kings 23: 9,[44] and the evidence of the cooperation among the priests and Levites in II Chr. 35. [45]

---

[40] See, for instance, A. Yerushalmi, מפעלות יאשיהו ודורו א-ב (Tel Aviv, 1935); Y. Kaufmann, האמונה הישראלית (Tel Aviv, 1968), Vol. III, pp. 34-9, 81-112; S. Yeivin, ספר דינבורג (Jerusalem, 1949), pp. 31ff.; Th. Oestreicher, *Das Deuteronomische Grundgesetz* (Gütersloh, 1923); G. Hölscher, *Eucharistrion 1* (Göttingen, 1923), pp. 206-213; H. Gressmann, "Josia und das Deuteronomium," *ZAW* 42 (1924), 313-337; A. Bentzen, *Die Josianische Reform und ihre Voraussetzungen* (Kobenhavn, 1926); H. H. Rowley, *Studies in OT Prophecy Presented to Th. H. Robinson* (Edinburgh, 1950), pp. 157-174; S. Yeivin, "Davidic Dynasty," *VT* 3 (1953), 164; A. Alt, *Kleine Schriften I* (München, 1959), pp. 250 ff.

[41] See M. Rehm, *Das Zweite Buch der Könige*, p. 223; and M. Noth, *The History of Israel*, p. 339.

[42] "If a Levite moves from one of your towns anywhere in Israel where he is living, and comes in all earnestness to the place the Lord will choose, he may minister in the name of the Lord his God like all his fellow Levites who served there in the presence of the Lord. He is to share equally in their benefits...."

[43] The Korah rebellion relates only one such episode. Concerning the issue of the Levites' status, see the comprehensive summary in *Encyclopedia Biblica*, Vol. IV (Jerusalem, 1962), s.v. "Levy, Levites."

[44] In II Kings, we have no indication of the duties of which the provincial priests were relieved, nor of those commissions for which they remained authorized. Although the text does not mention any official duty, it does not seem reasonable that they received a perpetual share of the priests' allowances without performing any work. The expression "they ate unleavened bread" is also obscure, and does not grant us a precise idea of

We do not know precisely what sacrificial performances were carried out by the priests at the high places,[46] if any, since it is well known that lay people were performing their own sacrifices at these local shrines. Scripture offers abundant evidence in this respect; the Talmud acknowledges this evidence, and modern scholarship substantiates it. From Noah[47] on through the Patriarchs,[48] Moses[49] and later biblical personalities,[50] com-

---

the extent and type of their recompense. The Levites are not mentioned at all in II Kings. On the other hand, we do find in II Chr. chap. 35 comprehensive attestations of the cooperation between the priests and Levites, and evidence of a "division of labour" among them.

[45] If we compare this pericope with Ezekiel's accusations against the Levites in chap. 44, and contrast his suggestion there that their inferior status is a punishment for their evil deeds with the favourable attitude towards them in the Chronicles narrative, which is unquestionably of a later date, we must deduce that either their status was in flux, with various ups and downs before a final settlement of their rank and privileges, or that the author of Chronicles described conditions as he considered they "ought to be" instead of as they actually were.

[46] We have some indications of the priestly duties in I Sam. 2: 28; the interpretation of this verse is an issue much debated by scholars, and I too will later discuss its authenticity. On the other hand, this pericope refers to the priestly duties at Shilo, a central temple controlled by priestly families, at which the priests obviously enjoyed a preferential position. This was not the case at the local shrines; we may observe the striking difference between the custom at Shilo, and that at a local shrine. We read in I Sam. 2: 13-14: "Now it was the practice of the priests with the people that whenever anyone offered a sacrifice and while the meat was being boiled, the servant of the priest would come with a three-pronged fork in his hand...and the priest would take for himself whatever the fork brought up"; the priests, the "guardians" of the holy shrines, took a part of the flesh, and, as it seems from the text, the best part which they or their servants chose. On the other hand, in I Sam. 9, we read "for the people have a sacrifice at the high place (v.12)"; there are no priests, and the best portion of flesh, the thigh, the part of the sacrifice which was traditionally given to the priests (Lev. 7: 32), is offered to Saul (v. 24). The priests received their remuneration for their guardianship of the holy shrine, and not for the performance of the sacrifice. One must assume that there were certain priests of the high places who did receive recompense for their services, and who were compensated for the loss caused by king Josiah's reform (II Kings 23: 9).

[47] Genesis 8: 20.

[48] Genesis 22: 13; 46:1. (I have omitted occurrences which describe the altars built by the Patriarchs in which the sacrificial act is not explicitly mentioned.)

[49] Exod. 24: 5-6.

[50] Jethro, Exod. 18: 12; Gideon, Jud. 6: 19-21; Manoah, Jud. 13: 19; Elkanah, I Sam. 1: 3ff. I have not included Absalom (II Sam. 15: 12) and Adonijah (I Kings 1: 9), since Scripture does not state specifically that the "slaughterings" mentioned in these verses were "offerings" to the Deity; they may have been a type of "bribery" to the masses, similar to the well-known *panem et circenses*.

munities,[51] prophets[52] and kings,[53] many performed sacrifices and were not censured. The Talmud too acknowledges the fact that individual sacrifices were offered at the high places, and according to Rabbi Judah, a priest was not required in this case.[54] As to modern scholarship, I shall quote Rendtorff as representative of those who address this subject.[55] From the use of alternate subjects within Lev. chap. 1,[56] Rendtorff perceives traces of a transition from private offerers to priests in the various stages of the sacrifice. The offerer is cited in singular וְשָׁחַט, וְהִפְשִׁיט, וְנִתַּח, יִרְחַץ, יַקְרִיבֶנּוּ, יַקְרִיב, וְסָמַךְ and the priests in plural וְהִקְרִיבוּ, וְזָרְקוּ, וְנָתְנוּ, וְעָרְכוּ.[57] Further, at some stage of this transfer of the sacrificial performances from offerer to priest, the priests were certainly receiving a share of the offering. We observe this development even within the P source. In Lev. chap. 3, although we already find a division of functions between the offerer and the priest, which was probably a later revision of the original text,[58] there is no mention of any compensation to the priest. Such a regulation appears only

---

[51]   The "people of Beth-Shemesh [who] offered burnt offerings (I Sam. 6: 15)," a legitimate act, but who were punished "because they had looked into the ark of the Lord (v. 19)"; the people present at the inauguration of Solomon's temple.

[52]   Samuel, I Sam. 7: 9; Elijah, I Kings 18: 31ff.

[53]   Saul, I Sam. 13: 9 (he was reprimanded by Samuel for not awaiting the appointed time, but not for his sacrificial performance *per se*); David, II Sam. 24: 25; Solomon, I Kings 3: 4, and 8: 5.

[54]   We read in Mishnah Zebahim 14: 10: קרבנות הצבור קרבים במשכן, וקרבנות היחיד בבמה... ר"י אומר אין מנחה בבמה וכיהון "Public sacrifices are offered at the Temple, individual sacrifices [are offered] at the high place...R. Judah says: There is no *Minhah* at the high place, [nor] priesthood." (Rashi explains: וכיהון, כהונה דאפילו זר בבמת יחיד כשר "Priesthood, since even [the performance of] a lay person is proper at the individual high place.")

[55]   Rolf Rendtorff, *Studien zur Geschichte des Opfers im Alten Israel*, p. 111: "Allerdings wissen die älteren Texte nichts von einer Trennung der Funktionen des Opfernden und des Priesters. Vom Priester ist überhaupt fast nie die Rede; vielmehr zeigen die Texte z.T. eindeutig, dass der ganze Opfervorgang vom Opfernden selbst vollzogen wird." ("Certainly the older texts do not know of a division of functions between the offerer and the priest. There is almost no mention of the priest; rather some texts show unequivocally that the entire offering procedure was performed by the offerer himself.")

[56]   p. 100.

[57]   K. Elliger, *Leviticus*, pp. 27ff extensively analyzes Rendtorff's literary analysis of this pericope and the question of its period of redaction, as both issues relate to the demarcation between the offerer and the priest and their sacrificial performances.

[58]   See Elliger, *Leviticus*, pp.47 ff.

in Lev. 7: 29-35,[59] where it is justified by the Deity's surrendering of His share and assigning it to the priests. The institution of the priest's share of the sacrifices may have been a consequence of this gradual shift in the sacrificial functions, but might also have been an earlier custom, attached to a certain category of high place at which the sacrifices were performed.[60] M. Weinfeld[61] distinguishes between private and provincial high places, and the Talmud differentiates between במה גדולה "a great *Bamah*," and במה קטנה "a small *Bamah*,"[62] and between במת יחיד "an individual *Bamah*,"

---

[59] "From the fellowship offerings of the Israelites, I have taken the breast that is waved and the thigh that is presented and have given them to Aaron the priest and his sons as their regular share from the Israelites (v. 34)."

[60] We observe the differences between the regional and the local or personal sanctuaries. There was no involvement of a priest at Gideon's offerings, either at the one laid on the rock, or on the one offered on the built altar (Jud. 6: 20-28). At the local communal *Bamah* ("for the people have a sacrifice at the high place," I Sam. 9: 12), the thigh, the traditional priestly allotment, was given to Saul (Sam. 9: 23-24). On the other hand, at Shiloh, the regional sanctuary, the priests took "whatever the fork brought up (I Sam. 2: 14)." The priests' misdeed here was not the receipt of the flesh, but merely their seizing it by force, before the burning of the fat. Further evidence of the priests' financial interest in the sacrifices at the Temple is encountered in II Kings 12: 17: כסף אשם וכסף חטאות לא יובא בית ה', לכהנים יהיו "The money from the guilt offerings and sin offerings was not brought into the temple of the Lord; it belonged to the priests (v.16 in NIV)." The simple meaning of the text conveys the idea that the priests took for themselves all the monies for the trespass and sin offerings, but it is obvious that the Sages could not accept such an act, which was contrary to Scripture. We read therefore in Mishnah Sheqalim 6: 4: זה מדרש דרש יהוידע כהן גדול אשם הוא אשם אשם לה' זה הכלל כל שהוא בא משום חטאת ומשום אשמה ילקח בהן עולות, הבשר לשם והעורות לכהנים, נמצאו שני כתובין קיימין אשם לה' ואשם לכהן ואומר כסף אשם וכסף חטאות לא יובא בית ה' לכהנים יהיו "This homily [on the verse in Lev. 5: 19] was proposed by Jehoiada the High Priest [the High Priest involved in these matters]: 'It is a guilt offering; he has been guilty of wrongdoing against the Lord' [the English translation does not convey the idea of the Hebrew homily, which is based on the triple mention of the word אשם in this verse. Although the text is impeccable according to grammatical and syntactical rules, since a redoubling of a verb to emphasize it is common in biblical texts, it nevertheless allows for interpretative homily, to deduce some additional meaning]. This is the rule: Whatever is left over from [i.e. the surplus money after having bought] a sin offering and a trespass offering, burnt offerings should be bought from it, the flesh [goes] to the Deity, and the skins to the priests. Hence, we have two phrases: trespass to God and trespass to the priest, as it is said 'The money from the guilt offerings and sin offerings was not brought into the temple of the Lord; it belonged to the priests [II Kings 12: 17; verse 16 in NIV].'"

[61] מיהושע עד יאשיהו, p. 98.

[62] We read in Mishnah Megillah 1: 10: אין בין במה גדולה לבמה קטנה אלא פסחים "There is no difference between a great *Bamah* and a small *Bamah*, except the Passover sacrifice

and במת ציבור "a public *Bamah*." It seems that the priests were not involved at all in the private, small *Bamoth* and did not have any economic
interest in them. We read in Zebahim 119b: חזה ושוק ותרומת לחמי תודה
נוהגין בקדשי במה גדולה ואין נוהגין בקדשי במה קטנה "The breast and the
shoulder and the offering of thanksgiving bread are celebrated at the 'Great
Bamah' and are not celebrated at the 'Small *Bamah*.'" On the other hand,
it is evident that the priests did have a strong economic interest in their
recompense from the sacrifices at the "Great *Bamoth*" and at the Temple.
In the prophecy uttered against Eli's priestly family, concerning their exclusion from service, we read in I Sam. 2: 36: "Then everyone left in your
family line will come and bow down before him for a piece of silver and a
crust of bread and plead, Appoint me to some priestly office so I can have
food to eat." We encounter the same economic concern after Josiah's reform, as Josiah had to find a way for the disallowed priests to eat of the
"unleavened bread with their fellow priests (II Kings 23:9)."

6.2.2 Financial Aspects

The priests initially received their remuneration as "guardians" of the public holy shrines; it is evident that the financial situation of the Jerusalem
priesthood improved dramatically after Josiah's reform, when they attained
their unique and exclusive position as sole guardians of the single temple at
which sacrifices could be offered. Such a "windfall" event must have had a
number of significant consequences on the further development of the cult
and the empowerment of an oligarchic priestly class. The concentration of
the sacrificial cult in a single place, controlled by a particular group or clan

---

[which is not allowed at the small *Bamah*]." In other occurrences in the Mishnah and
B.T. we find the other set of expressions. In Mishnah Zebahim 14: 10, we read
ומה בין במת יחיד לבמת ציבור "What is the difference between an individual *Bamah*
and a public *Bamah*"? The same nomenclature also appears in B.T. Pesahim 9a; Aboda
Zara 24b; Zebahim 11a, 119b, 120a; Bekhoroth 14b; Temurah 14b; Meila 3a. I do not
know the reason for the different names in the Talmud, but it seems that במה קטנה is
identical to במת יחיד, and במה גדולה to במת ציבור. Rashi on Mishnah Megillah states
with respect to במה קטנה: לבמה קטנה מזבח של יחיד שכל יחיד ויחיד עושה במה לעצמו: במה קטנה
"An altar of an individual; each individual makes a *Bamah* for himself." This equation
is also seen in the Talmud. We read in Zebahim 119b: אימא נוהגין בבמה גדולה ואין
נוהגין בבמה קטנה "I would say: It applies to a great *Bamah* and it does not apply to a
small *Bamah*," followed by ופליגא דרבי אלעזר, דאמר רבי אלעזר עולת במת יחיד "and
that is in opposition to Rabbi Elazar, since Rabbi Elazar said 'an individual *Bamah*'...."
We thus observe that the Talmud equates במה קטנה and במת יחיד.

of priests, enabled the priests to "institutionalize" the system and create precise rules and regulations for the various cult celebrations; the consolidation allowed the creation of an elaborate sacrificial system with precise regulations for the various offerings, and with an established rhythm of daily and yearly cycles. It gave these priests the authority to divide the sacrificial functions between the offerers and the priests. In contrast to the earlier custom, in which the offerer performed the actual act of sacrifice, the priests transferred most of the incidents of sacrifice to themselves, and left to the offerer only minor tasks, such as the placing of the hands on the animal's head, and its slaughtering, flaying, dissecting and washing. And with the growth of the priestly functions came the expansion and methodical definition of the priestly remuneration.[63] The establishment of an orderly system of compensation marked the culmination of the shift in priestly duties from the earlier assignments, such as guardians of the ark[64] and oracle,[65] to the performance of the sacrifices. One may thus speculate that Josiah's reform had an overwhelming influence on the "institutionalization" of the cult in all its aspects, and in the creation of a two-tier priestly class, as we have seen in II Kings 23: 9. The latter was a radical innovation, which might have constituted the ground for a vehement and relentless struggle between the two classes of priests,[66] hints of which seem to have been retrojected into the alleged Korah rebellion. Theocratic power and

---

[63] Concerning the link between cult centralization and the conveyance of the tenth portion to the clerical class in Jerusalem, see Hölscher, "Komposition und Ursprung des Deuteronomiums," *ZAW* 40 (1922), p.184.

[64] We observe in I Sam 7: 1 that the people "consecrated Eleazar his [Abinadab's] son to guard the ark of the Lord." Scripture does not inform us whether he was a Levite or a priest, but he must have been consecrated. We observe in II Sam. 6: 3-7 that as long as the ark was in the house of Abinadab (Eleazar's father), none were harmed, but when Uzzah, an unfit person "reached out and took hold of the ark of God...the Lord's anger burned against Uzzah because of his irreverent act; therefore God struck him down and he died there beside the ark of God."

[65] The priests were chosen "to wear an ephod in my presence (I Sam. 2: 28)"; David used the Ephod as an oracle: "And David said to Abiathar the priest, the son of Ahimelech, Bring me the ephod (I Sam. 30: 7)." Weinfeld, p. 108 and note 37, states that this is the last time we find the use of the Ephod as God's oracle before Solomon deposed Abiathar (I Kings 2: 26-27).

[66] As well as the basis of the struggle between Aaronites and Levites, an issue which is beyond the scope of this study. Concerning this issue of the Levites' status, see the comprehensive summary in *Encyclopedia Biblica*, Vol. IV (Jerusalem, 1962), s.v. "Levy, Levites."

economic interests[67] were firmly interwoven as a result of Josiah's reform;[68] this combination may serve to illuminate many issues, such as the exclusive political power of the priesthood in the post-exilic era, and the shift in importance of the incense celebration from an insignificant performance in the pre-exilic period to a rite of cardinal significance in the later period.

Josiah's reform induced, as we have seen, a polarization in the cult system, between the Jerusalem priesthood who aspired to centralize the cult and concentrate it in their own hands, and the common people who struggled to keep their high places and their accustomed spontaneous and personal worship in their own neighborhoods.[69] One must not discount an economic motive behind the people's struggle – that is, the desire to avoid paying the priestly compensation; but the people's persistence in keeping their old customs may be explained otherwise. What better solution to their problem existed than the practice of burning cakes and incense at their private shrines in their homes, roofs, and gardens? The coincidence of all the factors enumerated above served their needs perfectly. As I argued above, one has the impression that initially there was no opposition to this type of

---

[67] See Appendix II on the issue of the financial interests of the priests, and the development of the relationship between king and priest.

[68] As we have seen, the power struggle of the priests might have started earlier (this depends on the dating of the current final edition of the relevant pericopes). It is reasonable to speculate that in Josiah's period the priests, and especially the High Priest (if this title existed at that time) or the representative of the Jerusalem Temple priests, achieved dominance and collaborated with (or even induced) the king to impose the reform, as well as the prohibition against and destruction of the *Bamoth*, and the centralization of the sacrificial worship in Jerusalem. See Adam Welch, "The Death of Josiah," *ZAW* 43 (1925). For the sake of objectivity, I wish to note that Budde, in his essay "Das Deuteronomium und die Reform König Josias," *ZAW* 44 (1926), pp.177-244, states (p. 203) that the exclusion of the provincial priests from the sacrificial service in Jerusalem need not necessarily have been motivated by the financial greed of the Zadokite priests; their opposition to the provincial priests might have been driven by their religious concern, and anxiety to ensure that the pure and exact ritual of the Temple in Jerusalem was uniformly observed, as against the various customs prevailing at the provincial sanctuaries. We may note the parallelism in the narratives concerning the collection of money for the repair of the house of the Lord, by Joash in II Kings chap. 12, and by Josiah in II Kings chap. 22. In both sources, the High Priest is involved, and in Kings the title הכהן הגדול appears here for the first time after its mention in chap. 12.

[69] In his essay "The Post Exilic Origin of Deuteronomy," *JBL* 47 (1928), pp. 322-379, L. B. Paton expresses himself forcefully in this respect: "Drastic reforms do not at once win universal recognition. Ancient religious ways persist with extraordinary tenacity (p.335)."

worship at the private *Bamoth*, if it were not devoted to idols. This is the view of most of the scholars;[70] and it also seems to be confirmed by the fact that Ezekiel, a later prophet than Jeremiah, does not criticize the burning of incense *per se* by the seventy ancients of the house of Israel (Ezek. 8:10-12). The exclusive control by the priesthood of this type of worship had not yet been established, and it might legally be performed by anyone.

Upon the return from Babylonian exile, the zeal for reconstruction of the Temple in Jerusalem and the restoration of the sacrificial cult is understandable, and one must assume that this state of affairs allowed the priests an increased political influence. Scripture states[71] that Cyrus was commanded by God "to build a temple for him at Jerusalem in Judah (Ezra 1: 2; II Chr. 36: 23)."[72] The building of the Temple was seen as God's prin-

---

[70] In a recently published essay by M. Haran, 'מזבחות הקטורת' והפולחן של צבא השמים במלכות יהודה *Tarbiz* 61/3 (1992), he states (p. 330): "...a modest offering which consisted exclusively of cake and libation was also offered by individuals in places other than in the Temple in Jerusalem. But in the actual conditions prevailing after Josiah's cult reform, every offering brought outside the Temple in Jerusalem must have been considered as outside the legitimate worship of God." He does not offer any evidence to substantiate this statement; he merely quotes Isa. 57: 6, in which the prophet condemns the offerings of cakes and libations in many places. As Haran himself states, the prophet censures there the offerings to idols, together with other types of offerings such as the slaughtering of children שחטי הילדים, and the offerings of animals לזבח זבח. Moreover, this prophecy originates from a later date; therefore, I do not comprehend whence Haran deduces his postulate that private offerings of cakes were considered illegitimate right after Josiah's reform. However, even if this were the case my thesis would not be contradicted, since the issue would remain whether it was in the power of the authorities, political and religious, to enforce the prohibition against privately performed celebrations.

[71] The text demonstrates how the people of Judah viewed Cyrus' edict. For my thesis, the actual text of the edict is of no importance; it is only the manner in which it was interpreted by the Jews which is significant.

[72] In fact it was the policy of Cyrus and Darius to offer reverence to the deities of conquered peoples and to rebuild their destroyed temples. Cyrus returned the exiled gods to Babylon, according to *The Cambridge Ancient History*, Vol. IV (London, 1926), p. 13; and "Darius adopted as king of Egypt a name, Stitu-Re, that proclaimed his devotion to the god Re. He repaired the temple of Ptah at Memphis, and built the great temple in the oasis Khargah. He made offerings to the god and gifts to the priests (ibid. p. 25)." It was part of the Persian kings' administrative policy to attempt to legitimize their conquests: "As the empire grew and incorporated ancient empires of other faiths, the Persian kings sought and obtained the sanction of the religion of these countries for their sovereignty; Cyrus was called to the throne of Babylon by Marduk, and Cambyses and Darius in Egypt took names claiming relationship with the Egyptian god Re (ibid., p.185)." The recital of Cyrus' edict in Scripture is therefore certainly faithful to the

cipal objective, and the return of the exiles was merely a subordinate event, to provide the builders. Cyrus' edict in Ezra 1: 3 states: "Anyone of his people among you...let him go up to Jerusalem...and build the temple of the Lord." We observe the constant involvement of the priesthood and the High Priest in the post-exilic writings. This emphasis becomes more evident when we compare the narrative of the building and consecration of Solomon's temple in I Kings chaps. 7-8, in which the priests are mentioned only with reference to the ark.[73] In the later writings there are manifold instances of the involvement of the priests and the High Priest in all aspects of public life: political,[74] cultural and legal,[75] the Temple, the building of the wall and fortifications, and sacrificial service.

---

facts, if not to the letter, and one may perceive the advances which the priests gained in their relationship with political power, as a result of the edict. It is possible that the decline of Zerubbabel, and the Davidic royal family which he represented, started at this juncture in Israelite history. Building activities regarding the Temple had until then been the function of the kings; David planned its construction, Solomon built it, and Joash and Josiah initiated its repair. In Ezra, Haggai, and Zechariah, however, Zerubbabel is always encountered together with Jeshua the priest in connection with activities referring to the building of the altar and Temple.

[73] See M. Noth, *Könige*, pp. 177ff. who states that mentions of priests in the respective verses concerning the carrying of the ark are a later addition of the P school, to harmonize these verses with the regulations in Num. 4: 15. Regarding the phrase in I Kings 8: 3b וישאו הכהנים את הארון "and the priests took up the ark," he writes: "mit ihm hat ein Späterer von vornherein sicherstellen wollen, dass die heilige Lade nur priesterliche Händen anvertraut war." ("With it [the addition of this phrase], a later [editor] attempted to bespeak [the idea that] from the start the holy ark was entrusted only to the priests.")

[74] Ezra was a priest who initiated political decisions, and also arranged for the donations to the Temple (Ezra chap. 7).

[75] We read in Deut.17: 9: ובאת אל הכהנים הלוים ואל השפט אשר יהיה בימים ההם ודרשת והגידו לך את דבר המשפט "Go to the priests, who are Levites, and to the judge who is in office at that time. Inquire of them and they will give you the verdict." In the earlier writings, priests are not mentioned among the legal officers. We have a clear distinction between the priestly and judicial authorities and functions, in Jos. 8: 33: וזקניו ושטרים ושפטיו עמדים מזה ומזה לארון נגד הכהנים הלוים נשאי ארון ברית ה' "[The people] with their elders, officials and judges, were standing on both sides of the ark of the covenant of the Lord, facing those who carried it – the priests who were Levites." The judgement of Naboth the Jezreelite took place before הזקנים והחרים "the elders and nobles," as we read in I Kings 21: 11.

6.2.3 Divine Legitimation of Priestly Status

Upon carefully analyzing the text, we observe further significant changes in the status and concerns of the priesthood in the post-exilic period: in particular, divine involvement in the establishment of their status. Josiah's reform had created a division among the priests, based on the merits of their previous activity: whether they had been on the high places,[76] or in the Temple in Jerusalem.[77] Now we witness a new and original criterion, a genealogical standard. We read in Ezra 2: 61-62 and in Nehemiah 7: 63-64, "And from among the priests: the descendants of Hobaiah...these searched for their family records but they could not find them...." It is no longer the king who determines appointment to the priesthood, as David[78] and Solomon[79] did; it is genealogical descent, a choosing by God, which is determinant. The Korah rebellion and the Nadab and Abihu episode confirm the significance of appropriate lineage with respect to the various sacrificial performances, and are retrojected into ancient Israelite history to legitimate the move to divinely sanctioned exclusivity.

In the earlier discussion of these topics above, I cited numerous quotations from Chronicles which also point to the significance of the "right" descent; by this time it was therefore impossible to contest the priests' privileged status in the cult. The concentration of the cult in one location, in the hands of a divinely chosen oligarchy, miraculously validated by God, provided the priests with a great power; then, as today, power and wealth went hand in hand, creating a well-defined social establishment, and enabling their possessors to reach ever higher objectives.[80] That economic fac-

---

[76] II Kings 23: 9.

[77] We find an interesting parallel in Mishnah Menahoth 13: 10:הכהנים ששמשו בבית חניו לא ישמשו במקדש שבירושלים ... שנא' אך לא יעלו כהני הבמות וכו' ... הרי אלו כבעלי מומין חולקין ואוכלין ולא מקריבין "The priests who ministered at Onaias' temple should not minister at the Jerusalem Temple...since it is said 'The priests of the high places' etc. [II Kings 23: 9]...and they are like priests with blemishes, they divide and eat [the priestly allotment], but do not sacrifice."

[78] See II Sam. 8: 17, and I Chr.24: 3-6.

[79] I Kings 2: 35: "The king...replaced Abiathar with Zadok the priest."

[80] Maccabees II offers us an insight into the extent of the political power and wealth attained by the High Priests in the period of the Second Commonwealth, and the ensuing struggle to be appointed to this highly rewarding office. In 2: 3, we read of the great wealth in the Temple treasury, and in 4: 8-9, we observe the great amounts of money promised by Jason to the Seleucid authorities to ensure his appointment as High Priest. In 4: 24, we read that Jason's brother Menelaus further increased the

tors played an important part in the functioning of the priestly exclusivity
is evident from many scriptural texts. We encounter the issue of the allowances for the priests of doubtful origin, or Levites, a matter which had, as
it seems, a long period of struggle and development with rising and de-
scending intermediate periods,[81] until it reached its final stage. Contrary to

---

amount of the bribery, to ensure control of this office. Such sums would not have been
paid if the high priesthood had not been so financially rewarding.

[81]   An interesting sequence of events concerning the Levites' remuneration is encountered
in Nehemiah. We read in 12: 27: ובחנכת חומת ירושלם בקשו את הלוים מכל מקומתם
להביאם לירושלם לעשת חנכה ושמחה "At the dedication of the wall of Jerusalem, the
Levites were sought out from where they lived and were brought to Jerusalem, to
celebrate joyfully." Scripture does not tell us what their clerical activities and means of
subsistence had been up to that time, but we apprehend that from now on they would
receive their compensation from the treasury of the collected tithes and donations. We
read in v. 44: ויפקדו ביום ההוא אנשים על הנשכות לאוצרות לתרומות לראשית ולמעשרות
לכנוס בהם לשדי הערים מנאות התורה לכהנים וללוים "At that time men were appointed
to be in charge of the storerooms for the contributions, first-fruits and tithes. From the
fields around the towns they were to bring into the storerooms the portions required
by the Law for the priests and the Levites." But, as often happens, the greed of certain
individuals overpowered all regulations and good intentions, and we read in 13: 10 the
following sad account: ואדעה כי מניות הלוים לא נתנה ויברחו איש לשדהו הלוים והמשררים
עשי המלאכה "I also learned that the portions assigned to the Levites had not been given
to them, and that all the Levites and singers responsible for the service had gone back
to their own fields." Scripture does not tell us exactly what happened, and who precisely
did not give the Levites their share. Was it a result of the priests' control of the Temple
chambers (as we see in Neh.13: 5), where the tithes were stored, so that the priests did
not hand out the Levites' share to them, or did the people not bring the tithes allocated
for the Levites? Rashi, zealous to defend the priests' honour and reputation, writes:
שלא נתנו ישראל שם המתנות ועל כן ברחו והלכו להם "because the Israelites did not give
the donations there, they fled and left"; however, I think that from the context one may
deduce that it was the priests who did not give the Levites their share of the donations
brought by the people of Judah. We read in v. 13 the measures taken by Nehemiah to
avoid the same situation and to ensure that the Levites received their share and stayed
at the Temple: ואוצרה על אוצרות שלמיה הכהן וצדוק הסופר ופדיה מן הלוים ועל ידם חנן
בן זכור בן מתניה כח נאמנים נחשבו ועליהם לחלוק לאחיהם "I put Shelemiah the priest,
Zadok the scribe, and a Levite named Pedaiah in charge of the storerooms and made
Hanan son of Zaccur, the son of Mattaniah, their assistant, because these men were
considered trustworthy. They were made responsible for distributing the supplies to
their brothers." It is evident that such a committee, consisting of members of the
interested parties, the priests and Levites, together with a scribe to register the details
of the quantities received and distributed, and a faithful arbiter who enjoyed the confidence of both parties, would only be necessary to resolve the contentious issue of
distribution between the Levites and priests. This was clearly the mandate of the committee, "distributing the supplies to their brothers"; the committee was not instituted,
and had no power, to force the people to bring their tithes.

Josiah, who provided the ousted priests with the priestly allowance,[82] the post-exilic priests excluded them from partaking in their economic benefits.[83] We read in Ezra 2: 63 and Nehemiah 7: 65: "The governor (Tirshatha) ordered them, not to eat any of the most sacred food."[84]

Between Josiah and Ezra and Nehemiah, there is another post-exilic source referring to the relations between the priests and Levites. We read in Ezek. 44 about the abominations and sins of the Levites, and their demotion to an inferior status as punishment. On the other hand, there is complete silence there about their remuneration, although the prophet has an expanded narrative on the rules of the various donations to the "priests, the Levites the sons of Zadok (v. 15)." We observe another economic aspect of the cult centralization in the centralization texts themselves: Deut. 14: 22-27,[85] and 15: 19-20. The tithes and the first-born are to be brought exclusively to the central sanctuary.[86] We may also contrast the narrative of

---

[82] II Kings 23: 9.

[83] H. Gressmann writes in his essay "Josia und das Deuteronomium," *ZAW* 42 (1924), 313-337: "So allein ist die Entwicklung begreiflich...dass das Dtn mit seinem 'ideologischen' Charakter in der nüchterner Wirklichkeit sich nicht durchsetzem konnte." ("Only thus is the development comprehensible, that Deuteronomy, with its 'ideological' character, could not succeed in the first instance against stark reality.")

[84] Hölscher, p. 203, quotes L. Horst, *Revue de l'histoire des religions* XXVII 162ff., that it was logical that the Jerusalemite priests would oppose Josiah's rule requiring them to divide their allowances with the provincial Levites who had lost their privilege to perform sacrifices. "Croit-on que les prêtres de Jérusalem auraient jamais accepté cette concurrence"? ("Can one believe that the Jerusalemite priests would ever accept this competition"?)

[85] עשר תעשר את כל תבואת זרעך ... ואכלת לפני ה' אלהיך במקום אשר יבחר "Be sure to set aside a tenth of all that your fields produce....Eat the tithe...in the presence of the Lord your God at the place he will choose", and ואכלת ... בו ה' אלהיך אשר יבחר אל המקום שם לפני ה' אלהיך "and go to the place the Lord your God will choose ..eat there in the presence of the Lord your God (vv. 22-26)"; כל הבכור אשר יולד ... תקדיש לה' אלהיך לפני ה' אלהיך תאכלנו ... "Set apart for the Lord your God every firstborn male of your herds and flocks...eat them in the presence of the Lord your God (vv. 19-20)."

[86] R.P.Merendino writes in *Das Deuteronomische Gesetz* (Bonn, 1969), p. 383, concerning these verses: "Feststehende Traditionen, wie etwa die Abgabe des Zehnten vom Feldertrag oder das Opfer der Erstgeburten aud dem Gross- und Kleinvieh, wurden 'zentralisiert'. Diese Kulthandlungen durften nicht mehr am Lokalheiligtum stattfinden, sondern nur an jenem von Gott erwählten Heiligtum, in dem der 'Namen' Gottes wohnte." ("Entrenched traditions, such as the tithe of a tenth of the harvest, or the offering of the first-born of the herds and flocks, were 'centralized'. These cult activities were not allowed to be performed any longer at the local sanctuaries, but only at the divinely-chosen sanctuary, where the 'name' of God dwells.") The economic implications of these regulations, to the advantage of the Jerusalemite priests, are evident.

Hezekiah's reign in II Kings 18-20, and its parallel in II Chr. 29-32. The centralization of the Passover in Jerusalem, so vividly portrayed in II Chr. chap. 30, is immediately followed by the regulations of the tithes and donations to the priests and Levites. In II Kings, on the other hand, the initiation of the centralization process by Hezekiah is a contentious matter among scholars. It is certainly not clearly defined in II Kings, and there is no mention of the first centralized Passover ceremony; nor do we encounter there regulations for the distribution of the tithes to the clerics. The later editor of Chronicles, who had the ability to consider events from a later perspective, saw that the distribution of tithes was economically linked to the cult centralization process.

This monopoly had only one competitor, and that was the incense-burning celebrations of the private individuals; these, as we have seen, were not disallowed, or eradicated by Josiah's reform. The ready availability[87] of frankincense, and the sophistication of the fumigation celebration as a result, must have kindled a red light in the eyes of the priests, who attempted for their own reasons to maintain their exclusive control of the cult. The blending of frankincense with the *Minhah*, the cake sacrifice, which as we have seen in Jeremiah was celebrated by individuals in their dwellings, obviously encouraged this kind of ritual; as its practice expanded, it began to constitute a threat to the priestly monopoly of the cult. It would only have been natural for the priests to undertake some drastic measure to neutralize this danger, and at the same time to take control of the extremely lucrative incense trade, which was growing in importance in that period (the fifth century B.C.E.[88]) as it expanded into the Greek and Roman world. The alleged difficulties in the production of frankincense,[89] and the

---

[87] We observe the accumulation of frankincense in the Temple chambers (Neh. 13: 5, 9), and the occurrences of the term in Jer. (6: 20; 17: 26; 41: 5), II Isa. (43: 23; 60: 6; 66: 3), and Cant. (3: 6; 4: 6; 4: 14).

[88] Max Löhr, in *Das Räucheropfer im Alten Testament* (Halle, 1927), p. 157 states that Xenophanes (sixth century) mentions frankincense for the first time, but we encounter frequent occurrences in *The Histories* of Herodotus (Books III: 107-110; IV: 75; VI: 97; VII: 54) in the fifth century. Nigel Groom, in *Frankincense and Myrrh* (London, 1981), therefore states on p. 231: "The earliest classical author to provide evidence for the use of frankincense and myrrh from Arabia is Herodotus."

[89] Herodotus, *The Histories*, transl. A.D. Godley, Book III: 107: "Arabia...is the only country which yields frankincense and myrrh and cassia and cinnamon, and gum-mastich. All these but myrrh are difficult for the Arabians to get. They gather frankincense by burning that storax which Phoenicians carry to Hellas; this they burn and so get the frankincense; for the spice-bearing trees are guarded by small winged snakes of varied colour, many round each tree; these are snakes that attack Egypt. Nothing

high cost of transport, gave rise to high prices,[90] and assured its traders great profits. A protected monopoly for the supply of incense to the Temple service would guarantee consistently high profits, and constituted a strong incentive to the priesthood to dominate and manipulate the substance.

A simple prohibition would not have been effective in obliterating the private incense fumigation ceremonies.[91] The high places were forbidden, apparently successfully, as we have no record of their renewal, but incense-burning was now practised in private dwellings,[92] not on the high places as before.[93] A more sophisticated and positive strategy had to be devised. Thus the incense celebration was elevated from its usual category of common, or even auxiliary and secondary, worship, and became exalted through its appeal to the highest cult objective, namely theophany. Direct contact with the Deity was already subject to an ingrained set of restrictions in Israel, and these might easily be accommodated to this new objective; the fire and smoke created at the incense-burning ceremony matched perfectly the entrenched types of theophany already prevalent in Israelite mythology.

---

save the smoke of storax will drive them away from the trees. (109) The Arabian winged serpents do indeed seem to be many; but it is because these are all in Arabia and are nowhere else found."

[90] Groom, p. 8 writes: "Demand exceeded the supply...consequently the cost of frankincense and myrrh was considerable...the price could be equated to gold." Walter W. Müller mentions in his article "Der Weihrauchhandel der Südaraber in der Antike," in *Die Königin von Saba* (Stuttgart, 1988), p. 49, that Plinius complained about the unjustifiably high price of frankincense, caused not by alleged difficulties in its harvesting, but as a result of stringent religious regulations governing its collection.

[91] I wish to refer again to the above-quoted extended essay of Hölscher. We need not accept his statement concerning the origin of Deuteronomy, but it is interesting to note that he often considers the issue of whether the various rules imposed by Josiah's reform and the system of priestly remuneration were achievable in practice, or were merely idealistic theories.

[92] "...all the houses where they burned incense on the roofs to all the starry hosts... (Jer. 19: 13)"; "...they will burn it down, along with the houses where the people provoked me to anger by burning incense on the roofs to Baal (Jer. 32: 29)." As we have established, Jeremiah's censure of these deeds was due to their idolatrous dedication, not because they were an illegitimate act of worship per se.

[93] The censure in Kings states stereotypically: "The high places, however, were not removed; the people continued to offer sacrifices and burn incense there (II Kings 12: 4 in MT, 12: 3 in NIV)"; there are numerous other occurrences.

6.2.4 The Relationship Between Theophany and Incense

Smoke, cloud and fire are associated in Israelite mythology and in Scripture with the presence of the Deity.[94] For our purposes, it is immaterial whether the Deity appears as fire and smoke, or is curtained in a cloud[95] to disguise the presence; the theophany of the unseen Israelite God is portrayed in Scripture in all these ways. We can now approach the pericope in Lev 16 as a whole, and in particular vv. 2 and 12-13, which discuss the relationship between the smoke of the incense celebration and God's presence. We read in v. 2:

דבר אל אהרן אחיך ואל יבא בכל עת אל הקדש מבית לפרכת אל פני ...
הכפרת אשר על הארן ולא ימות כי בענן אראה על הכפרת

> ...Tell your brother Aaron not to come whenever he chooses into the
> Most Holy Place behind the curtain in front of the atonement cover
> on the ark, or else he will die, because I appear in the cloud over the
> atonement cover.

The stylistic difficulties of this pericope, due to the interjections of apparently unconnected verses which disrupt the natural flow of the commands, are discussed by Noth[96] and Elliger,[97] and I shall refer only to those discussions which are directly relevant to my hypothesis.

---

[94] For instance, the first covenant with Abraham, in Gen. 15: 17: והנה תנור עשן ולפיד
אש אשר עבר בין הגזרים "a smoking firepot with a blazing torch appeared and passed
between the pieces"; the guide in the desert: וה' הלך לפניהם יומם בעמוד ענן לנחתם
הדרך ולילה בעמוד אש להאיר להם "By day the Lord went ahead of them in a pillar of
cloud to guide them on their way and by night in a pillar of fire to give them light
(Exod. 13: 21)"; the revelation at Mount Sinai, in Exod. 19: 18: והר סיני עשן כלו מפני
אשר ירד עליו ה' באש ויעל עשנו כעשן הכבשן "Mount Sinai was covered with smoke,
because the Lord descended on it in fire. The smoke billowed up from it like smoke
from a furnace"; at the consecration of the Tabernacle in Exod. 40: 34: ויכס הענן את
אהל מועד וכבוד ה' מלא את המשכן "Then the cloud covered the Tent of Meeting, and
the glory of the Lord filled the tabernacle"; the Deity's encounter with Moses: וירד
ה' בעמוד ענן ויעמד פתח האהל "Then the Lord came down in a pillar of cloud; he stood
at the entrance to the Tent (Num. 12: 5)"; and even an outright description of the
Deity: ומראה כבוד ה' כאש אכלת "... the glory of the Lord looked like a consuming fire
(Exod. 24: 17)."

[95] There are numerous verses in Scripture concerning the theophany, all in connection
with cloud, smoke and fire, but different passages give different details. See Appendix
III for an examination of the relevant passages.

[96] M. Noth, *Leviticus*, p. 118 ff.

[97] K. Elliger, *Leviticus*, pp. 202-3.

The phrase כי בענן אראה על הכפרת, "because I appear in the cloud over the atonement cover," leaves us perplexed as to its exact meaning. In particular, the phrase כי בענן אראה "because I appear in the cloud" is, to say the least, ambiguous; does it mean that the Deity appears as a cloud; or does it refer to God's concealment in a cloud, or does it mean God will appear within the smoke of the incense brought in by Aaron? In Appendix III I discuss whether the cloud is God's image, or a concealing curtain, and indicate many citations which may be interpreted in different ways concerning the definition of the cloud. Another significant problem arises in the interpretation of the second part of v. 2, namely whether the Deity dwells continuously on the atonement cover, or descends there at the appropriate time for particular rituals. Elliger declares that this phrase does not indicate God's appearance on the atonement cover,[98] but rather the merciful concealment of the Deity's awe-inspiring presence. Beyond this, I have not encountered any scholarly discussion as to whether this specific phrase should be understood as meaning that God dwells on the atonement cover, which must then be concealed by the smoke of the incense, or that the Deity will appear at Aaron's invocation with the incense smoke;[99] it may be that this topic is considered to be subsumed within the general enigma of the character of the theophany. The traditional commentators were also aware of the enigmatic message of this text, and attempted various interpre-

---

[98] He states (p. 203) that this verse merely indicates the specific form of God's presence, illustrating his merciful protective concealment. On p. 211 he adds that the prohibition against meeting "Yahweh" at any desired time may be the result of an opinion that the Deity had taken up His dwelling there, as is suggested by I Kings 8: 11-12. The idea that the incense smoke functions as a merciful protective concealment of the Deity is a later theological development. Elliger considers the end of v. 2, "because I appear in the cloud over the atonement cover," and vv. 12-13, as additions made at the final redaction of this pericope.

[99] With respect to the Sinai theophany, in Exod. 19: 1-20: 21, both Noth, in *Exodus* (Philadelphia, 1962), pp.159-160, and Beyerlin in *Origins and History of the Oldest Sinaitic Traditions* (Oxford, 1965), pp. 6-11, consider this an issue of contention between the E and J sources. According to E, the mountain is seen as Yahweh's dwelling place, whereas for J the mountain is merely the place to which He descends. G. von Rad in "The Tent and the Ark" in his *The Problem of the Hexateuch and other Essays* (New York, 1966), pp. 105-6, declares that according to the P source, the Deity does not dwell constantly in the tent. Israel Knohl in מקדש הדממה, p. 150, n. 136 proposes contrasting opinions between P and D in this regard; whereas P's concept affirms God's constant dwelling in the Temple, D denies such a continuous presence. The character of the Deity's epiphany is the core of the divergence between the two sources.

tations.[100] One may even speculate that the same dilemma, regarding the referent of the cloud, was at the core of the known dispute between the Pharisees and Sadducees concerning the exact procedure of the incense celebration on the Day of Atonement.[101] The philosophy behind such ar-

---

[100] Rashi states, כי בענן אראה. כי תמיד אני נראה שם עם עמוד ענני. ולפי שגלוי שכינתי שם,
be-..." יזהר שלא ירגיל לבא, זהו פשוטו, ומדרשו לא יבא כי אם בענן הקטרת ביום הכפורים
cause I am always present there with my cloud, and since the revelation of my glory is there, he should be careful not to get used to coming; that is the simple meaning. And the homiletic interpretation is: he should not come except within the smoke of the incense on the Day of Atonement." Rashi's simple interpretation of the verse is that the phrase כי בענן refers to the Deity, and indicates that God dwells on the atonement cover; the homiletic interpretation, on the other hand, is that the phrase refers to the cloud of incense inside which the priest should enter in order to meet the Deity. Ramban interprets the phrase in a similar way to Rashi's midrashic interpretation. Radak proffers another midrashic interpretation, using I Kings 8: 10-12: the phrase "because I appear in the cloud over the atonement cover" in Lev.16: 2 refers to the Deity's dwelling in future on the atonement cover in Solomon's temple, as is written in I Kings: ...the cloud"והענן מלא את בית ה'... אז אמר שלמה ה' אמר לשכן בערפל filled the temple of the Lord...Then Solomon said, 'The Lord has said that He would dwell in a dark cloud....'" Abarbanel, in his commentary on Lev. 16, disputes Rashi's simple interpretation that כי בענן refers to the Deity, and asserts that it refers to the cloud of the incense. He demonstrates that the simple meaning of the text does not correspond to Rashi's proposal: the text does not declare that the Deity is dwelling in the cloud, and further, the preceding phrase "or else he will die" has no logical connection to "because I appear in the cloud"; there is no reason for the priest to die should the Deity appear in the cloud. On the other hand, the connection between death and the cloud of incense is well established in v. 13: וכסה ענן הקטרת את הכפרת אשר על העדות ולא ימות "...and the smoke of the incense will conceal the atonement cover above the Testimony, so that he will not die." Rashbam understands that the phrase שהרי מתוך עמוד הענן אני נראה כל שעה על הכפרת ... does refer to the Deity: כי בענן ואם יראה הכהן ימות "since I am seen all the time in the cloud upon the atonement cover...and if the priest sees (me), he would die"; therefore God has commanded that the priest must burn incense first, to darken the house with the incense cloud when he enters. Ibn Ezra cites both possible interpretations: he (the priest) should make a cloud of incense, since I will show myself to him in the cloud, so that he may not die; and the second meaning, since I dwell in the cloud. We thus observe the difficulties encountered with the interpretation of this phrase by the commentators. As for the Sages, they proposed in B.T. Yoma 53a: כי בענן אראה. מלמד שנותן בה מעלה עשן"We deduce from this phrase that he [the priest] places a 'smoke generating' substance [in the incense]." The Talmud, as we see, considers that the phrase כי בענן refers to the incense, and thus that God will appear through the cloud of incense; but it does not elaborate upon whether the Deity dwells there continuously, or whether He descends for the epiphany upon performance of the prescribed ritual, and is then concealed by the cloud of the incense.

[101] We read in B.T. Yoma 53a ת"ר ונתן את הקטרת על האש לפני ה', שלא יתקן מבחוץ ויכניס

guments would be consistent with their general conceptions and social status.[102] Nonetheless, whether the Deity descends for the epiphany with the High Priest through the invocation of the incense ritual, or makes

---

להוציא מלבן של צדוקין שאומרים יתקן מבחוץ ויכניס. מאי דרוש: כי בענן אראה על הכפרת,
מלמד שיתקן מבחוץ ויכניס. אמרו להם חכמים והלא כבר נאמר ונתן את הקטרת על האש
לפני ה'? אם כן מה ת"ל כי בענן אראה על הכפרת? מלמד שנותן בה מעלה עשן. "They
taught in a *Beraita*: [it is written] 'He is to put the incense on the fire before the Lord'
[Lev. 16: 13], [that means] he should not prepare [put the incense on the coal] outside,
and then bring it in[to the Holy of Holies]. [This is said] to contest the pronouncement
of the Sadducees that he should prepare outside and carry it inside. What is their
interpretation? 'Because I appear in the cloud over the atonement cover' [in the cloud
of the incense, therefore Aaron must come into the Holy of Holies with the incense on
the fire]. The Sages replied: But has it not been said 'He is to put the incense on the
fire before the Lord'? Then what is meant by [the phrase] 'because I appear in the cloud
over the atonement cover'? That teaches us that he has to place a smoke-producing
substance on it." It is true that according to this rhetoric in the Talmud the Pharisees
also understood the "cloud" to refer to the cloud of incense, but the Talmud's rhetoric
is later, and does not preclude the existence of a different opinion regarding the core of
the Pharisee-Sadducee dispute. In fact the Maharasha refers to the above-cited interpretation of Rashi, and wonders that his midrashic interpretation – "he should not
come except within the smoke of the incense on the Day of Atonement"- could be
considered as a Sadducee opinion. He does not elaborate upon the Pharisees' conception, but we observe that the Maharasha connects the notion that the "cloud" refers to
the cloud of incense with the Sadducees' interpretation of this phrase. One might
assume that the Pharisees' conception was the complete antithesis. I have the feeling
that Maimonides also considered the meaning of the "cloud" the core issue of the
Pharisee – Sadducee dispute. In הלכות עבודת יוה"כ פ"א ה"ה he writes: ... ויצאו בצדוקין
והיו אומרין שקטרת של יום הכפורים מניחין אותה על האש בהיכל חוץ לפרוכת וכשיעלה
עשנה מכניס אותה לפנים לקדש הקדשים. הטעם זה שכתוב בתורה כי בענן אראה על הכפרת
אמרו כי הוא ענן הקטרת "And there came the Sadducees...and said that one places the
incense of the Day of Atonement on the fire in the Holy Place outside the veil, and
when the smoke rises, he carries it into the Holy of Holies. The reason for it [is that]
since it is written in the Torah 'because I appear in the cloud over the atonement cover'
they said that it is the cloud of the incense." By the talmudic principle מכלל לאו אתה
שומע הן "from the negative, you learn the positive," which Maimonides certainly
applies in his conjectures, one may deduce that the Pharisees interpreted the "cloud" as
referring to the Deity, in opposition to the Sadducees' opinion that it refers to the
cloud of incense.

[102] Even if we do not endorse the previously accepted idea that the Sadducees were mainly
a priestly movement, there is a general consensus that a number of High Priests were
Sadducees. Talmudic sources also confirm this situation, as we see from the oath and
admonitions recorded in Mishnah Yoma 1: 5, effected in order to ensure that the High
Priest did not perform the incense celebration in the mode of the Sadducees. As a result
of these circumstances, the Sadducees had an interest in enhancing their status, and the

possible the epiphany to the High Priest through His concealment by the incense smoke, does not affect the indisputable relationship between the incense ritual and Aaron's meeting with the Deity. We observe such a relationship from verses 12-13[103] of the pericope which establish the rules of this encounter; one must also consider whether these verses are related to the end of v. 2, though there are different opinions as to whether they are additions by the same hand or not. The location of these two verses regarding the incense celebration in the midst of regulations on animal sacrifices[104] is only one of the perplexities[105] in the structure of this pericope

---

importance of their ritual performances. The interpretation of the scriptural text to mean that the Deity will appear in the cloud of the incense brought in by the High Priest bestows enormous significance on the priest's act and status; he brings about God's appearance. On the other hand, the Pharisaic interpretation diminishes the significance of the High Priest's act. God is veiled in His cloud, and the incense celebration does not cause the theophany; it is merely a highly important celebration during the exclusive entrance of the High Priest into the Holy of Holies, and, consequent upon a later addition, performed only once a year. This incense performance is of great importance and associated with tremendous awe, as the High Priest encounters the Deity's presence, but it is not the celebration which invokes the theophany.

[103] vv. 12-13: וְלָקַח מְלֹא הַמַּחְתָּה גַּחֲלֵי אֵשׁ מֵעַל הַמִּזְבֵּחַ מִלִּפְנֵי ה׳ וּמְלֹא חָפְנָיו קְטֹרֶת סַמִּים דַּקָּה וְהֵבִיא מִבֵּית לַפָּרֹכֶת. וְנָתַן אֶת הַקְּטֹרֶת עַל הָאֵשׁ לִפְנֵי ה׳ וְכִסָּה עֲנַן הַקְּטֹרֶת אֶת הַכַּפֹּרֶת אֲשֶׁר עַל הָעֵדוּת וְלֹא יָמוּת "He is to take a censer full of burning coals from the altar before the Lord and two handfuls of finely ground fragrant incense and take them behind the curtain. He is to put the incense on the fire before the Lord, and the smoke of the incense will conceal the atonement cover above the Testimony, so that he will not die."

[104] Karl Elliger declares (p. 204) that these two verses concerning the incense ritual found amid the blood ceremony are a later interpolation. Like Abarbanel, he connects the end of v. 2 with vv. 12-13: "Es spricht alles dafür, dass 12f. mit 2 bg zusammengehört und ebenso sekundär ist." ("Everything illustrates that v. 12 belongs together with v. 2b and is likewise secondary [namely a later interjection].") He also asserts on p. 213 that the incense scene is post-exilic. Noth in *Leviticus*, p. 122 writes, "It could be regarded as a later addition," but also contemplates the possibility that "this censing belonged from the start to the material of this ritual" as preparatory to the blood sprinkling, and the verses describing it would be in the right sequence of the complex ritual. He then adds: "The act of burning incense does not yet assume the special altar of incense in Exod. 30: 1-10"; I will return to this statement below. It is interesting to note that Seforno, the traditional commentator, also questioned the insertion of the incense ritual into the blood sprinkling, and explains that after the slaughtering of the sin sacrifices Aaron's sins are forgiven, and he is now prepared to encounter the "light" of the Deity.

[105] Martin Noth writes in *Leviticus*, p.117: "It is evident at the first glance that the chapter is in its present form the result of a probably fairly long previous history that has left its traces in a strange lack of continuity and unity about the whole."

concerning the great cultic atonement celebration, the "kernel of the chapter, to which in the course of a fairly long time, and very unsystematically, many other elements have attached themselves."[106]

Beyerlin[107] understands the phrase כי בענן in Lev. 16: 2 to refer to the smoke derived from the "censer full of coals of fire in Yahweh's shrine," in which God appears above the atonement cover of the ark.[108] Noth considers the incense celebration by the High Priest approaching the atonement cover as an apotropaic measure: "The burning of incense would make the mercy seat above the ark, specially 'dangerous' through the divine presence, invisible."[109] As we have seen, he speculates that the "censing belonged from the start to the material of this (special atonement) ritual," but even in that case, the putting of "the incense on the fire before the Lord, [so that] the smoke of the incense will conceal the atonement cover...so that he will not die (Lev 16: 13)," is closely related to the presence of God at this ritual. However one interprets the phrase כי בענן , one cannot dissociate the latter parts of verses 2 and 13: ולא ימות כי בענן אראה על הכפרת "or else he will die, because I appear in the cloud over the atonement cover (v. 2)" and וכסה ענן הקטרת את הכפרת אשר על העדות ולא ימות "and the smoke of the incense will conceal the atonement cover above the Testimony, so that he will not die (v. 13)." Elliger has therefore concluded that the end of v. 2, and vv. 12-13, are an addition of the final redactor.

Whether or not we would agree with Beyerlin's theory that the appearance of a cloud "reflects a cultic arrangement from the earliest period of the Yahwistic community,"[110] "this does not at all require that the complete

---

[106] ibid. p. 123.

[107] Beyerlin, p. 134 ff.

[108] Beyerlin considers that the incense ceremony which served to hide Yahweh during the festival cult was actually the primordial theophany, from which descriptions of the Sinai theophany and its accompanying phenomena derived. Thomas W. Mann contradicts this assertion in "The Pillar of Cloud in the Reed Sea Narrative," *JBL* 90 (1971), pp.15-30, and contends that "the incense ceremony is from the late Priestly tradition"; he declares that "the link between the cloud of incense and the cloud phenomenon of Exod. 13: 21ff. (and the Lord went before them by day in a pillar of a cloud...and by night in a pillar of fire), is a later secondary accretion (p.19)." Mann does not dispute the connection between the cloud of incense and God's presence, but merely challenges Beyerlin's opinion concerning the primordial origin of Yahweh's portrayal in a cloud of smoke.

[109] Noth, *Leviticus*, p. 123.

[110] Beyerlin, p. 147.

gamut of cultic practices was also present at that time," as Mann rightly contends.[111] Regardless of when the cultic incense performance is thought to have originated in ancient Israel, there is no scholarly disagreement, it seems to me, that the incense celebration described in Lev. 16 is anything other than a priestly rendering. This statement reverts back to my thesis that the cultic association between the incense celebration and theophany, as well as the danger, were utilized, if not exploited, by the priests, or more precisely by certain aristocratic priestly families in Jerusalem, to secure the rights to an exclusive cultic performance of the highest degree and importance. Upgrading the significance of the incense celebration, and relocating it from the "commonplace" to the Holy of Holies, where an old established "taboo" prevented the lay person's entrance, made it impossible for lay people and common priests to perform the ceremony, and facilitated the acquisition of a total monopoly of the incense supply and of the celebration by these priestly families.

The achievement of this goal was not the consequence of a single decree, but rather the outcome of a lengthy development, likely with grim struggles between the interested parties, as we may observe from critical text analysis. Before speculating on the possible stages of this process, I would like to note that although the prohibition against any person, including a priest, being present in the Tabernacle was specified solely for the "atonement celebra-

---

[111] Mann, p. 19.

[112] We read in Lev. 16: 17: וכל אדם לא יהיה באהל מועד בבאו לכפר בקדש עד צאתו "No one is to be in the Tent of Meeting from the time Aaron goes in to make atonement in the Most Holy Place until he comes out...." It is not clear whether this phrase is part of the oldest text, or was added only later together with the inclusion of the incense ceremony in the atonement celebration. Noth, in Leviticus, p. 119, writes: "It must also be remembered that even elucidation of the pre-literary or literary growth-process still cannot decide the relative ages of the cultic customs and ideas contained in the separate elements." At any rate, the strict prohibition against any man's presence is limited to this specific atonement ceremony, and there is no indication anywhere else in Scripture of a similar interdiction at the daily incense celebration.

[113] We read in Mishnah Tamid 6: 3: פרשו העם והקטיר והשתחוה ויצא "The people withdrew, and he [the priest] burned the incense, prostrated himself and came out." Maimonides, commenting on this Mishnah, observes that "people" implies שיצאו כל הכהנים מבין האולם ולמזבח "that all the priests left the site between the Temple and the altar," that is, they had to leave not only the Temple itself at the time of the incense celebration, but also the section between the Temple and the altar. He relies on a statement in Mishnah Kelim 1: 9: ופורשין מבין האולם ולמזבח בשעת הקטרה "And [the priests – the subject of the antecedent rulings] withdrew from [the site] between the Temple and the altar at the time of the incense celebration."

tion,"[112] the same rule was applied at the daily incense celebration in the last period of the Second Temple.[113] The interdiction against approaching the censing performance was expanded both concerning time (every day, instead of only at the atonement ritual) and space (around the Temple, instead of solely in the Tabernacle). This prudence was due to the great danger related to the theophany at the incense celebration.[114] The admonition ולא ימות "so that he will not die," indicated solely for the atonement celebration, now encompassed the daily incense performance.

The element of theophany involved in the atonement celebration was also extended to the daily ceremony.[115] The announcement by an angel of

---

[114] I wish to remind the reader of the various midrashim I have cited in this essay concerning the dangers related to the incense celebration. I may also add the statement in Mishnah Yoma 5: 1: "ולא היה מאריך בתפילתו שלא להבעית את ישראל" "And he [the High Priest] did not lengthen his prayer [in the Holy of Holies] in order not to scare [the people of] Israel [who might be concerned that he had been injured during the dangerous theophany]." We also find an interesting midrash in Midrash Tanhuma *Parshat Tezaveh* 14 ד"ה ועשית מזבח מקטר קטרת: וכשהיה ענן הקטרת מתמר ועולה ופונה למעלה ונעשה כאשכול היה יודע שנתכפרו עונות ישראל ... ואם לא כסה ענן הקטרת (את הכפורת) היה יודע שהוא מת, שנא', וכסה ענן הקטרת את הכפרת ולא ימות, נמצאת אומר דכ"ג וכל ישראל מרתיתים בשעה שכ"ג נכנס לפני ולפנים עד שהיה יוצא משם בשלום "And when the cloud of incense spiralled and rose upward like a cluster, he [the High Priest] realized that the sins of Israel were forgiven...[but] if the cloud of incense did not cover [the atonement cover], he knew that he was going to die, as it is said 'the smoke of the incense will conceal the atonement cover...so that he will not die.' It resulted therefore that the High Priest and all of Israel trembled when the High Priest entered the Holy of Holies, until he came out safely." These midrashim attest to the dangers and to the people's anxiety on the Day of Atonement, but we have another ancient source which reveals the same attitude towards the daily incense ceremony, and we have no reason to doubt its authenticity in this respect. We read in Luke 1:10: καὶ πᾶν τὸ πλῆθος ἦν τοῦ λαοῦ προσευχόμενον ἔξω τῇ ὥρᾳ τοῦ θυμιάματος "And when the time for the burning of incense came, all the assembled worshipers were praying outside." We observe the great reverence and awe bestowed upon the incense ceremony by the fact that all the people prayed at that specific time. Zechariah also had an encounter with an angel of the Lord at the incense celebration (v. 11), a duplicate of the High Priest's theophany, and the people were anxious because of his prolonged stay inside. We read in v.21: καὶ ἦν ὁ λαὸς προσδοκῶν τὸν Ζαχαρίαν καὶ ἐθαύμαζον ἐν τῷ χρονίζειν ἐν τῷ ναῷ αὐτόν "Meanwhile, the people were waiting for Zechariah and wondering why he stayed so long in the temple." *The Greek-English Lexicon of the New Testament* by Walter Bauer translates the verb θαυμάζω as "wonder, marvel, be astonished" (the context determines whether in a good or bad sense). We may assume that in this case the writer intended it to express "astonishment and concern." We also observe that no persons whatsoever, not even priests, were in the Temple at the time of the incense ceremony.

[115] Prof. Revell commented in a note to me: "Surely we see similar expansions of the domain of a decree in the late development of a practice with no other intention than

the birth of John the Baptist at an incense ceremony celebrated by his father is well known,[116] and we have a similar story narrated by Josephus in *Ant.* XIII: 282 concerning Hyrcanus, the Hasmonean King and High Priest, who received at his celebration of the incense ceremony a communication from the Deity that his sons had won in battle.[117] We observe a belief in the

---

'to keep man away from transgression' or to 'put a fence around the Torah.' When did this concept originate"? I cannot answer the last question, which would be much beyond the scope of my study. I wish to emphasize the structural and logical differences between the general concept of a "fence around the Torah" and the specific expansion of custom in this case. The prohibition against eating chicken together with milk, for example, is the result of a logical consideration; if one may eat chicken with milk, one might easily forget the difference between chicken and other meats and assume that the consumption of other meats is also not prohibited. In our case, it would be illogical to decree a prohibition against attendance during a daily celebration performed by common priests in the Holy Place on the golden altar, because of a possibility that it might be confounded with a specific, once-yearly performance of a censer celebration in the Holy of Holies by the High Priest. Moreover, the Sages had confidence that the priests were well trained, and not liable to errors. We read in Mishnah Sabbath 1: 11: ומאחיזין את האור במדורת בית המוקד "One [may] intensify the fire in the 'House of the Hearth' [a building in the Temple with a constant fire]"; i.e. this may be done on Friday before dusk, and one is not concerned that the priests might do this on Sabbath. The Talmud (Sabbath 20a) offers the reason: כהנים זריזין הן "the priests are alert" – they know the rules and would not err, as Rashi explains. The exhortation "No one is to be in the Tent of Meeting (Lev. 16: 17)" is considered by the Sages to be a warning against the imminent danger, rather than an admonition not to trespass against a command. The prohibition against the High Priest entering the Holy of Holies "whenever he chooses (Lev. 16: 2)" appears in Maimonides' count of the מצות לא תעשה "negative commands," and the transgressor is liable to death by a divine act (הל' ביאת המקדש פ"ב ה"ג); in contrast, the admonition "No one is to be" is not counted by Maimonides among the commands, and there is no punishment mentioned in Maimonides' הל' תמידין ומוספין פ"ג ה"ג. We read there: "At the time of the daily incense ceremony in the *Heichal*, all the people withdraw." Maimonides uses a neutral style, which gives the impression of a custom, rather than a prohibition. Based on the above, I suggest that the expansion of the prohibition against entering the Holy Place during the daily incense ceremony is due to precaution, to avoid danger, rather than to prevent a possible transgression.

[116] See previous note.

[117] We read there: παράδοξον δέ τι περὶ τοῦ ἀρχιερέως Ὑρκανοῦ λέγεται, τίνα τρόπον αὐτῷ τὸ θεῖον εἰς λόγους ἦλθεν. φασὶ γὰρ ὅτι κατ' ἐκείνην τὴν ἡμέραν καθ' ἣν οἱ παῖδες αὐτοῦ τῷ Κυζικηνῷ συνέβαλον, αὐτὸς ἐν τῷ ναῷ θυμιῶν μόνος ὢν ὁ ἀρχιερεὺς ἀκούσειε φωνῆς ὡς οἱ παῖδες αὐτοῦ νενικήκασιν·ἀρτίως τὸν Ἀντίοχον. "Now about the High Priest Hyrcanus an extraordinary story is told how the deity communicated with him, for they say that on the very day on which his sons fought with Cyzicenus, Hyrcanus, who was alone in the temple, burning incense as high priest, heard a voice saying that his sons had just defeated Antiochus." We cannot tell

incense ceremony as dangerous, on the one hand, and on the other hand as an efficacious means of approaching the Deity for forgiveness of sins and supplication for future support. It is no wonder that such belief enabled the priests to bolster and validate their unique status within the cult, and possibly within the political leadership of Judah, in the eyes of the lay public. We have no hint or indication of any hostility or opposition by the people to these conditions, which were the rule in Judah in the Second Temple period.[118] Nor did the monopoly of the incense supply for the Temple affect the interests of the people, or incite their protests.

6.3 The Struggle for Priestly Exclusivity

6.3.1 Priests Versus Levites

Resistance to this exclusivity arose from within the clerical class, be it from the Levites, or from those priests outside the few aristocratic priestly families who had gained the upper hand. The means by which these families gained control are not precisely known, and do not represent the main issue of our investigation. On the other hand, we have fairly well documented information concerning opposition within the clerical group to the

---

whether this happened on the Day of Atonement or on another day. The High Priest had the exclusive right to celebrate the incense whenever he wished to do so, without undergoing the usual lottery procedure mandatory for the simple priests. We read in Mishnah Yoma 1: 2: כל שבעת הימים הוא זורק את הדם ומקטיר את הקטורת ... ושאר כל הימים, אם רצה להקריב מקריב "All the seven days [before the Day of Atonement] he sprinkles the blood and burns the incense...and on all other days, if he desires to celebrate, he does so." Josephus also does not state whether Hyrcanus was celebrating inside the veil, which would have been on the Day of Atonement, or at the golden altar, the daily procedure. One might speculate that had it been on the Day of Atonement, Josephus would have emphasized this fact.

[118] Josephus, *Ant.* XI: 111-112, links the favourable attitude of the people toward the rule of the priests with the sacrificial cult: καὶ οἱ μὲν ὑπὲρ τούτων ἐπιδαψιλευόμενοι ταῖς θυσίαις καὶ τῇ περὶ τὸν θεὸν φιλοτιμίᾳ κατῴκησαν ἐν τοῖς Ἱεροσολύμοις, πολιτείᾳ χρώμενοι ἀριστοκρατικῇ μετ᾽ ὀλιγαρχίας. οἱ γὰρ ἀρχιερεῖς προεστήκεσαν τῶν πραγμάτων ἄχρις οὗ τοὺς Ἀσαμωναίου συνέβη βασιλεύειν ἐκγόνους. "And so with lavishness of sacrifice in return for these favours and with magnificence in their worship of God, they dwelt in Jerusalem under a form of government that was aristocratic and at the same time oligarchic. For the high priests were at the head of affairs until the descendants of the Hasmonean family came to rule as kings."

control by such families of the incense supply[119] and of the celebrations. The deaths of Nadab and Abihu, portrayed as the sons of Aaron, the primeval Deity's chosen priest, due to the offering of alien incense within the Holy Place, and the rebellion of Korah, a Levite leader who protested Aaron's exclusive right to the incense celebration, offer us a realistic illustration of the intensity of the struggles, and of the cruelty of the solution: the total annihilation of those who contested the established order. The dissident act of Nadab and Abihu concerning the incense celebration is linked in Scripture[120] with the theophany at this ceremony, and the deadly danger associated with it. As we have seen previously, chapter 16 in Leviticus consists of a conglomeration of verses or parts of verses from different periods and editorial hands, each with its specific message. I cited Noth's assessment in this regard, and add now his remark that "the connecting thread (of the chapter) is probably not so much literary as textual and historical."[121] I intend, therefore, to speculate on the historical conditions and *Sitz im Leben,* as we may best envisage them, and attempt to compose a sequence of events which will give us a reasonable portrayal of the development of the incense ceremony. Derived from textual analysis of the various sources, such a conjecture will attempt to elucidate the stages which advanced the incense ceremony to the climax of the cult, and its consequential political and economic implications.

---

[119] We have some confirmation from Josephus concerning the controls on the use of incense, in his narration of the Nadab and Abihu story. Josephus states clearly that they were punished because they brought incense of a type used previously. We read in *Ant.* III: 209: δύο οἱ πρεσβύτεροι Νάβαδος καὶ Ἀβιοῦς κομίσαντες ἐπὶ τὸν βωμὸν οὐχ ὧν προεῖπε Μωυσῆς. θυμιαμάτων ἀλλ' οἷς ἐχρῶντο πρότερον, κατεκαύθησαν τοῦ πυρὸς "The two eldest, Nadab and Abihu, having brought to the altar, not the incense which Moses had prescribed, but such as they had used aforetime, were burned to death, the fire etc...." This demonstrates that at each specified time only incense of a specific origin was considered appropriate to be offered, and the use of any other incense, even if used before, was strictly prohibited and punishable by death. Prof. Revell asks if it is possible that Josephus was "just at a loss to explain the passage, as so many others"? I would answer that the passage still corroborates the fact that in Josephus' time only incense of a specific composition was considered appropriate, a fact which is confirmed from talmudic sources. If any type of incense were legitimate, Josephus could not have invented such a severe proscription, a transgression punishable by death.

[120] I cited previously various midrashic homilies which connected the Nadab and Abihu story with the Korah rebellion and king Uzziah's punishment (Azariah in II Kings), all related to the incense ceremony.

[121] Noth, p. 119.

I suggest that the biblical narratives point to a struggle which took place in three main stages during the development of the final form of the incense ceremony. It seems to me that with the elevation of the status of the incense celebration, through the link between its cloud of smoke and the Sinaitic cloud theophany, the first objective of the aristocratic priestly families involved the exclusion of the Levites – whatever this name and concept represented – from this significant and rewarding cultic performance. The narrative of the rebellion of Korah the Levite fits well[122] within this stage. The Korah clan was undoubtedly a prestigious family which zealously fought for its own interests, and was the leading power of the Levite group. Then as today, the leaders of a movement, who are generally its main beneficiaries, attracted a clientele, which conferred upon them the appearance of strength and merit. The prominence of the Korah clan appears clearly in Scripture. Exod. 6: 16-27 records the genealogical tree of the Levites, in order to demonstrate the lineage of Moses and Aaron. The lists starts with Levi in the first generation, and continues through the second and third; however, in the fourth generation, the list of descendants contracts, and in the fifth generation only the sons of Aaron and Korah are enumerated. This demonstrates the pre-eminence and power of the Korah clan. Since the Aaronite family won supremacy, only Aaron's descendant Pinehas is recorded in the sixth generation. The Levites lost their right to perform the incense ceremony, and were finally demoted to an inferior position.[123] It is

---

[122] It seems to me unnecessary to discuss the complexity of this narrative in Num. chaps. 16, 17 and 18. I may refer to Noth, who writes in *Numbers*, p. 120: "It is abundantly clear from the present text that in this complex of traditions several different elements have been united...that several, already fixed, literary sources have been worked together by a redactor." With this declaration he expresses a generally accepted scholarly theory on this issue. If we carve out the Korah mutiny from the conflated narrative, as well as the division of functions and rewards in the following chaps. 17 and 18, we see clearly that this text refers to an Aaronite – Levite conflict, with tragic consequences for the latter: we hear of no further claim or sedition on their part. We read in Num. 18:2: וגם את אחיך מטה לוי "your fellow Levites from your ancestral tribe"; in v. 6: ואני הנה לקחתי את אחיכם הלוים "I myself have selected your fellow Levites." Concerning the division of the rewards, we read in v. 21: ולבני לוי הנה נתתי "I give to the Levites," and in v. 26: ואל הלוים תדבר "Speak to the Levites." The entire chapter regulates the relations between the Aaronites and Levites. Noth gives the heading "Priests and Levites" to the pericope 17: 12-18: 32.

[123] We read in Num. 18: 2 concerning the Levites וילוו עליך וישרתוך ואתה ובניך אתך לפני אהל העדות "...to join you and assist you when you and your sons minister before the Tent of the Testimony." The Levites serve the priests, and the priests serve the Deity. The concept of the verb "minister", the Greek λειτουργέω used by the LXX in this

likely, however, that the members of the Korah clan retained their pre-eminent position. In the narrative of the Korah struggle in Num. 16: 32, we read that all of Korah's descendants perished: ותפתח הארץ את פיה ותבלע אתם ואת בתיהם ואת כל האדם אשר לקרח " And the earth opened its mouth

---

verse, has acquired a cultic meaning relating to a dignified religious or public service, but the Hebrew expression signifies a generic "service" in material affairs, when not in direct relation to the "service" of the Deity. We read in Gen. 39: 4: וימצא יוסף חן בעיניו וישרת אתו "Joseph found favor in his [Potiphar's] eyes and became his attendant," and in Gen. 40: 4: וישרת אתם "and he [Joseph] attended them [Pharaoh's officers]." Onkelos in Num. 18: 2 translates וישרתוך as וישמשנך from the root שמש. Sokoloff translates this verb in his *Dictionary of Jewish Palestinian Aramaic* as "to minister, serve, copulate," and the noun as "attendant, sexton, servant." In any case, whatever we perceive in the verb שרת in this respect, the Levites were finally subordinated to the Aaronite families, as is repeated in Num. 18: 6: לקחתי את אחיכם הלוים מתוך בני ישראל לכם מתנה נתנים נתנים לה׳ "I myself have selected your fellow Levites [the literal translation is "your brothers the Levites"] from among the Israelites as a gift to you...." Here they are further degraded, as in my opinion the expression "from among the Israelites," without any genealogical rank, stands in contrast to אחיכם "your brothers," a genealogical attribute. The same epithet appears in Num. 3: 9 and 8: 19, as Noth has correctly observed. And as a consequence of the "division of labour" in the cultic performances, a separation and differentiation were also established in the rewards. The priests receive the best parts of that offered to the Lord: כל חלב יצהר וכל חלב תירוש ודגן ראשיתם אשר יתנו לה׳ לך נתתים "I give you all the finest olive oil and all the finest new wine and grain they give the Lord as the firstfruits of their harvest (Num. 18: 12)"; בכורי כל אשר בארצם אשר יביאו לה׳ לך יהיה "All the land's firstfruits that they bring to the Lord will be yours (v. 13)." All the best of the land to the priests, in comparison to the inferior common parts to the Levites: ולבני לוי הנה נתתי כל מעשר בישראל לנחלה חלף עבדתם "I give to the Levites all the tithes in Israel as their inheritance in return for the work they do (v.21)." The Levites' inferiority is quite blatant in this verse; God communicated directly to Aaron regarding his rewards וידבר ה׳ אל אהרן ואני הנה נתתי לך את משמרת תרומתי "Then the Lord said to Aaron, 'I myself have put you in charge of the offerings presented to me...(v.8),'" but it seems from the context that the nature of the Levites' rewards was communicated to them through Aaron as intermediary. (As already noted above, this is one of the few occurrences in which God spoke directly to Aaron, without Moses as intermediary, and demonstrates the overall spirit of this regulation.) Further, a condition was attached to the Levites' reward: חלף עבודתם "for the work they do." We may note that when Scripture addresses the issue of the Levites and their reward, the verb עבד, which carries an association of a more inferior status than שרת, is utilized, to emphasize the distinction. Moreover, the Levites are commanded to offer a tenth of their tithes to Aaron מעשר מן והרמתם ממנו תרומת ה׳ "you המעשר must present a tenth of that tithe as the Lord's offering (v. 26)," and again ונתתם ממנו את תרומת ה׳ לאהרן הכהן, "you must give the Lord's portion to Aaron the priest (v. 28)." One has the impression that the literary style of this pericope on the Levites' compensation suggests castigation and punishment for their leader Korah's rebellion, narrated in the previous pericope, rather than reward for their proficient and meaningful services. It is conceivable that as a result of the decisive defeat of the Levites,

and swallowed them, with their households and all Korah's men."[124] It is clear that the all-inclusive expression כל האדם comprises all his family, and certainly his sons. Yet we read the opposite in Num. 26: 11, also part of the P section, following the statement that the earth swallowed Korah: ובני קרח לא מתו "Notwithstanding[125] the children of Korah died not." This statement must have been added so as to reconcile the narrative in Num. 16: 32 with the realities in that period: we encounter Korahites as various ritual performers in the Temple – as musicians,[126], gate keepers,[127] and

---

in their struggle for equality with the Jerusalemite priests, they also lost their share of the other sacrificial duties (assuming that Josiah's reform was not entirely successful in this respect, and certain Levites and provincial priests continued to perform some sacrificial, and not merely lower rank, duties). The narrative of the Korah rebellion does not portray the whole story of the intra-clerical struggle, with its probable fluctuations, and the transient victories and defeats of each party; it conveys only the final stage of affairs, after the Levites' conclusive defeat.

In Ezek. 44 we find a post-exilic accusation of another kind against the Levites, used as a pretext for their inferior status. There they are denounced for idolatrous practices, a charge for which we find no record in any other source. We find in vv. 12-13 very grave accusations, such as ישרתו אותם לפני גילוליהם ... ונשאו כלמתם ותועבותם אשר עשו "...they served them in the presence of their idols...they must bear the shame of their detestable practices."

[124] This is the NIV interpretation, which harmonizes with Num. 26: 11, but the plain meaning of the verse is that all the people of his family perished.

[125] The KJV adds this term, likely to reconcile between the conflicting verses. The LXX and Onkelos follow the MT text exactly, but Jonathan quotes midrashic explanations that Korah's sons were not involved in the rebellion, but rather sided with Moses, and therefore were not burnt by the fire or swallowed by the earth.

[126] We read in I Chr. 6: 16 (6: 31 in KJV) ואלה אשר העמיד דויד על ידי שיר "And these are they whom David set over the service of song"; in verses 22-23 "(37-38 in KJV) we read the lineage of certain Temple functionaries: בן אסיר בן אביאסף בן קרח בן יצהר בן קהת בן לוי ... "... the son of Assir, the son of Ebiasaph, the son of Korah, the son of Izhar, the son of Kohath, the son of Levi. We also read in II Chr. 20: 19 ויקמו הלוים מן בני הקהתים ומן בני הקרחים להלל לה׳ אלהי ישראל בקול גדול "And the Levites, of the children of the Kohathites, and of the children of the Korahites, stood up to praise the Lord God of Israel with a loud voice." There is no doubt that the term הקרחים "the Korahites" is identical with the sons of Korah; we observe this explicitly in I Chr. 9: 19 בן אביסף בן קרח ואחיו לביח אביו הקרחים "the son of Ebiasaph, the son of Korah, and his brethren, of the house of his father, the Korahites." The LXX translates the family names Kohathites and Korahites simply υἱῶν Κααθ and υἱῶν Κορε.

[127] We read in I Chr. 9: 19 הקרחים על מלאכת העבדה שמרי הספים לאהל "the Korahites were over the work of the service, keepers of the gates of the tabernacle." and in I Chr. 26: 19 אלה מחלקות השערים לבני הקרחי ולבני מררי "These are the divisions of the porters among the sons of Kore and among the sons of Merari." I have no explanation as to why the KJV uses here the name Kore instead of the usual Korah; in I Chr

Habitim[128] makers in Chronicles, and as musicians in Psalms.[129] One must assume that some compromise ended the struggle between the Aaronites and Korahites. The latter kept their status as a prominent priestly clan, and likely retained most of the benefits attaching to this status; however, they lost all rights with respect to incense.

The same incense ceremony which, when performed by the Levites, brought them death by "fire [which] came out from the Lord (Num. 16: 35)," served to commute God's anger, procure the benevolent, apotropaic aspect of the theophany,[130] and stop the plague,[131] when it was celebrated by Aaron, the appropriate priest.

6.3.2 Internecine Struggle

As commonly occurs when a particular group succeeds in securing for itself certain privileges, a struggle began among the members of the group for a greater share, or for the exclusive right to the acquired advantages.[132] The

---

9: 31 the same MT term הקרחי is translated in the KJV as "the Korahite". It is possible that the name "Kore" was taken from the LXX, where Kore is used for Korah.

[128] We read in I Chr. 9: 31 ומתתיה מן־הלוים הוא הבכור לשלם הקרחי באמונה על מעשה החבתים "And Mattithiah, one of the Levites, who was the firstborn of Shallum the Korahite, had the set office over the things that were made in the pans." It is not clear whether the term "Habitim" concerns "pans", as the KJV translates according to the LXX τοῦ τηγάνου, or the special daily Minhah of the High priest called חביתין in the rabbinical literature. The traditional commentator Radak considers it as "pan", but Mezudat David interprets it as the special Minhah of the High priest.

[129] For instance, in chapters 42, 44, 45, 46, 47, 48, 49, 54, 84, 87, 88 etc.

[130] The plague described in 17:13-14 (16: 48-49 in NIV) is introduced by the Deity's appearance in the cloud: והנה כסהו הענן וירא כבוד ה' "suddenly the cloud covered it and the glory of the Lord appeared (17: 7; 16: 42 in NIV)."

[131] ותעצר המגפה "and the plague stopped (17: 13; 16: 48 in NIV)."

[132] See, for example, Thomas Hobbes, *Leviathan*, ed. E. Curley (Indianapolis, Reprint 1994), Part I, chap. XI [2]: "...a general inclination of all mankind, a perpetual and restless desire of power after power, that ceaseth only in death...because he cannot assure the power and means to live well which he hath present, without the acquisition of more"; and in [3] "Competition of riches, honour, command, or other power, inclineth to contention, enmity, and war." In chapter XIII [3], we read: "And therefore, if any two men desire the same thing which nevertheless they cannot both enjoy, they become enemies." F. S. McNeilly, *Anatomy of Leviathan* (New York, 1968), p. 138, concludes Hobbes' opinion: "Because the power of one man resisteth and hindereth the effects of the power of another, power simply is no more, but the excess of the power of one above that of another: for equal powers opposed, destroy one another."

story of Nadab and Abihu represents this second stage of the contest for preeminence in the incense celebration; I suggest that the celebration had in the meantime been further upgraded in significance and exaltation, through its transfer from outside the Temple into the Holy of Holies. This measure ensured the exclusion of Levites and/or other eventual pretenders from its performance. We observe that the entire drama of the Levite-Korah rebellion was enacted outside the Tabernacle of the congregation,[133] whereas the Nadab and Abihu event seems, from the context and the midrashim, to have taken place in the Temple,[134] or in the Holy of Holies. In the case of Nadab and Abihu, we have a conflict among members of the same aristocratic priestly family; both were the sons of Aaron, who were allowed to enter the Temple, but were excluded from the highest-ranking ceremony, the incense celebration leading to the theophany.

The Levite-Korah rebellion reflects a public issue, a conflict between two large groups with vested interests, and was conducted before the entire people,[135] whereas the Nadab and Abihu struggle and its tragic outcome

---

[133] We read in Num. 16: 18: ויעמדו פתח אהל מועד "and stood... at the entrance to the Tent of Meeting."

[134] We read in Lev. 10:1: ויקריבו לפני ה' אש זרה "they offered unauthorized fire before the Lord," in v. 2: ותצא אש מלפני ה' "So fire came out from the presence of the Lord," and in Lev. 16: 1: בקרבתם לפני ה' וימתו "who died when they approached the Lord." Expressions such as "before the Lord" convey a direct encounter in the realm of the Holy Place. I have cited many midrashim which interpret these verses to mean that the sin of Nadab and Abihu consisted of their entry into the Holy of Holies.

[135] We read in Num. 16: 19: ויקהל עליהם קרח את כל העדה "When Korah had gathered all his followers in opposition to them...." It is unclear whether v. 17: 6: וילנו כל עדת בני ישראל ממחרת על משה ואהרן "But when the assembly gathered in opposition to Moses and Aaron (16: 42 in NIV)" referred originally to the Korah Levite rebellion, or to the Dathan and Abiram insurrection, due to the intermingling of "different traditions" (Noth, *Numbers*, p. 120) in this narration; however, other verses of this pericope, demonstrating the public interest in the dispute, must be related to the Korah rebellion, with its interdiction against incense celebrations by Levites and lay people. We read in 17: 3: ויהיו לאות לבני ישראל "Let them be a sign to the Israelites (16: 38 in NIV)." In v. 5, the message and its addressees are made even more explicit: זכרון לבני ישראל למען אשר לא יקרב איש זר אשר לא מזרע אהרן הוא להקטיר קטרת לפני ה' "This was to remind the Israelites that no one except a descendant of Aaron should come to burn incense before the Lord (16: 40 in NIV)." The exclusivity of the incense ceremony claimed by the Aaronites was at the core of the dispute, and one may assume from this text that a segment of the people sided with Korah, and opposed the change enacted by the priests. The teaching of the narrative is directed to the people, and not only to the Levites. The text refers here to the incense ceremony, the core of the rebellion; however, Onkelos and the other translators, who wrote their interpretations

echoes an internal affair among the priests. Contrary to the Korah affair, in which the people were involved both at the insurrection and its consequent lessons, there is no public involvement in the Nadab and Abihu narrative. Moses communicates God's message and admonitions about future conduct only to Aaron[136] and his two remaining sons.[137] The corpses of the deceased sons were carried out of the Temple by close relatives of the same Aaronite family;[138] the people were not involved in this drama, they had no interest in it, and they are not mentioned at all in this pericope. The internal nature of this conflict, and the exclusion from the priestly privileges of the losing branch of the Aaronite clan, is further substantiated in Num. 3: 4: וימת נדב ואביהו לפני ה׳ ... ובנים לא היו להם ויכהן אלעזר ואיתמר על פני אהרן אביהם "Nadab and Abihu, however, fell dead before the Lord....They had no sons; so only Eleazar and Ithamar served as priests during the lifetime of their father Aaron." Scripture testifies that they died childless, and this was the most effective way to exclude eventual "pretenders": descendants who might have tried to solicit priestly privileges on account of an Aaronite genealogy.

There was no incense altar at this stage,[139] and I would speculate that the first part of Lev. 16, which concerns the atonement celebration, originates from this intermediate period in the development of the incense ceremony.[140] Aaron was commanded to celebrate the incense element of the

---

at a much later date when all except the Aaronites were excluded from every legitimate sacrificial service, translated the verb קטר here with the term סלק, which includes all aspects of the sacrificial cult, and not only the incense celebration.

[136] We read in Lev. 10: 3: ויאמר משה אל אהרן הוא אשר דבר ה׳ "Moses then said to Aaron, 'This is what the Lord spoke of....'"

[137] Lev. 10: 6: ויאמר משה אל אהרן ולאלעזר ולאיתמר בניו "Then Moses said to Aaron and his sons Eleazar and Ithamar...."

[138] Lev. 10: 4: ויקרא משה אל מישאל ואל אלצפן בני עזיאל דד אהרן ויאמר אלהם קרבו שאו את אחיכם "And Moses summoned Mishael and Elzaphan, sons of Aaron's uncle Uzziel, and said to them, 'Come here, carry your cousins....'"

[139] Scripture records an incense ceremony with censers: ויקחו איש מחתתו ויתנו בהן אש וישימו עליה קטרת ויקריבו לפני ה׳ "[Nadab and Abihu each] took their censers, put fire in them and added incense; and they offered [unauthorized fire] before the Lord (Lev. 10: 1)." There is no indication of any golden or other specific incense altar.

[140] B. Levine, Leviticus, *The JPS Torah Commentary*, in his Commentary to Lev. 4: 6, finds an interesting comparison between the highly unusual blood rites prescribed for the sin offering of the anointed priest in vv. 16-21, and the Yom Kippur ritual, as set forth in chap. 16. In Lev. 16: 18 we read: ויצא אל המזבח, concerning the altar to be sprinkled with the blood of the offering. Levine interprets this as the incense altar, contrary to all other modern scholars with whose works I am familiar, and contrary to

atonement ritual with a censer[141] מבית לפרכת "behind the curtain (Lev. 16: 12)" so that וכסה ענן הקטרת את הכפרת אשר על העדות "the smoke of the

---

the simple understanding of the text. He writes: "In verse 12, 'the altar before the Lord' referred to the altar of burnt offerings; here, according to the context, it must refer to the incense altar. The sense of 'going out' should, therefore, be understood not as an indication that the High Priest left the Tent itself, but only that he came out of the Holy of Holies to the outer chamber of the Tent." For the sake of harmonizing Lev. 16 with Lev. 4, or to illustrate that there was no incense altar at the time when the Day of Atonement celebration was instituted, Levine interprets this phrase contrary to the text and context; this, of course, is equivalent to the rabbinic position, as we read in Mishnah Yoma 5: 5: זה מזבח הזהב : ויצא אל המזבח אשר לפני ה', and a clear retrojection of later ideas. The context does not require the interpretation of this altar as the "incense" altar; this is simply his opinion, based on other texts. In addition to the difficulties which even the traditional interpreters encountered with this interpretation (see the following notes), I would like to add that in Lev. 4: 18, the text is clear, stating: ומן הדם יתן על קרנת המזבח אשר לפני ה' אשר באהל מועד, whereas in Lev. 16: 18 we read: ויצא אל המזבח אשר לפני ה' וכפר עליו; the description of the place is absent. Further, we read in the preceding v. 16: וכפר...וכן יעשה לאהל מועד; hence the inner tabernacle was already purified before the priest's exit. We find the same order in the concluding verse 20: וכלה מכפר את הקדש ואת אהל מועד ואת המזבח, and here we must surely assume that the holocaust altar is meant; there is no other provision for its purification. There is also no rule concerning where to pour the remaining blood, as in 4: 7, and we must assume that since Scripture speaks about the holocaust altar, there is no need to specify it. On the other hand, in 4: 7, since the sprinkling is on the incense altar, there is a need to emphasize that the remaining blood is to be poured out at the holocaust altar. The similarities between the rules in Lev. chaps. 4 and 16 are striking and the necessity of comparing them is evident, but an examination of all aspects of these pericopes points clearly to the fact that the rules in Lev. 4 concerning the High Priest's sin offering were fashioned on the cult forms of Lev. 16, and not vice-versa. At the time of the writing of chap. 4, the golden incense altar was already in place. See further the next note.

[141] Noth writes in *Leviticus*, p. 122: "The act of burning incense does not yet assume the special altar of incense in Exod. 30: 1-10." The מזבח "altar" to be atoned for in Lev. 16 definitely refers to the outer holocaust altar; only in Exod. 30: 10, in the pericope commanding the construction of the incense altar, is there a connection between the latter altar and atonement: וכפר אהרן על קרנותיו אחת בשנה מדם חטאת הכפורים "Once a year Aaron shall make atonement on its horns. This annual atonement must be made with the blood of the atonement sin offering...." Elliger, in his analysis of the text (*Leviticus*, p. 200), does not explicitly declare that the outer altar is meant, but translates ויצא "dann geht er hinaus zum Altar" which must be interpreted "he went outside [the Tabernacle] to the altar," hence to the outer one. On p. 214, in his exegesis of the entire pericope, he writes that the cleansing of the sanctuary refers to its totality: "...des gesamtes Heiligtums mit Einschluss des im Hof stehenden Altars" ("...of the entire sanctuary, inclusive of the altar placed in the courtyard.") Here he states explicitly that in his opinion the altar refers to the outer altar.

incense will conceal the atonement cover above the Testimony (v. 13)";
there is no mention of a specific altar in this pericope. We do not know with

---

It is obvious that the Talmud does not agree with such an interpretation, and declares
at Mishnah Yoma 5: 5: ויצא אל המזבח אשר לפני ה׳ זה מזבח הזהב "'Then he shall come
out to the altar that is before the Lord [Lev. 16:18],' this is the golden altar." From the
context one must assume that this v. 18 refers to the outer holocaust altar; the previous
verse states: וכל אדם לא יהיה באהל מועד בבאו לכפר בקדש עד צאתו וכפר בעדו "No one
is to be in the Tent of Meeting from the time Aaron goes in to make atonement in the
Most Holy place until he comes out, having made atonement for himself...," which
demonstrates that the priest was in the Tabernacle, and then went out towards the
holocaust altar. His task is finished only when he has cleansed the Tabernacle and the
atonement cover inside, and the altar outside, as we read in v. 20: וכלה מכפר את הקדש
ואת אהל מועד ואת המזבח "When Aaron has finished making atonement for the Most
Holy Place, the Tent of Meeting and the altar..."; the altar here is unequivocally the
outer altar, to which he went out previously. The Talmud and Sifra are aware of the
textual difficulty in trying to interpret the term ויצא without implying the priest's exit
from the Tabernacle, and B. T. Yoma 58b and Sifra on v. 18 interpret the phrase to
mean "inside" the altar (that is, the priest stays between the golden altar, inside the
Tabernacle, and the veil), and "outside" (the priest stays on the outer side of the altar).
Thus the priest would stay behind the golden altar and sprinkle the blood upon it.
Malbim states clearly in his commentary to Sifra: עד עתה בעת הזיית הדם על הפרכת עמד
לפנים מן המזבח והצריכו הכתוב שיצא חוץ למזבח כולו "Until now, at the sprinkling of
the blood on the veil, he stood inside of [between] the altar [and the veil], and [there-
fore] Scripture said [that] he should [now] move to the [farther] side of the whole
altar." Neither the Talmud nor Sifra relies on the term לפני ה׳ "[the altar] before the
Lord," to imply the golden altar inside the Tabernacle, but Rashi in his commentary
to the above-cited Mishnah in Yoma states: דאילו מזבח החיצון לא לפני ה׳ הוא "since
the outer altar does not stay 'before the Lord' [but in the courtyard]." It seems that
Rashi distinguishes between the expression לפני ה׳ which refers to the golden inner
altar, and מלפני ה׳ which would refer to the outer altar. We read in v. 12 ולקח מלא
המחתה גחלי אש מעל המזבח מלפני ה׳ "And he shall take a censer full of burning coals
of fire from off the altar before the Lord." This verse refers unequivocally to the outer
altar, and contains the phrase "before the Lord." There are no coals of fire on the golden
altar; the Talmud in B.T. Yoma 45b deduces from this verse that coals should be taken
from the outer altar not only on the Day of Atonement but also for the daily incense
celebration. We read there: איזהו מזבח שמקצתו לפני ה׳ ואין כולו לפני ה׳, הוי אומר זה
מזבח החיצון "Which is the altar which is partly before the Lord, and not entirely before
the Lord? You must say: This is the outer altar." Rashi explains there that the added
preposition מ "from" gives the expression a partitive implication, and therefore it is
interpreted as "partly before the Lord." Only Ibn Ezra states expressly in his commentary to v. 16: 18: ויצא אל המזבח. הוא מזבח העולה "'Then he shall come out to the
altar.' That is the holocaust altar." But his own commentator could not conceive that
Ibn Ezra would interpret a verse in explicit contradiction to a Mishnah, and proposed
that the text of Ibn Ezra was erroneously printed as referring to v. 18, and really applies
to v. 24. The comment would be appropriate to that verse from the homiletic aspect,
but, in my opinion, does not fit from the textual and literary aspects.

what frequency[142] the atonement ritual commanded in Lev. 16: 1-28 was practised before the establishment of the once-yearly ritual, as imposed by the supplementary verses 29-34.[143] We must ask what the motive would have been in limiting Aaron's entrance into the Holy of Holies with the incense to once a year; we must also ask the reason for equipping the Temple, at a certain stage, with a new, specific altar for the burning of incense, and providing the means for individuals other than the aristocratic Zadokite priests[144] to gain a foothold in this mystical and exalted ceremony.

---

[142] Verses 29-34, which establish a precise date for the once-yearly atonement ritual, are a later addition to this pericope, according to scholarly opinion (see Noth, *Leviticus*, p. 126, and Elliger, *Leviticus*, pp. 200 ff ; the latter considers them as originating in the last redaction of the pericope). It seems obvious that the fixed date for the ritual, at the end of the pericope, contrasts with the introductory verses ואל יבא בכל עת אל הקדש "not to come whenever he chooses into the Most Holy Place (v.2)." Aaron's prescribed entry is not contingent on a certain date, but on a specific ritual, as follows in v. 3: בזאת יבא אהרן אל הקדש "This is how Aaron shall come into the sanctuary area." There is no indication, where one would expect it, "of a particular time or occasion when entrance was allowed or commanded," as Noth observes. The traditional commentators were also aware that the text, specifically the phrase בזאת יבא אהרן "This is how Aaron shall come," refers to the ritual which allows him to enter, and not to a date when he may go in. Rashi, in his commentary to Lev. 16: 3 writes: אף זו לא בכל עת, כי אם ביום הכפורים כמו שמפרש בסוף הפרשה "But with this [the following sacrifices] too, not at any time, but only on the Day of Atonement, as is elucidated at the end of the pericope." Ramban also addressed this apparent contradiction in the text, and states: שכבר הזכיר יום הכפורים שאמר וכפר אהרן על קרנותיו אחת בשנה ... אמר בכאן ואל בשום עת אל הקדש רק בזאת, כלומר ביום אשר יקריב הקרבנות האלה לכפורים בעבור יבא "Since He already mentioned the Day of Atonement, as He said 'Once a year Aaron shall make atonement on its horns' [Exod. 30: 10]...he said here [Lev. 16: 2-3] 'not to come whenever he chooses into the Most Holy Place'; only 'Thus', that is to say, on the day in which he shall offer these sacrifices for atonement." Due to the complexity of this pericope, it is impossible to determine what the previous custom was before the regulation to limit Aaron's atonement ritual in the Holy of Holies to a single and annual event. I would speculate that in the preceding period the High Priest, the winner of the right to enter the Holy of Holies with the cloud of incense and to be present at the theophany, would perform this ritual whenever he deemed appropriate. This might have occurred in periods of trouble, such as war, drought, plague, or similar calamities, when the High Priest's meeting with the Deity was expected to set in motion the apotropaic effect of the incense celebration.

[143] Noth, in *Leviticus*, p. 126 writes: "The position at the end shows the supplementary character of the date fixing," and substantiates this declaration by further textual analysis of these concluding verses of the pericope.

[144] Although only Aaron is mentioned in the pericope concerning the daily incense celebration (Exod. 30: 1-10), and not his sons (though the latter are mentioned with respect to many other sacrificial duties), from textual evidence in various sources, some

6.3.3 The Final Stage of the Struggle – Compromise

I would suggest that this significant development, which represents the final version of the incense celebration in the last period of the Second Temple, is the result of the third stage in the struggle for participation in this ceremony. Since this stage too was an internal feud among the priestly families, and not a matter relevant to the people, and since it was not resolved by a dramatic event, but ended rather with a compromise, we have no textual record of this last struggle and the final conclusion of the extended contest. But the fact that Scripture can be interpreted as having retained the details of the various stages of the development of the incense ceremonies offers us some rational basis from which to deduce that there was a settlement of the struggle through concessions by both parties.[145] We can only speculate on the historical circumstances[146] which might logically have caused this innovation, assisted by literary and textual analysis of the available sources which point to this significant transformation in the incense ceremony. I would suggest that there was an appropriation of the

---

of which I have cited in this study (chap. 6, sec. 6.3.3 and notes 146, 147 and 148), there is no doubt that the regular priests did celebrate this daily ritual, by lot.

[145] I am indebted for this last suggestion to Prof. Fox.

[146] We do not possess any textual or other references on which to speculate about the period in which this innovative daily incense altar celebration was instituted, and the possible stages of such a development; that is, whether the establishment of a daily censer incense celebration anticipated the construction of a special altar, which would seem a logical expansion of the existing practice, or whether the compromise induced an extreme reform of the incense cult, both in its method and frequency. I note again the various citations from Ecclesiasticus, in which we found occurrences of the use of incense, but no mention of a daily incense ceremony on a specific golden altar. Although the absence of such mention does not offer us definite evidence of the lack of such an altar, it adds to the circumstantial evidence in this regard, a helpful technique in historical research. On the other hand, though the Temple Scroll also has no reference to a daily incense ceremony, the fact that it does mention an incense altar for the burning of the frankincense from the showbread may allude to another scenario. It is possible that a small specific altar was placed inside the Temple for the burning of the בזיכין after the introduction of the frankincense into the cult ceremonial; later the celebration of the daily "special incense compound" on this altar was instituted; and the burning of the frankincense of the showbread was moved to the outer altar, to differentiate between the two distinct rituals. The sect of the Temple Scroll objected to this innovation. They saw no reason to burn the frankincense outside the Temple, when it was placed on the showbread inside the Temple; their opposition was valid, based on the maxim מעלין בקדש ולא מורידין (B.T. Berakhoth 28a; Yoma 20b; Megillah 21b and others): "one may elevate sanctity, but one may not lower it."

incense ceremony by a single aristocratic priestly family, and that this appropriation was met with a strong opposition from other Jerusalemite families; they continued to challenge the exclusivity and monopoly of this ceremony, which had now become the most significant and rewarding ritual, as I shall discuss later. We do not know the pattern of this struggle, whether it was violent or not, but we may assume that there was also a threat to establish new, rival temples by the contesting families.[147] Such a considera-

---

[147] For instance, the temple built and put in operation by Onias in Heliopolis-Leontopolis, Egypt, to compete with the Jerusalem Temple. Josephus reports on this temple on many occasions; I shall set out several representative quotes which suggest Onias' real motives for the establishment of the temple. We read in *Wars* VII: 431: οὐ μὴν 'Ονίας ἐξ ὑγιοῦς γνώμης ταῦτα ἔπραττεν, ἀλλ' ἦν αὐτῷ φιλονεικία πρὸς τοὺς ἐν τοῖς 'Ιεροσολύμοις 'Ιουδαίους ὀργὴν τῆς Φυγῆς ἀπομνημονεύοντι, καὶ τοῦτο τὸ ἱερὸν ἐνόμιζε κατασκευάσας εἰς αὐτὸ περισπάσειν ἀπ' ἐκείνων τὸ πλῆθος "In all this, however, Onias was not actuated by honest motives; his aim was rather to rival the Jews at Jerusalem, against whom he harboured resentment for his exile, and he hoped by erecting this temple to attract the multitude away from them to it." The competition motive is evident in this narrative, but in *Ant.* XIII: 63, he adds other interesting and enlightening purposes; for instance: βουλόμενος αὐτῷ μνήμην καὶ δόξαν αἰώνιον καρασκευάσαι "desiring to acquire for himself eternal fame and glory"; and a further crucial motive, relevant to my thesis, καὶ Λευίτας καὶ ἱερεῖς ἐκ τοῦ ἰδίου γένους καταστήσῃ "and to appoint Levites and priests of his own race." The ruling priestly clan certainly had valid reason to be apprehensive about the dangers of alienation within the priestly society.

Josephus is not consistent in all his records concerning Onias' priestly status, or perhaps he had in mind different priests with the same name; Onias is sometimes described as ἀρχιερεύς, "High Priest" (*Wars* I: 33), and sometimes, as in I: 31, he is only 'Ονίας μὲν εἷς τῶν ἀρχιερέων "one of the chief priests." In *Ant.* XII: 387, Onias is described as the son of the chief priest Onias, who fled to Egypt to the Ptolemaic kings when the Seleucid king killed Menelaus and nominated Alkimus as High Priest. However, it is evident that he was a member of the most noble priestly family, and the struggle for supreme priestly power was at the core of his incentive to establish his own temple. The notion of a plurality of High Priests in office naturally does not occur either in Scripture or in talmudic sources, though the plural referring to High Priests in general does occur. Thus, Josephus (for example in *Ant.* VIII: 93 : στολὰς δὲ ἱερατικὰς τοῖς ἀρχιερεῦσι "the priestly vestments for the High Priests"), and Luke (20: 1 ἐπέστησαν οἱ ἀρχιερεῖς καὶ οἱ γραμματεῖς "the chief priests and the teachers of the law, together with the elders"), do mention them in plural. This may demonstrate that relations between the High Priest and his dominant priestly clan were not always precisely established, and left open possibilities of rivalry. It is also interesting to note here the story in B.T. Menahoth 109b of the rivalry between Onias and Shimi, both sons of the High Priest Simon the Righteous, concerning the status of High Priest. At any rate, the sages did not condemn the rituals at Onias' temple as idolatrous; it seems they were fairly lenient in their judgment. We read in Mishnah Menahoth 13: 10: הרי עלי עולה

tion might have been one of the factors motivating a compromise with the rival factions, to avoid a proliferation of competing temples in the Diaspora, and possibly also in Judah. The retention of one central sanctuary in Jerusalem was considered the most vital concern, for which some degree of compromise was deemed worthwhile.[148]

יקריבנה במקדש; ואם הקריבה בבית חוניו לא יצא;שאקריבנה בבית חניו יקריבנה במקדש, ואם הקריבה בבית חוניו יצא ... הכהנים ששמשו בבית חניו לא ישמשו במקדש בירושלים ואין צריך לומר לדבר אחר "If one pledges to bring a holocaust offering, he should offer it in the Temple, and if he offered it at the House of Onias, he has not discharged his pledge. [If he pledges] to offer it at the House of Onias, he should offer it in the Temple [in Jerusalem], if he offered it at the House of Onias, he has discharged his pledge...the priests who served at the House of Onias should not serve at the Temple in Jerusalem, nor needless to say [if they served] idols." We observe an interesting distinction in how the sages considered the actions of lay persons versus those of the priests. The lay person was obliged to discharge his obligation when he pledged to offer at the House of Onias; he was commanded to bring his offering to the Temple, but he fulfilled his pledge by bringing it to Onias' House. If his act had been a severe violation of the rules, his pledge would not be binding. On the other hand, the priest who served at the House of Onias was not allowed to serve at the Temple, because of Josiah's regulation אך לא יעלו כהני הבמות על מזבח ה׳ בירושלים "Nevertheless the priests of the high places did not come up to the altar of the Lord in Jerusalem," as the Mishnah explains. Such a lenient attitude by the sages towards the people who would eventually bring offerings to a rival temple must have been a signal even to the audacious priests, and tempered any possible adversarial stance.

Similarly, in talmudic writings the plural term כהנים גדולים is well attested. We have, for example, the expression בני כהנים גדולים "the sons of the High Priests" as a designation for a group of sages, in Ketuboth 13: 1; I would suggest that this term does not demonstrate the co-existence of many High Priests, but rather denominates an aristocratic group whose members were descendants of the families from whom High Priests were usually chosen. We have a similar expression in B.T. Gittin 58a, where we read: אני כהן בן כהנים גדולים "I am a priest, a son of High Priests." Here, the speaker uses the expression merely to emphasize his aristocratic lineage. We have another occurrence in B.T. Yoma 59a: אמר רבי ישמעאל: שני כהנים גדולים נשתיירו במקדש ראשון "Said Rabbi Ishmael: Two High Priests remained [from] the First Temple."Again, although the expression in plural does not necessarily imply that they ministered at the same time, Rabenu Hananel is aware of a possible misunderstanding, and explains: "כלומר, אירע קרי באחד מהן ונכנס השני ושמש תחתיו ונשתיירו שניהן..."...that is to say: one [of the priests] had a nocturnal emission and the second substituted for him, and so there remained two [High Priests who ministered on the Day of Atonement, the issue in the Talmud]."

[148] I am intentionally avoiding any reference to the Samaritan temple in Samaria, because we do not know precisely what event triggered the building of this temple. We have no reason whatsoever to consider it a result of a rivalry between two priestly families at that time. The story in Ezra chap. 4, which is not very clear, is generally assumed to portray the beginning of the Judean-Samaritan split, which led ultimately to the construction of a separate temple in Samaria.

The institution of an incense altar in the Temple was the core of the compromise. The incense celebration in the Holy of Holies was further exalted in its significance and purpose,[149] and linked to a once-yearly singular ritual of atonement and theophany. On the other hand, the other priests were granted the right to perform the incense celebration in the Temple. The hierarchical division between the High Priest and the other priests remained in force; the High Priest had the exclusive privilege of meeting the Deity in the Holy of Holies, while the other priests could only celebrate in the Temple. The people, the laics, were definitely excluded, if there were still some pretenders to the incense celebration at that time, by a drastic change in the character and pattern of the celebration. The incense ritual was finally transformed, from the previous censer ceremony at unspecified locations, to an altar celebration within the Temple. Only the incense ritual on the Day of Atonement remained a censer celebration, because of its specific and unique character. Further, there was no altar in the Holy of Holies, and the censer had to be placed between the staves of the ark to cover the atonement cover[150] with its smoke, or on the rock, in the Second Temple.[151]

---

[149] Noth, *Leviticus*, p. 118, analyzes the literary style of the pericope in Lev. 16, and demonstrates the oddities created by the different names for the "people" in this chapter. We find there the terms עם, קהל, עדה, and עם הקהל. Noth further emphasizes the inconsistencies between the offerings of Aaron and those of the people, a fact which in itself demonstrates the different strata of the pericope. I would suggest that we should consider the possibility that the atonement-cleansing ritual was originally a priestly ritual which did not affect the people. This ceremony was later elevated in status and significance to encompass the atonement and cleansing of all the people, who took part in a different manner, through their self-affliction on the Day of Atonement. The first part of the pericope has no indication of the people's participation in the ritual; whereas the later development of this holy day, in contrast, demonstrates the significance and awe bestowed upon this day even up to the present because of the association of the comprehensive atonement-cleansing ritual with the High Priest's incense ceremony in the Holy of Holies.

[150] We cannot date the different accretions to the atonement ritual pericope in Lev. chap. 16, but it certainly contains some archaic passages, as for example the ritual of the two he-goats; as argued by Noth, *Leviticus* p. 119, "Its material makes a distinct impression of antiquity." We have, on the other hand, implicit indications of an early cloud-producing ceremony in the Temple, though with no details as to who performed it. We read in I Kings 8: 10: ויהי בצאת הכהנים מן הקדש והענן מלא את בית ה' "When the priests withdrew from the Holy Place, the cloud filled the temple of the Lord." It is interesting to note that Josephus, describing this event at the consecration of Solomon's Temple in *Ant*. VIII: 106, states in a previous verse (*Ant*. VIII: 102) καὶ θυμιῶντες

This seems to me, in broad outline, the evolution of the third and final stage of the incense ceremony, and the establishment of an orderly relationship between the High Priest and his close entourage, and the other common priests. However, we might also propose certain variations in this comprehensive scenario, some of which are alluded to in biblical, talmudic and other sources. The pericope of Exod. 30: 1-10 commends the daily incense ceremony exclusively to Aaron; there is no mention of his sons, as there is concerning the other sacrifices. On the other hand, we have ample proof from talmudic,[152] historical,[153] and New Testament[154] sources that

---

ἀπειρόν τι θυμιαμάτων πλῆθος, ὡς ἅπαντα τὸν πέριξ ἀέρα πεπληρωμένον καὶ τοῖς πορρωτάτω τυγχάνουσιν ἡδὺν ἀπαντᾶν, καὶ γνωρίζειν ἐπιδημίαν θεοῦ καὶ κατοικισμὸν κατ᾽ ἀνθρωπίνην δόξαν εἰς νεοδόμητον αὐτῷ καὶ καθιερωμένον χωρίον. καὶ γὰρ οὐδ᾽ ὑμνοῦντες οὐδὲ χορεύοντες ἕως οὗ πρὸς τὸν ναὸν ἦλθον ἔκαμον "...and burning so vast a quantity of incense that all the air around was filled with it and carried its sweetness to those who were at a great distance; this was a sign of God's being present and dwelling – according to human belief – in the place which had been newly built and consecrated to him." The linkage between incense and theophany is recorded by Josephus as the belief of the people. There is no mention of incense-burning in I Kings, and one has the impression that Josephus was attempting to prepare the reader for the event of the appearance of the cloud in verse 106, and offer, if only indirectly by allusion, a rational explanation for that miraculous event. M. Noth, *Könige* (p. 180), suggests that this verse in I Kings and the following v. 11 concern the same wondrous event described in Exod. 40: 34-35, and originate from a secondary **P** imagination interjected into Kings. This, however, would still not preclude there having been some form of a cloud ritual, carried out at the First Temple before the ark. There is no dispute among scholars concerning the antiquity of the relationship between the cloud and theophany in Israelite mythology. See also Beyerlin and Mann; Mann considers the idea as originating from Canaanite mythology, whereas Beyerlin perceives it as a Sinaitic idea. In any event, both admit its ancient roots.

[151] We read in Mishnah Yoma 5: 1-2 concerning the incense ceremony on the Day of Atonement: הגיע לארון נותן את המחתה בין שני הבדים. צבר את הקטורת על גבי הגחלים ונתמלא כל הבית כולו עשן ... משנטל הארון אבן היתה שם מימות הנביאים הראשונים ... ועליה היה נותן "When he reached the ark, he placed the censer between the staves [of the ark], heaped the incense upon the coals, and the whole house was filled with smoke...After the ark was carried away, there was a rock there from the period of the first prophets... and on it he placed [the censer]."

[152] We read in Mishnah Tamid 5: 2: אמר להם חדשים לקטרת בואו והפיסו "[The supervisor] said to them: 'New ones [priests who had never before performed the incense celebration], come and cast the lot!'" It is evident that this lot was cast every day among the simple priests for the performance of the daily incense ceremony.

[153] We find in Philo (*The Special Laws* I: 171) and in Josephus (*Wars* I: 150; V: 231; *Ant.* III: 199, 209; IV: 32ff) many references to the incense celebration, but no requirement that it be the High Priest who performs it. I did not find a direct statement to this effect, but it seems to me that from the context of these numerous occurrences, one may safely deduce this.

the common priests celebrated the daily incense ceremony. It is therefore possible that the daily incense ritual was originally instituted to be celebrated exclusively by the High Priest and members of his aristocratic clan,[155] in order to increase the use of incense and the profits deriving from its supply; the shift to enable the common priests to celebrate the ceremony may have been as a result of their struggle, as suggested above. Or it is possible that the daily ritual may have been established only after the resolution of the conflict, with the purpose of granting the common priests participation in the incense ceremony.

We also detect another development in the significance of the daily incense ceremony. As already pointed out, there was no prohibition against being in the Temple at the daily incense celebration; the interdiction in Lev. 16: 17[156] refers unequivocally to the incense celebration on what came to be the Day of Atonement with its specific celebration mechanism by the High Priest. From the New Testament and the Talmud, as cited previously, we know that the same ban prevailed in the latter part of the Second Temple period. Thus the daily ceremony came to have bestowed upon it an association with theophany, so that it resembled to a certain extent the High Priest's Day of Atonement celebration. This exaltation of the daily ceremony must have been the result of a later development. It might have been the outcome of a continuing struggle by the common priests for an enhancement and glorification of their share in the ritual; or it might have been influenced by popular imagination and credence, which conferred an aspect of theophany upon every incense ceremony, as a consequence of the deep-rooted cloud mythology.

---

[154] We read in Luke 1: 10 that Zechariah, a simple priest, performed the incense celebration at the Temple.

[155] As cited above, we encounter in Josephus and the New Testament the concept of High Priests, in plural, which may be evidence of a group of priests, lower in status than the one High Priest, but with a higher rank in duties and remunerations than the simple priests. In a transitional period, the members of this group may have been the only priests who performed the incense celebration, in addition to the High Priest. It is not impossible that such a situation prevailed even at the end of the Second Temple period; we observe, as I will discuss later on, that the priestly Abtinas family had a monopoly on the incense supply, for what seems to have been a long period.

[156] וכל אדם לא יהיה באהל מועד בבאו לכפר בקדש עד צאתו וכפר בעדו ובעד ביתו ובעד כל קהל ישראל "No one is to be in the Tent of Meeting from the time Aaron goes in to make atonement in the Most Holy Place until he comes out, having made atonement for himself, his household and the whole community of Israel." Such a general atonement ritual takes place exclusively on the Day of Atonement.

6.3.4 The Incense Monopoly

I have already cited above certain scriptural evidence regarding the economic issues and interests involved in the control of the Temple ritual,
evident both in Josiah's reform and in the concerns of the Tirshatha upon
the return from exile (Ezra 2: 62). I wish now to discuss certain evidence
which further substantiates the importance of the financial aspect of the
incense celebration. First, as I briefly discussed above, there is the complete
absence in Scripture of any opportunity for an individual to offer incense;[157]
this is in contrast to the holocaust, meal offerings, peace offerings, and sin
offerings, which may be offered both by the individual and by the community.[158] There are a number of other sacrifices which are offered exclusively
by the individual on special occasions, such as the trespass offering, the
thanksgiving offering, the childbirth offering, the offering for leprosy and
other diseases, the jealousy offering and the Nazirite offering. Only the
incense offering has no individual counterpart to the public offering. In this
respect it is similar, according to Scripture, to oil and wine[159] for libations.

---

[157] I cited above the midrashic homily (Numbers Rabba, *Parshah* 13; Pesiqta Rabbati,
Parshah 5; Midrash Tanhuma, *Parshat Naso*) which recounts that even the offering of
incense by the princes (Num. chap. 7) was not deemed appropriate by the Deity,
though Scripture does not tell us it was of the same composition as that required for the
daily celebration in the Temple. In B.T. Menahoth 50a, a Beraita tells us that it was by
an extraordinary edict that the princes were permitted to offer incense. R. Simeon ben
Josina declares in Cant. Rabba 5: 1: "Nowhere does the individual offer incense, but
here [concerning the princes] it was [permitted]." One may observe that the sensitivity
in this case concerned the exclusivity of supply, not an offering on the altar by the
princes, an act which is not mentioned in this chapter.

[158] This is evident from Scripture, and we read in *Ant*.III 224: δύο μὲν γάρ εἰσιν ἱερουργίαι,
τούτων δ' ἡ μὲν ὑπὸ τῶν ἰδιωτῶν ἑτέρα δ' ὑπὸ τοῦ δήμου "There are two kinds of
sacrifice – one offered by individuals, the other by the community."

[159] Although there is no indication in Scripture of a separate offering of oil and wine, and
they are used merely as an ancillary to other offerings, the Rabbis discussed the possibility of such an independent donation. We read in Mishnah Menahoth 12: 4: אין
מתנדבין לוג שנים וחמשה אבל מתנדבין שלשה וארבעה וששה ומששה ומעלה "One does
not donate one, two and five *logim* [wine], but one may donate three, four, six and from
six onward." It is Rashi who explains that the rule of the Mishnah concerns a donation
of wine for libation, independent of the sacrifice. It is strange that the Mishnah utilizes
the measure *log* for wine, whereas in Scripture the oil measure is called *log*. The measure
הין *hin* appears in Scripture for both oil and wine, but *log* is used exclusively for oil. It
is possible that Rashi decided to interpret the Mishnah in this way because the Talmud
first asks concerning the Mishnah: יש קבע לנסכים או אין קבע לנסכים "Is there a fixed

This similarity may suggest a common, and ancient, origin for both the incense celebration and the libations, as ancillary components of the cultic celebration rather than as independent offerings. Thus the people could

---

quantity for libation, or not"? However, I do not see any reason to interpret the Mishnah as solely concerning wine; it could also be oil, or both, since the quantities are equal for each animal offering. The different quantities refer to specific sacrifices. The minimum requirement for a lamb is a quarter of a *hin* = three *log*, for a ram a third of a *hin* = four *log*, and for a bullock half a *hin* = six *log*. The greater quantities could be divided for the offering of more than one animal. The Mishnah does not specify what to do with the wine or oil: to offer the libation separately as an independent offering, or to attach the libation to another offering which was brought without libation or to a public offering, instead of taking the wine or oil from the public chambers. In the following Mishnah, we find a dispute between the sages concerning donations of wine and oil: מתנדבין יין ואין מתנדבין שמן דברי רבי עקיבא, רבי טרפון אומר מתנדבין שמן "'One donates wine and one does not donate oil,' are the words of Rabbi Akiba, Rabbi Tarfon says 'one donates oil.'" Only from the following debate between the two Rabbis do we learn that Rabbi Tarfon asserts that one donates both oil and wine, and we get a glimpse of their conceptual differences. We read there: אמר רבי טרפון מה מצינו ביין שהוא בא חובה ובא נדבה, אף שמן שהוא בא חובה בא נדבה "Rabbi Tarfon said to him: What we find for wine, which is offered as an obligation and as a free-will offering, so we find for oil, which is offered as an obligation and as a free-will." Rabbi Akiba retorted: לא אם אמרת ביין שכן קרוב עם חובתו בפני עצמו תאמר בשמן שאינו קרוב עם חובתו בפני עצמו "They are not equal, since wine is offered apart [on the altar], though it is brought together with the main sacrifice as an obligatory ancillary, whereas oil is not offered apart [on the altar but is mingled with the semolina]." We observe here an interesting criterion, which governs their dispute: if the item is offered distinctly and separately on the altar, that establishes its character as an independent offering. The incense offering, which is always celebrated on its own, would therefore be the perfect example of an individual free-will offering; as we have seen, however, such an offering by the princes was considered wrong by the midrashic sources. Maimonides rules that one donates both wine and oil. We read in הל' מעשה הקרבנות, פי"ד ה"א: ומתנדב או נודר יין בפני עצמו או לבונה בפני עצמו או שמן בפני עצמו או עצים למערכה מפני שהם כקרבן שנא', ולקרבן העצים "And one donates or makes a vow of wine separately, or of frankincense separately, or oil separately, or wood for the arrangement [on the altar], since they are as an offering, as it is said 'and for the wood offering [Neh. 10: 35, 10:34 in NIV].'"

In the opinion of the sages, everything could be offered as a private donation, except the incense compound. According to the Talmud, ancillary items were offered separately on the altar, an issue left open in the Mishnah, as noted above. We read in B. T. Menahoth 74b that Samuel said: המתנדב יין מביאו ומזלפו על גבי אישים, המתנדב שמן קומצו ושיריו נאכלין "The one who offers wine, brings it, and [the priest] sprinkles it on the fire [upon the altar]; the one who brings oil, [the priest] takes off the handful, and the rest is eaten [by the priests]." Incense is the singular exception, even in the opinion of the sages, who admit of independent offerings of ancillary substances without the main offering to which they are regularly attached.

offer only money to purchase the incense compound,[160] which was made available exclusively from the Temple stores. This circumstance is also confirmed by talmudic evidence.

We should also recall here another oddity, previously discussed, regarding the remarkable specific limitations regarding incense: the extraordinary and singular interdiction against preparation, not merely use, of the specific incense compound utilized in the Temple. We have evidence that the preparation of the incense compound,[161] and by implication the supply of the finished product, was firmly in the hands of a prominent priestly clan, the Abtinas[162] family. They kept the secret of the preparation,[163] they taught

---

[160] We read in a *Beraita* in Ketuboth 106b: הקטורת וכל קרבנות הציבור באין מתרומת הלשכה "The incense and all the public sacrifices come [are bought of the money] from donations to the Temple chamber." Mishnah Sheqalim 4: 1 does not explicitly mention the incense, but uses the generic concept וכל קרבנות הציבור "and all public offerings." The commentators interpret this clause to include the incense, and Maimonides, when he sets out the *Halakha* corresponding to the above Mishnah, adds explicitly והקטורת ושכר עשייתה "...and the incense and the cost of its preparation (Hilkh. Sheqalim 4: 1)."

[161] We read in a *Beraita* in B. T. Ketuboth 106a: נשים האורגות בפרכות ובית גרמו על מעשה "The לחם הפנים, ובית אבטינס על מעשה הקטרת, כולן היו נוטלות שכרן מתרומת הלשכה women who wove the veils, the House of Garmu who [were appointed] for the task of the showbread, and the House of Abtinas [who were appointed] for the task of the incense, all received their compensation from donations to the Temple chamber." The women who wove the veils are not specified, and anyone might have participated in this chore, but the preparation of incense was reserved exclusively to the Abtinas family. It seems that certain other rewarding tasks were also the sole preserve of a number of specific aristocratic priestly families.

[162] Mishnah Sheqalim 5: 1 recounts the names of the various officers in the Temple: אלו הן הממונין שהיו במקדש ... בית אבטינס על מעשה הקטרת "These are the officers in the Temple ...the House of Abtinas on the task of the incense."

[163] We read in Mishnah Yoma 3: 11: ואלו לגנאי. של בית גרמו לא רצו ללמד על מעשה לחם הפנים. של בית אבטינס לא רצו ללמד על מעשה הקטורת "And these were remembered with disgrace: the House of Garmu [who] did not consent to teach [others] about the task of the showbread; the House of Abtinas [who] did not consent to teach [others] about the task of incense." The B.T. at Yoma 3a and the Y. T. at Yoma chap. 3 hal. 9, 41a enlighten us concerning the extraordinary and exclusive skill of this clan: ולא רצו ללמד שלחו והביאו אומנים מאלכסנדריאה והיו בקיין במעשה הקטורת ובמעלה עשן לא היו בקיאין; של בית אבטינס היתה מתמרת ועולה ופוסה ויורדת ושל אילו היתה פוסה מיד ...and they [the Abtinas clan] did not consent to teach, so they brought artisans from Alexandria, [but] they were proficient in the composition of the incense, not in the [preparation] of the smoke-producing substance. The [smoke of the] House of Abtinas rose up, spread and moved downward, [whereas] theirs [the Alexandrians'] spread right away." This issue demonstrates both the importance bestowed upon the smoke, and its relevance to the theophany. An interesting midrash offers us an insight into the aura of

the High Priest the correct ritual procedure,[164] and the storage[165] of the incense was in their ceremonial house, called specifically by their clan name בית אבטינס "the House of Abtinas," within the precinct of the Temple.[166] These facts are evident from the talmudic texts, in which some of the references are certainly authentic, and we have no reason to doubt them. At the very least they contain a "kernel" of truth from which we may infer that this clan had the best relations with the office of the High Priest, and wielded much power in the Temple bureaucracy. They assured for themselves the highly lucrative right to be the exclusive purveyors of incense for the daily celebrations, paid for by public funds. In fact, at the end of the

---

mystery surrounding the special tools employed by the House of Abtinas for the preparation of the incense. We read in תשעה דברים קסב: עמ' (אייזנשטיין) אוצר המדרשים: העשויין וגנוזין הן ... אבל מכתשת של בית אבטינס שולחן ומנורה ופרוכת וציץ עדיין מונחין ברומי "Nine artifacts [from the Temple] are hidden [by a Divine act]…but the mortar of the House of Abtinas, the table and the veil and the plate [on Aaron's mitre] are still deposited in Rome."

[164] We read in Mishnah Yoma 1: 5: והעלהו לעליית בית אבטינס והשביעוהו "And they [the elders of the priests] brought him up to the upper chamber of the House of Abtinas, and took his oath [that he would perform the incense ceremony in the correct Pharisaic manner]." The Talmud adds to this Mishnah ללמדו חפינה "[they brought him to the House of Abtinas] to teach him the [intricate method] of grabbing the incense in the hollow of his hand." In B. T. Yoma 47ab, the Talmud describes this complex technique, and declares: וזו היא עבודה קשה שבמקדש "and this is the fastidious work in the Temple." The significant incense ritual on the Day of Atonement was guided in all its many aspects by the compelling control of the House of Abtinas.

[165] We read in a *Beraita* in B.T. Yoma 47a: הוציאו לו כף ריקן מלשכת הכלים, ומחתה גדושה של קטורת מלשכת בית אבטינס "They brought him an empty spoon from the equipment chamber, and a censer heaped with incense from the chamber of the House of Abtinas."

[166] We read in Mishnah Tamid 1: 1 and in Mishnah Midoth 1: 1: בשלשה מקומות הכהנים שומרים בבית המקדש בבית אבטינס בבית הניצוץ ובבית המוקד "At three locations in the Temple the priests keep guard: at the House of Abtinas, at the House of the Spark, and at the House of the Fire." (I do not wish to expand here on the purpose of the last two buildings, since in my opinion their use is not entirely clear from the talmudic sources, and their precise use does not affect my thesis.) It is interesting for our purposes to observe that while the Houses of the Spark and the Flame were situated at corresponding gates, the Gate of the Spark and the Gate of the Flame (as we learn from Midoth 1· 5*), and the placing of guards there was thus justified, the House of Abtinas was not located at a gate, but within the precinct of the Temple court, and the placing of a guard there must have been motivated by another concern. This might have been to safeguard the secret of the incense compound formula and its method of preparation, or to protect against burglary of such a costly substance, or for both reasons. ובצפון שער הניצוץ ... שני לו שער הקרבן שלישי לו בית המוקד*) "And [the gates at the north were] the Gate of the Spark…next to it the Gate of the Sacrifice, the third from it the House of the Fire."

Second Temple period, we encounter an interesting development concerning the supply in general of the animals and other substances for the offerings. The offerer did not bring his own flour and wine for the libations at the Temple; he had to buy them there from the special repositories instituted and managed by some of the aristocratic priestly clans. This we know from talmudic reports;[167] here too, the many insignificant details contained in the narratives, and the apparent lack of any homiletic or other motive on the part of the *Tannaim*, bestow a certain aura of authenticity upon these records.

We would call this, in modern language, an efficient, monopolistic business enterprise, managed with great acumen and sufficient foresight to take advantage of every possible opportunity. In considering the motives behind the priestly regulation of the supply of incense, as well as the other components for the Temple ceremonies, we must not exclude financial incentive. The Talmud, in B.T. Yoma 38a and in Y.T. Yoma 3: 9, tells us why the House of Abtinas refused to teach the secrets of the incense preparation:[168] they simply wanted more money. We read there: שלחו להם חכמים ולא באו, כפלו להם שכרן ובאו. בכל יום היו נוטלין שנים עשר מנה, והיום עשרים וארבעה "The Sages sent for them [the artisans from the House of Abtinas, to come and prepare the incense] and they did not come; they doubled their pay, [then] they came. Every day [before that] they used to receive twelve units [of payment] but from now on twenty four."[169] Similarly reprehensible behaviour by both common priests and those of elevated rank is encountered in a *Beraita* in B.T. Pesahim:

---

[167] We read in Mishnah Sheqalim 5: 3-4: ארבעה חותמות היו במקדש וכתוב עליהן ענל זכר גדי וחוטא ... מי שהוא מבקש נסכים הולך לו אצל יוחנן שהוא ממונה על החותמות ונותן לו מעות ומקבל ממנו חותם; בא לו אצל אחייה שהוא ממונה על הנסכים ונותן לו חותם ומקבל ממנו נסכים "Four seals were in the Temple and there was imprinted upon them: calf, ram, goat, and sinner [sacrifice of the leper]...[the libations were different for each of these four classes of sacrifices]...Whoever needed libations would go to Johanan, the executive of the seals, give him money and receive from him a[n appropriate] seal; he then would go to Ahaia, the executive of the libations, give him the seal, and receive from him the libations."

[168] Such retention of a formula is also a way of controlling its development. For instance, modern manufacturers constantly reproduce old recipes with inferior ingredients under the old name.

[169] We must admit that the text of this story is somewhat perplexing and not entirely accurate. The Mishnah and the *Beraita* start their narration with the declaration that the House of Abtinas did not consent to teach others the secret of the preparation of the incense, but from the continuation of the story, one has the impression that it was their own preparation which was in dispute; when the sages doubled their remunera-

ת"ר בראשונה היו מניחין עורות קדשים בלשכת הפרוה לערב היו מחלקין
אותן לאנשי בית אב והיו בעלי זרועות נוטלין אותן בזרוע התקינו שיהיו
מחלקין אותן מערב שבת לע"ש דאתיין כולהו משמרות ושקלן בהדדי ועדיין
היו גדולי כהונה נוטלין אותן בזרוע

The Sages taught: At the beginning one would place the skins of the
sacrifices [which were given to the officiating priests] in the Fur
Chamber, and in the evening they were distributed among the
members of the family [which performed the service on that day];
[but] there were "rowdies" who took them [for themselves] by force;
[so] it was devised that they would distribute them once weekly, on the
eve of the Sabbath, when all the priests of the weekly shift come and
count [them] together, [but] still the prominent priests[170] took them
[for themselves] by force.

It is interesting to note that in the first episode, the evil elements who took
the skins are called "rowdies," but in the second episode it is the "prominent" priests who did the same. Although in both cases the *Beraita* declares
that the skins were taken בזרוע "by force," I would speculate that the
"prominent" priests took them by their authority and political power, and
that the term "by force" was repeated automatically in the second episode.

All the narratives outlined above, including Mishnah Yoma 3:11, agree
on the hold of the House of Abtinas and their connection to the significant
incense ritual.[171] If even a single detail of the stories told is authentic, then
it must likely originate from the time of the Temple. Other small details in
the narratives which refer to the Temple reinforce this conclusion. However, it appears that at a later date, after the destruction of the Temple, the

---

tion, the House of Abtinas started to work again. The terms בכל יום "every day," and
והיום "and today" might imply that they prepared incense afresh every day; I have put
a different interpretation on these terms, as "before" and "from today," since it seems
to me more appropriate in the context. Further, a daily preparation of incense would
be in conflict with a statement in a *Beraita* in B.T. Keritoth 6a: ת"ר קטורת היתה נעשית
שס"ח מנה שס"ה כנגד ימות החמה שלשה מנין יתירין שמהן מכניס כ"ג מלא חפניו ביו"כ "The
Sages taught: Incense was prepared in the quantity of three hundred and sixty-eight
portions; three hundred and sixty-five for the days in the solar calendar, and from the
remaining three portions, the High Priest would fill his handfuls on the Day of Atonement." According to this *Beraita*, incense was prepared once yearly. I do not pretend
that every detail of these stories is authentic, but there is a kernel of truth in them, and
an implication that some priestly families took advantage of their status for their personal financial benefit.

[170] As Rashi explains: גדולי כהונה: שרים שבהן "the chief priests."
[171] Both sources agree that the Abtinas clan had a monopoly on the preparation of the
incense compound.

longing for its former ceremonies and their glorification did not seem to harmonize with certain deprecating allegations against some of the highest-ranking priestly families. We therefore find several talmudic accounts[172] in B.T. Yoma 38a and Y.T. Yoma 4a, following the above-cited denunciations, which are intended to moderate the repulsive image resulting from the declaration in Mishnah Yoma 3: 11. I consider these to be of less weight,[173] insufficient to negate either the previous declarations, or the general portrayal of the circumstances prevailing at the Temple. The above-cited Mishnah which curses the House of Abtinas so vehemently with ושם רשעים ירקב "the name of the wicked will rot (Prv. 10: 7)," the story in Pesahim about the misdeeds of even the "prominent" priests, and the many other circumstantial narratives cited above, tend to bestow authenticity upon these declarations, rather than upon the later,[174] clearly apologetic,

---

[172] We read there: אמרו להם חכמים מה ראיתם שלא ללמד? אמרו יודעין היו של בית אבא שבית זה עתיד להיחרב אמרו שמא ילמוד אדם שאינו מהוגן וילך ויעבוד עבודת כוכבים ועל דבר זה מזכירין אותן לשבח מעולם לא יצאת כלה מבושמת מבתיהן וכשנושאין אשה ממקום אחר מתנין עמה שלא תתבסם שלא יאמרו ממעשה הקטורת מתבסמין לקיים מה שנא' והייתם נקיים מה' ומישראל "The sages asked them: Why were you adamant about not teaching [the preparation of the incense]? They said: Our father's house knew that this house [the Temple] would be destroyed, and they said it may be that some unfit man will learn it, and will serve idols [with it]. And on this issue they [the House of Abtinas] were remembered for praise: A bride never came out perfumed from their dwellings, and when they married a woman from another place [family], they made a condition that she might not perfume herself. This, that one should not murmur that they perfume themselves from the [substances used for the] preparation of the incense; as it is said 'to be free from your obligation [guiltless] before the Lord and to Israel [Num. 32: 22].'" I put a full stop before the phrase "And on this issue," to imply that it refers to the following narration, not to the previous. There are no punctuation marks in the Talmud, and one must effect the division among the phrases according to the context. I deduce that the sages did not accept the plea of the House of Abtinas, since we read in the story that they prepared the incense only when their recompense was doubled; hence their motivation was purely financial and not ideological. The sages remembering them for praise refers to the second part of the narrative, concerning their excessive care in avoiding any rumour that they used Temple substances for their personal use. I found that the Maharasha, a traditional commentator, interprets this passage in the same way. Several similar stories justifying the conduct of the House of Abtinas, in a different style and wording, follow in the Talmud at this point.

[173] I also point in this regard to Rabbi's editorial judgement; he included in the Mishnah the accusatory version with its grim malediction, and ignored the apologetic *Beraitot*.

[174] Abba Saul, who denounces so bitterly the evil conduct of the High Priests, was a *Tanna* of the first generation (H. Albeck, מבוא למשנה, Jerusalem, 1959, p. 225), and his manifesto is brought in the name of Abba Joseph ben Hanin, a *Tanna* from the time of the Temple (ibid. p. 221). The apologetic utterances are made by Rabbi Ishmael,

counterclaims. It is no wonder that the Babylonian Talmud Pesahim 57a continues with a grievous complaint against the unconcealed nepotism of the High Priests, as a burden and affliction to the people. We read there a lament by Abba Saul, after a long list of High Priestly families, (such as אוי לי מאגרופן (בית בייתוס, בית חנין, בית קתרוס, בית ישמעאל בן פיאכי שהם כהנים גדולים ובניהם גזברין וחתניהם אמרכלין ועבדיהן חובטין את העם במקלות "Woe is to me from their power! as they are High Priests[175] and their sons [are] treasurers, and their sons-in-law [are] administrators, and their servants strike the people with sticks." Reading this passage, one cannot but compare it to a similar charge in the Commentary on Nahum from the Dead Sea Scrolls, on verse 2: 13:[176] "[*I will burn up your multitude in smoke*], *and the sword shall devour your young lions*. I will [cut off] your prey [*from the earth*] [interpreted]...*your multitude* is the bands of his army...and his *young lions* are...his *prey* is the wealth which [the priests] of Jerusalem have [amassed], which...Israel shall be delivered." Further, in the Commentary on Habakkuk on verses 2: 5-6 we read: "...the wicked priest...when he ruled over Israel his heart became proud, and he forsook God and betrayed the precepts for the sake of riches. He robbed and amassed the riches of the men of violence who rebelled against God, and he took the wealth of the peoples...." The possibility that this reprehensible conduct by the priests was a catalyst in the creation of certain sects in the last period of the Second Temple, and/or that the wealth amassed by the aristocratic priestly families favoured their control of political power in Judah, is a matter to be investigated in a separate study.

Thus the various talmudic texts attest to the importance of financial interests among the higher-ranking priests in their management of the Temple rituals, with special emphasis on the economic aspects of the incense ritual and the supply of its components. We find a parallel to this

---

Rabbi Akiba and Rabbi Johanan ben Nuri, all *Tannaim* of the second generation (ibid. pp. 225-226).

[175] We observe here too that the expression כהנים גדולים "High Priests," in plural, refers to the families from whose members High Priests were chosen, or nominated. Concerning some of these names, we also have substantiation from other sources, such as Josephus, and other talmudic narratives. We encounter a story in B.T. Yoma 47a about the High Priest Rabbi Ishmael ben Kimhith who became ritually unclean from the saliva of a pagan, and his brother substituted for him at the service on the Day of Atonement. The Talmud then recounts that his mother had seven sons and all ministered as High Priests. As we observe, these High Priests did not serve together, merely alternately, but were always from the same family.

[176] G. Vermes, *The Dead Sea Scrolls* (London, 1987).

situation in antiquity, in the control of the extremely lucrative incense trade by the sanctuaries in South Arabia, the place of origin of frankincense. Basing himself on ancient sources, Walter Müller[177] informs us that the harvest of frankincense was considered a sacred activity in South Arabia, and further, that the origin of the frankincense was kept secret by the traders, to preclude competition and to allow them considerable profit. Müller describes the method of the collection and sale of the frankincense, in which the sanctuaries had a significant practical and financial involvement. The collected frankincense was first deposited in piles at the sanctuary of the sun god,[178] with the weight and requested price attached to it. When the buyer agreed to the terms, he took the goods and put the money in its place. A third of the proceeds went to the sanctuary.[179] Müller speculates that since the whole process of storage and sale took place in the sanctuary, it is possible that the frankincense was considered to be a sacred element fit for the gods, and therefore a large portion had to be offered to them before it could be used by humans. Although there is no evidence of a formal monopoly of the frankincense trade by the sanctuaries, such a logical result accords with the general circumstances in South Arabia at that period, about the 4th century B.C.E.. We need not necessarily assume that the Jerusalemite priests apprehended the concept of holiness of the frankincense, and the commercial opportunities associated with it, as a result of influence from the South Arabian priests; but at the same time we cannot exclude reciprocal influence in this respect between these two groups. It may be assumed that the leaders of the caravans carrying frankincense traded not merely commodities, but also information of all kinds.

We may now examine a piece of folkloric evidence which suggests a link between incense and financial payback; though an indirect source, it is

---

[177] "Der Weihrauchhandel der Südaraber in der Antike," in *Die Königin von Saba* (Stuttgart, 1988), pp. 49ff. Müller's essay is based on Theophrastus' records of various reports concerning the nature of the frankincense and myrrh plants, their harvest and trade, in his book *Enquiry into Plants*. In the following notes I will quote passages from this work.

[178] ibid. IX. iv. 5: ὅτι συνάγεται πανταχόθεν ἡ σμύρνα καὶ ὁ λιβανωτὸς εἰς τὸ ἱερὸν τὸ τοῦ ἡλίου. τοῦτο δ᾽ εἶναι μὲν τῶν Σαβαίων ἁγιώτατον δὲ πολὺ τῶν περὶ τὸν τόπον, τηρεῖν δέ τινας Ἄραβας ἐνόπλους "...that the myrrh and frankincense are collected from all parts into the temple of the sun; and that this temple is the most sacred thing which the Sabaeans of that region possess, and it is guarded by certain Arabians in arms."

[179] ibid. IX. iv. 6: καὶ τὸν ἱερέα παραγενόμενον τὸ τρίτον μέρος λαβόντα τῆς τιμῆς τῷ θεῷ τὸ λοιπὸν αὐτοῦ καταλιπεῖν "...and then the priest comes and, having taken the third part of the price for the god, leaves the rest of it where it was."

nonetheless not to be disregarded. This is the aphorism: "Rich as Korah."
This aphorism, which is used even in our time, reflects an idea of ancient
origin, since we find it in talmudic midrashim which describe Korah's
wealth and attempt to provide an explanation for it. We read in B.T.
Pesahim 119a and B.T. Sanhedrin 110a: עשר שמור לבעליו לרעתו, אמר רבי
שמעון בן לקיש זו עשרו של קרח "'Wealth hoarded to the harm of its owner
[Eccl. 5: 13 in NIV, v. 12 in MT],' Rabbi Simeon ben Lakish said: This is
Korah's wealth." The Talmud then goes on to discuss the vastness of his
wealth; this is undoubtedly an exaggeration, but illustrates the extent of
popular fancy in this respect: ואמר ר' לוי משוי שלש מאות פרדות לבנות היו
קרח מפתחות של בית גנזיו של קרח "And Rabbi Levi said: Three hundred
white mules carried the keys of Korah's treasuries." We read in Exodus
Rabba, *Parshah* 31: 3: ד"ה א"א אם ... עושה רע לבעליו זה עשרו של קרח שהיה
עשיר מכל ישראל "'[Wealth] which hurts its owner,' this is Korah's wealth,
who was the richest in all Israel." It is obvious that we would not expect the
Talmud to tell us that Korah made his money through the supply of incense, and that that was the reason behind his clash with the Aaronites;
another explanation had to be found. We read in the continuation of the
above-cited talmudic discourse: אמר רבי חמא בר חנינה שלש מטמוניות הטמין
יוסף במצרים, אחת נתגלה לקרח "Rabbi Hama son of Hanina said: Joseph
hid three vaults in Egypt, one was revealed to Korah." In Y.T. Sanhedrin
27d we find a similar midrash: קרח עשיר גדול היה היה תיסברין של פרעה נגלה לו
בין מגדול ובין הים "Korah was a very rich man, Pharaoh's treasuries were
revealed to him [hidden] between Migdol and the Sea." The Talmud may
in this case have been attempting to contradict a popular supposition that
Korah's wealth originated from his dealings with incense, by attributing his
wealth to the discovery of some legendary treasure; but, as we have seen and
shall see further, on other occasions the Talmud definitely confirms the
linkage between incense and wealth.

We read in Mishnah Tamid 5: 2: אמר להם חדשים לקטרת בואו והפיסו
"[The supervisor] said to them: 'New ones [priests who had never before
performed the incense celebration] come and cast the lot!'" In Yoma 2: 4,
the Mishnah contains the same declaration, in a slightly different style, and
the Talmud there explains the meaning of "new ones" and the reason for
this limitation. We read in B.T. Yoma 26a: תנא מעולם לא שנה אדם בה. מ"ט
א"ר חנינא מפני שמעשרת "Never did a man [perform the incense celebra-
tion] twice. What is the reason?...because it enriches [the performer]." Rashi
explains that therefore they did not allow any one person to perform it twice
(so as not to create great income gaps among the priests, and to grant each
one a chance of enrichment; Rashi does not elaborate, but he refers – as I

understand it – to issues of social justice and equality). The Talmud also attempts to explain the apparently implausible axiom that the performance of incense enriches. One may perceive that the priests would be motivated to perform other sacrifices to achieve economic benefits, since with the *Minhah, Shelamim* and sin offerings the officiating priest, or his clan, received a significant share; but incense evaporated in smoke, and nothing was left to the celebrating priest. The solution to this difficulty is based on an interpretation of Deut. 33: 10 and 11, concerning the blessing of (the tribe of) Levi, where we read: ישימו קטורה באפך וכליל על מזבחך ברך ה' חילו ופעל ידיו תרצה "They offer [in the NIV it is "he offers"] incense before you and whole-burnt offerings on your altar.[180] Bless all his skills, O Lord, and be pleased with the work of his hands." Whether or not we accept the talmudic solutions, we observe a notion of incense related to wealth. This may be a source of the myths ingrained in Israelite folk tales, concerning not only the wealth of the Abtinas priestly family, but also of Korah, whose Levite family fought for similar rights.[181] Undoubtedly, these notions result from some ancient popular wisdom, the exact details of which were lost during the ages, or were deliberately obfuscated by concerned parties who attempted to modify the popular memory.

---

[180] Rav Papa asks why the same benefit would not also affect someone performing the whole-burnt offering; the Talmud answers: הא שכיחא והא לא שכיחא "this occurs often, and that does not occur often." There are different interpretations of this enigmatic retort; I prefer the explanation of the *Tosafot Yeshanim* that many whole-burnt sacrifices are offered on behalf of the public and by individuals, but incense is offered on behalf of the public only twice daily.

[181] Korah's struggle was attributed, as we have seen, to the incense monopoly of the Aaronites.

7. Conclusion

The hypothesis I postulated offers solutions to most of the questions posed during the course of this study. A punctilious examination of the texts has revealed the long and complex path the incense ceremony followed until it reached the last stage in its development, as we know it from the P section of the Pentateuch, the Talmud, the New Testament, and other writings from the end of the Second Temple period. I also demonstrated the significance of financial interests in the development of the incense ceremony, as well as the overall economic concerns of the priesthood. I showed the impact of such concerns on matters of cult, and probably, as a consequence, on the issue of political power; a close correlation exists between the achievement of wealth by the priesthood and their attainment of political power in the period of the Second Temple.

I defended most of my propositions through examination of the various texts, from the literary, historical and rational points of view; this has led, in my view, to the satisfactory resolution of the various issues. I wish nevertheless to revert to a number of these questions. The first issue of my study was the examination of the term קטר, used indiscriminately in the P section of the Pentateuch for the burning both of substances not intended to produce vapour and of incense, instead of the term להעלות עולה, which appears in Genesis and the first part of Exodus, including the Sinai narrative.[1] Moreover, it is utilized in a directional sense, such as והקטיר המזבחה with the directional *heh*, where the verb קטר in the sense of burning is inappropriate. One almost has the impression that the term והעלה המזבחה was "carelessly" replaced by the term והקטיר; or rather, the motive of the final redactor in executing this emendation was to emphasize the unity of all cult celebrations, and to impose this concept on the people by insinuat-

---

[1] B. A. Levine translates the term והקטיר (Lev. 1: 9) in *The JPS Torah Commentary* as "turn the whole into smoke." This is the precise sense of the Hebrew *hiqtir*, a verb derived from the noun *qiter* or *qitor*, "smoke". However, he does not comment on the directional meaning of the expression והקטיר הכהן את הכל המזבחה, a form which is not appropriate in this context, or question why this term appears only in P, contrary to the other sections of the Pentateuch, where the appropriate term להעלות עולה is used.

ing into the daily language a unified terminology. I shall elaborate upon this concept further.

I also questioned the appropriateness of the term מזבח for an implement which had no connection whatsoever with the term זבח, "slaughter." According to my thesis, the priests had a strong interest in coordinating and unifying the two main ceremonial systems, the burning of animals and the burning of incense. As we deduced from Ezekiel, in the early period of the Second Temple lay people offered incense, while the burning of animal sacrifices was already the exclusive prerogative of the priests, on the altar in the Jerusalem temple. The social and psychological impact of using a common term for both types of ceremony was probably recognized by the priestly class, and they undertook all the necessary measures to achieve the desired outcome. Thus, as evidenced in the MT, Hebrew is the only language[2] in which the term מזבח is used for the censing implement, contrary to other ancient Near Eastern records, where such an expression is not encountered. At the same time, we have the verb קטר as a *terminus technicus* embodying all types of sacrificial worship, including the whole-burnt עולה, for which the term להעלות, as used in other than the P section, is more appropriate.

It is interesting to note that the verb קטר as a technical term for offering, whether of incense or anything else, appears outside the specific sacrificial rules only in the aetiological verse Num. 17: 5 (16: 40 in NIV) after the Korah rebellion; this verse serves as a ratification of the exclusive Aaronite cultic privileges and as an admonition illustrating the fate of those who might attempt to challenge such privileges.[3] In the narrations of the actual incense celebrations performed by Nadab and Abihu and by the Korah group, the verb קטר is not yet in use. We read in Lev. 10: 1: ויתנו בהן אש שני בני אהרן בקרבתם; in Lev. 16: 1:[4] וישימו עליה קטרת ויקריבו לפני ה׳; in וזתנו בהן אש ושימו עליהן קטרת לפני ה׳; in Num. 16: 7: לפני ה׳ וימתו; in 16: 18: ונתתם עליהם קטרת והקרבתם לפני ה׳; in Num. 16: 17: ויתנו עליהם.

---

[2]   I have demonstrated that Onkelos, the LXX and the Peshitta have all translated the term קטר, when it is used for the burning of substances not intended to produce fumes, with verbs denoting "to carry up, to offer, to put on, to raise up," which is quite appropriate when the term appears with a directional sense.

[3]   We observe the explicit texts: ויהיו לאות לבני ישראל "Let them be a sign to the Israelites (17: 3; 16: 38 in NIV)"; זכרון לבני ישראל ... ולא יהיה כקרח וכעדתו "This was to remind the Israelites... or he would become like Korah and his followers (17: 5; 16: 40 in NIV)."

[4]   The verb קטר also does not appear in the other short narratives of the death of Nadab and Abihu, in Num. 3: 4 and 26: 61.

מקריבי הקטרת ;in 16: 35: אש וישימו עליהם קטרת. Even in Num. 17: 11
(16: 46 in NIV), which describes incense offered by Aaron to stop the
plague, a legitimate act commanded by Moses, we still read: קח את המחתה
ותן עליה אש מעל המזבח ושים קטרת. Thus in none of these incense offerings
do we encounter the verb קטר[5] to describe the ceremony; the term obviously appears exclusively in the specific rules for the offering of sacrifices.

Etymologically, the term קטר is exclusively linked to smoke and vapours, and this linkage is also corroborated from the ceremonial aspect.
However we interpret the phrase כי בענן אראה על הכפרת "because I appear
in the cloud over the atonement cover (Lev. 16: 2)," whether as the cloud
of the incense, or the cloud representing the Deity, I contend that the verse
וכסה ענן הקטרת את הכפרת אשר על העדות ולא ימות "and the smoke of the
incense will conceal the atonement cover above the Testimony, so that he
will not die (Lev. 16: 13)" illustrates that the purpose of the incense was to
produce smoke to conceal the theophany. In contrast, it was the production
of fire and flame which was the sacred purpose of the whole-burnt sacrifice,
as it was the smell of meat and fragrant wood at an earlier stage. We read
in Lev. 6: 2: זאת תורת העלה היא העלה על מוקדה על המזבח כל הלילה עד
הבקר ואש המזבח תוקד בו "These are the regulations for the burnt offering:
the burnt offering is to remain on the altar hearth through the night, till
morning, and the fire must be kept burning on the altar (6: 9 in NIV)."
There is no allusion to smoke on the מזבח העלה "altar of burnt offering,"
the specific name of the altar on which the parts of the sin offering and the
peace offerings were burned. The generation of smoke was the only purpose
of the incense celebration, the placing of the קטרת on coal, and the term
קטר is exclusively appropriate for this act.[6] We also have evidence in this

---

[5]   I have not translated these verses, since the particular translations used by the English
      texts for this term are not relevant to the discussion.

[6]   The theological basis of the incense ceremony was certainly different from that of the
      surrounding cultures at that period. Israel adopted many practices and ideas from the
      surrounding peoples, but adapted them to its own theology before integrating them
      into its culture. This is an issue which cannot be dealt with in the framework of this
      study, but it will suffice for our purposes to reiterate the proposition that the concept
      of the sweet savour, ריח ניחוח, which supplements almost every animal sacrifice, is
      entirely absent in the incense pericope. On the other hand, the concept of the smoke
      is in the foreground of the incense celebration on the Day of Atonement. It should be
      no surprise that the theological basis of a cultic custom in Judah, in the later period of
      the Second Temple, in a resolutely monotheistic society, is different from the idola-
      trous theology of the earlier Mesopotamian culture. The basic procedure and technique
      may remain identical or similar, but the underlying philosophy changes. We have

respect from the talmudic sources in B.T. Yoma 3a, in which it is recorded that the Alexandrian artisans succeeded in creating incense of the same composition, but could not emulate the smoke produced by the Abtinas experts. The latter received double recompense for their work, because the generation of the appropriate smoke was the primary purpose of the incense ceremony. Incense no longer had the purpose of generating a fragrant odour for the pleasure of the Deity; I emphasized that the relevant pericope[7] concerning the composition of the incense, Exod. 30: 34-37, does not mention the expression ריח ניחוח לה׳ "an aroma pleasing to the Lord," customary at the burning of animal and vegetable sacrifices.[8] The incense does emit an odour, and it is forbidden for a man to enjoy its smell, as is written in v. 38: איש אשר יעשה כמוה להריח "Whoever makes any like it to enjoy its fragrance"; but its odour is not intended for the Deity.

Following upon the unification of the technical terms for both the cultic acts as well as their ceremonial *loci*, all the sacrificial cultic celebrations were now the exclusive prerogative of the priests, both in practice and symbolically. Among the priests, a further demarcation was instituted, to distinguish between the High Priest, or Priests, and the ordinary members of the group. But this distinction was applied merely with respect to their enjoyment of certain exclusive financial privileges, and to the celebration inside the curtain. Concerning the burning of the sacrifices and the censing of incense, all priests were equal; the only relevant distinctions were now between priests and Levites, who were demoted to inferior duties, and between priests and Israelites, who were gradually excluded from approaching the precinct of the sanctuary.[9] A complete transformation was accomplished,

---

many occurrences in Scripture in which we observe a shift in theology, and others in which such a shift is discernible from the context.

[7]   Concerning the possibility that a certain portion of this pericope is of ancient origin, while other elements are post-exilic additions, see the extensive textual analysis in the previous section of this study. The absence of the phrase "an aroma pleasing to the Lord" likely demonstrates a post-exilic development.

[8]   This fact corroborates the postulate that the incense celebration was instituted at a later date, at a time when the editor would have been sensitive to anthropomorphic expressions. The commands concerning the holocaust and other offerings originate from an earlier period, when such expressions were not yet considered impious.

[9]   A remnant from some distant period in which the people took a more active part in the cult celebrations may be observed in a custom in which the table is exhibited to religious pilgrims. We read in B.T. Menahoth 96b and in other talmudic sources: מלמד שמגביהין אותו לעולי רגלים ומראין בו לחם ואומרים להם ראו חיבתכם לפני המקום "We learn [from an aforesaid verse] that [the priests] raised [the table] and showed the showbread on it to the pilgrims and said to them: See the Deity's fondness towards you."

from total public participation in the cult performances to the people's final and emphatic exclusion, to the advantage of one specific clan; as I suggested, the incense ceremony had a significant part in this metamorphosis. The increasing importance of the incense celebration, and the parallel advancement of the economic power and the political supremacy of the High Priest and his entourage, point unmistakably in this direction; I presented, assisted by textual analysis, a plausible hypothesis regarding the sometimes tortuous route of this evolution.

I reiterate that I do not consider it necessary to elaborate further rebuttal to the proposition that archeological finds of incense implements are evidence of the performance of incense ceremonies in the ancient Israelite cult. Haran, who initially considered such finds as convincing proof, has himself changed his mind in this respect, in a later study. The sudden appearance of a remarkable number of stationary censers in Judah around the 5th century B.C.E.[10] may even confirm my thesis that there was an expansion in the use of incense by lay people in that period,[11] a fact which served as a trigger to the priests to induce a radical shift in this ritual. I wish to revert to Haran's textual evidence, based on Deut. 33: 10: יָשִׂימוּ קְטוֹרָה בְּאַפֶּךָ "they offer [NIV has "he offers"] incense before you," and in particular on I Sam 2: 28: וּבָחֹר אֹתוֹ מִכָּל שִׁבְטֵי יִשְׂרָאֵל לִי לְכֹהֵן לַעֲלוֹת עַל מִזְבְּחִי לְהַקְטִיר קְטֹרֶת לָשֵׂאת אֵפוֹד לְפָנָי "I chose your father out of all the tribes of Israel to be my priest, to go up to my altar, to burn incense, and to wear an ephod in my presence." I wonder that Haran has chosen this verse, "a staff of broken reed,"[12] as evidence of an incense celebration at such an early stage as the period of the creation of the book of Samuel.[13] The authenticity of

---

[10] See Nelson Glueck, "מזבחות קטורת" *Eretz-Israel* 10 (1971), pp. 120-125 concerning the Tell el-Hulefi excavations, and W. Zwickel, *Räucherkult und Räuchergeräte* (Göttingen, 1990), p. 86ff. See also Introduction pp. 15ff.

[11] See Introduction p. 13 concerning a study by N. M. Sarna.

[12] Isaiah 36: 6.

[13] In *Temples and Temple-Service in Ancient Israel*, pp. 237-8, he states: "If anyone wishes to prove the antiquity of this use [of incense in the Temple alone], but does not consider the traditions recorded by P as ancient enough for his purpose, he can safely take his stand on such evidence as Deut. 33: 10; I Sam. 2: 28." I do not intend to evaluate the merit of the verse in Deut. יָשִׂימוּ קְטוֹרָה בְּאַפֶּךָ "they offer incense before you," since the date of the final editing of Deuteronomy is itself a contentious issue; moreover, this verse does not indicate a particular incense celebration on an altar, unlike Exod. 30: 7. As I have argued, the placing of spices and incense on a table as complements to a meal was a widespread custom in the ancient Near East, in the home and in the temple.

this verse and the time of its inclusion in the present text is a matter of contention among scholars;[14] and I wish to add another proposal, which seems to me to have been overlooked,[15] regarding the late origin of I Sam. 2: 28 quoted above.

---

[14] K. Nielsen, in *Incense in Ancient Israel*, p. 102, quotes the different scholarly opinions concerning the date of this verse. It seems that all agree that vv. 27-36 are not of the "Urtext"; the controversies are limited to the questions of whether they are "reworked" or completely later additions, and the issue of the *terminus ante*, the earliest date of editing.

[15] W. Nowack states in his work *Handkommentar zum Alten Testament, Richter, Ruth u. Bücher Samuelis* (Göttingen, 1902), p. 14: "Diese Vv. [27-36] sind als Einarbeitung von allen Seiten annerkannt." ("These verses are acknowledged by all as interpolations.") He interprets v. 36 "Then everyone left in your family line will come and bow down before him for a piece of silver and a crust of bread" as referring to Josiah's reform, and the alms-basket support granted to the provincial priests, described in II Kings 23: 9. Karl Budde, in *Die Bücher Samuel* (Tübingen, 1902), p. 22, also connects the prophecy to Josiah's reform, and adds that therefore the prophecy pericope cannot be dated before 621 B.C.E. M. Tsevat writes in "Studies in the Book of Samuel," *HUCA* 32 (1961) p. 193: "The connection of v. 36 with this [Josiah's] reform is strengthened," and adds: "Whether v. 36 is contemporaneous with the situation it describes – priests in distress seeking relief through association with well-provided priestly offices – cannot be said with certainty, but it is unlikely that it is much later." Peter Mommer in *Samuel* (Neukirchen, 1991), p.11 states that vv. 27-36 are an inseparable pericope, and affirms that it refers to the situation of the provincial priests after Josiah's reform; hence that is the *terminus a quo*. P. D. Miscall, in *I Samuel* (Bloomington, 1986), does not refer to the dating of this pericope, but states on p. 21: "There are priests in Kings, but no houses, of Eli or otherwise, which support the supposition that Eli's house is the house of Aaron." Miscall expresses, in a different manner, my thesis that the concept of a specific tribe chosen by God for His priestly service does not appear in Kings, and certainly not in Samuel. R. H. Pfeiffer, in *Introduction to the Old Testament* (New York, 1941), writes on pp. 368-9: "There is, of course, a great variety of opinion about I Sam. 2: 27-36," and "A well intentioned reader living demonstrably after the publication of the Priestly Code, if not after the codification of the Pentateuch about 400 B.C., could not resist the impulse to put on paper his muddled ideas about the vicissitudes of the priesthood in ancient Israel....In conformance with the teaching of the Priestly Code, he regarded all priests of Israel as descendants of Aaron." Pfeiffer corroborates here my thesis that the genealogical requirement for priesthood was a Priestly Code innovation.

Only M. Noth, in "Samuel and Silo," *Vetus Testamentum* 13 (1963), pp. 393-4, does not consider the prophecy as referring to the status of the provincial priests after Josiah's reform, but rather to some struggle between the Jerusalemite priests and priests from Shilo, who tried to regain their lost position after the consecration of Solomon's Temple. The degradation of Abiathar, the last Shilonite priest, by Solomon, terminated the priestly status of this family. Noth therefore considers this passage as appropriate to the early monarchic period, after Solomon's death. None of these scholars

My argument consists of the fact that genealogy as a prerequisite for priesthood is a late P postulate, and hence this verse, which concerns the choosing of priests out of a specific tribe, must be of a late, post-exilic date. There is nowhere an indication that Eli was a descendant of Aaron. As previously argued, the issue of legitimate family or tribal origin appears in late, post-exilic books: Ezra and Nehemiah. In the Sinai narrative, while Nadab and Abihu appear along with Aaron, they are not described as his sons,[16] and neither they nor Aaron are designated as priests; on the contrary one may assume from the context that Aaron was not considered among the priests.[17] Nor is there mention of Levites in the Sinai narrative. The genealogical prerequisite for priests and Levites is anchored in the P section. We read in Exod. 28: 1: ואתה הקרב אליך את אהרן אחיך ואת בניו אתו מתוך בני ישראל "Have Aaron your brother brought to you from among the Israelites,"[18] and similarly concerning the Levites, in Num. 3: 12: ואני הנה לקחתי את הלוים מתוך בני ישראל "I have taken the Levites from among the Israelites." The parallelism of these verses, each of which establishes lineage as a precondition for cultic service (for priests on the one hand and Levites on the other), is striking; both reflect a P section requisite and

---

considered the issue of priests chosen from a specific tribe, a circumstance which prevailed only in the post-exilic period, later than Josiah's reform, as I have demonstrated; this is also suggested by G.F.Moore, *The International Critical Commentary. A Critical and Exegetical Commentary on Judges* (2nd ed. Edinburgh, 1898), XVII: 7, p. 383, as explained in detail in note 28.

[16] We read in Exod. 24: 1: עלה אל ה׳ אתה ואהרן נדב ואביהוא ושבעים מזקני ישראל "Come up to the Lord, you and Aaron, Nadab and Abihu, and seventy of the elders of Israel"; and in v. 9: ויעל משה ואהרן נדב ואביהוא ושבעים מזקני ישראל "Moses and Aaron, Nadab and Abihu, and the seventy elders of Israel went up."

[17] We read in Exod. 19: 24: "...ועלית אתה ואהרן עמך והכהנים והעם אל יהרסו לעלות go down and bring Aaron up with you. But the priests and the people must not force their way through to come up to the Lord." Aaron and the priests are separated. The offering of sacrifices is not associated with the priesthood or a specific lineage, as we read in Exod. 24: 5: וישלח את נערי בני ישראל ויעלו עלת ויזבח זבחים שלמים "Then he sent young Israelite men, and they offered burnt offerings and sacrificed young bulls as fellowship offerings." Priestly status is not contingent upon genealogy, as we read in Exod. 19: 6: ואתם תהיו לי ממלכת כהנים "you will be for me a kingdom of priests."

[18] There is no longer a kingdom of priests; only Aaron and his descendants are now suitable for the priesthood.

[19] Exod. 32: 26 concerning the virtue of the Levites: ויאמר מי לה׳ אלי, ויאספו אליו כל בני לוי "...and said, 'Whoever is for the Lord, come to me.' And all the Levites rallied to him" is a late P addition to a story which may have been of earlier origin. Noth states in *Exodus* p. 245: "Now in any case it is clear that the Levite-passage is to be judged a later addition; its real claim is not to describe the punishment of Israel but to narrate

custom.[19] Genealogy is of no importance in the appointment of priests, or High Priests, in the early writings;[20] here, lineage and tribal association are not mentioned.[21]

We encounter an interesting exception to this rule, an occurrence in which an ideological motive is discernible, and where we may positively

---

and give reasons for the entrusting of the priestly office to the Levites, and in so doing it presupposes the occasion of this punishment." W. Beyerlin, in *Origins and History of the Oldest Sinaitic Traditions*, writes on p. 18 ff concerning Exod. chap. 32: "It is clear that this chapter also is not a unity....The action of the Levites in exacting vengeance is not presupposed. The report of this was obviously inserted later." And on p. 132, we read: "Similarly the tradition of vv. 25-29 which has been added to the E-source has been determined by the group interests of the Levitical priesthood, which found in it the aetiological explanation and defence of their right to the priesthood." This quotation also corroborates my thesis concerning the struggles of various groups for the domination of the sacrificial cult, and the attempts of each party to create, by all available means, including the invention of myths, a legitimation of their viewpoint and conduct. E. Meyer, in *Die Israeliten und Ihre Nachbarstämme* (Halle, 1906), states on p. 82: "...der Segen Jakobs von der Identität von Lewit und Priester nicht nur nichts weiss, sondern sie gerade ausschliesst." ("Jacob's blessing [Gen. 49: 5-7] not only does not know anything concerning the identity of Levite and priest, but moreover forthrightly excludes it.") The issue of the Levites is much debated, and I wish to quote from the introduction of a study by K. Mohlenbrink, "Die Levitische Überlieferung des Alten Testaments," *ZAW* 11 (1934) pp. 189-231. He states:"...wie wichtig einerseits die Geschichte des israelitischen Priestertums für alle Zweige der ATlichen Wissenschaft ist, und wie sehr anderseits die Auffassung der Fachvertreter immer noch divergieren." ("...on the one hand, how important the history of the Israelite priesthood is for all branches of the OT discipline, and on the other hand how divergent are the conceptions of the specialized scholars of this field.") Mohlenbrink quotes in note 2 a substantial list of these different opinions. The issue of the Levites is not a primary objective of this study, and I will therefore not enlarge its discussion further than necessary in relation to my thesis. At any rate, it seems to me that notwithstanding the different opinions, there is no dispute among scholars that the lineage issue of the priesthood is of a later date than Samuel's original redaction.

[20] See discussion and substantiation in Appendix IV.

[21] Even in the post-exilic Ezekiel, where we read והכהנים הלוים בני צדוק אשר שמרו את משמרת מקדשי בתעות בני ישראל מעלי "But the priests who are Levites and descendants of Zadok and who faithfully carried out the duties of my sanctuary when the Israelites went astray from me (44: 15)," it is the sons of Zadok who are appropriate to "stand before me to offer sacrifices" rather than the sons of Aaron. Further, the reason is not a genealogical preference, but their loyalty to the Lord at a time when the other group of Levites misbehaved: כי אם הלוים אשר רחקו מעלי בתעות ישראל "The Levites who went far from me when Israel went astray (44: 10)." A study of the definition of the term שבט and its connection to the genealogical issue of the Levites is offered in Appendix V.

assume a later interjection into an earlier text. We read in I Kings 12: 31, concerning the priests appointed by Jeroboam: ויעש את בית במות ויעש כהנים מקצות העם אשר לא היו מבני לוי "... built shrines on high places and appointed priests from all sorts of people, even though they were not Levites."[22] In the following chapter 13, the איש אלהים, "man of God," foretells the destruction of the altar and the slaughtering of its priests by Josiah. However, it seems inexplicable that at the fulfillment of this prophecy, as narrated in II Kings 23: 20 ויזבח את כל כהני הבמות אשר שם על המזבחות "...slaughtered all the priests of those high places on the altars," the fact that these priests were usurpers of levitical privileges is not brought against them as a motive for their execution; their only sin was their ministering at the בתי הבמות אשר בערי שמרון אשר עשו מלכי ישראל להכעיס "... shrines at the high places that the kings of Israel had built in the towns of Samaria that had provoked [the Lord] (23: 19)." Further, the term כהנים, "priests", appears often in II Kings within the narrative of Josiah's kingship, but generally without an association to lineage; only in II Chr. 35: 14 do we read: כי לכהנים בני אהרן "because the priests, the 'descendants of Aaron'...."

It seems that the terms "Levite" and כהן "priest" corresponded in the monarchic period to a "guild" of professionals,[23] who probably tried to keep strangers and newcomers from entering this undoubtedly rewarding occupation, and that it was the king who had the power and the privilege to nominate his friends and loyal subjects to membership in these "guilds." Solomon nominated Zadok, who anointed him as king: ויקח צדוק הכהן את קרן השמן מן האהל וימשח את שלמה "Zadok the priest took the horn of oil from the sacred tent and anointed Solomon (I Kings 1: 39)"; Solomon also deposed Abiathar, who sided with Adonijah, his rival for the kingship, as we have seen. One may also speculate that Jehoiada, who rescued Joash, was

---

[22] This issue is, as one may expect, much more elaborately described in II Chr. 11: 13-17. There we read that the priests and Levites left the Northern Kingdom כי הזניחם ירבעם ובניו מכהן לה' "because Jeroboam and his sons had rejected them as priests of the Lord (v.14)."

[23] See E. Meyer, *Die Israeliten und Ihre Nachbarstämme*, p. 52: "Die Priesterschaft bildet ein Berufsstand, der, wie so scharf wie möglich ausgesprochen ist, nicht auf Abstammung beruht, sondern auf freier Berufswahl." ("The priesthood constitutes a professional association, which, to express it as precisely as possible, did not depend on lineage, but free choice.") G. B. Gray, in *Sacrifice in the Old Testament* (Oxford, 1925), speculates that there was a progressive narrowing of the priesthood, and writes on p. 240: "Whatever sense we place on 'Levite', whether a tribal or a professional, the last narrative makes it clear that there were priests who were not Levites, as well as priests who were Levites."

not a priest before this event, and that he received his nomination to the priesthood from the king as a reward for his loyalty and assistance in crowning him king. In the first appearance of Jehoiada, in II Kings 11: 4, at the start of his enterprise to rescue the king, he does not have the title priest;[24] he is called merely Jehoiada, and was probably a high court official who had authority over the Royal Guard, as we read: ובשנה השביעית שלח יהוידע ויקח את שרי המאיות לכרי ולרצים "In the seventh year Jehoiada sent for the commanders of units of a hundred, the Carites and the guards." It is only after the event that Jehoiada is called by the title הכהן "the priest."[25] Indirect evidence appears in II Kings 10: 11: ויך יהוא את כל הנשארים לבית אחאב ביזרעאל וכל גדליו ומידעיו וכהניו "So Jehu killed everyone in Jezreel who remained of the house of Ahab as well as his chief men, his close friends and his priests." We may assume that the priests were not merely neutral clerics, since in that case it is unlikely that they would have been killed among the king's loyal political and administrative state officers; they were more likely friends and associates of the king, who were rewarded with titles for their faithful service in other fields.

There is also evidence that "Levite" was a technical term for a man trained as a ritual celebrant, rather than an indication of a specific lineage.[26]

---

24 In II Chr. 22: 11 we find the first occurrence in which Jehoiada has his title of priest הכהן; however, in our consideration of the date of this source, we must conclude that this phrase in II Chr. is a later insertion into the earlier text of II Kings 11, which was likely the primary source taken over by II Chr. The editor of II Chr. was probably faced with the problem of how to explain the fact that Jehoiada showed the king's son to his allies, "the commanders of units of a hundred.[II Kings 11: 4]"; the child was hidden by Jehosheba, king Joram's daughter and Ahaziah's sister. As is common in other similar occurrences, the editor of Chr. attempts to explain the *lectio difficilis* of the earlier texts, and adds: יהושבעת בת המלך יהורם אשת יהוידע הכהן Now we have an excellent rationalization for Jehoiada's involvement in the rescue and crowning of Joash: Jehoiada was married to Jehosheba, king Joram's daughter. On the other hand, in II Chr. 23, in which Jehoiada's plan and actions are described in parallel to the text in II Kings chap. 11, Jehoiada appears without any title, exactly as in II Kings.

25 Verse 17, in which he made the "covenant between the Lord, the king and the people," is the one additional occurrence in which he appears without this title.

26 With respect to the term כהן, there is no issue concerning its meaning in the P section. On the other hand, there are some odd occurrences of this term in this Micah narrative, such as his utterance והיה לי לאב ולכהן "and be my father and priest (Jud.17:10)"; וימלא; מיכה את יד הלוי ויהי לו הנער לכהן "Then Micah installed the Levite, and the young man became his priest (v.12)," and כי היה לי הלוי לכהן "since this Levite has become my priest (v. 13)." One has the impression that while the term Levite signifies a member of an exclusive professional "clerical guild," one becomes a כהן by nomination, by the will and resolution of a person who has the authority to appoint someone to this

We read in Jud. 17: 7: ויהי נער מבית לחם יהודה ממשפחת יהודה והוא לוי
והוא גר שם "A young Levite from Bethlehem in Judah,[27] who had been

---

special office. We encounter the term מלא יד in Num. 3: 3:אשר מלא יד הכהנים בני אהרן
ידם לכהן "...who were ordained to serve as priests," but also in Exod. 32: 29: ויאמר
משה מלאו ידכם היום לה׳ "Then Moses said, 'You have been set apart to the Lord
today,'" in a matter which has no reference to a ritual appointment, but to a nomination as "distinctive soldiers" who are permitted to kill their kinfolk for the glorification
of the Deity. We find a more explicit statement of this idea in II Sam 8: 18: כהנים היו
ובני דוד "and David's sons were royal advisers." It is obvious that the term כהנים could
not have meant "priests" here, since in v. 17, previously cited, Zadok and Ahimelech
are the priests. The Targum translates this term as רברבין, that is, "great men" or
"great officers"; the LXX has αὐλάρχαι,"chiefs of the court," and the NIV has also
interpreted accordingly. Ramban in his interpretation of Gen. 41: 45 states כי לשון
שרות, אבל לא לאלהות בלבד, כי הנה ובני דוד כהנים היו, ובמקומו בדברי הימים והאמת
כהונה המלך ליד הראשונים דוד ובני (יז :יח .א) "...really the term כהונה [signifies]
'service, ministry', but not exclusively to the Deity, since [we see that in lieu of the
expression] 'and the sons of David were כהנים' we [have] in I Chr. 18: 17 [the same
declaration, reading] 'And the sons of David were הראשונים [literally the first] chief
about the king.'" Radak and Ralbag also interpret the term כהנים as chief officers. A
midrash in B.T. Nedarim 62a deduces that David's sons were "great in the knowledge
of the Torah"; the term רברבין in the Targum also lends itself to such a homily.
On the other hand, concerning the term כהן in II Sam. 20: 26: וגם עירא היארי היה
כהן לדוד, we find divergent interpretations. The LXX translates this as ἱερεύς and,
likely following this, the NIV uses "priest." A midrash in B.T. Erubin 63a also assumes
Ira was a priest, to whom David granted all his tithes, and that is the reason for the
expression כהן לדוד, literally a "priest to David." But the Targum translates this as
רב לדוד, a chief officer. Rashi quotes the above-cited midrash, but adds that the simple
meaning is a chief officer; other traditional commentators, such as Radak, Ralbag, and
Mezudat David, translate similarly. In I Kings 4: 5 וזבוד בן נתן כהן רעה המלך, the
Targum translates this as רבא שושבינא דמלכא "officer [who is] counselor to the king,"
the LXX uses ἑταῖρος "friend," and the NIV interprets it as "a priest and personal
adviser to the king." The traditional commentators similarly interpret "chief officer and
counselor," David's steady companion. Thus we observe that the term כהן in the early
writings indicated a person nominated for a special assignment of various types, not
necessarily related to ritual duties.

27 The Sages were aware of this apparent contradiction to the Pentateuch, and we read in
B.T. Baba Batra 109b a lengthy discussion of this verse. The Talmud attempts to
demonstrate that one's mother's family, not merely his father's, is also considered as his
family, and brings evidence from this verse: אמרת והוא לוי – אלמא מלוי אתי,ממשפחת
יהודה יהודה – אלמא מיהודה אתי. אלא לאו דאבוה מלוי ואימיה מיהודה וקאמר ממשפחת
"It says 'and he is a Levi' – you might say he [originates] from [the tribe of] Levi, [but
then it says] 'of the family Judah' – you might say he [originates] from [the tribe of]
Judah. It is that his father [originates] from [the tribe of] Levi, and his mother from
[the tribe of] Judah, and [Scripture] calls [him] of the family of Judah." The Talmud
continues with its rhetoric and comes up with other solutions to this riddle (for instance, that his name was Levi, but he did not originate from the tribe of Levi), and

living within the clan of Judah." In vv. 12-13 we read: וימלא מיכה את יד
הלוי ויהי לו הנער לכהן ... ויאמר מיכה עתה ידעתי כי ייטיב ה׳ לי כי היה לי
הלוי לכהן "Then Micah installed the Levite, and the young man became
his priest....And Micah said, 'Now I know that the Lord will be good to me,
since this Levite has become my priest.'" It is obvious that this Levite was
a member of the tribe of Judah, and Micah consecrated him as a priest.
Micah was exhilarated to have a trained celebrant as his priest, and therefore
assumed he would receive favour from God; it was this training that was the
Levite's qualification, and the fact that he was of the tribe of Judah was of
no relevance to his aptitude to minister as a priest.[28] We also observe in 18:
30 that the Levites' descendants were probably priests to the Dan tribe. We
read there: ויהונתן בן גרשם בן מנשה הוא ובניו היו כהנים לשבט הדני עד יום
גלות הארץ "... and Jonathan son of Gershom, the son of Moses, and his
sons were priests for the tribe of Dan until the time of the captivity of the
land." There is no mention of an Aaronite genealogy in any of these occurrences.

It is remarkable, yet typical, that the Samaritans also retroject to the
period of Eli their own genealogical dispute with Judah concerning the
legitimacy of the High Priest's family,[29] a contention which is considered a

---

ends its eloquent deliberations with the conclusion that since the Levite עשה מעשה
מנשה דאתי מיהודה – תלאו הכתוב ביהודה "acted like Manasseh [the malefactor king],
who originated from [the tribe of] Judah, Scripture associated him with the [tribe of]
Judah." The Talmud similarly explains v. 18: 30: Jonathan son of Gershom was really
a son of משה Moses, not of מנשה Manasseh, but since he acted like Manasseh, he was
called his descendant. The *nun* of מנשה appears as a superscript in the MT, hence the
association with משה. Mezudat David, a traditional commentator, offers another explanation; he states that the words "of the family of Judah" refer to the town of Bethlehem,
not to the young man, who was a Levite who merely lived in Bethlehem.

[28] *The International Critical Commentary, Judges*, XVII: 7, p. 383, rejects the different
theories brought by various scholars to explain the phrase והוא לוי, and states: "The
true explanation probably is that *Levite* here designates his calling, not his race. He was
a regularly trained priest, who possessed the traditional religious lore, and especially the
art of using and interpreting the oracle. The calling was doubtless, like all others,
ordinarily, though not exclusively, hereditary; and in later times all Levites were supposed to be descended from an eponymous ancestor, Levi. This *genealogical fiction* [the
stress is mine] was made the easier...." This postulate corresponds to my thesis; the
author articulates the meaning of Levite "here", but one has the impression from his
ongoing explanation that the same definition would be generally valid. The use of the
term כהן, as shown, also corroborates this thesis.

[29] John MacDonald, *The Theology of the Samaritans* (London, 1964), Introduction, p.
17: "Eli's sin was that he coveted the High-Priesthood for himself."

late post-exilic[30] development. The Samaritans had to impute the split with
Judah to that period, to justify the existence of the sanctuary at Shilo instead of Mount Gerizim; and a genealogical disqualification[31] served to
discredit Eli,[32] who set up the rival sanctuary. There must have been some
vague recollection in the minds of the people of a rivalry between the various sanctuaries, especially concerning the Shilo shrine, and that theme was
later altered and adapted to provide a legitimate motive for the split with
Judah. The genealogical issue regarding the High Priest cannot be considered authentic, since Uzzi, the son of Bukki, the legitimate Samaritan High
Priest at the time of Eli,[33] is also mentioned in the priestly lineage in the
Judean chronology, in I Chr. 5: 31: ואבישוע הוליד את בקי ובקי הוליד את
עזי "Abishua the father of Bukki, Bukki the father of Uzzi (6: 5 in NIV)."
I do not wish to expand upon this issue of lineage as an absolute prerequisite for ritual and other nominations, but merely state that one has the
impression that such a concept, in its broadest applications, became a problem only in the post-exilic period. Intermarriages were also not censured
before that period, and we have seen that questions of priestly lineage, as
well as the issue of intermarriage, arise for the first time in the Ezra and
Nehemiah narratives. In conclusion, we must agree that I Sam. 2: 28,
declaring that the priests were specially chosen from all the other tribes,[34] a
concept which also appears in the narrative of the Korah rebellion and its
aftermath in Num. chaps. 16-17, is of post-exilic date and belongs to the P
edition.

---

[30] See Menachem Mor,"The Persian, Hellenistic and Hasmonean Period," in *The Samaritans*, ed. A.D. Crown (Tübingen, 1989), p. 2: "Our knowledge of the Samaritans begins at the time of Nehemiah's governorship in Judea."

[31] John MacDonald, *The Theology of the Samaritans*, p. 17: "Eli came of the Ithamar branch of the priesthood, and the Samaritans ever since his time have rejected the claims of that branch in favour of the sons of Phinehas."

[32] ibid p. 17: "His [Eli's] covetousness led him to gather all sorts of malcontents to him, and he moved to Shiloh, where he set up a sanctuary in rivalry to that on Mount Gerizim."

[33] See John Bowman, trans. and ed., *Samaritan Documents Relating to their History, Religion and Life* (Pittsburgh, 1977), p. 89.

[34] From the literary point of view, one has the impression that the narrative prepares the reader for the replacement of the Elides by Samuel, who was not from the tribe of Levi; he was an Ephraimite (I Sam. 1: 1). This is one of the reasons for Budde's assertion, cited above, that the pericope 27-36 is a later interpolation. He states, p. 22: "Denn die Erzählung zielt bis zu Ende von Cap. 3 und wieder von Cap. 7 an durchaus auf einen Ersatz der Eliden durch Samuel ab, und gerade der findet in v. 27-36 gar keine Stelle." ("Because in all respects the narrative up to the end of chap. 3, and again from chap.

I suggested that the Pi'el of קטר is appropriate for the burning of incense in a censer, whereas the Hiph'il is the suitable form for the bringing of the incense up onto an altar. The term קטר in the sense of going up in smoke is probably an ancient element in the Hebrew language, as in other Semitic languages, but we do not know when it became a term applied to a ritual act of burning some form of incense, or bread, or fat of animals; we have no authentic texts to establish this, considering that the term does not appear in the patriarchal or Sinai narratives of the Pentateuch. It does not appear in Judges, and I discussed its solitary[35] occurrence in Samuel. The occurrences in Kings cannot serve as evidence, since we must admit that in many cases the appearance of the term is a later interjection whose motive is evident. For instance, the stereotypical accusation העם מזבחים ומקטרים בבמות "the people continued to offer sacrifices and 'burn incense' [this is the interpretation of the NIV, but it is not necessarily accurate[36]] there [in the high places]," occurs frequently before Josiah's reform; its very frequency tends to weaken its authenticity. I would like to quote one interesting occurrence of such an interjected phrase to demonstrate its lack of coherence and rationale. We read in I Kings 3: 2-3: רק העם מזבחים בבמות כי לא נבנה בית לשם ה' עד הימים ההם. ויאהב שלמה את ה' ללכת בחקות דוד אביו רק בבמות הוא מזבח ומקטיר "The people, however, were still sacrificing in the high places, because a temple had not yet been built for the name of the Lord. Solomon showed his love for the Lord by walking according to the statutes of his father David, except that he offered sacrifices and burned incense on the

---

7, aims at a replacement of the Elides by Samuel, and in contrast, he [Samuel] is not mentioned in vv. 27-36.") Nowack, *Handkommentar zum Alten Testament, Richter, Ruth u. Bücher Samuelis*, p. 14, affirms the same idea, in different words. Eli's lineage from the tribe of Levi is also never mentioned.

[35] The term קטר appears twice more in Samuel, also in chap. 2, vv.16-17, and can therefore not serve as evidence, since the entire Eli narrative, the misdeeds of his sons, and the prophecy of his punishment, have their own motive. We do not find any other occurrences in Samuel of the term קטר, although there are many instances of sacrifices in Samuel (I Sam. 1: 3, 21, 24; 6: 14-15; 7: 9; 9: 12; 10: 8; 13: 9, 13; 15: 21-22; 16: 2, 3, 5; II Sam. 6: 16; 24: 22, 24, 25). It is interesting to note that in I Sam. 15: 22, the fat of animals is mentioned, but not the term קטר. We read there הנה שמע מזבח טוב להקשיב מחלב אילים "To obey is better than sacrifice, and to heed is better than the fat of rams."

[36] Noth, in *Könige*, p. 49, states on this phrase: "...wahrscheinlich eine herkömmliche Wortzusammenstellung, die in der Bedeutung 'schlachten und verbrennen' allgemein das kultische Opfer ohne Bezug auf bestimmte Opferarten meint." ("...probably a common literary compound, meaning 'slaughtering and burning', a generic ritual sacrifice without any indication of a specific type.")

high places." The insertion of v. 2 concerning the people's sacrificial cus-toms right after the narrative of Solomon's marriage to Pharaoh's daughter clearly demonstrates its intrusion into an inappropriate spot.[37] The text itself displays incoherence; verse 2 starts in an accusatory manner, with the conjunction רק,[38] but ends with a vindication.[39] On the other hand, v. 3 addresses the same accusation against Solomon, but provides no excuse for his behaviour. The legitimacy of the people's custom to sacrifice at the high places is established, "because there was no house built"; this makes the accusatory phrase "only he [Solomon] sacrificed..." entirely redundant, and absolutely unjustified. The authenticity of these two accusatory phrases, and similar ones in I and II Kings, must be considered with skepticism.[40] Thus,

---

[37] Verse 1 fits well in the context as a continuation of the last v. 46 of chapter 2, which ends with והממלכה נכונה ביד שלמה "The kingdom was now firmly established in Solomon's hands." King Solomon's marriage to the daughter of the Pharaoh, the ruler of a great and prestigious kingdom, gives further evidence of Solomon's achievement and prominent status. The initiation of a new chapter and an entirely different subject matter with the term רק seems peculiar, to say the least, and there is suggestion of a similarity with the stereotypical phrase רק הבמות לא סרו "But the high places were not taken away." One must assume that the two verses 2 and 3b, concerning the offering at the *Bamoth*, are later glosses; without them, the text would be perfect. The phrase "The people, however, were still sacrificing at the high places (v. 2)" has no relevance within the context of the narrative, and it is only the first part of v. 3 which harmonizes with the story. The phrase "Solomon showed his love for the Lord" is an impeccable start and explanation for the succeeding narrative concerning Solomon's remarkable "thousand burnt offerings." The phrases referring to the offerings in high places are thus an unconnected intrusion into the narrative. It is difficult to perceive whether both glosses are from the same author; in the event that they originate from two different authors, it is also not clear whether the comment concerning Solomon exonerates the king, or censures him. Still, however we perceive the author's intentions, we can deduce his motive in interjecting the comments. From verse 1 it appears that Solomon built the "temple of the Lord," and therefore Solomon's sacrifice at the high place in Gibeon would have amounted to a transgression according to the views held in the editor's time. He therefore had to insert his gloss to justify the people's conduct, and/or Solomon's.

[38] For example, see II Kings 12: 4; 14: 4 and other instances, where רק unequivocally implies an accusation.

[39] The people are entirely exonerated, since there was no prohibition against sacrificing at high places before the construction of the Temple, even according to the P code.

[40] As we have seen, Haran does not rely on the various verses in Kings to defend his theory of incense celebration at that period, probably for the same reason, and brings as evidence only the two verses in Samuel and Numbers.

In a recent review of Rubenstein's *The History of Sukkoth in the Second Temple and Rabbinic Periods* (E-mail Ioudaios), Professor Basser suggested: "Perhaps models of

from textual evidence, the earliest date we can establish for the use of the term קְטֹר in connection with legitimate ritual procedure would be the period of Isaiah (perhaps as early as Isa. 1: 13, although we have there only קְטֹרֶת as a noun; as a verb the root occurs only in chap. 65). This date would well match the situation I described, namely the arrival and wider distribution of frankincense in the region, and the Mesopotamian influence. As I noted earlier, Mesopotamian influence gained the upper hand in Northern Israel somewhat earlier than in the South, and this explains the findings of censer artifacts there from an earlier period than in the South. The same consideration also applies to the occurrences of the term קְטֹר in Amos and Hosea, prophets who were active in a slightly earlier period than that of Isaiah. In any event, these occurrences of קְטֹר do not confirm an independent daily incense celebration on a specific separate altar; incense in Isaiah and Amos is linked to meal offerings, and that in Hosea is associated with alien idolatrous rituals.

There is an inherent difficulty in finding convincing attestations which prove the negation of some event or deed. Direct evidence of something which did not exist is a contradiction in terms. The proposition that a daily incense celebration on a special altar did not exist in the pre-exilic period can therefore be demonstrated only by circumstantial evidence. I am confident that a sufficient level of valid text-critical analysis, dependable historical documentation, and logical conjecture has been presented to prove my case beyond an assertion *ex silentio*. A rational explanation of the many etymological, textual and literary questions posed moves beyond a mere assertion of what did not happen, and forms itself into a tenable theory of what did happen. The course of the development of the incense celebration

---

simultaneous developments might make more sense in the studies of ancient texts...and the ramifications of such approaches might be considered." Such speculation would perhaps lead us to consider the antiquity of sweet-smelling smoke theophany as earlier than the incense offering in Isaiah, and to consider the verses in Samuel and Kings not as interjections but as evidence of other types of ritual cultic practice. This would, however, result in positing institutional practice with no evidence beyond the *en passant* references of these few verses. Indeed the ancient traditions may hide such complexities, but it has proven sufficiently difficult to unravel and demonstrate one rational course out of the evidence considered; to attempt the demonstration of rival models based on no further evidence would yield nothing more than idle speculations and the paraphrase of verses. No model of antiquity can account for every loose detail; it is perhaps impossible, and certainly beyond the ability of this scholar, to deal with "many things [that] happen at once in every period" and only come to our attention at the surface of many texts, reflecting very little of the time periods at issue.

in ancient Israel is deduced from critical analysis of the biblical texts and contrasting documentation from other sources. The significance of the incense celebration in the last period of the Second Temple, and the financial concerns of the priesthood, are documented in these sources, and the hypothesized developmental stages of the incense ritual are revealed through critical analysis of the biblical narratives concerning incense and its correlated events. The post-biblical texts substantiate the validity of my interrogation, confirming the reality of the contradictions between certain biblical pericopes, and the ambiguous statements in others. It is evident that the solutions posited in those texts are divergent from mine; the Sages' explanations necessarily had to conform to their own frames of reference.

In conclusion, I would like to quote Professor Haran, in an article which appeared in 1995 in a weekly supplement to the Israeli newspaper *Haaretz*: "In the Humanities, it is impossible to physically go and control the facts; it is not a discipline [in which facts are] verifiable. It is [a discipline] based in part on the creative imagination of the researcher (and it is important that his imagination be concrete and well-based), but primarily on a faculty of rational argumentation. I am convinced that those whose argumentation is stronger, and more reasonable, come close to truth, in the science of Humanities." I hope to have justified this conviction.

Appendix I
List of 44 Occurrences of the Verb קטר in MT Pentateuch

	MT	Onkelos	Samaritan	Neophyti	LXX
Group 1, Subgroup 1.1					
Ex 29:13	והקטרת המזבחה	ותסיק	ותועד	ותסדר	ἐπιθήσεις
Ex 29:18	המזבחה ... והקטרת	ותסיק	ותועד	ותסדר	ἀνοίσεις
Ex 29:25	והקטרת המזבחה	ותסיק	ותועד	ותסדר	ἀνοίσεις
Lev 1: 9	המזבחה...והקטיר	ויסיק	ויועד	ויסדר וי	ἐπιθήσουσιν
Lev 1:13	והקטיר המזבחה	ויסיק	ויועד	ויסדר	ἐπιθήσει
Lev 1:15	והקטיר המזבחה	ויסיק	ויועד	ויסדר	ἐπιθήσει
Lev 1:17	והקטיר המזבחה	ויסיק	ויועד	ויסדר	ἐπιθήσει
Lev 2: 2	המזבחה .. והקטיר	ויסיק	ויועד	ויסדר	ἐπιθήσει
Lev 2: 9	והקטיר המזבחה	ויסיק	ויועד	ויסדר	ἐπιθήσει
Lev 3: 5	המזבחה ... והקטירו	ויסקון	ויועדון	ויסדרון ויסדרון	ἀνοίσουσιν
Lev 3: 11	המזבחה ... והקטירו	ויסיקיניה	ויועד	ויסדר	ἀνοίσει
Lev 3: 16	המזבחה ... והקטירם	ויסיקינון	ויועדון	ויסדר	ἀνοίσει
Lev 4: 19	והקטיר המזבחה	ויסיק	ויועד	ויסדר	ἀνοίσει
Lev 4: 26	יקטיר המזבחה	יסיק	יועד	יסדר	ἀνοίσει
Lev 4: 31	המזבחה .. והקטיר	ויסיק	ויועד	יסדר	ἀνοίσει
Lev 4: 35	והקטיר המזבחה	ויסיק	ויועד	יסדר	ἐπιθήσει
Lev 5: 12	והקטיר המזבחה	ויסיק	ויועד	ויסדר	ἐπιθήσει
Lev 6: 8	והקטיר המזבח	ויסיק	ויועד	ויסדר	ἀνοίσει
Lev 7: 5	המזבחה ... והקטיר	ויסיק	ויועד	ויסדר	ἀνοίσει
Lev 7: 31	המזבחה ... והקטיר	ויסיק	ויועד	ויסדר	ἀνοίσει
Lev 8: 16	המזבחה ... ויקטר	ואסיק	ואועד	וסדר	ἀνήνεγκεν
Lev 8: 21	המזבחה ... ויקטר	ואסיק	ואועד	וסדר	ἀνήνεγκεν
Lev 8: 28	המזבחה ... ויקטר	ואסיק	ואועד	וסדר	ἀνήνεγκεν
Lev 9: 10	הקטיר המזבחה	אסיק	אועד	סדר	ἀνήνεγκεν
Lev 9: 14	המזבחה ... ויקטר	ואסיק	ואועד	וסדר	ἐπέθηκεν
Lev 9: 20	המזבחה ... ויקטר	ואסיק	ואועד	וסדר	ἀνήνεγκεν
Lev 16: 25	יקטיר המזבחה	יסיק	יועד	יסדר	ἀνοίσει
Num 5: 26	והקטיר המזבחה	ויסיק	יועד	ויסדר	ἀνοίσει

Group 1, Subgroup 1.2

Lev 4: 10	והקטיר... על	ויסדר ויועדנון ויסיקינון	ויסדר	ἀνοίσει
Lev 6: 5	והקטיר עליה	ויסיק ויועד	ויסדר	ἐπιθήσει
Lev 9: 13	ויקטר על	ואסיק ואועד	וסדר	ἐπέθηκεν
Lev 9: 17	ויקטר על	ואסיק ואועד	וסדר	ἐπέθηκεν

Group 1, Subgroup 1.3

Ex 30: 20	להקטיר אשה	לאסקה	למסדרה למועדה	ἀναφέρειν
Lev 2: 11	לא תקטירו ... אשה	תסקון	תקרבון תקרבון	προσοίσετε
Lev 2: 16	והקטיר ... אשה	ויסיק	ויועד ויסדר	ἀνοίσει
Lev 8: 20	ויקטר את הראש	ואסיק	ואועד וסדר	ἀνήνεγκεν
Lev 17: 6	והקטיר החלב	ויסיק	ויועד ויסדר	ἀνοίσει
Num 18:17	חלבם תקטיר	תסיק	תועד תסדר	ἀνοίσεις

Group 1, Subgroup 1.4

| Lev 6: 15 | כליל תקטר | תחסק | תתועד תסתדר | ἐπιτελεσ-θήσεται |

Group 2

Ex 30: 7	והקטיר ... קטרת	ויקטר	ויועד* ויסדר	θυμιάσει
Ex 30: 7	יקטירנה	יקטרינה	יועדנה* יסדר	θυμιάσει
Ex 30: 8	יקטירנה	יקטרינה	יועדנה* יסדר	θυμιάσει
Ex 40: 27	ויקטר ... קטרת	ואקטר	ואעד וסדר	ἐθυμίασεν

*Chap. 25 in the Samaritan Pentateuch

Group 3

| Num 17: 5 | להקטיר קטרת | לאסקה | למסדרה למועדה | ἐπιθεῖναι |

Appendix II
Financial Interests of Priests and Relations between King-Priest

In the period of king Joash (II Kings 12: 11) we already encounter a concentration of temple donations in the hands of the High Priest Jehoiada, and the inappropriate behaviour of the other priests, who did not apply the money designated for the repair of the Temple as they were supposed to do. The king's subsequent relapse after the High Priest's death, as narrated in II Chr. chap. 24, where we find significant disagreements between the two sources, casts doubts on the complete authenticity of all the particulars of these narratives. In II Kings 12: 9 we read: ויאתו הכהנים לבלתי קחת כסף מאת העם ולבלתי חזק את בדק הבית "The priests agreed that they would not collect any more money from the people and that they would not repair the temple themselves (verse 8 in NIV)." The reason behind this behaviour of the priests seems, to say the least, strange. Why would they not cooperate in the restoration of the Temple, if it was not at their own expense? I detect in the style and language of the king's words מדוע אינכם מחזקים את בדק הבית an expression of reproach, similar to the opening phrase in II Chr. 24: 6, in which the king's words are unmistakably meant to reprehend. Rehm (p. 125) maintains that he does not discern in the text the mood in which the king's conversation with the priests occurred; in his opinion, one observes merely the king's disappointment, but not a suspicion of corruption on the priests' part. I agree that an accusation of corruption is not perceivable in the king's words, but I cannot escape wondering whether financial interests were at the core of some dissension between the king and the priests, regarding their conceptions of priestly remuneration, and that for reasons of "rectifying censorship" the editor undertook some "ameliorative" amendments. As we shall see, the record of this meeting in Kings contrasts considerably with the report in Chronicles, so that a certain "correction" in Kings should also not be considered extraordinary.

We do not know to what category these priests belonged, and whether they ministered in Jerusalem, or at the high places. Moreover, this verse seems in contradiction to II Kings 12:17, which states that the priests took some sort of remuneration for the sin and trespass offerings; it is not clear whether the wording in this verse means that the priests took the sacrifices, or the money. There is a general consensus among scholars that these two sacrifices are of a later origin (see Elliger, *Leviticus*, p. 11; Noth, *Leviticus*, p. 36: exilic or post-exilic; Rendtorff, *Studien zur Geschichte des Opfers im Alten Israel*, pp. 53ff. and 240-241). Whether these sacrifices were instituted before or after the exile, we observe at any rate the importance of financial issues in the relationships between the king and the priests, and, most importantly, between the priests and the people. In the speculations of these scholars concerning the institution of the sin and trespass sacrifices, I have not encountered significant evidence which, in my opinion, would tip the scale in favour of a post-exilic conclusion. Lev. 4: 22 sets out the characteristics of the sin sacrifice of the נשיא "leader", not of the "king", the title of the political sovereign in the First Temple period. Moreover, one may observe this ruler's inferior status in comparing his sacrifice and corresponding ritual ceremony with that of the High Priest. This is a long way from the conditions prevailing in the First Temple period; we read, for instance, in the narrative in II Kings 16 that Ahaz instructed Uriah the priest to build an altar according to his specifications, and that a special royal burnt offering was sacrificed (probably daily, as one may assume from the context) before the people's offering. There is no such king's offering in Leviticus.

In II Chr. 24: 5-6, the story has an interesting twist. Whereas in II Kings all the blame is thrown on the priests because of their unreasonable refusal to cooperate, the reproach in Chronicles is directed exclusively at the Levites. We read there (vv. 5, 6):

> He called together the priests and Levites and said to them, "Go to the towns of Judah and collect the money due annually from all Israel, to repair the temple of your God. Do it now." But the Levites did not act at once. Therefore the king summoned Jehoiada the chief priest and said to him, "Why haven't you required the Levites to bring in from Judah and Jerusalem the tax...."

There is no mention of the priests' objection to collecting the money, but only of the negligence of the Levites in fulfilling their duty. The priests are exempted from any wrongdoing, and this modified text in Chronicles offers us an insight into the endeavour of the priestly editor of Chronicles (or at least of this pericope) to delegitimize the Levites and degrade their status. Verse 12:17 of II Kings (verse 16 in NIV), concerning the benefit of the guilt and sin offerings granted to the priests rather than to the house of God, is, as expected, missing in II Chr. In II Kings, we read in v.14 (13 in

NIV) that vessels for the temple were not made from the collected money, but in II Chr. 24: 14, we read the contrary, namely that there "were made articles for the Lord's temple." Nonetheless, from both sources we acquire an awareness of the importance of economic issues to the priesthood, and of financial irregularities or embezzlement among some groups of priests.

On the other hand, II Chr. emphasizes the righteousness of the High Priest, who died at the age of one hundred and thirty years, and succeeded during his lifetime in ensuring the correct conduct of the king. It seems to me that this event is possibly the most important principle conveyed in the naration in II Chr., namely, the relationship between priest and king, church and state. The editor offers us a justification for the High Priest's superiority to political authority; the king acted lawfully as long as he remained under the High Priest's influence, and lapsed into sinful acts after his demise (II Chr. 24: 17-22). The king's collusion with the princes of Judah, possibly against the powerful authority of the successor High Priest, Jehoiada's son, and the assassination of the High Priest at the king's command, are presented in Chronicles as the reasons for the king's own military defeat and assassination. H. Tadmor (*Encyclopedia Biblica,* Vol. III, s.v. יהואש (יואש) בן אחזיה מלך יהודה) speculates that Joash came into conflict with the priests, who opposed his taking the hallowed items and the gold of the Temple treasury to give to the king of Syria, as set out in II Kings 12: 19; again, this narrative is contrary to that in II Chronicles. Tadmor concludes that the spoliation of the Temple treasury might also have been the reason for Joash's assassination. However, II Kings does not expressly mention any conflict on this issue between the king and the priests. It seems that it was a later P editor, post-Josiah's reform, who added the stereotypical phrase in II Kings 12: 3 "The high places, however, were not removed...." It is also interesting to note the subtle syntactical modification performed in II Chr., in order to achieve a significantly different meaning than its parallel in II Kings. We read in II Kings 12: 3 (v.2 in NIV): ויעש יהואש הישר בעיני ה' כל ימיו, אשר הורהו יהוידע הכהן. In II Chr. 24: 2, we read: ויעש יואש הישר בעיני ה' כל ימי יהוידע הכהן. In Kings, the meaning is "Joash did what was right in the eyes of the Lord all the years Jehoiada the priest instructed him," but in Chronicles he did right only during "all the years of Jehoiada the priest."

This narrative in II Kings is the first occurrence in this book of the title הכהן הגדול "the High Priest," and if authentic, as it seems to be, it demonstrates the emergence of the priestly power and its involvement in the political affairs of the kingdom. The priestly thrust for power probably waxed and waned, and we observe that later, in Ahaz's reign, the king ordered

Uriah the priest to build the "altar in accordance with all the plans that
King Ahaz had sent from Damascus (II Kings 16: 11)." Uriah has neither
the title כהן גדול, "High Priest", nor כהן הראש; the latter is another
significant title which appears much later in Zedekiah's period, in II Kings
25: 18 and in Jeremiah 52: 24, as well as in the post-exilic Ezra 7: 5 as
Aaron's denomination. As expected, in the narration of Josiah's reign and
cult reform (II Kings 22: 4, 8 and 23: 4) there is a greater incidence of the
title כהן גדול and increasing evidence of this individual's control of the
Temple funds. The title הכהן הגדול, and evidence of a division within the
priestly ranks, are even more prominent in the post-exilic writings of Haggai
(1: 1, 12, 14; 2: 2, 4), Zechariah (3: 1, 8; 6: 11), Nehemiah (3: 1, 20; 13:
28), and II Chronicles (34: 9). There is one mention of the title in Jos. 20:
6, an earlier writing, with reference to the cities of refuge, a regulation of
late Deuteronomic origin: הכהן הגדול אשר יהיה בימים ההם "the high priest
who is serving at that time." M. Noth (*Numbers, A Commentary*, p. 253)
states: "The present passage [Num. 35: 1-34, regarding the cities of refuge,
which contains occurrences of the title הכהן הגדול] then, also belongs to
the redactional unification of Pentateuchal narrative and deuteronomistic
historical work." This differentiation among the attendants of the cult, and
the creation of various classes and categories with separate duties and remuneration, appear only after Josiah's reform, apparently as a consequence of
it.

Professor Revell has commented, "Both the Temple Scroll from Qumran
(in the section dealing with the duties) and the Samaritan Chronicle (in the
section describing the acts of 'King Gideon' and other judges) envisage the
pre-exilic king as wholly under the control of the priesthood, presumably
reflecting the post-exilic situation; the Samaritan Chronicle is, of course, of
uncertain value." I fully agree with this remark. As I argued above, the
author of the Temple Scroll wrote from the perspective of "what ought to
be," and it was his opinion, based on the situation in his time, that the
High Priest, the spiritual leader and the Deity's most exalted servant, was
superior to everyone, including the king, the representative of political
power. The purpose of the Samaritan Chronicle, as one may conclude from
the spirit of the narration, was the glorification of the Samaritan High
Priests and their legitimacy as against the unauthorized Judean priests. The
split between the Samaritans and Judah started, from their viewpoint, from
the time of Eli's setting up of a rival sanctuary.

Appendix III
Theophany as Cloud, Fire and Smoke in Biblical Verses

The Deity as fire, or cloud

At Abraham's covenant, in Gen. 15: 17 cited above (sec. 6.1.8), one has the impression from the context that the Deity passed in the image of תנור עשן ולפיד אש a "smoking firepot with a blazing torch," since v. 18 declares in continuation, ביום ההוא כרת ה׳ את אברם ברית "On that day the Lord made a covenant with Abram."

ומראה כבוד ה׳ כאש אכלת "... the glory of the Lord looked like a consuming fire (Exod. 24: 17)," during the revelation at Mount Sinai, and in Exod. 19: 18 והר סיני עשן כלו מפני אשר ירד עליו ה׳ באש, where the mount was "covered with smoke, because the Lord descended on it in fire."

והיה כבא משה האהלה ירד עמוד הענן ועמד פתח האהל ודבר עם משה "As Moses went into the tent, the pillar of cloud would come down and stay at the entrance, while the Lord spoke with Moses (Exod. 33: 9)." Here, it is the Deity in the image of the cloud who speaks with Moses. In other verses, as we shall see, we have a different expression; a distinction is made between the cloud and the Deity, who speaks from "out of the fire" מתוך האש (Deut. 4: 12).

ויכס הענן את אהל מועד וכבוד ה׳ מלא את המשכן ולא יכל משה לבוא אל אהל מועד כי שכן עליו הענן וכבוד ה׳ מלא את המשכן "Then the cloud covered the Tent of Meeting, and the glory of the Lord filled the tabernacle. Moses could not enter the Tent of Meeting because the cloud had settled upon it, and the glory of the Lord filled the tabernacle (Exod. 40: 34-35)." This description appears almost verbatim at the Temple consecration in I Kings 8: 11 and with minor difference in II Chr. 5: 14: ולא יכלו הכהנים לעמד לשרת מפני הענן כי מלא כבוד ה׳ את בית ה׳ "And the priests could not perform their service because of the cloud, for the glory of the Lord filled his temple." This description does not appear at the consecration of the Second Temple in Ezra, but we find it in II Maccabees 2: 8 καὶ τότε ὁ κύριος ἀναδείξει ταῦτα καὶ ὀφθήσεται ἡ δόξα τοῦ κυρίου καὶ ἡ νεφέλη, ὡς καὶ ἐπὶ Μωυσῇ ἐδηλοῦτο, ὡς καὶ ὁ Σαλωμῶν ἠξίωσεν ἵνα ὁ τόπος καθαγιασθῇ μεγάλως. "And then the Lord will disclose these things, and the glory of the Lord and the cloud will appear, as they were shown in the case of Moses, and as Solomon asked that the place should be specially consecrated." כי...לי אוי ואמר עשן ימלא והבית "And the temple was filled with smoke. 'Woe את המלך ה' צבאות ראו עיני to me!' I cried ...'my eyes have seen the King, the Lord Almighty' (Isa. 6: 4- 5)."

The Deity distinct from a cloud, smoke or fire

הנה אנכי בא אליך בעב הענן בעבור ישמע העם "I am going to come to you in a dense cloud, so that the people will hear... (Exod. 19: 9)." The cloud is distinct from the Deity, and serves as a medium or instrument to conceal the Deity from the eyes of the Israelites, and allow them only to hear His voice.

וידבר ה' אליכם מתוך האש "Then the Lord spoke to you out of the fire (Deut. 4: 12)." Here too the fire is distinct from the Deity; this expression מתוך האש appears often in Scripture.

וירד ה' בענן וידבר אליו "Then the Lord came down in the cloud and spoke with him (Num. 11: 25))."

Indeterminate quotations

וה' הלך לפניהם יומם בעמוד ענן לנחתם הדרך ולילה בעמוד אש להאיר להם "By day the Lord went ahead of them in a pillar of cloud to guide them on their way and by night in a pillar of fire to give them light (Exod. 13: 21)."

וישקף ה' אל מחנה מצרים בעמוד אש וענן "The Lord looked down from the pillar of fire and cloud at the Egyptian army (Exod. 14: 24)."

Cloud or fire as the Deity's messengers

ויסע מלאך אלהים ההלך לפני מחנה ישראל וילך מאחריהם ויסע עמוד הענן מפניהם ויעמד מאחריהם "Then the angel of God, who had been traveling in front of Israel's army, withdrew and went behind them. The pillar of cloud also moved from in front and stood behind them (Exod. 14: 19)."

וירא מלאך ה' אליו בלבת אש מתוך הסנה "There the angel of the Lord appeared to him in flames of fire from within a bush (Exod. 3: 2)"; but in continuation, we read in v. 4 וירא ה' כי סר לראות ויקרא אליו אלהים מתוך הסנה "When the Lord saw that he had gone over to look, God called to him from within the bush." We have here two types of theophany, as well as both J and E terminology, which makes it difficult to attribute the variance to distinct sources.

Hermann Gunkel, in his commentary to Genesis concerning the description of the Deity as a fire torch at Abraham's covenant, writes: "Solche

Beschreibung des Aussehen Gottes ist sehr naiv und gewiss sehr alt; doch beachte man, wie vorsichtig der Erzähler spricht: er sagt nicht geradezu, dass diese Erscheinung Jahve gewesen ist, sondern lässt es erraten; auch hat Abraham Jahves Gesicht nicht gesehen." ("Such a portrayal of God's image is very naive and certainly very old, but one perceives how cautiously the narrator speaks; he does not say overtly that this vision was the Deity, but merely lets us conjecture it; Abraham too has not seen the Deity's face.") Gunkel comments that this is the only occurrence in Genesis of God's theophany as a fire torch, in comparison with the many occurrences in the Moses narrations. In his opinion, this description seems to be an interjection of a later mythological image into the patriarchal narratives, where such imagery was absent. In the continuation of his study in this respect, he reaches an important conclusion, which I think should guide us in our analysis and speculation about the various strata of the biblical pericopes: "Es ist ein Zeichen für das hohe Alter der Vätersagen, dass selbst solche Stücke, die zu den spätestens gehören, doch noch einzige sehr alte Züge enthalten." ("It is an indication of the archaic period of the patriarchal mythologies, so that even such pericopes attributed to the later periods still contain some very old features.")

Appendix IV
Genealogical Requirements for the Priesthood

In the Eli pericope, the prophet states והקימתי לי כהן נאמן "I will raise up for myself a faithful priest (I Sam. 2: 35)"; there is no lineage requirement for the priesthood. We read in II Sam. 8: 16-17, concerning David's appointments for various offices: ויואב בן צרויה על הצבא ויהושפט בן אחילוד מזכיר וצדוק בן אחיטוב ואחימלך בן אביתר כהנים ושריה סופר "Joab son of Zeruiah was over the army; Jehoshaphat son of Ahilud was recorder; Zadok son of Ahitub and Ahimelech son of Abiathar were priests; Seraiah was secretary...." Again, there are no differences among the various officers regarding their lineage; only their fathers' names are mentioned, probably for identification purposes. It seems that the narrator had forgotten the name of Seraiah's father. Although there is no indication that the priests were appointed by David in repayment for their loyalty to him, we may assume that the king appointed the priests according to his will and discretion, as he did concerning other officers. We observe in I Kings 2: 27 – ויגרש שלמה את אביתר מהיות כהן לה' "So Solomon removed Abiathar from the priesthood of the Lord" – that king Solomon dismissed Abiathar, the priest appointed by David, and replaced him, in the same way as he proceeded against his army commander; we read in I Kings 2: 35 ויתן המלך את בניהו בן יהוידע תחתיו על הצבא ואת צדוק הכהן נתן המלך תחת אביתר "The king put Benaiah son of Jehoiada over the army in Joab's position and replaced Abiathar with Zadok the priest."

The list of Solomon's appointments in I Kings 4: 2-6 does give rise to many questions: for instance, the sudden appearance of Abiathar as priest, together with Zadok, after his banishment by the king; the duties of Azariah, the son of Zadok the priest, and Zabud the son of Nathan, כהן רעה, translated by the NIV as "a priest and personal adviser to the king." However, there is still no mention of any Aaronite lineage.

Hilkiah, the first High Priest, named in II Kings 22: 4 and 8, also appears without any mention of an Aaronite lineage, as do the other High Priests: "Seraiah the chief priest, Zephaniah the priest next in rank (II Kings 25: 18)"; even in Zechariah 3: 1, Joshua the High Priest is mentioned without further indication of genealogy, and in 6: 11, only his father's name appears: "the high priest, Joshua son of Jehozadak ."

In Jeremiah 1: 1 we encounter the prophet's own identity and status, in the phrase מן הכהנים אשר בענתות, "[he was] one of the priests at Anathoth," with no claim of Aaronite lineage. In 29: 25-26, we read of the substitution of certain apparently high-ranking priests: ה' נתנך כהן תחת יהוידע הכהן להיות פקדים בית ה' "The Lord has appointed you [Zephaniah] priest in place of Jehoiada to be in charge of the house of the Lord." (Zephania, the new priest, is probably the priest next in rank mentioned in II Kings 25: 18: את שריה כהן הראש ואת צפניהו כהן משנה "Seraiah the chief priest, Zephaniah the priest next in rank.") Again, there is no indication that lineage was the motive for the change of appointment.

Appendix V
A Study on the Hermeneutics of שבט

There are two quotations in Deuteronomy referring to the Levites as a שבט "tribe". In 10: 8 we read: בעת ההוא הבדיל ה׳ את שבט הלוי "At that time the Lord set apart the tribe of Levi," and in 18: 1 לא יהיה לכהנים הלוים כל שבט לוי חלק ונחלה "The priests, who are Levites – indeed the whole tribe of Levi – are to have no allotment or inheritance." I shall not enter into a discussion concerning the final redaction of Deuteronomy, but shall merely analyze these verses on their own merit.

G. Seitz, in *Redaktionsgeschichtliche Studien zum Deuteronomium,* establishes the context of these two verses. He writes (p. 206): "Für die letzte Stufe des Priestergesetzes, die sich im Zusatz כל שבט לוי in v. 1a und in v. 2.5 niedergeschlagen hat, ist die Verwandschaft mit 10, 8 zu beachten. Meist wird angenommen, dass 10, 8 f. das Priestergesetz beeinflusst hat." ("For the last stage of the Priestly Code, which shows itself in the accretion of [the phrase] כל שבט לוי in vv. 1a and 2.5, one has to consider its affinity with vv. 10: 8ff. Generally, it is considered that vv. 10: 8ff have influenced the Priestly Code.") Verse 10: 8 is intrinsically intertwined with Exod. 32: 25-29, which, as we have seen, is considered as a later priestly accretion with an aetiological motive. Seitz also demonstrates that Deut.10: 6- 9 is not an integral part of Moses' Horeb narrative in the previous verses of the pericope. He states (p. 57): "Von diesen Einschüben entfernt sich der Passus 10, 6f. am weitesten von der Mosesrede." ("In these interjections, passage 10: 6ff deviates most from Moses' speech.") We observe that even the fictitious concept of the Levites as a tribe related by blood, instead of a professional association, is of a late date.

There is another element of this debate to which I wish to draw attention, and that is the concept of שבט used in many occurrences in Scripture with respect to cultic issues. We read in Deut. 12: 5 כי אם אל המקום אשר יבחר ה׳ אלהיכם מכל שבטיכם "...the place the Lord your God will choose from among all your tribes," and in v. 14, a similar phrase: כי אם במקום אשר יבחר ה׳ באחד שבטיך "...the place the Lord will choose in one of your tribes." These associations of the term שבט with a site, or a locality, as

opposed to a group of people, with respect to the choosing of Jerusalem as
the locus of the sanctuary, is further emphasized in Kings. We read in I
Kings 8: 16 לא בחרתי בעיר מכל שבטי ישראל לבנות בית להיות שמי שם "I
have not chosen a city in any tribe of Israel to have a temple built for my
Name to be there"; in 11: 32 ולמען ירושלם העיר אשר בחרתי בה מכל שבטי
ישראל "But for the sake of... the city of Jerusalem, which I have chosen out
of all the tribes of Israel." Similar connections of the term שבט with a "site"
occur in I Kings 14: 21, in II Kings 21: 17, and in I Kings 11: 36, where
we read: ולבנו אתן שבט אחד למען היות ניר לדויד עבדי כל הימים "I will give
one tribe to his son so that David my servant may always have a lamp before
me in Jerusalem."

The NIV has interpreted the term ניר in I Kings 11: 36 as if it were נר,
a "lamp" or "light", while the usual meaning is "arable soil," as in Jer. 4: 3:
נירו לכם ניר ואל תזרעו אל קצים "Break up your unplowed ground and do
not sow among thorns"; Hos. 10: 12: זרעו לכם לצדקה קצרו לפי חסד נירו
לכם ניר "Sow for yourselves righteousness, reap the fruit of unfailing love,
and break up your unplowed ground [where no meaning other than "plow
a furrow" is conceivable]"; and in Prv. 13: 23 רב אכל ניר ראשים, translated
by the NIV as "A poor man's field may produce abundant food." The
traditional commentators such as Rashi, Ibn Ezra and Ralbag interpret the
term as referring to plowing. Ibn Ezra, the grammarian, compares I Kings
11: 36 with the above-cited verse from Jeremiah and states: יתכן להיותו שם
ניר "It is possible that it is akin to ניר לכם פועל מן נירו לכם ניר in
Jeremiah," where its interpretation is unequivocal. Thus it is likely the NIV
interpreted the term in I Kings 11: 36 as "lamp" because a translation of
"field" did not seem to the translator as appropriate in the context. The
LXX interpreted the verse as τῷ δὲ υἱῷ αὐτοῦ δώσω τὰ δύο σκῆπτρα
ὅπως ᾖ θέσις τῷ δούλῳ μου Δαυιδ "And to his son I will give the two
'scepters' [or 'royalty, kingly power, rule, etc.' according to Liddell and
Scott], so that it might be a *situs* [or 'situation, of a city' according to Liddell
and Scott] to my servant David all the days before me." The LXX has
interpreted the verse metaphorically, but in essence the term ניר signifies a
locus, certainly not a light. The Targum translates בדיל לקימא מלכו לדוד
"in order that a kingdom be secured to David." Rashi states: ממשלה וניר
לשון עול "a government, and ניר 'has an affinity' with a yoke." Both
interpretations are metaphoric, but both also relate the definition of ניר to
the concept of a territory, or a realm, not to a "lamp" or "light".

In I Kings 15: 4, כי למען דוד נתן ה' אלהיו לו ניר בירושלם, the NIV
translates consistently: "Nevertheless, for David's sake the Lord his God
gave him a lamp in Jerusalem," an interpretation which does not make

sense at all. The LXX translates the term ניר here with κατάλειμμα, "a remnant – what was left"; this interpretation does make sense, since it refers to the one "tribe" left to David's descendants when the other ten were torn away, as portrayed in the parable of the twelve rent pieces of garment in I Kings 11: 30-36. The Targum here also translates ניר metaphorically as מלכו "kingdom". Ralbag explains the logic of the metaphor, stating: ניר הוא הארץ הנעבדת באופן שיהיו הצמתים אשר בה פרים ובזה יאמר כי לולא דוד לא היה השם יתברך נותן לו בירושלים זרע שימשול בו "'Nir' is the land which is worked in such a way that its furrows are fertile, and what is meant by that is that if it were not for David, God, blessed be He, would not have given him 'progeny' in Jerusalem, to rule it." There is a similar verse on the same topic in II Kings 8: 19: למען דוד עבדו כאשר אמר לו לתת לו ניר לבניו. The LXX, is, alas, inconsistent here with respect to its previous interpretations, and translates ניר as λύχνον, "light". The Targum translates with its usual מלכו, "kingdom", and Rashi states ממשלה "government". Radak attempts to translate it כמו נר בצרי על דרך ערכתי נר למשיחי, "as *Ner* with a *Zerei* vocalization, akin to '...and set up a lamp for my anointed one' [Psalms 132: 17]," but adds that both Jonathan and Onkelos translated it with "kingdom". Onkelos has also translated ונירם in Num. 21: 30 as ומלכו. It seems to me that in Psalms not only is the term נר written without a "י", but the context also requires the interpretation of "lamp" with the verb ערך: that is, "to prepare, to arrange, to put" a light, to illuminate the way for the anointed. In II Kings 8: 19, on the other hand, the verb is נתן, and a more logical translation here is "to give, to grant" a realm to David's sons.

I therefore beg to differ with Noth (*Könige* p. 240), who interpreted the term ניר in I Kings 11: 36 as "eine Lampe," "a lamp." He then discusses this apparently "strange" interpretation (pp. 243ff.) and notes that J. W. Wevers suggested "royal prerogative," based on the Akkadian *neru*.[1] Noth comments that this solution cannot be substantiated, and therefore suggests the customary translation, the "lamp" of the NIV (p. 244). In Num. 21: 30 Noth translates ונירם as "We have gained the upper hand." He does not elucidate his reason for this translation; perhaps he considered it a form of the verb רום. Even-Shoshan in his Concordance classifies ונירם under the verb ירה, "to shoot arrows," "to throw," whereas Mandelkern in his Concordance classifies the term (with a question mark) under ניר, thus as "their

---

[1]   J. W. Wevers, *Oudtestamentische Studien* 8 (1950), pp. 300-322, at p. 316.

field" with a suffix. I would consider the traditional interpretation as entirely valid. The term נִיר, as we have seen, signifies a furrow, a field, and
metaphorically a place and a property. This interpretation is certainly more
appropriate to the context of all the above-cited verses, declaring that God
has given to David an estate, an inheritance.

Now, if נִיר conveys the concept of a "place, a territory," we have a
perfect parallel to the term שבט לדויד in I Kings 11: 36: שבט אחד למען
היות ניר לדויד (though the NIV has translated "one tribe ...so that David
my servant may always have a lamp," the more appropriate translation here
is "realm"). Such an interpretation of שבט as a territory inhabited by a
specific group of people would also explain the "strange" idea of "the city
which I have chosen out of all the 'tribes' of Israel," in the various citations
above. A city is a locality, and the common concept of שבט as a "tribe", a
group of people, is not appropriate as an entity to be chosen as a *situs*; but
a territory in which a specific group of people dwells is an entity in which
a site for a sanctuary can be chosen. And as we know, the tribal jurisdiction
of Jerusalem, whether under Judah or Benjamin, is not well-defined; again,
the choice of "tribes" for the sanctuary is not appropriate.

In *The History of Israel*, pp. 55ff, M. Noth writes: "The name Judah is
not related to any well-known type of Semitic personal name and can hardly
have been a personal name originally....It is probable that the clans which
settled in this area called themselves later the 'people of Judah,' 'Judeans'
(בני יהודה), and thus became the 'tribe of Judah'....The name 'Ephraim' is
obviously not a personal name, but the name of a place, as is already indicated by its ending, which often occurs in the names of places and countries." He writes further on p.72: "Some of the Israelite tribes bear names
that were originally place-names and derived from the areas in which the
tribes in question settled [Judah, Ephraim, Benjamin and probably Naph-
tali]; in another case a tribe derived its name from the particular circumstances in which it had acquired its land [this is true of Issachar]." On p.
106, he writes: "The tribes...were formed only when they reached Palestine
as part of the historical process of the occupation of the land and consisted
of the clans which settled in a particular limited area and were not simply
held together by bonds of kinship." One wonders that Noth, who held the
idea that "tribe" meant initially a group of people living together in a
defined area, does not interpret the term נִיר in a manner consistent with
this concept.

I do not know the etymological development of the two meanings of the
term שבט: a "stick" or "staff" and a "tribe". There is unquestionably an
association between the two concepts; we have the parallel set of synonyms

מטה "stick" and מטה "tribe". I cannot conceive of an association between a "group of people" and a "stick", but it seems to me that an association between a stick and a territory is entirely rational. A stick might have served as a medium for measuring a field or a territory; in fact, we have in Jer. 51: 19 the expression שבט נחלתו (which the NIV has translated as "the tribe of his inheritance," though the more appropriate translation is "rod"), similar to חבל נחלתו "the lot [or cord] of his inheritance (Deut. 32: 9)," (which the NIV has translated as "his allotted inheritance"). Use of the cord as a method of measuring is a known fact, and from its parallel to שבט נחלתו, we may deduce the same function for the rod. The stick can also represent a weapon, a spear, a pike – that is, a medium to defend the territory inhabited by the group, and a symbol of power; the "sceptre" in the form of a rod, שבט, therefore implies the concept of a territory, and of a group of people living on a specific territory. (As we have seen, the LXX translates שבט as σκῆπτρον; according to Liddell and Scott, this term means "I. a staff or stick, II. a staff as a badge of command, a sceptre.") Thus שבט does not imply a common ancestry and blood relationship. The Levites, a group of professional clerics, could not live together in one specific territory, since their occupation required them to provide their cult services to all the people, over the entire land. Therefore, they had no שבט, a specifically defined territory, and that is confirmed by Num. 26: 62: כי לא נתן להם נחלה בתוך בני ישראל "they received no inheritance among [the Israelites] ."

Citation Index

Subject Index

Bibliography

Abbreviations

ANET	Ancient Near Eastern Texts, J. B. Pritchard, ed.
HUCA	Hebrew Union College Annual
JBL	Journal of Biblical Literature
JQR	Jewish Quarterly Review
VT	Vetus Testamentum
VTS	Vetus Testamentum, Supplements
ZAW	Zeitschrift für die alttestamentliche Wissenschaft

Academy of the Hebrew Language, ed., ספר בן סירא, המקור, קונקורדנציה, וניתוח אוצר המלים, המילון ההיסתורי ללשון העברית. Jerusalem, 1973.

Aland, K., M. Black, C. Martini, B.M. Metzger and A.Wigkren, edd. *The Greek New Testament*. 3rd revised edition. Stuttgart, 1966.

Albeck, H. מבוא למשנה. Jerusalem, 1953.

Alt, A. *Kleine Schriften zur Geschichte des Volkes Israel*, I. München, 1953.

Anderson, Gary A. *Sacrifices and Offerings in Ancient Israel*. Atlanta: Scholars Press,1987.

Anderson, George W., H. Cazelles, D.N. Freedman D.N., S. Talmon and G.Wallis. *Theologisches Wörterbuch zum Alten Testament*. Stuttgart, 1970.

Avishur, I., ed. עיונים בספר יחזקאל. Jerusalem, 1982.

Baentsch, B. *Exodus, Leviticus, Numeri. Handkommentar zum Alten Testament*. Abt. I, Band 2. Göttingen, 1902.

Bar – Ilan, M."האם מסכתות תמיד ומדות הן תעודות פולמוסיות?" In *Sidra*. Edited by. Z.A. Steinfeld. Ramat Gan, 1989.

Bauer, Walter. *A Greek-English Lexicon of the New Testament and Other Christian Literature*. Translated by W.F. Arndt and F.W. Gingrich. Second edition. Revised by F.W. Gingrich and F. Danker from 5th German edition, 1958. Chicago, 1979.

Bentzen, A. *Die Josianische Reform und ihre Voraussetzungen*. Kobenhavn, 1926.

Benziger, I. *Hebräische Archeologie*. Tübingen, 1927.

Bergstrasser, G., ed. *Hebräische Grammatik*. Mit Benutzung der von E. Kautzsch bearbeiteten 28. Auflage von Wilhelm Gesenius. Leipzig, 1909.

Bertholet, A. *Leviticus. Kurzer Hand-Commentar zum Alten Testament*. Edited by K. Marti. Tübingen, 1901.

Beyer, Klaus. *Die Aramäischen Texte vom Toten Meer*. Göttingen,1984.

Biblia Sacra, Iuxta Latinam Vulgatam Versionem, ad Codicum Fidem, Libros Exodi et Levitici. Romae, 1929.

Beyerlin, W. *Origins and History of the Oldest Sinaitic Traditions*. Translated by S. Rudman.Oxford, 1965.

Bird, P. "The Place of Women in the Israelite Cultus." In *Ancient Israelite Religion, Essays in Honour of F. M. Cross*, pp. 397-419. Edited by P.D. Miller Jr., P.D. Hanson and S. D. McBride. Philadelphia,1965.

De Boer, P.A.H. "An Aspect of Sacrifices, Divine Bread." In *Studies in the Religion of Ancient Israel. Supplements to VTS* Vol. XXIII (1972), pp. 27-47.

Bowman, John, ed. *Samaritan Documents Relating to their History, Religion and Life.* Pittsburgh, Pennsylvania, 1977.

Brody, A. *Der Mishna Traktat Tamid.* Uppsala, 1935.

Budde, K. "Das Deuteronomium und die Reform König Josias." *ZAW* 44 (1926), pp. 177-244.

– *Die Bücher Samuel. Kurzer Hand-Commentar zum Alten Testament.* Edited by K. Marti. Tübingen und Leipzig, 1902.

Burkert, W."Offerings in Perspective." In *Gifts to the Gods. Proceedings of the Uppsala Symposium 1985*, pp. 43-50. Edited by T. Linders and G. Nordquist. Uppsala, 1987.

Bury, J., ed. *The Cambridge Ancient History.* Vol. IV. London, 1926.

Charles, R. H., ed. *The Apocrypha and Pseudepigrapha of the Old Testament.* Oxford, 1913.

Charles, R. H. and Cowley, A. "An Early Source of Testaments of Patriarchs." *JQR* 19 (1906), pp. 566-583.

Chusid, I. A.and Siani, S., edd. *Keter Hatora, The Great Tag', Torah Hadura* פרשה תאנ'. Reprinted Jerusalem, 1971.

Conrad, D. "Zu Jes. 65 3b." *ZAW* 80 (1968), pp.232-234.

Curley, E.,ed. *Hobbes' Leviathan, with Introduction and Notes with Variants from the Latin Edition of 1668.* Reprinted Indianapolis, 1994.

Dalman, Gustaf. *Aramäisches Neuhebräisches Handwörterbuch zum Targum, Talmud und Midrash.* Dritte unveränderte Auflage. Göttingen, 1938.

Davies, Peter. *Roots, Family Histories of Familiar Words.* New York, 1981.

DeLagarde, Paul, ed. *Veteris Testamenti, Fragmenta apud Syros servata quiunque.* Göttingen, 1880. Reprinted 1971.

Dever, W. G. "The Contribution of Archeology to the Study of Canaanite and Early Israelite Religion." In *Ancient Israelite Religion, Essays in Honour of F. M. Cross*, pp. 209-247. Edited by P.D. Miller Jr., P.D. Hanson and S. D. McBride. Philadelphia, 1965.

Dillmann, A. *Die Bücher Exodus and Leviticus. Kurzgefasstes Exegetisches Handbuch zum Alten Testament.* Leipzig, 1886-1897.

Ebeling, E. *Parfümrezepte und Kultische Texte aus Assur*, Roma: Pontificium Institutum Biblicum, 1950.

Ebeling, E. and Meissner, B., edd. *Reallexicon der Assyriologie.* Berlin, 1932

Encyclopedia Biblica. Jerusalem, 1964. S.v. מזבח, דברי הימים, לוי, יהואש, כהנא, דניאל

Eerdmans, B. D., *Das Buch Exodus. Alttestamentliche Studien*, Vol. IV. Giessen, 1908-1912.

Elliger, Karl, *Leviticus. Handbuch zum Alten Testament*, Erste Reihe, 4.Tübingen, 1966.

Englund, G. "Gifts to the Gods." In *Gifts to the Gods. Proceedings of the Uppsala Symposium 1985* , pp. 57-64. Edited by T. Linders and G. Nordquist. Uppsala,1987.

Even Shoshan, Avraham. קונקורדנציה חדשה לתנ"ך. Revised edition. Jerusalem, 1989.
– המילון החדש. Revised edition. Jerusalem, 1974.

Feliks, J. עולם הצומח של התנ"ך Jerusalem, 1968.
Fitzmyer, Joseph A. "The Targum of Leviticus from Qumran Cave 4." *Ma'arav* 1/
     1(October, 1978), pp. 5-23.
Flavius, Josephus. *Antiquities*. Edited and translated by H. St. J. Thackeray, R. Marcus,
     and H. Feldman. 10 vols. London: The Loeb Classical Library, 1926-1965.
– *Life*. Transated by. H. St. J. Thackeray. The Loeb Classical Library,1926.
– *The Jewish War*. Translated by H. St. J.Thackeray. 2 vols. The Loeb Classical
     Library, 1927-1928.
Furlani, Giuseppe *Il Sacrificio nelle Religione dei Semiti di Babylonia e Assiria*, Serie VI,
     Vol. IV, Fascicolo III. Roma, 1932.

Galling, K. *Der Altar in den Kulturen des Alten Orients*. Berlin,1925.
Gehring, A. *Index Homericus*. Hildesheim, 1970.
Ginzberg, L. "Tamid, the Oldest Treatise of the Mishna." *Journal of Jewish Lore and
     Philosophy* I (1919), p. 265-295.
Glueck, Nelson."מזבחות קטורת" *Eretz Israel* 10 (1971), pp. 120-125.
Gradwohl, R. "Das Fremde Feuer." *ZAW* 75 (1963), pp. 289-296.
Gray, G. B. *Sacrifice in the Old Testament*. Oxford, 1925.
Gressmann, H. "Josia und das Deuteronomium." *ZAW* 42 (1924), pp. 313-337.
Groom, Nigel. *Frankincense and Myrrh: A Study of the Arabian Incense Trade*. London,
     1981.
Grossfeld, B. "ערק – אזל" *ZAW* 91 (1979), pp. 107-123.
Gunkel, H. *Genesis. Handkommentar zum Alten Testament*. 5. unveränderte Auflage.
     Göttingen, 1922.
Gur, Yehuda. מלון עברי Tel Aviv, 1946.

Hallo, W. W. "The Origins of the Sacrificial Cult." In *Ancient Israelite Religion, Essays
     in Honour of F. M. Cross*, pp. 3-13. Edited by P.D Miller Jr., P.D. Hanson and S.D.
     McBride, Philadelphia,1965.
Hanhart, R., ed. *SEPTUAGINTA, Vetus Testamentum Auctoritate Academiae
     Scientiarum Gottingensis editum*: Vol. VIII, 4: *Iudith*. Göttingen, 1979.
Haran, Menahem. *Temples and Temple-Service in Ancient Israel*. Oxford,1978.
– "מזבחות הקטורת" *Tarbiz* 61/3 (1992), pp. 321-332.
Hartom, A.S., ed. Hebrew text according to Cassuto, בן סירא. Tel Aviv, 1963.
Hayman, A. P., ed. *The Old Testament in Syriac according to the Peshitta Version*. Num-
     hers. Part I, 2, Leiden, 1991.
Heidel, A. *The Gilgamesh Epic and Old Testament Parallels*. Chicago, 1946.
Herodotus. *The Histories*. Translated by A.D. Godley. 4 vols. London: The Loeb Clas-
     sical Library, 1920-1925.
Holladay, J. S. Jr. "Religion in Israel and Judah under the Monarchy: An Explicitly
     Archeological Approach." In *Ancient Israelite Religion, Essays in Honour of F. M.Cross*,
     pp. 249-299. Edited by P.D. Miller Jr., P.D. Hanson and S. D. McBride. Philadel-
     phia, 1965.

- "The Kingdom of Israel and Judah: Political and Economic Centralization in the Iron IIa-b (ca 1000-750 B.C.E.)." Reprinted in *The Archeology of Society in the Holy Land*, pp. 1-85. Edited by Th. E. Levy. London, 1994.
- "The Use of Pottery and other Diagnostic Criteria, from the Solomonic Era to the Divided Kingdom." In *Biblical Archeology Today, 1990: Proceedings of the Second International Congress on Biblical Archeology, Jerusalem, June-July 1990*. Edited by A. Biran, J. Aviram, with A. Paris-Shadur. Jerusalem, 1993.

Hollander, H. W. and De Jonge, M., trans. *The Testaments of the Twelve Patriarchs, A Commentary*. Leiden, 1985.

Hoffmann, D., *Leviticus*. Berlin, 1905.

Hölscher, G. "Komposition und Ursprung des Deuteronomiums." *ZAW* 40 (1922), pp.161-255.

- "Das Buch der Könige, Quellen und seine Redaktion." In *Eucharistrion 1, Studien zur Religion und Literatur des Alten und NeuenTestaments, zu Ehren von H. Gunkel*, pp. 158-213. Edited by H. Schmidt. Göttingen, 1923.

Holzinger, Heinrich. *Exodus. Kurzer Hand-Commentar zum Alten Testament*. Tübingen, 1900.

Horst, L. "Étude sur le Deuteronome." *Revue de l'Histoire des Religions* XXVII (1893), pp. 119-176.

Hurowitz, V. "Salted Incense." *Biblica* 68. 2 (1987), pp. 178-194.

- *I Have Built You an Exalted House*. Sheffield, 1992.

Ibn G'anach, Yona. ספר השרשים. Berlin, 1896. Reprint Jerusalem, 1966.

Jastrow M. *A Dictionary of the Targumim, the Talmud Babli and Yerushalmi, and the Midrashic Literature*. Philadelphia, 1903.

Kahane, A., transl. and ed. הספרים החיצונים: אגרת אריסטיאס, ספר היובלים, ספר המקבים, יהודית, ספר בן סירא, צוואות השבטים. Tel Aviv, 1959.

Kaufman, A. כלי המשכן. MA Dissertation. Tel Aviv University, 1966.

Kaufmann, Y. תולדות האמונה הישראלית. Vol. III. Tel Aviv, 1968.

Kirschner, Robert. "The Rabbinic and Philonic Exegesis of the Nadab and Abihu Incident." *JQR* LXXIII, No. 4 (April 1983), pp. 373-93.

Knohl, I. מקדש הדממה. Jerusalem, 1992.

Koehler, L. and Baumgartner, W., *Lexicon in Veteris Testamenti Libros*. 2 vols. Leiden 1958.

Koster, M. D., ed. *The Old Testament in Syriac according to the Peshitta Version: Exodus*. Part I,1, Leiden, 1977.

Kutscher, E.Y. *Toldoth Haaramith: A History of Aramaic, Part I*. Jerusalem, 1973.

Labat, Rene. *Le Poème Babylonien de la Création*. Paris, 1935.

Laughlin, J. C. "The 'Strange Fire' of Nadab and Abihu." *JBL* 95/4 (1976), pp. 559-65.

Levine, B.A. *Leviticus* ויקרא. *The JPS Torah Commentary*. Philadelphia, 1989.

Levine, B.A. and W. Hallo. "Offerings to the Temple Gates at Ur." *HUCA* 38 (1967), pp. 17-58.

Liddell, H.G and R. Scott. *Greek-English Lexicon. A New Edition and Augmented throughout by H.S. Jones.* 9th edition. Oxford, 1940.

Loew, I. *Die Flora der Juden.* Wien - Leipzig, 1928.

Löhr, Max. *Das Räucheropfer im Alten Testament.* Halle: Schriften der königlichen gelehrten Gesellschaft, 1927.

MacDonald, John. *The Theology of the Samaritans,* New Testament Library. London, 1964.

Macho, Alejandro Diez, ed. *Neophyti, Targum Palestinense,* MS de la Biblioteca Vaticana. Madrid, 1971.

Mandelkern, S. *Veteris Testamenti Concordantiae.* 4th revised edition. Jerusalem, 1959.

Mann, Thomas W. "The Pillar of Cloud in the Reed Sea Narrative." *JBL* 90 (1971), pp.15-30.

McNeilly, F. S. *Anatomy of Leviathan.* New York, 1968.

Merendino, R.P. *Das Deuteronomische Gesetz. Bonner Biblische Beiträge.* Bonn, 1969.

Metzger, B. M. and R. E. Murphy, edd. *The New Oxford Annotated Bible with the Apocrypha, An Ecumenical Study Bible.* Revised and enlarged. New York, 1991.

Meyer, E. *Die Israeliten und Ihre Nachbarstamme.* Halle, 1906.

Milgrom J. *Numbers,* במדבר.*The JPS Torah Commentary.* Philadelphia, 1990.

- "Qumran's Biblical Hermeneutics: The Case of the Wood Offering." *Revue de Qumran* 16, (1994), pp. 449-456.

Milik J. T. "Les Papyrus Araméens d' Hermoupolis: Dieux Madbah et Masga-dâ." *Biblica* 48 (1967), pp. 546-623.

Miscall, P. D. *I Samuel. Indiana Studies in Biblical Literature.* Bloomington, Indiana,1986.

Mohlenbrink, K. "Die Levitische Überlieferung des Alten Testaments." *ZAW* 11 (1934), pp. 189-231.

Mommer, Peter. *Samuel, Gechichte und Überlieferung. Wissenschaftliche Monographien zum Alten und Neuen Testament 65.* Neukirchen, 1991.

Moore, G. F. *The International Critical Commentary. A Critical and Exegetical Commentary on Judges.* 2nd. ed. Edinburgh, 1898.

Mor, Menachem. "Samaritan History, The Persian, Hellenistic and Hasmonean Period." In *The Samaritans,* pp. 1-18. Edited by A.D. Crown. Tübingen, 1989.

Morgenstern, J. *The Ark, The Ephod and Tent of Meeting.* Cincinnati,1945.

Müller, Walter W. "Der Weihrauchhandel der Südaraber in der Antike." In *Die Königin von Saba,* pp.49-54. Stuttgart, 1988.

Murphy, R. E. *An Ecumenical Study Bible.* Revised and enlarged New York, 1991.

Nielsen, Kjeld. *Incense in Ancient Israel. Supplements to VT,* Vol. 38. Leiden, 1986.

Noth, Martin. *The History of Israel.* Translated from German and revised by P.R. Ackyrod. London, 1960.

- *Exodus, A Commentary, The Old Testament Library.* Translated from German by J. S. Bowden.London, 1962.

- "Samuel and Silo." *VT* 13 (1963), pp. 393-4.

- *Leviticus, A Commentary. The Old Testament Library.* Translated from German by J. E. Anderson. London, 1965.

– *Numbers, A Commentary. The Old Testament Library.* Translated from German by J. D. Martin. Philadelphia, 1968.
– *Könige. Biblischer Kommentar Altes Testament* IX/1. Neukirchen, 1968.
Nowack, W. *Richter, Ruth und Bücher Samuelis. Handkommentar zum Alten Testament.* Göttingen, 1902.

Oestreicher, Th. *Das Deuteronomische Grundgesetz.* Gütersloh, 1923.

Paley, F. A. *English Notes to the Iliad.* London, 1866.
Paton, L. B. "The Post Exilic Origin of Deuteronomy." *JBL* 47 (1928), pp.322-379.
Pfeiffer, Samuel. R. H. *Introduction to the Old Testament.* New York, 1941.
Philo. *The Special Laws.* Translated by F.H. Colson. 10 vols. London: The LoebClassical Library, 1939.

Qimron, Elisha. ארמית מקראית. Jerusalem, 1993.

Rabin, Ch., ed.and transl. *Zadokite Documents.* Oxford, 1954.
Rad, G. von. *Theologie des Alten Testaments.* Band 1. Zweite revidierte Ausgabe. München,1962.
– "The Tent and the Ark." In *The Problem of the Hexateuch and Other Essays.* Translated by E. W. Trueman. Dicken, N.Y.,1966.
Rahlfs, Alfred, ed. *Septuaginta, Id est Vetus Testamentum graece LXX interpretes.* Stuttgart, 1935.
Rehm, Martin. *Das Erste Buch der Könige. Ein Kommentar.* Eichstatt, 1979.
– *Das Zweite Buch der Könige.* Eichstatt, 1979.
Reiner, E., ed. *The Assyrian Dictionary of the Oriental Institute of the University of Chicago*, vol. 13. Chicago, 1982.
Rendtorff, R. *Studien zur Geschichte des Opfers im Alten Israel. Wissenschaftliche Monographien zum Alten und Neuen Testament.* Neukirchen,1967.
Robertson Smith, W. *The Religion of the Semites.* Cambridge, 1889. First paperback edition New York, 1972.
Rosenthal, Franz. *A Grammar of Biblical Aramaic.* Wiesbaden, 1961.
Rowley, H. H. "The Prophet Jeremiah and the Book of Deuteronomy." In *Studies in OT Prophecy Presented to Th. H. Robinson*, pp.157-174. Edited by H. H. Rowley. Edinburgh,1950.
Ryckmans, G. "Sud-Arabe *Mdbht* = Hébreu *Mzbh* et Termes Apparentés." In *Festschrift Werner Caskel*, pp. 253-260. Edited by E. Gräf. Leiden, 1968.

Sachs, A., transl. "Akkadian Rituals." In *ANET.* 2nd edition. Edited James B. Pritchard. Princeton, 1955.
Sanderson, J. E. *An Exodus Scroll from Qumran. 4QpaleoExod and the Samaritan Tradition.* Atlanta, 1986.
Sarna, N. M. "The Psalm Superscriptions and the Guilds." In *Studies in Jewish Religious and Intellectual History*, pp. 281-300. Edited by S. Stein and R. Loewe. University, Alabama, 1979.
Schmökel, H. *Ur, Assur und Babylon, Grosse Kulturen der Frühzeit.* Stuttgart, 1955.
Segal, Moshe Zvi. ספר בן סירא השלם. Jerusalem, 1972.

Segert, Stanislav. *Altaramäische Grammatik*. Leipzig, 1975.

Seitz, G. *Redaktionsgeschichtliche Studien zum Deuteronomium*. Stuttgart, 1971.

Shenan, A. "ל"חז באגדת ואביהוא נדב של חטאיהם". *Tarbiz* 3/4 (1979), pp. 201-214.

Sokoloff, Michael. *Dictionary of Jewish Palestinian Aramaic*. Ramat Gan, 1990.

Speiser, E. A., transl. "Akkadian Myths and Epics." In *ANET*. 2nd edition. Edited by James B. Pritchard. Princeton, 1955.

Sperber, A., ed. *The Bible in Aramaic. The Pentateuch According to Targum Onkelos*. Leiden, 1959.

Stäubli, Thomas. *Das Image der Nomaden*. Freiburg, 1991.

Tal, Abraham, ed. לתורה השומרוני התרגום. Tel Aviv, 1980-1982.

Theophrastus. *Enquiry into Plants, and Enquiry into Odours*. Translated by A. Hort. London: Loeb Classical Library,1961

Tsevat, M. "Studies in the Book of Samuel." *HUCA* 32 (1961), pp. 191-216.

Thureau-Dangin, F. *Rituels Accadiens*. Paris, 1921.

Vaux, R. de. *Ancient Israel, Its Life and Institutions*. Translated by J. McHugh. London, 1973.

Vermes, G., ed. and transl. *The Dead Sea Scrolls*. Reprinted with revisions, London, 1968.

Weinfeld, Moshe. יאשיהו עד מיהושע. Jerusalem, 1992.

Welch, Adam C. "The Death of Josiah." *ZAW* 43 (1925), pp. 255-260.

Wellhausen, Julius. *Prolegomena to the History of Ancient Israel*. 5th edition. Edinborough, 1885.

Wevers, John W. "Exegetical Principles Underlying the Septuagint Text of I Kings ii 12 - xxi 43." *Oudtestamentische Studien* 8 (1950), pp.300- 322.

– *Notes on the Greek Text of Exodus. Septuagint and Cognate Studies* 30. Atlanta, 1990.

– "The Composition of Exodus 35 to 40." In *Text History of the Greek Exodus. Mitteilung des Septuaginta* XXI, pp. 117-146. Göttingen, 1992.

– *Notes on the Greek Text of Genesis. Septuagint and Cognate Studies* 35. Atlanta, Georgia, 1993.

– ed. *SEPTUAGINTA, Vetus Testamentum Auctoritate Academiae Scientiarum Gottigensis editum*: Vol. I: *Genesis*. Göttingen, 1974;

– Vol. II, 1: *Exodus*. Göttingen, 1991;

– Vol. II, 2: *Leviticus*. Göttingen, 1986;

– Vol. III, 1: *Numeri*. Göttingen, 1982;

– Vol. II, 2: *Deuteronomy*. Göttingen, 1977.

Wigand, K. *Thymiateria*. Bonn, 1913,

The Wisdom of Ben Sira. Translated with Notes by P. W. Skehan. Introduction and Commentary by A. A. Di Lella. The Anchor Bible, vol. 39. New York, 1987.

Yadin, Y. *The Temple Scroll*. Jerusalem, 1977 (Hebrew), 1983 (English).

Yerushalmi, A. ודורו יאשיהו מפעלות. Tel Aviv, 1935.

Yeivin S. דינבורג ספד Jerusalem, 1949.

– "Social, Religious and Cultural Trends in Jerusalem under Davidic Dynasty." *VT* 3 (1953), pp. 149-166.

Ziegler, J. ed. *SEPTUAGINTA, Vetus Testamentum Graecum Auctoritatae Societatis Litterarum Gottingensis editum*: Vol. XIV: *Isaias*. Göttingen, 1939;
– Vol. XIII: *Duodecim Prophetae*. Göttingen, 1943;
– Vol. XV: *Ieremias*. Göttingen, 1976;
– Vol. XVI: *Ezechiel*. Göttingen, 1977.
Zimmerli, W. *Ezekiel*. *Biblischer Kommentar zum Alten Testament*, Band 13. Neukirchen, 1969.
Zimmern, H. *Beitraege zur Kenntnis der Babylonischen Religion* Leipzig,1901.
Zohary, M. *Plants of the Bible*. Cambridge-Tel Aviv: Cambridge University Press, 1982.
Zwickel, W. *Räucherkult und Räuchergerate*. *Orbis Biblicus et Orientalis* 97. Göttingen, 1990.